Conscripts and Volunteers

Maryland Studies in Public Philosophy

Series Editor: The Director of
The Center for Philosophy and Public Policy
University of Maryland, College Park

Also in this series

INCOME SUPPORT
Conceptual and Policy Issues
Edited by Peter G. Brown, Conrad Johnson, and Paul Vernier

BOUNDARIES
National Autonomy and Its Limits
Edited by Peter G. Brown and Henry Shue

THE BORDER THAT JOINS
Mexican Migrants and U. S. Responsibility
Edited by Peter G. Brown and Henry Shue

ENERGY AND THE FUTURE
Edited by Douglas MacLean and Peter G. Brown

LIBERALISM RECONSIDERED
Edited by Douglas MacLean and Claudia Mills

Forthcoming

THE GOOD LAWYER
Lawyers' Roles and Lawyers' Ethics
Edited by David Luban

Conscripts and Volunteers

Military Requirements, Social Justice, and the All-Volunteer Force

Edited by

Robert K. Fullinwider

ROWMAN & ALLANHELD
Publishers

ROWMAN & ALLANHELD

Published in the United States of America in 1983
by Rowman & Allanheld, Publishers
(A division of Littlefield, Adams & Company)
81 Adams Drive, Totowa, New Jersey 07512

Library of Congress Cataloging in Publication Data
Main entry under title:

Conscripts and volunteers.

  (Maryland studies in public philosophy)
  Includes bibliographical references and index.
1. Military service, Voluntary—United States—
Addresses, essays, lectures. 2. United States—Armed
Forces—Recruiting, enlistment, etc.—Addresses,
essays, lectures. I. Fullinwider, Robert K., 1942-
II. Series
UB323.C59.   1983   355.2'2362'0973   83-3095
ISBN 0-8476-7224-7
ISBN 0-8476-7264-6 (pbk.)

83 84 85/ 10 9 8 7 6 5 4 3 2 1

Printed in the United States of America

Contents

Tables and Figures

Preface

The Center for Philosophy and Public Policy was established in 1976 at the University of Maryland in College Park to conduct research into the values and concepts that underlie public policy. Most other research into public policy is empirical: it assesses costs, describes constituencies, and makes predictions. The Center's research is conceptual and normative. It investigates the structure of arguments and the nature of values relevant to the formation, justification, and criticism of public policy. The results of its research are disseminated through workshops, conferences, teaching materials, the Center's newsletter, and through books like this one.

This is the fifth volume of Maryland Studies in Public Philosophy. Previous volumes, listed across from the title page, dealt with the welfare system, the significance of national boundaries, immigration, and energy policy. Forthcoming studies will look at issues concerning risk policy, air pollution, endangered species, and a number of other areas of public policy.

The chapters in this book grew out of the meetings of the Center's Working Group on Voluntary versus Non-Voluntary Military Service, which met on three occasions in 1980–81 to discuss the all-volunteer policy of military recruiting and its alternatives. Papers produced for the meetings were subjected to criticism and comment by the whole group and were revised and rewritten for this volume.

In addition to the authors of the essays in this book, others who participated in all or some of the meetings were Richard V. L. Cooper, Director of Management Consulting Services, Coopers and Lybrand, and author of *Military Manpower and the All-Volunteer Force* (Santa Monica, Calif.: Rand Corporation, 1977); Edward Frankle, Associate Director for Policy Development and Administrative Legal Systems, Selective Service System; Philip Bobbitt, Professor at the University of Texas School of Law and at the time of the Working Group meetings Associate Counsel to the President of the United States; and Charles Moskos, Professor of Sociology, Northwestern University, and author of *The American Enlisted Man: The Rank and File in Today's Military* (New York: Russell Sage Foundation, 1970). Their participation added substantially to the value of the meetings and the quality of the essays included in this book.

Financial support for the Center's project on military service was provided by the Ford Foundation. General support for the Center is provided by the Rockefeller Brothers Fund. The views expressed by the individual contributors are, of course, their own and not necessarily those of the Center or its sources of support, or of the institutions and agencies for which the contributors work.

The successful completion of this book is due in no small measure to the resourceful and patient editorial efforts of Claudia Mills and the devoted and expert labor of Robin Sheets, Rachel Sailer, and Virginia Smith. Murrell Hawke rates special thanks for her skilled organization of the meetings of the Working Group.

RKF

Introduction

Recent years have seen the beginnings of a renewed national debate about military conscription.[1] These beginnings are more than likely to flower into broader controversy and political division as the decade unfolds. A growing awareness, justified or not but shared by increasing numbers, is that the All-Volunteer Force (AVF) is unsatisfactory and that a return to some form of compulsory service is desirable. Polls have revealed substantial segments of the American public who express a willingness to return to a draft.[2]

A little more than a decade ago, resistance to and hostility toward the Vietnam War draft led to the collapse of political support for conscription. Between 1969 and 1971 there was a flurry of draft reform—ending student and occupational deferments, changing to a lottery and a youngest-first order of selection, adopting a uniform national call—but widespread resentment remained, and conscription was eliminated altogether in 1973. The main objections to the draft were that (a) it bore heaviest against minority and lower-class youth and was thus inequitable,[3] (b) it coerced conscience and violated personal liberty,[4] and (c) it made it too easy for the nation to engage in military adventures.[5] Raising as they did fundamental questions about equity of service, the justification of compulsion, the nature of coercion, and the means to peace, these objections were clearly moral in nature.

To those who still vividly remember the criticisms of the draft in the late 1960s, it must seem ironical that two of the most common criticisms of the AVF are that it is an inequitable means of distributing service and that it enables the country too easily to go to war.[6] These two complaints might be termed as coming from the "left"; from the "right" come criticisms that the all-volunteer policy costs too much,[7] that it cannot produce enough recruits,[8] and that it yields soldiers of inferior quality.[9] These diverse grounds of unhappiness have led to calls from both "right" and "left" that the all-volunteer policy be abandoned.

A full debate about the desirability or undesirability of a change in military manpower policy must include many elements—economic, technical, military, diplomatic, as well as moral. Nevertheless, even many apparently economic or technical issues involve, at bottom, moral presuppositions or controversies. For example, debates about whether the AVF costs too much are, in the final analysis, less about the total dollar figures for alternative defense structures than about who shall bear what share of the burden of supporting defense. Shall the full burden be reflected in the budget of the United States and thus be paid for out of tax revenues, or shall the tax support for defense be reduced by shifting a major portion of the burden to young men (and women) through a levy on their labor? This essentially distributive question invokes relevant principles of distributive justice. Likewise, apparently technical debates about how to measure quality of recruits and what minimum quality is necessary to man increasingly complex and sophisticated weapons systems are also, in effect, debates about the composition of the force. Thus, such debates are inextricably linked to questions about representativeness in the ranks and about the fair allocation of the burden of service.

Moreover, even when moral concerns do not arise immediately, those who argue for a return to compulsory service generally seek to buttress their cases by positing a duty or obligation of young people to serve the country, and they thus implicate in the draft debate one of the oldest and most enduring questions in philosophy—the reality of political obligation. Thus, in the debate of the 1980s, just as in the debate of the 1960s, moral issues and moral principles are going to have central roles. This volume seeks to aid a more fertile engagement with the moral dimensions of the manpower debate by bringing together the reflections of seven philosophers—Simmons, Gewirth, Coleman, Piper, Childress, Fullinwider, and Ruddick—on some of the issues where moral concern is most prominent.

A. John Simmons (Chapter 5) and Alan Gewirth (Chapter 6) tackle the difficult question of political obligation. Simmons examines a variety of grounds for asserting there is a moral obligation to serve, but concludes that "citizens generally do not have a moral obligation or duty to serve in the military." Gewirth argues that the "obligation to obey and support the laws of some state can be justified" if that state is "minimal, supportive, and democratic," and that this can carry through to a justification of conscription in the right circumstances.

Jules Coleman (Chapter 7) looks at what must be presupposed if we object that the all-volunteer policy is intolerable because large numbers of poor and minorities enlist. We must either hold that these enlistments are not voluntary in some significant sense, or that the voluntariness of enlistments is not sufficient to make morally acceptable the resulting pattern of service. Coleman advocates the second possibility and clarifies some of the concepts and beliefs associated with the ideas of bargaining strength and fair bargains, allowing us better to understand what sort of judgment we want to make about the accusation that the all-volunteer policy takes "unfair advantage" of poor and minority youth.

Adrian Piper (Chapter 8) considers whether it is rational for a disadvantaged young person to choose military service as a means of self-advancement and contends that it is not. James Childress (Chapter 9), while surveying the challenging problem of justifying policy about conscientious objection, can find no compelling justification for treating selective objectors differently from universal objectors. Robert Fullinwider (Chapter 11) examines the increasing racial imbalance in the military and considers the arguments for concluding that this imbalance indicts the all-volunteer policy. He finds the arguments far from convincing. Sara Ruddick (Chapter 14) takes up a question new to our nation's debates about peacetime conscription: should women be included in a draft? In looking at how this question might be addressed, she explores at length the idea of fairness (involved in the contention that, out of fairness to men, women ought to be drafted if men are) and the claim that women have a distinctive capacity for peace (leading some to urge that women should be drafted in the interests of peace and others to urge that they should be excluded).

These chapters of philosophical investigation are joined to essays by six non-philosophers—D. Segal, M. Segal, Hunter, Coffey, Marlowe, and Butler (with Holmes)—who are experienced and respected students of military personnel policies. These essays provide the reader with some of the factual information relevant to assessing an all-volunteer versus a compulsory service policy. Moreover, they expose the reader to the considered judgments of individuals who have frequently had a hand in making and executing military manpower policy as well as in studying it.

David Segal (Chapter 1) looks at some of the current manpower problems and suggests that it is simplistic to blame them on the AVF. Some of the trends causing concern arose before the AVF was established; still other problems that emerged after the creation of the all-volunteer policy would have occurred even if a draft had been retained. In addition, argues Segal, much of what is wrong with readiness and performance can be laid to bad management and inadequate training within the services. Richard Hunter (Chapter 2) views the accomplishments of the AVF to date and assesses its prospects for the future. Whereas Hunter takes a somewhat positive view of the AVF, David Marlowe (Chapter 3) urges a return to the draft, arguing that the stringent demands of modern ground combat require capabilities which the AVF cannot supply.

Kenneth Coffey (Chapter 4) considers what a draft might actually do for the military. He postulates different-sized draft calls and different minimum entrance standards, and examines their results for racial composition of the force and for intelligence level of the enlistees (as measured by mental category scores). John Butler and Malcolm Holmes (Chapter 10) survey the history of blacks in the services and hypothesize that as the military becomes more like civilian institutions in organization, management, and ethos, race relations in the military will mirror race relations in society at large.

David Marlowe, in his second appearance (Chapter 12), argues that distinctive biological differences between males and females fit them for different fighting roles. Women, he claims, "should be excluded from offensive ground combat roles but not from combat roles in the air or at sea, and not from ground combat support and service support roles that may require possible defensive combat operations." Mady Segal (Chapter 13) surveys the changing role of women in the military and examines the controversy about their assignment to "combat" specialties.

Taken together, these fourteen essays should provide a useful context within which the reader may sharpen and refine his thinking about military manpower policy. The quality of the future debate will have much to do with the quality of future policy.

Notes

1. See Brent Scowcroft, ed., *Military Service in the United States* (Englewood Cliffs, N.J.: Prentice-Hall, 1982, sponsored by The American Assembly); Report of the Atlantic Council's Military Service Working Group, Andrew J. Goodpaster and Lloyd Elliot, co-chairmen, and J. Allan Hovey, rapporteur, *Toward a Consensus on Military Service* (Elmsford, N.Y.: Pergamon Press, 1982); and William J. Taylor, Eric T. Olson, and Richard A. Schroder, eds., *Defense Manpower Planning: Issues for the 1980s* (Elmsford, N.Y.: Pergamon Press, 1981).

2. See the data from a Gallup Poll in June 1981 and an Associated Press/NBC Poll in July 1981, both cited in Atlantic Council Policy Paper, *Toward a Consensus on Military Service* (Washington, D.C.: Atlantic Council of the United States, June 1982), p. 60, n. 51.

3. This objection is summarized in Lawrence M. Baskir and William A. Strauss, *Chance and Circumstance* (New York: Random House, 1978).

4. See *The Report of the President's Commission on an All-Volunteer Armed Force* (New York: Collier Books/The Macmillan Company, 1970); Bruce Chapman, *The Wrong Man in Uniform* (New York: Trident Press, 1967); and James C. Miller III, ed., *Why the Draft? The Case for a Volunteer Army* (Baltimore: Penguin Books, 1968).

5. See, for example, Richard Flacks, "The Draft in a Democratic Society," in Sol Tax, ed., *The Draft: A Handbook of Facts and Alternatives* (Chicago: University of Chicago Press, 1967), p. 197; and *The Draft? A Report Prepared for the Peace Education Division of the American Friends Service Committee* (New York: Hill and Wang, 1968), pp. 68ff.

6. For the first complaint, see Joseph Califano, "Playing the Draft Card," *The Washing-*

ton Post, 27 January 1980, B7; James Fallows, *National Defense* (New York: Random House, 1981); Richard Cohen, "Draft," *The Washington Post,* 28 July 1981, B1; *Hearings on Military Posture,* Committee on Armed Services, House of Representatives, 96th Congress, 1st Session, February–April 1979, Part 5, p. 182. The second argument is given voice in, among other places, Cohen, "Draft."

7. See, e.g., Cynthia Roberts, "We Must Reinstate the Draft," *The New York Times,* 25 February 1982, A31.

8. See Eliot A. Cohen, "Why We Need a Draft," *Commentary* 74 (April 1982), and the exchange of letters in *Commentary* 74 (July 1982).

9. See Cohen, "Why We Need a Draft," and J. L. Reed, "An Analysis and Evaluation of the United States Army," appendix to *Status of the All-Volunteer Armed Force,* Hearing Before the Subcommittee on Manpower and Personnel, Committee on Armed Forces, U. S. Senate, 95th Congress, 2nd Session, 20 June 1978.

Part I

The All-Volunteer Force and Its Prospects: Conditions and Alternatives

1

Military Organization and Personnel Accession: What Changed with the AVF . . . and What Didn't

DAVID R. SEGAL

Introduction

Criticisms of America's all-volunteer military force have become commonplace in the nation's media.[1] In the early 1980s, the public was reminded daily by magazine articles, television documentaries, and newspaper stories that our fiscal year 1979 recruiting efforts fell short by about 25,000 personnel in the active duty forces, that shortages in the reserve components were even worse, and that the personnel who were joining the service were of poor quality. The low grade of recruits and reductions in the training system were thought to be the reasons for personnel who could not do their assigned jobs. In addition, the force was and is becoming increasingly unrepresentative of the American sociodemographic population, as it becomes ever more dependent upon black and, more recently, Hispanic personnel. The services are also increasingly dependent upon female personnel, although women are excluded by statute and by regulations from direct combat roles and are proportionally underrepresented in the armed forces. An increasing fraction of the force is married or is composed of single parents, two categories that cause special deployment problems. All these difficulties at the lower military grades are aggravated by an exodus from the service of mid-level noncommissioned and commissioned officers, particularly those trained in technical specialties. Large numbers of junior personnel leave the service before completing their obligated tours, and personnel who remain in the service are hypothesized to be motivated more by pecuniary incentives than by a desire to serve the nation.[2]

All these factors are thought to add up to a military force incapable of meeting America's national security needs: a credible deterrent and constabulary force to keep the peace, and a military machine capable of fighting and winning a war if deterrence and constabulary operations prove insufficient. In addition to its operational problems, the American military establishment is extremely expensive. The existence of this expensive but seemingly ineffective military system is widely blamed on the fact that, in 1973, the United States stopped drafting young men through the Selective Service System and adopted a military manpower system based wholly on volunteer personnel. It is further argued that our military force would become less expensive and more effective if we were to revert to military conscription.

It is my thesis that many of the problems of the American military that are attributed to the All-Volunteer Force in fact preceded the end of the draft. Others, which evolved after 1973, would have appeared even if conscription had not been abolished. To be sure, the change to an all-volunteer format did have an impact on our armed forces, yet that impact is probably not as great, in terms of cost and effectiveness, as would appear at first blush. And while return to a conscription system would again have an impact on our armed forces, such a reversion would not necessarily reduce the cost or increase the effectiveness of our military establishment. Indeed, the greatest impact of a reintroduction of a military draft, or of some other form of national service for American youth, is likely to be seen not in the military per se, but in the nature of the relationship between the armed forces and American society.

Personnel Recruitment

In the early 1970s, when America abolished the draft and shifted to an all-volunteer format, the economy was in a shambles, youth unemployment was high, the last cohorts of the post–World War II baby boom were coming of military-age eligibility and, for a brief period of time, individuals entering the military could earn about as much as their civilian counterparts. The armed forces were able to recruit sufficient young people to man the force on an all-volunteer basis. We may have converted to an All-Volunteer Force at the only time in recent history when it had a chance of working.

By the late 1970s, however, the economy had improved, youth unemployment had dropped, pay caps kept military pay lagging behind civilian compensation, and the baby boom bubble had burst. Recruiting shortfalls began to appear, first affecting the ground combat forces, but ultimately spreading to all the services. In fiscal year 1976 the armed services achieved 100.6 percent of their recruiting objectives for non-prior-service personnel. By FY 1979, the figure had fallen to 92.8 percent. One of the results of this decline was that, near the end of 1979, the Army, which had the greatest recruiting difficulty, had a shortage of trained personnel of about 29,000 people.

Much of the decline in recruiting toward the end of the seventies can be attributed to the pay caps of 1975, 1978, and 1979. The pay of first-term junior enlisted personnel, which in 1972 was 115 percent of the federal minimum wage, had fallen to 84 percent by 1979. In the early 1980s, with youth unemployment again pushed up by inflation, the services are again meeting their recruitment goals. Nevertheless, to have our ability to meet national security manpower needs dependent upon major economic disruptions in American society is highly unsatisfactory.

One way to attract sufficient armed forces personnel on a routine and continuing basis is to reintroduce military conscription, or some more general program of national service within which military service in either the active forces or the reserve components would be among the options available. As long as public opinion did not oppose such a program, America's youth could routinely be registered, classified, and called up as needed. As the experience of the past has shown, some "draft-motivated volunteers" would enlist rather than waiting to be drafted, in order to retain some control over their enrollment date, which service they joined, what skill training they received, and where they served. Other young people would enlist for nonconscription-based reasons. Whatever manpower needs then remained in the active forces could be met through a draft.

Likewise, the reserves would find their ranks swollen by young people who preferred to avoid active service by incurring a reserve service obligation of greater duration. And under involuntary service schemes, remaining shortfalls in the reserve components could be made up by having a draft for the reserves, or by having reserve service as one of the options in a broader national service system. It is not comforting, however, to have our mobilization base in the event of war made up largely of people who join the reserves specifically to avoid active military service.

Any workable conscription system would have to be supported by the public and, ironically, our manpower needs are not sufficiently great to mobilize the needed public support. While widespread sentiment currently supports the concept of national service, the transfer of that support to an operating draft assumes that the draft will be perceived as equitable. The major determinant of perceptions of equity seems to be the proportion of the eligible population that is in fact drafted. If almost everyone must serve, the system is regarded as equitable. If only a few are called, it is unlikely that the system will be seen as equitable, regardless of how those few are chosen. Randomness, as in a draft lottery, is not the equivalent of equity. Our manpower shortfalls in the active duty forces are too low to be filled by conscription and have that conscription regarded as fair.

Another way to attract the requisite numbers into the All-Volunteer Force is to raise the military wage scale. When the President's Commission on an All-Volunteer Armed Force submitted its recommendation that we end the draft, it made the assumption that the wages paid to America's volunteer service people would be competitive with the civilian labor market, as indeed they were in the early 1970s.[3] But the pay caps on general schedule civil service salaries, to which military pay has been tied, until recently have prevented their keeping pace with the economy. Thus, high school graduates in June 1979 who went into the military, for example, earned about 18.5 percent less than their peers who entered the full-time employed civilian labor force. Perhaps before we reject the concept of an All-Volunteer Force, we should try it, by making the investment in people that it was assumed would be made.[4]

It is not clear that the reserve components can be manned as easily on the basis of remunerative considerations under all-volunteer conditions as they might be manned under a conscription system. Neither is it clear, however, that the reserves continue to play a significant role in our defense posture. They were not used in the Vietnam engagement, and we currently lack the means to get them to a war in Europe. If they are merely an artifact of past conceptions of military organization, we might be able to stop worrying about how to raise the manpower to fill them. That there is a role for the reserves in a protracted engagement, if we develop the means to move them, is unquestionable. In a brief war, however, it is unlikely that reserve forces could be mobilized rapidly enough to participate. I shall return to these points later.

Qualifications of Personnel

Much of the concern about the All-Volunteer Force has focused on the numbers who seek to enlist who have no high school diplomas, and on the proportion of enlistees who fall into the lower mental categories on the Defense Department's aptitude test, the Armed Forces Qualification Test (AFQT). In 1964, the last year

before the Vietnam War, about 29 percent of the draftees entering the Army had
not graduated from high school. The figure was 10 percent higher for volunteers.
During the all-volunteer era, the figure has been even higher, averaging more than
40 percent between 1975 and 1979. During this period, less than a quarter of all
males aged 18–24 did not graduate from high school. Thus, this lower educational
stratum is overrepresented in the All-Volunteer Force.[5] As in the case with
numbers of personnel, improvements can probably be made in quality through
reimposing the draft, or indeed through raising military compensation to make it
competitive with civilian pay levels. The extent of these improvements, however,
has probably been overestimated by those who think that reinstitution of the draft
would solve the problem.

It is obvious that, in a healthy economy, a system based upon compulsion
would be more effective in bringing people who have finished college, or at least
high school, into the enlisted ranks where, under the current all-volunteer format,
the college graduate is almost extinct. It is not clear, however, how many college
graduates, whose skill might be better applied elsewhere, we really need in our
enlisted force. The greatest gains here might be among *college-bound* youth, who
would enter the military with above-average mental aptitudes to fulfill their
military obligations prior to completing higher education. The services are
currently trying to attract this kind of person on an experimental basis with
enhanced educational incentives. While the aptitudes they would bring are
probably useful to the services, it is unclear whether it is more effective to attract
them with the carrot of educational incentives or drive them with the stick of
compulsion.

A military draft does give the defense establishment some leverage in increasing the representation of high school graduates in the enlisted ranks, and a long
history of social science research in the military shows that high school graduates
adapt more successfully and perform better in military environments than do
nongraduates. The possibility exists, however, that the achievements represented
by a high school diploma may have altered in U. S. society. Performance
indicators of high school seniors have reflected a nationwide decline, and it may
well be that the high school diploma represents less accomplishment and adaptability today than it did thirty years ago.

The issue of qualification test scores is even more complex. The norms used
until 1982 to classify volunteers by mental category were developed during World
War II, when millions of young men were tested and when a sufficient data base
existed for precise psychometric calibration of the AFQT. In subsequent years,
the test had not been renormed. To apply the World War II norms to the first
decade of All-Volunteer Force recruits required the assumption that the distribution of mental aptitudes in the youth population had not changed in the intervening four decades. The AFQT itself had been replaced by more recently developed
tests, parts of which have been used to estimate the World War II norms on the
AFQT. During 1980, the services discovered that an error had been made in
estimating these norms, so that a larger proportion than desired of Category IV
volunteers (the lowest acceptable mental category, including the tenth to the
thirtieth percentiles on mental aptitude) had been admitted to the service. Thus,
while the Army thought it had recruited less than 10 percent Category IV
personnel in 1979, it found that more than 45 percent of its 1979 recruits were in
Category IV, once test scores were corrected.

Beyond the psychometric errors of misnorming, however, which in any case
are relatively easy to correct in the short run, lies the very basic question of
whether the World War II norms credibly describe the mental aptitudes of

American youth in the 1980s, as measured by standardized tests. Scores on the other standardized tests administered to young Americans have been declining, and there is no reason to believe that AFQT scores and their surrogates would be an exception to this trend. If this is the case, the population mean on the AFQT might be lower today than in the 1940s, as might the cut-off points for the mental categories used by the services. If, for example, the 10th percentile occurred at a lower absolute score today than it did in 1940, then people in the bottom decile by the World War II norms, who by that standard would be in Category V and unacceptable for military service, might in terms of the 1980 norms become Category IV personnel, eligible to serve. In other words, considerably more than 10 percent of today's youth population might fall within the World War II definition of the bottom decile. Perhaps more important, at the other end of the distribution, were we to introduce widespread testing and classification, we might well find fewer Category I and II people in the population than we would expect on the basis of the World War II norms. In 1982, the classification test was finally renormed.

Minority Representation

About a quarter of all new recruits to the All-Volunteer Force are black. This proportion is higher in the Army than in the other services, and in the ground maneuver elements in particular. In our combat divisions, it is not uncommon to find units that are 50 percent black. (These units, in the event of combat, would sustain the greatest number of casualties and fatalities.) The representation of Hispanics in these same elements is growing as well. Is it fair to expect those segments of the population that have benefited least from the affluence of American society to bear most heavily, and out of proportion to their representation in the population, the casualties and fatalities of wartime military engagement? And would a draft guarantee proportional representation of the population in the ranks of the armed forces?

While the answer to the first question, in terms of morality, is probably no, let us consider another side of the question. Minorities have come to perceive, probably correctly, that although discrimination against them exists in the armed forces, it is less than the discrimination they might encounter in the civilian sector.[6] Volunteering for military service is a rational economic move for them. They will ''do better'' in the service than they would in the civilian labor market, and once they leave the service, they will ''do better'' in the civilian labor market than their peers who did not serve in the military.[7] In short, the military has been shown to be a mobility channel for minority males. Would it be ethical to restrict their access to this channel? And more important, perhaps, could we? Even under the draft, we have never had a totally conscripted force of first-term soldiers, but instead a mixture of volunteers and conscripts; historically, far more of our personnel have been volunteers than draftees. If opportunities were perceived by minority members to be more advantageous in the military than in the civilian sector, even under a conscription system, minority members would be likely to enlist in numbers disproportionately larger than their representation in the civilian population. Moreover, both draftee and volunteer minority members would be likely to reenlist in numbers greater than their proportional representation, and thus they would be overrepresented in the career nucleus of the forces, as well as among first-term junior personnel. The operating dynamic is external to the military: the process of discrimination in the civilian labor market.

Nor is there a guarantee of racial representation among those drafted, because here again external forces are at work. Major social inequalities exist in American society, and these inequalities have historically been reflected in all our major social institutions, including the draft. Conscription has never produced a socially representative armed force in the United States. Rather, it has reflected the distribution of privilege existing in society at large. Davis and Dolbeare, for example, found the poor to be overrepresented among draftees, a fact that was especially impressive since those with low incomes were also much more likely to be found mentally, morally, or physically unfit for service. In short, men with low incomes who were qualified for service were far more likely to be drafted than men with high incomes who had similar qualifications.[8] Davis and Dolbeare also found blacks to be overrepresented among draftees, but only as a function of their representation in low-income strata; blacks were drafted in the same proportions as whites of the same economic strata. In other words, blacks drafted through the Selective Service System were victims of economic, not racial, discrimination.

During the Vietnam War, individuals from lower socioeconomic backgrounds, once they were drafted, were also more likely to be channeled into the ground combat forces than into branches requiring technical aptitudes. They were, therefore, also more likely to be wounded or killed than were persons of higher socioeconomic backgrounds.[9] Again, blacks were overrepresented in these strata and, again through socioeconomic background rather than racial discrimination, were overrepresented among casualties. Recognition of these inequities in the Vietnam era draft contributed to opposition to the draft.

During the Vietnam War, in contrast to previous American wars, education was inversely related to military service. Student deferments in effect became student exemptions and had a statistically significant effect on the draft.[10] In an effort to make military conscription more equitable, the system of deferments that allowed people to escape the draft was revised, as was the method of selection for service. These steps were too late to save the Selective Service System, or perhaps could not have saved it in any case, for draft calls were too low for selection to be regarded as equitable, no matter how fair the selection procedures were. In 1967, eligibility for student deferments was reduced to age 24 or four years of study, whichever occurred first. In 1968, deferments were ended for all graduate study except medicine and allied fields. In 1970, much of the discretionary power of local Selective Service boards was eliminated by the establishment of the draft lottery. This lottery assigned Selective Service registrants priorities for conscription on the basis of their birth dates. These changes increased the likelihood that males from higher socioeconomic backgrounds would be drafted. The administration, responding to criticisms from liberals that the draft was inequitable, increased the risk of conscription of middle-class youth and thereby increased middle-class opposition to the draft. In January 1973, six months earlier than required by the Congress, Secretary of Defense Melvin Laird announced the end of peacetime conscription.

It is ironic that the criticisms of the inequities of conscription that contributed to its demise and to the establishment of the All-Volunteer Force are now being used as a justification for reinstituting conscription. Will a draft guarantee proportional representation of racial, ethnic, and socioeconomic groups in the armed forces? The lessons of recent history suggest it would not. In the past, the draft has not produced a proportionally representative force, although there was greater representation of more highly educated white males in the enlisted ranks than we have today. As Kenneth Coffey points out, a draft of 16,000 people would reduce the representation of blacks among new accessions by only 3 percent, from 37 to 34 percent. Drafting 57,000 people would reduce the percentage to 24.

Further reductions could be achieved by drafting from an increasingly narrow band of the population spectrum and rejecting for service increasingly large numbers of people who want to volunteer.[11] A draft that turns away large numbers of people from lower social strata, who see military service as an opportunity for a job or for social mobility, and places liability for conscription disproportionately on the middle strata of society is not likely to be supported by either segment of the population. A draft acceptable to those in privileged positions in society is likely to reflect society's inequalities and to place the burdens of enlisted service elsewhere. A draft that increases, through equity considerations, the liability of the middle class to serve in the enlisted grades is likely to be opposed by the middle class. In any case, minorities are likely to continue to be overrepresented among volunteers, unless we are willing to draft more than 100,000 people.

Women and Dependents

If blacks are the overrepresented minority in the armed forces, women are the underrepresented majority. Although they comprise more than 50 percent of the adult population, they represent less than 10 percent of the active forces, and are projected to make up no more than 12 percent of the force by 1984. These figures, however, represent a major increase over 1970 and reflect the growing dependence of our armed forces on female personnel to meet numerical strength objectives. In the early 1970s, women constituted only 2 percent of our military personnel. Not until the shortfalls in male enlistments in the early years of the All-Volunteer Force were the enlistment goals for women increased.[12] Many critics of the All-Volunteer Force regard warfare as man's work and see reinstitution of conscription as a means of reducing our dependence on female military personnel. The failure of then-President Carter to gain approval from Congress for his plan to register both young men and young women for Selective Service in 1980 was a reflection of a lack of national consensus on the appropriate role of women in national defense.

Again, the resolution of the issue of women in the military is likely to be driven not by decisions to introduce conscription or to raise military pay, but by social changes in American society external to the military. As a nation, we are undergoing a large-scale redefinition of appropriate gender-role behaviors. Increasingly, women are moving into domains that have been exclusively or predominantly masculine, and are proving themselves successful. In arenas such as athletics, education, and employment, the courts have upheld the principle of gender equality. Under a continued all-volunteer format, women will continue to demand the right to volunteer for the military activities that men are allowed to perform and, projecting from recent trends, their roles in the military will continue to be expanded in the long run, although there may well be short-term fluctuations from this trend. In the event of a draft, if women are not included in a system of compulsory service, that system is likely to be challenged in the courts by both women and men. As odious as war may be, some elements of the women's movement will find a statutory definition of gender differences in citizenship obligations still more odious. Men, on the other hand, are likely to oppose such a system because exempting any large segment of the population from military responsibilities would increase the likelihood that another segment will be called upon to make great sacrifices for the nation, thus depriving them of equal protection under the law. It is impossible to predict what the outcome of such challenges would be, but the recent judicial history would seem to favor rulings of gender equality.

The issue of women in the military is directly related, in the minds of many, with family responsibilities. In terms of traditional gender-role definitions, women serving in the military, or indeed in the civilian labor force, are seen as unable to fulfill their roles as wives and mothers. It is important to note here that the major changes have taken place outside the military, and changing gender roles within the military merely bring our armed forces into synchronization with civilian patterns.

Of greater pragmatic concern is the ability of the military to deploy female personnel who have dependent children. Where the military mother has a civilian spouse, the solution seems clear-cut, even if individual couples may have to wrestle with the particulars of application: the civilian spouse will have to take responsibility for the children while the military member of the family is away, as is common with male military personnel who have civilian wives. Where both spouses are in the armed forces, the services currently require that arrangements for childcare in the event of deployment be made beforehand. Monitoring of this requirement is honored more in the breach than in the practice, and increased attention will have to be paid to this area under either conscription or all-volunteer conditions.

The same requirement for back-up childcare arrangements exists for single parents in the military. Although there are proportionately more female than male single parents, there are numerically more males than females in the armed forces with sole responsibility for dependent children, because there are so many more men than women in uniform. The family issue is not just a female issue, and it is not going to go away even through the reimposition of a male-only draft.

A renewed draft is unlikely to keep women, or male sole parents, out of the armed forces. If they are excluded by statute, the statute is unlikely to go unchallenged in the courts.

Attrition

Another major concern voiced about the All-Volunteer Force is that of first-term attrition. By the late 1970s, more than a third of our volunteer enlisted personnel were leaving the armed forces prior to completing their initial enlistment. This is costly in terms of both the training wasted on those who leave prior to completing their obligated tours, and the cost of recruiting their replacements. It is not clear, however, that a return to the draft would be necessary, or even effective, in resolving this problem. Three points in particular are worthy of note.

First, while the loss of a third of our personnel seems high, under conscription in the early 1970s, we lost about a quarter of our personnel before they completed their first tours. Thus, the comparison is not zero-attrition under the draft versus one-third under the All-Volunteer Force, but a difference of one-quarter versus one-third.

Second, the long-term trend in first-term attrition has been one of fluctuation, and a figure of one-third is not a new historical peak. Indeed, the records of the War Department reveal that a century ago, the attrition pattern was similar to what it is today in terms of numbers: more than a third of our personnel did not complete their obligated tours of service. What differed were the reasons for attrition, and this leads to the third, and perhaps most important, point.

A hundred years ago, the most common reason for first-term attrition was purchase: personnel were able to buy their way out of military obligations. This military personnel policy does not depend on the existence of a particular system of conscription. Indeed, the British currently have a purchase system under an

All-Volunteer Force. By contrast, U.S. personnel today do not have to buy their way out of the force. The services have made it increasingly easy—for example, through the Navy's experimental Voluntary Discharge Program and the Army's Trainee Discharge and Expeditious Discharge programs—for personnel to receive honorable discharges and leave the service prior to the completion of their obligated tours; and the current system of benefits, including eligibility for unemployment compensation after 90 days of active duty, rewards them for so doing. As a matter of policy, this trend could be counteracted if the services would make it increasingly difficult to leave the force with an honorable discharge, or indeed at all, prior to completion of an obligated tour of duty, and Congress could restrict the benefits available to those who leave the service early for other than medical or compassionate reasons. First-term attrition in this case would be expected to decrease. This could be accomplished without resorting to a military draft.

The Cost Factor

Many of the arguments in favor of a return to the draft have been couched in terms of expense. In the late 1960s, under a draft, about 46 percent of the Defense Department budget went to manpower costs. That figure is currently 50 percent but is projected to decrease through 1985, assuming no real increases in military compensation over the next five years.[13] The assumption of no compensation increase seems unrealistic, so the decline in proportional expenditures on manpower is unlikely to occur. On the face of it, therefore, one might infer significant savings through a return to the draft.

Such an inference would be misguided. Actually, the personnel costs of the All-Volunteer Force would seem less excessive if we subtracted those costs that are after-effects of the mobilization for the Vietnam War rather than of the conversion to an All-Volunteer Force. Retirement costs in the defense budget in constant dollars, for example, increased from about $5 billion in 1974 to almost $14 billion in 1981. With regard to potential savings in recruiting costs, these costs must be weighed against the cost of establishing and maintaining a selective service system or a national service system plus maintaining as much of a recruiting system as we had during previous periods of military conscription. We never depended wholly on drafted personnel; therefore the issue is not one of high recruiting costs versus no recruiting costs.

In regard to savings in compensation, it is important to recall that the President's Commission on an All-Volunteer Armed Force separated the issue of compensation level from that of conscription. The argument made was that a differential in compensation that favored the civilian labor force did not represent a saving, but rather a reallocation of cost, so that it was borne by those who served rather than by the taxpayers. The commission felt this "conscription tax" was inequitable and recommended that even if military conscription were maintained, military compensation should be brought into line with the civilian labor market. As noted earlier, we managed to do just the opposite: we have abolished conscription and allowed military compensation to fall behind civilian pay levels.

The analysis of economic costs must also take into account the cost of veterans' benefits, particularly those related to education and training. One of the major justifications for benefits under the original G.I. Bill was the assumption that those who served under the draft would be economically disadvantaged relative to their peers who did not serve, and that assistance in achieving higher education or job training might resynchronize them with their age cohorts. These G.I. Bill benefits were among the casualties of the end of conscription. Although the Defense Department is currently experimenting with additional educational incentives, there has been no thorough accounting of the costs and benefits of military educational benefits.[14]

The Office of the Assistant Secretary of Defense has estimated that there would be net savings if we returned to a draft, but that these savings would be unlikely to amount to more than a half a billion dollars a year.[15] On the other hand, economists have pointed out that while the budget costs are less with a draft than under the All-Volunteer Force, the true costs of the draft are greater than those of an All-Volunteer Force. The differential is reflected in such factors as the "conscription tax" borne by those drafted, the productive activities forgone by the individuals assigned to military service, and the inefficient allocation of resources under a distorted incentive system.[16] Clearly, much economic analysis is yet to be done on military manpower issues. It is unfortunate that, should these analyses be undertaken, they will have to be interpreted in the light of a recent history of economic analyses of military manpower issues that, for the most part, have been incorrect.

What Then Has Changed?

The end of the draft was followed by recruiting shortfalls in the active forces in the late 1970s. These presumably could be corrected by increased youth unemployment, by reinstitution of a draft, or by paying military personnel a competitive wage and providing other economic incentives. It is not clear that the draft is either the best or the worst of these alternatives.

The end of the draft was followed by a reduction in the enlisted ranks of people with higher education, or at least aspirations for higher education. Either a draft or increased educational incentives might produce improvements here. The end of the draft was followed by an increase in female, racial, and ethnic minority personnel in the armed forces. It is unlikely that a return to the draft alone would greatly alter this composition. The end of the draft greatly altered the nature of the relationship between the individual and the state in America, in what I regard to be an undesirable direction. In this area there is a need for institution building, an issue that I shall return to later.

If there is anything for which the end of the draft was *not* responsible, it was the transformation of our military machine from an effective to an ineffective fighting force. If we ever had a truly effective fighting machine, a transformation to ineffectiveness took place under conscription (though the All-Volunteer Force may have exacerbated these changes). Had we not abolished conscription in 1973, I believe our armed forces would be no more effective than they are today.

American Military Organization and Performance

That we had an heroic and effective fighting force under conscription is, it seems to me, a romantic myth. While we like to believe that we won World War II in Europe because of the brilliance of our commanders and the bravery and commitment of our soldiers, and while it is clear that some units and some personnel manifested truly outstanding military performance, the German commanders were at least as brilliant and, for most of the war, the German soldiers were at least as brave and committed as our own. Our advantage in World War II, and what I heretically suggest led to our victory, was a seemingly inexhaustible manpower supply and a North American industrial base to support the war effort that was impervious to attack by the military technologies of the day. Our two major post-World War II military engagements in Korea and Vietnam, which we fought with large numbers of draftees, we failed to win. Our one dramatic military operation of the post-Vietnam era, the aborted 1980 attempt to rescue our hostages in Iran, was also a failure, but that had nothing to do with our having an All-Volunteer Force—the problems were in organization, planning, and hardware. To assert that problems of military effectiveness will be resolved by returning to a draft is akin to asserting that a flat tire can be repaired by adding air on the bottom. In my view, the manpower issue has become a smokescreen to mask the fact that, for reasons that have little to do with manpower, we have an ineffective military force. While this situation is not new, in the current international environment it can be regarded as a crisis of major proportions.

For at least two decades, important analyses have suggested major problems of organizational design in the U. S. forces. These include insufficient preparation of management personnel, overlapping management jurisdictions, ineffective coordination, the absence of some basic organizational functions such as planning, and personnel policies that undermine, rather than support, effective organizational functioning.[17] For most of this period we had a conscription-based force. Within the Army itself, for example, during the past twenty years a series of internal studies has recommended sweeping changes in personnel management to reduce redundancy and ambiguity, and to assure that someone be allocated responsibility for manpower functions that were not being performed at all. Only partial attempts have been made to meet the identified problems, and the organization has become even more chaotic. It was under conscription, not under the All-Volunteer Force, that the defense establishment moved most rapidly toward terminal organizational confusion.

One major factor increasing the complexity of modern military organization is the increased complexity of weapons systems in an age of new technologies. Historically, the core of the weapon system was the individual soldier, equipped in a way that made him most effective on the battlefield. Prior to the use of tanks, airpower, and increasingly accurate cannons and missiles (now directed by radar, lasers, and computers), the soldier was an infantryman, and his weapons were a rifle and a bayonet. Training in their use and eventually in the use of machine guns and grenades was relatively straightforward.

The advent of sophisticated tanks and antitank weapons, military aircraft and antiaircraft weapons, radar, computers, and lasers with military application changed this basic philosophy. Instead of equipping the man, we now man the equipment. We start with the hardware systems and then seek ways to train people to use them effectively on, or in support of, the battlefield. Too often, we find that the men can't use the equipment effectively. We have become gadget-happy, and this has costs in terms of military performance. These costs are not a function of the All-Volunteer Force.

The costs of our gadget-happiness are reflected in what we buy. Things that go bang are popular, so we buy expensive planes and tanks. Spare parts are not popular, so many of our expensive tanks and planes sit unused, either because components have broken down and cannot be replaced from inventory, or because parts have been removed through "irregular logistical procedures," i.e., cannibalized, to provide parts to keep other tanks or aircraft in operation. These priorities in resource allocation, which contribute to ineffectiveness, are not a product of the All-Volunteer Force.

While tanks and planes are popular, machines that move them—and indeed that move people—are not. We have not been investing in transport aircraft and ships to move our tanks and troops to foreign theaters. We talk about a "total force," in which troops in a foreign theater such as Germany or Korea will be reinforced and supported by active-duty personnel from the continental United States, by reserve and National Guard units, and ultimately by the mobilization of new personnel in the event of a war. Yet we do not at present have the means to get these additional personnel and their equipment to the war. For this reason I question whether the reserve components are anything other than anachronistic. If indeed we have to fight a "come as you are" war, the party will be over before they get there.

The concern with gadgets has also contributed to redundancy. The Air Force has invested in high-performance aircraft, in which pilots must spend a great deal of flying time to maintain their combat skills. Equipment failures and the cost of fuel keep such practice at a suboptimal level. Perhaps more important, these fancy machines are not appropriate for air mobility and close support of ground combat personnel. The Army and the Marine Corps have had to develop their own air technology for these functions. Indeed, the U. S. Army is the third-largest air force in the world, behind the U. S. and Soviet air forces. These redundancies and inefficiencies are not functions of the All-Volunteer Force and would not disappear with the reinstitution of the draft.

The organizational and resource problems can be exemplified by the state of training in the U. S. Army. Among the many criticisms of the Army under conscription during the declining years of the Vietnam War were frequent references to the poor state of training, and the extent to which Army personnel spent their time at housekeeping tasks, rather than training for mission effectiveness.[18] In 1971, Army Chief of Staff General William C. Westmoreland, recognizing the poor state of training, appointed a board of officers, the Board for Dynamic Training, to study the situation. The board was chaired by Brigadier General Paul F. Gorman.

General Westmoreland attributed the Army's training problems not to general organizational issues that might be long-lasting, but to "the Vietnam straitjacket." That is, he felt that providing personnel and logistical support for American troops in Vietnam had forced the Army to disregard training in other areas. A corollary to the straitjacket hypothesis was that with the withdrawal of American troops from Vietnam, high-quality personnel could be assigned to training duties, and the training system would be improved.

The Board for Dynamic Training rejected the straitjacket hypothesis and suggested that "the Army has marginally adequate training not because of inadequate trainers, but because of *systematic difficulty in assigning and articulating training objectives for its trainers and providing them with adequate resources.*"[19] In transmitting the Board's report to General Westmoreland, General Gorman sounded a note of pessimism: "The Board discovered no managerial 'quick fix' nor magic gadgetry that will swiftly and surely lead to . . . improvement . . . the Board calls attention to the fact that its recommendations, even if fully accepted, would impact . . . only after many months—conceivably years— of concerted effort at all echelons of the Army." The Army did try to improve its training system. But when the system was reevaluated in the spring of 1978 by the Army Training Study (ARTS), what was most apparent was the similarity to the findings of the Board for Dynamic Training.

What is true of training is also true of other areas of military organization and performance. There are major inefficiencies in the system; they are not the result of the conversion to an all-volunteer armed force; reinstitution of the draft will not make them go away.

What Will a Change Accomplish?

If the reinstitution of a draft will not solve the problems of military effectiveness, are there other reasons for continuing to regard it as a useful alternative? I believe there are. One function of national service, whether manifested as a military draft or as a broader set of activities, is to establish a principle of citizenship responsibility, a behavioral link between the individual and the state, and a social link between the manifold elements of civilian society and the armed forces that protect them. These functions were all filled by the draft in the United States and, to greater or lesser degrees, were lost with the conversion to an All-Volunteer Force.

The association of the right to bear arms with the role of citizen grew out of the American and French revolutions. Morris Janowitz notes that

> The political democracies which these revolutionary movements sought to establish rested on their having armed their citizens, who in turn demonstrated their loyalty through military service. . . . Military service emerged as a hallmark of citizenship and citizenship as the hallmark of a political democracy.[20]

The recognition that citizenship involves obligations, such as military service, as well as rights was in a sense lost when we moved away from a draft and toward an all-volunteer system. Replacing the draft with a broader national service system was considered, and indeed, at a 1966 conference on the draft, Janowitz argued in favor of replacing the Selective Service with a system of national service, with service in the military one of the alternatives available to American youth.[21] Correctly anticipating the events that were to unfold, he suggested that "an Armed Forces based on 'competitive' salaries is not a real possibility. . . . The military would always be disadvantaged relative to the private sector."

The assumption of pay comparability between the military and civilian sectors under market conditions cannot be met as long as military pay is determined by rank rather than by occupational task. In the civilian sector, a technician is paid a market wage based upon the demand for his skills and the number of people with those skills in the market. In the armed services, however, the basic pay of an E-4 computer operator is keyed not to what computer operators receive in the civilian economy, but to what E-4 combat infantrymen, tank turret repairmen, or truck drivers in the armed forces receive. The imposition of a market model of military manpower on the armed services without a major change in the structure of military compensation virtually assures that skilled technicians will be difficult to attract, and that armed forces personnel who are trained in technical skills while in the armed forces will be difficult to retain. This, of course, has been the lesson of recent history.[22]

Janowitz's arguments in favor of national service were not based primarily on market principles. Rather, he saw it as an opportunity to build a new social institution that would constructively help to direct social change. He saw the new system as more broadly distributing the burden of national defense and as helping to equalize educational and social welfare opportunities. Perhaps most important, although more implicit, national service was seen to establish linkages between the armed forces and civilian society, and between the behavior of the individual citizen and national purpose. The participation of the individual in the state, rather than the fact of military service, is crucial in this formulation, and in a world devoid of military threats to the state, a national service scheme might in fact exclude military service. But in a world with more than thirty ongoing armed conflicts which involve more than eight million military and para-military personnel, and in which potential adversaries have widely announced hostile intentions, the defense of the state becomes one of the most central forms of citizen participation.

When the All-Volunteer Force became a reality in the early 1970s, both the linkage between the armed forces and civilian society and the linkage between individual behavior and national purpose became important issues. In a presentation focusing on enlisted personnel, at the 1973 meeting of the American Sociological Association, Charles Moskos noted, almost in passing, "an organizational shift from a predominantly institutional format (i.e., legitimized by normative values) to one more resembling that of an occupation (i.e., akin to civilian marketplace standards)."[23] This typology in fact referred to the nature of military organization rather than to the nature of military service, but as it developed, it came to focus on both levels of analysis. By 1976, Moskos had identified a sense of calling as the individual orientation associated with the institutional format, and a sense of job as the individual orientation associated with the occupational format.[24] Policymakers in the United States have been greatly influenced by Moskos's typology, and have come to believe that a choice must be made between the definition of military service as a *calling* and as a *job*.

I do not mean to suggest that the idea of the military as a job was new in the 1970s. Indeed, it was anticipated by Janowitz, who, in discussing the officer corps in 1960, noted that "those who see the military as a calling or a unique profession are outnumbered by a greater concentration for whom the military is just another job."[25] Neither am I suggesting that the econometric pressures to redefine service originated in the debates on the termination of conscription in the late 1960s. They can certainly be traced back at least as far as Robert McNamara's emphasis on operations research and systems analysis in the Department of Defense. Nor am I suggesting that a model of military service as a calling requires that we pay military personnel less than a fair market wage. Indeed, I feel strongly that whether our military manpower system is based on voluntarism, conscription, or some combination of the two, the economic costs of military service should not be borne disproportionately by those who serve. Nonetheless, I believe that economic incentives by themselves are not sufficient to maintain an effective fighting force. The empirical question is whether soldiers motivated by the same factors that recruit workers for an automobile assembly line are any more willing to risk their lives for the nation, or to take the lives of enemy soldiers in combat, than are those assembly line workers. In a survey of the Army chain of command in 1978, more than 86 percent of the officers and NCOs surveyed felt that soldiers today think of their service primarily as a job, and more than a third questioned whether soldiers who see their service as a job will perform well in combat.[26] The bulk of the historical evidence suggests that troops perform well in combat because of solidarity, rather than remunerative incentives.[27] Reestablishing the norm of service as a citizen duty will, I believe, contribute to the sense of collective purpose that has been on the wane in the American armed forces under individualistic econometric management.

At the aggregate level, the organizational health of the military is also affected by the degree to which it enjoys broad popular support and trust. In a democracy, responsibility for defense of the state ideally is shared by all strata of society. To the extent that this ideal is met, all segments of society feel that they have a stake in the armed forces. Where purely economic incentives produce a force in which some communities are entirely unrepresented, however, these communities are likely to feel estranged from the armed forces which protect them. The issue of representation, as I see it, is not one of *proportional* representation, with which other scholars seem concerned,[28] but rather one of the isolation of the military from large segments of civilian society, and the potential resulting distrust and lack of interest that might evolve between those segments and the armed forces.[29] The overrepresentation of blacks in the Army, from this perspective, is not, in and of itself, problematic.[30] The nonrepresentation of the white middle class, however, would be.

A military organization that increasingly resembles industrial organization and a societal context that becomes progressively more rationalized and alienating contribute to heightened individualism, increasing disengagement, and a weakening of social control.[31] The available evidence suggests that, as a nation, we have lost sight of the fact that citizenship involves responsibilities as well as rights. The advent of the All-Volunteer Force both reflected and contributed to the redefinition, and reduction in moral valence, of that responsibility. Much of the contemporary discussion of registration or reintroduction of a draft, of compulsory or voluntary national service, and of tying some of the benefits of citizenship, such as financial assistance for higher education, to fulfillment of citizenship responsibilities implicitly addresses the issue of responsibility to the state. Sociologists have begun to address the issue explicitly as well, but increased attention is warranted.[32] This is the area where the effect of an All-Volunteer Force has probably been most pervasive.

Notes

1. See, for example, William P. Snyder, "Son of Sad Sack," *The New Republic,* 5 and 12 July 1980, pp. 20–23; and John J. Fialka, "Can the U.S. Army Fight?" *Washington Star,* five-article series, 15–19 December 1980, page 1 each day.

2. Charles C. Moskos, "From Institution to Occupation," *Armed Forces and Society* 4 (Fall 1977): 41–50.

3. President's Commission on an All-Volunteer Armed Force, *The Report of the President's Commission on an All-Volunteer Armed Force* (Washington, D.C.: Government Printing Office, 1970).

4. Melvin R. Laird, *People, Not Hardware* (Washington, D.C.: American Enterprise Institute, 1980).

5. Charles C. Moskos, "Saving the All-Volunteer Force," *The Public Interest* 61 (Fall 1980): 75–76.

6. John D. Blair, Richard C. Thompson, and David R. Segal, "Race and Job Satisfaction in the U.S. Army," in *Changing Military Manpower Realities,* edited by James Brown, Michael J. Collins, and Franklin D. Margiotta (Boulder, Colo.: Westview Press, 1983).

7. Melanie Martindale and Dudley L. Poston, Jr., "Variations in Veteran/Nonveteran Earnings Patterns Among World War II, Korea, and Vietnam War Cohorts," *Armed Forces and Society* 5 (1979): 219-43.

8. James W. Davis, Jr., and Kenneth M. Dolbeare, *Little Groups of Neighbors* (Chicago: Markham Publishing Co., 1968).

9. Gilbert Badillo and David G. Curry, "The Social Incidence of Vietnam Casualties," *Armed Forces and Society* 2 (1976): 397-406.

10. Jerald Bachman, John D. Blair, and David R. Segal, *The All-Volunteer Force* (Ann Arbor: University of Michigan Press, 1977), p. 14.

11. Kenneth J. Coffey, "If the Draft Is Restored: Uncertainties, Not Solutions," Chapter 4, this volume.

12. Mady W. Segal, "Women in the Military," *Youth and Society* 10 (December 1978): 101-26.

13. Lawrence J. Korb, "The FY 1981–1985 Defense Program: Issues and Trends," *AEI Foreign Policy and Defense Review* 2, no . 2 (1980): 7.

14. See David R. Segal and Melanie Martindale, "The Role of Military Service in the Status Attainment Process," paper presented at the International Sociological Association Symposium on Social Stratification and Intellectual Skills, Austin, Texas, 4–7 February 1980.

15. Office of the Assistant Secretary of Defense (Manpower, Reserve Affairs, and Logistics), *America's Volunteers: A Report on the All-Volunteer Armed Force* (Washington, D.C.: Department of Defense, 1978).

16. These issues are discussed by Richard V.L. Cooper, "Military Manpower Procurement: Equity, Efficiency, and National Security," paper presented to the Working Group on Voluntary versus Non-Voluntary Military Service, Center for Philosophy and Public Policy, Washington, D.C., 10 October 1980.

17. For discussion of these issues, see David R. Segal and Joseph J. Lengermann, "Professional and Institutional Considerations," in *Combat Effectiveness,* edited by Sam C. Sarkesian (Beverly Hills, Calif.: Sage, 1980), pp. 154–84; and David R. Segal, "Leadership and Management: Organization Theory," in *Leadership,* edited by James Buck and Lawrence Korb (Beverly Hills, Calif.: Sage, 1981), pp. 41–69.

18. See, for example, William L. Hauser, *America's Army in Crisis* (Baltimore: Johns Hopkins University Press, 1973).

19. Board for Dynamic Training, *Report of the Board for Dynamic Training* (Ft. Benning, Georgia: 1971). The italics are mine.

20. Morris Janowitz, "The All-Volunteer Military as a 'Sociopolitical' Problem," *Social Problems* 22 (February 1975): 435.

21. Morris Janowitz, "The Logic of National Service," in *The Draft,* edited by Sol Tax (Chicago: University of Chicago Press, 1967), pp. 73-90.

22. David R. Segal, "Military Service in the Nineteen Seventies," in *Manning the American Armed Forces,* edited by Allan R. Millett and Anne F. Trupp (Columbus, Ohio: The Merson Center of the Ohio State Universtiy, 1981), pp. 41-63.

23. Charles C. Moskos, "Studies on the American Soldier," paper presented at the 1973 Annual Meeting of the American Sociological Association.

24. Charles C. Moskos, "The Military: Occupation, Profession, or Calling?" in *The Changing World of the American Military,* edited by Franklin D. Margiotta (Boulder, Colo.: Westview Press, 1978), pp. 199-206.

25. Morris Janowitz, *The Professional Soldier* (New York: Free Press, 1960), p. 117.

26. John D. Blair and David R. Segal, *Perceptions and Evaluations of the Army Training System* (Washington, D.C.: Army Training Study, 1978).

27. See Segal, "Leadership and Management."

28. See, for example, Morris Janowitz and Charles C. Moskos, "Five Years of the All-Volunteer Force," *Armed Forces and Society* 5 (Winter 1975): 194–98.

29. For discussions of this more general issue of civilian-military institutional linkages, see David R. Segal, Mary Scheuer Senter, and Mady W. Segal, "The Civil-Military Interface in a Metropolitan Community," *Armed Forces and Society* 4 (Spring 1978): 423-47; and John D. Blair, "Internal and External Integration Among Soldiers," *Journal of Political and Military Sociology* 8 (Fall 1980): 227-42.

30. See Robert Fullinwider, "The All-Volunteer Force and Racial Balance," Chapter 11, this volume.

31. Morris Janowitz, *The Last Half-Century* (Chicago: University of Chicago Press, 1978).

32. See, for example, Morris Janowitz, "The Citizen Soldier and National Service," in *Evolving Strategic Realities,* edited by Franklin D. Margiotta (Washington, D.C.: National Defense University Press, 1980), pp. 127-44; and Janowitz, "Observations on the Sociology of Citizenship," *Social Forces* 59 (September 1980): 1-24.

2

An Analysis of the All-Volunteer Armed Forces—Past and Future

RICHARD W. HUNTER

Introduction

To assess the performance of the All-Volunteer Force (AVF), we must ask, compared to what? It is always easy to criticize, to find fault and point out things that are not optimal. It is more difficult, but essential, to evaluate and compare the current system for staffing the military against alternative systems, and to pick the system that appears best overall.

The *first* requirement of a military manpower system is that it provide the armed forces with a sufficient number of people to meet manpower requirements under existing and potential operating conditions. *Second,* the system must provide people who have the skills required by the military, or who can be trained in the needed skills. The *third* criterion is attitudinal. Are those who are selected to serve motivated to carry out their duties? The *fourth* standard relates to experience, in two dimensions. One is the breadth of experience available to the military. How many people in the mobilization base (the number who can be called in an emergency) have had military experience? The other is the depth of the experience in the active force, which is a function of length of tours, turnover, reenlistments, etc. *Fifth,* the working of the manpower system must seem fair and justified to the public; and, *sixth,* the cost must be acceptable to the taxpayers and their elected representatives.

This chapter will review how the AVF has succeeded or failed in meeting these six requirements, then estimate how it and its leading alternatives are expected to fare against the same criteria in the rest of the 1980s. All alternatives are assumed to require an active armed force of about 2 to 2.5 million people in peacetime, with significant increases only during wars or national emergencies. The three basic options are (1) to continue the All-Volunteer Force or some modified version of it, (2) to reactivate the existing draft law or some modification of it, and (3) to start some form of national training or national service.

The current system recruits men and women volunteers primarily in their late teens to meet the peacetime requirement, but relies on conscription through a rapidly expanded Selective Service System to call up previously registered young men in war or major national emergency. Variations on this option could increase the level of the standby draft to include classification or even physical exams; women could be included as well as men. On the other extreme, registration could be dropped and draft authority permitted to expire, resulting in increased dependence on the AVF during emergencies.

The second option likewise could have many variations to try to increase fairness and acceptance. They range from conscripting small numbers of males to make up for shortages of AVF volunteers, to prohibiting volunteers altogether and conscripting the entire force. A number of bills introduced in Congress would legislate one or another variant of the third option, national training or national service. Some are not universal, and others would affect nearly all eighteen-year-olds. While each variation is unique and could be considered separately, the evaluation here will address the three broad groups.

Evaluation of the Current AVF

During the decade since the draft ended in 1973, the armed forces of the United States have met all manpower requirements by recruiting men and women volunteers. How well has that system met the needs of the military measured against the six criteria set out above?

QUANTITY

The total number of active-duty military personnel increased from 2.7 million to 3.5 million to meet Vietnam requirements, and after Vietnam declined to 2.1 million. Most of the change was in the size of the Army, but all the military services followed the same trend. The size of the post-Vietnam force is smaller than the pre-Vietnam force by some 600,000 people.

America's Volunteers, a report by the Assistant Secretary of Defense for Manpower, Reserve Affairs, and Logistics, claims that this decline was the result not of recruiting difficulties, but of more efficient use of personnel.[1] Considerable evidence supports this claim, and little or no evidence refutes it. Because people could no longer be forced into service, wages for all military personnel, but especially for junior enlisted personnel, dramatically increased. Recruit pay doubled.[2] As Richard Cooper pointed out in *Military Manpower and the All Volunteer Force,* as long as labor is cheap to the military, incentives remain to use more people than otherwise would be necessary.[3] By paying the market cost for labor under the AVF, the military has been encouraged to make the capital-labor substitutions found in other sectors of American society. This would account for the smaller post-Vietnam force size. Clearly, the smaller size was caused by the conditions of voluntary service, but is not a quantitative shortfall. The Reagan administration has suggested returning to a larger force that approaches pre-Vietnam levels, but this would represent an increase in capability, not a reversal of the capital-labor substitutions.

Active-duty force sizes seem to be in balance with other elements of the defense budget. In situations of great uncertainty, more is usually considered better, and it is easy to compare the U.S. armed forces with potential enemies and wish for much more of everything. One is not surprised when military leaders call for more people. What is important to note is that the size of the active-duty armed forces does not seem to be constrained by recruiting capability in the market, but rather by resources allocated to the defense budget within the national priorities established by the president and Congress.

The same argument does not apply to the reserve components of the armed forces. Recruiting difficulties have led to reduced reserve capability, especially in the land forces.[4] The purpose of the reserves is to provide trained people and operational equipment to augment the active forces in time of war. Some support units, such as field laundry units, field kitchens, mobile Army surgical hospitals (MASH), and airborne refueling squadrons, are needed only for very limited functions in peacetime but become very important in war. Such units may be placed in the reserves but must be called very early in a mobilization since they are essential to the operational effectiveness of the active forces. Other reserves provide both unit and individual replacements for casualties sustained in the early weeks of the war. Such replacements are planned to enter the combat theater thirty, sixty, ninety, or even more days after the start of a major war to maintain combat strength while untrained personnel are drafted and trained and additional equipment is produced and procured.

The reserves may be divided into two general groups: (1) the Selected Reserve, composed of units that train regularly, including the Army, Navy, Air Force, and Marine Corps reserves and the Army and Air Force National Guards; and (2) the Individual Ready Reserve (IRR), which does not have units and does not train, but in which reservists are available to be called to active duty to fill units that may have preemergency shortages or may sustain casualties.

The IRR does not recruit directly, as do the active and Selected Reserve forces. Rather, it is composed of those individuals who have left the active and Selected Reserve forces, but who still have a portion remaining of the six-year military obligation incurred by all who join the armed services (active or Selected Reserve). Thus the size of the IRR is directly proportional to the number of people being recruited and inversely proportional to how long they serve. Longer tours of active and Selected Reserve duty and higher reenlistment rates— normally considered desirable outcomes of an AVF—reduce the numerical strength of the IRR.

Prior to the Vietnam conflict, IRR strength varied between 800,000 and 1.5 million, increasing during periods of conflict or tension when higher draft calls were being made and decreasing during periods of calm. In 1963, 800,000 individuals were in the IRR as the Vietnam War began. IRR strength grew to a maximum of almost 1.6 million in 1971. Under the AVF it dropped precipitately to less than 400,000 at the low point in 1978, and it has increased slowly since then.

Changes in the Selected Reserve have not been nearly as dramatic, but still are of concern. In 1970 almost one million reservists were serving in organized Selected Reserve units. Since almost no reservists were called up for Vietnam, it was a popular way to avoid being drafted into active service. Recruiting and retaining college students was no problem at all, especially after college defer- ments were eliminated from the Selective Service procedures.

After the Vietnam War ended and the draft was terminated, one of the prime incentives to enlist in the reserves was gone. The end of the draft also greatly reduced an individual's incentive to complete his six-year service obligation in a drilling unit. Recruiting became difficult; many who did join left the units within a year or so as their educational, work, and personal preferences decreased the attractiveness of reserve duty. By 1978 Selected Reserve strength was down to 800,000. Almost all the drop was in the Army and Marine Corps and, especially, in the combat arms units of those organizations. Again, as with the IRR, there has been some improvement since 1978, but the reserves (Selected and IRR together) are about 250,000 people short of what most analysts believe is needed to sustain a protracted, high-intensity, conventional war in Europe.[5]

Under the AVF, the active force has been offering a full-time job that is competitive in the primary labor market. The reserve recruiting effort has been much less competitive in the part-time labor market. Relative to other part-time jobs the reservist's pay is low, but not unacceptably so. The major problem is a special condition of this part-time employment: an enlistee in the reserves must undergo several months of full-time training at a military installation outside the community. Usually this requirement is not compatible with his full-time job and thus rules out reserve service for many who otherwise would enlist in the reserves.

Perhaps the most important problem for the reserves, however, is their lack of priority within the Department of Defense. Making the AVF work for the active forces has been the first priority, and making it work for the reserve components has received concentrated management attention and resources only as time and money permitted.[6] In the 1975 to 1978 period, new enlistment incentives were developed for reserves, and training programs were redesigned to accommodate training with school and full-time jobs. In response to the recruiting shortfalls for the active force in 1978, almost all top management attention was turned to meeting active duty strength in 1979 and 1980. After increased recruiting success for the active forces, attention in 1981 again focused on the problems of reserve components.

The third priority, after active duty and reserve components, is mobilization of previously untrained personnel. During the early days of the AVF, draft registration and classification by the Selective Service System were continued. On March 3, 1975, however, registration based on birth date was suspended and periodic registration ordered by presidential proclamation.[7] This was understood to be an annual one-day registration for all eighteen-year-old males. The first annual registration, however, was not held for five years, until the summer of 1980, and was initiated by President Carter. The registration allows a newly up-graded Selective Service System rapidly to call up large numbers of draftees in case of an emergency mass mobilization.

QUALITY

Whenever one undertakes to evaluate the "quality" of human beings one is on uncertain ground. Yet the quality of military personnel may be more important to national security than the quantity. History supplies many examples of small groups of dedicated and committed soldiers who determined a favorable outcome against overwhelming opposition. It is unfortunate that we have no reliable tests to measure such dedication and commitment. In fact, troops that were extraordinary in one battle may be only mediocre in the next. Despite these limitations, the services must use some quantifiable measures for estimating quality. Instead of measuring dedication and commitment, they measure test scores and educational achievements.

One measure used to evaluate recruits is the aptitude testing for training in specific military occupational specialties.[8] On this measure, the AVF looks very good; all the services recruit more than enough personnel with scores above the minimum to meet training requirements. But, one can argue, a mix of personnel many of whose scores are well *above* minimum is needed for an effective force. An entire force of minimally qualified individuals is undesirable, but what are the standards for the correct mix? In fact, analyses done at the Center for Naval Analysis by Robert Lockman and James Thomason cast doubt on the reliability of the minimum scores.[9] Experiments show that youth just below the minimum requirement do about as well in training as those just above it. Lockman and Thomason are trying to develop more reliable selection instruments.

The aptitude tests given by the military for mechanical and other specific abilities are more reliable than the general aptitude scores on the Armed Forces Qualification Test. Notwithstanding, the general aptitude test that measures so-called mental group sets the legally required standards for enlistment.

During World War II all entering military personnel (officer and enlisted, draftee and volunteer) were classified into one of five mental groups, with mental group I having the highest scores and V the lowest. Those scoring below V were not allowed to serve. The same categorizations have continued in use since World War II, although the dividing boundaries among the groups probably have shifted as tests have changed and been renormed. Recently the Office of the Secretary of Defense found that both test compromise and errors in norming have resulted in many recruits being classified higher than they should have been.[10]

The test scores are believed to be fairly reliable for groups I and II, but there are more IVs and fewer IIIs than were previously believed. For example, in fiscal year 1979, about 30 percent of recruits for DOD overall and 47 percent for the Army were from category IV. Improved recruiting conditions and extra effort by the recruiting commands resulted in fewer Category IV recruits in 1981—only 18 percent of recruits overall. The Army had 31 percent, the Navy 12 percent, the Marine Corps 13 percent, and the Air Force 7 percent. Although many Category V people served in the armed forces in World War II, the services now are prohibited from enlisting people who score in this category.

Despite all the psychological testing that has been developed over the years, completion of high school is still one of the better predictors for successful completion of obligated service in the armed forces. For the active forces the percentage of accessions with high school diplomas has remained relatively constant. In FY 1978 and FY 1979, some military services elected to keep up high school graduate percentages even if strength shortfalls resulted. That is what occurred. In FY 1980 strengths were met, but high school graduate percentages were down to 68 percent from 73 percent in 1979 for all of DOD and down from 64 percent to 54 percent for the Army. In FY 1981 the market reversed. The percentages rose to 81 percent high school graduates overall, and to 80 percent in the Army. These improvements in part resulted from increased military pay and increased youth unemployment, but also from the assignment of Lieutenant General Maxwell Thurman to command the recruiting effort and an extraordinary commitment to recruiting high-quality youth for the Army.

The problem with restrictions of recruiting based on test scores and education is the problem common to all testing. What balance should be struck between type 1 and type 2 testing errors? (Type 1 error refers to the number admitted who should have been excluded; type 2 to the number excluded who should have been admitted.) As educational levels and test scores are lowered, more people who will eventually drop out before completing their tours are admitted. This is an increase in type 1 error, which increases training costs and causes turbulence. On the other hand, higher standards exclude many who could have succeeded. But type 2 error is often ignored.

The type 1 error for recruiting high school graduates only is a little more than 20 percent. For nongraduates, the type 1 error is almost 45 percent. At the margin, these figures indicate that about 55 percent of those rejected nongraduates would have succeeded and become good soldiers who completed their enlistments, if they had been permitted to enlist.

If strength shortfalls occur while a large number of potentially good recruits are being rejected, policy should be adjusted (and indeed was, from mid-1979 through FY 1980). When recruiting is good, standards should be raised by the services to reduce training costs. Occasional congressional restrictions on recruiting are not responsive enough to changing conditions. By the time Congress can act, the situation often has reversed.

Sliding standards may work, but a better solution would be improved selection tools—better ways of selecting youth, especially non-high-school graduates, to recruit higher percentages of those who will in fact succeed. The military services and their personnel laboratories and contractors have been addressing these issues and are continuing to search for better selection instruments.[11]

The change in education and test scores for recruits in the reserve and National Guard components is much more dramatic than for the active force. In 1970 almost 55 percent of recruits for the reserves had some college, and all but 6 percent were high school graduates. In 1980 this figure had reversed. Fewer than 10 percent had any college, and more than 50 percent had not graduated from high school. The reserves under the draft were much better educated than the active force. Now the two groups are very similar.

Many of those highly educated youth who enlisted in the reserve units during the draft years were really using the reserves as a draft-dodging vehicle. There is a real question how many would have reported for duty and how many would have reported to Canada had their units been activated. Also, no evidence exists to indicate that college-educated recruits make better soldiers than others. Training in military skills and effective leadership are probably more important than education and test scores.

ATTITUDE

Dedication to the cause and motivation to fight are the real quality determinants. Coupled with training, experience, and leadership, they make the difference between outstanding soldiers and mere file fillers. As mentioned above, we do not have good before-the-fact tests for these elements, but there is no reason to assume that this generation will be any less dedicated to the principles embodied in the Constitution or less motivated to defend their freedom than bygone generations.

Older generations always tend to remember "the good old days" as better than they were and to discount the commitment of the current younger generation, as the World War II writer Robert Sherrod wrote in *Tarawa*. He had asked an Army general, a friend of many years, his opinion of the American soldier. The general became depressed and said, "I'm afraid the Americans of this generation are not the same kind of Americans who fought the last war."[12] That conversation took place in 1942, not in the 1980s. To the older folks in World War II, the dog face was not up to the level of the brave lads at Verdun. During World War I, the doughboys were not as dedicated as the brave souls who stormed San Juan Hill or stood at Gettysburg. The tendency to underrate the current generation's patriotism and ability and to overrate that of previous generations is still alive and well in America.

While the youth of America can be expected to rise to meet a threat to our freedom as previous generations have done, morale problems are common to many peacetime armed forces. It is difficult to maintain good attitude and dedication. Garrison soldiers have problems staying ready. Nothing increases dedication, motivation, and morale of a fighting force like combat. A football training camp is not the same as Sunday afternoon in the stadium. (Increasing the stakes also has an effect—a preseason game is not the Super Bowl.) A firefighting crew can polish the fire engine only so many times a day without morale suffering, but as the engine races to a seven-alarmer with siren on and bells clanging, something happens to the crew that makes them heros who will risk their lives for others in distress.

I think the nostalgic tendency to romanticize the past and decry the present to some extent accounts for the negative reports circulated in well-meaning but unscientific surveys such as the *Beard Study* and the "ABC News Closeup . . . The American Army: 'A Shocking State of Readiness.' "[13] Even more scientifically oriented observers, such as Charles Moskos, have questioned the commitment of current military personnel based on attitudinal analysis that ignores the fact that peacetime soldiers, and especially garrison soldiers, always suffer from morale, motivational, and attitudinal problems that are best solved by exposing them to the combat stimulus and permitting them to do what they have trained to do in a situation where it really counts.[14]

I agree with the testimony of Lieutenant General DeWitt Smith before the Senate Armed Services Subcommittee on Manpower that, in spite of all the press excitement to the contrary, today's armed forces are among the best trained, best equipped, and most dedicated *peacetime* militaries the nation has ever had.[15] Serious problems remain, but most of them would not be alleviated by a return to a draft.

EXPERIENCE

Experience is a highly valued commodity among military leaders. Compared to the Soviets, who have few military personnel with combat experience and almost no field grade commanders or senior NCOs who have led Russian troops in action, the American forces, as a result of engagements in Korea and Vietnam, have a large relative advantage in combat experience. (The Russians may be increasing their experience levels in Afghanistan.)

Experience is more than just acquaintance with combat. Time in service also is important. The AVF provides a decided advantage over earlier drafted forces in this respect. Its longer initial enlistments and much higher first-term reenlistment rates provide a much more experienced force than existed under a draft. The comparative data are summarized in Tables 2.1 and 2.2.

First-term reenlistment rates for all the armed forces are up from 19 percent in 1972 to 43 percent in 1981. Career reenlistments have varied about 15 percentage points, from a high of 83 percent in 1973, to a low of 68 percent in 1979, and up to 76 percent in 1981. For the Army, first-term reenlistments are up from 10 percent in 1972 to 55 percent in 1981. Army career enlistments are up from 46 percent in 1972 to 73 percent in 1981.

Even under a draft, career personnel are volunteers. If the draft were reinstated and large draft calls made, one could expect that military leaders would soon lament the terrible problem of falling first-term reenlistment rates. That would soon be followed by shortages throughout the career force. Under a broad draft, fewer highly motivated people enter service, and therefore first-term reenlistment rates are lower. This smaller base results in career shortages even when mid-career reenlistments are high.

The Navy has been especially concerned with its career reenlistment rates, which sagged from more than 90 percent in 1972 and 1973 to a low of 62 percent in 1979. In the 1980s conditions have improved somewhat, but have not returned to the pre-AVF levels. With the ever-increasing complexity of weapons and support systems, the Navy needs more experienced personnel. This retention problem often is cited as a failing of the AVF. But I believe the Navy's experience problems would be worse, not better, if the draft were reinstated. First-term

Table 2.1   Length of Enlisted Commitment for DOD (percentage of active non-prior-service enlisted accessions)

Fiscal year	2 yr	3 yr	4 yr	5 yr	6 yr	Average length (years)
1964	33	27	40	1	1	3.1
1965	35	24	40	1	1	3.1
1966	47	19	34	1	1	2.9
1967	44	24	32	1	1	2.9
1968	51	22	27	1	1	2.8
1969	44	24	32	1	1	2.9
1970	48	23	29	1	1	2.9
1971	43	23	34	1	1	2.9
1972	21	20	50	4	5	3.5
1973	18	26	42	6	8	3.6
1974	13	41	39	1	7	3.4
1975	13	37	44	1	5	3.5
1976	1	41	54	1	5	3.7
1977	0	40	55	1	4	3.7
1978	0	39	56	1	4	3.7
1979	1	36	57	1	5	3.8
1980	1	34	58	1	6	3.8
1981	1	31	60	1	7	3.8

Note: Fiscal years 1964–1973 include draftees who had a two-year commitment.

Source: All data in this table and in other tables and figures in this chapter are from Office of the Assistant Secretary of Defense for Manpower, Reserve Affairs, and Logistics.

personnel who would enlist in the Navy to avoid being drafted into the Army would have very low reenlistment rates.

Under the AVF, the Army had the largest increase in experience both in terms of more years on initial enlistment and higher first-term reenlistment rates. This has led to proportionally more individuals with two-to-ten years of experience than ever occurred under the draft. Under a draft, all services would have greatly reduced experience levels and, one could argue, much less capability.

ACCEPTABILITY

In a democratic republic such as ours, conscription must be acceptable to the people, especially to those who must bear the burden of compulsory service. Its unacceptability to the youth of America was a basic factor leading to the end of the draft in 1973. The national attitude appears to be shifting as the memory of Vietnam fades and world tensions mount. The kidnapping of U.S. embassy personnel, abuses to other U.S. diplomats, the Soviet presence in South Asia, the

Table 2.2   Reenlistment Rates (percentages)

	1972	1973	1974	1975	1976	1977	1978	1979	1980	1981
First term										
Army	10	38	33	39	21	33	36	43	51	55
Navy	23	23	33	40	35	37	40	38	37	42
Marine Corps	12	13	17	20	26	29	29	20	23	27
Air Force	33	20	31	40	37	39	41	38	36	43
DOD	19	24	30	37	30	35	37	37	39	43
Career										
Army	46	63	74	75	71	70	69	66	69	73
Navy	91	92	80	80	75	68	64	62	67	73
Marine Corps	80	82	80	73	78	72	69	52	50	74
Air Force	94	93	90	90	82	86	82	82	82	86
DOD	74	83	81	82	76	75	72	68	70	76
Total										
Army	21	50	51	53	43	52	54	56	62	67
Navy	43	46	54	58	50	49	50	47	48	55
Marine Corps	22	26	29	34	41	43	42	34	35	43
Air Force	39	53	58	68	62	66	66	60	60	66
DOD	36	47	52	57	50	54	55	53	55	61

instability in Iran, the increasing tension overall, the failure of SALT II, and the erosion of détente have made many Americans more receptive to a draft.

Acceptability cuts two ways. Not only must the draft be acceptable to be reinstated, but the AVF must be acceptable to be continued. Since its inception, the voluntary nature of the AVF has been blamed in the press for all sorts of shortcomings. Drug use, poor equipment, low morale, poor training, reduced readiness, and almost every other imaginable problem have been blamed at least in part on the AVF.

In some cases, negative perceptions of the AVF are justified. In others, they unduly exaggerate normal peacetime problems of soldiers in garrison. In still other cases, the real problems may involve such non-AVF-related factors as fuel shortages, cost reductions, or limited training opportunities. Some critics simply remember the past as better than it was. Here let us briefly address some frequent criticisms that question the acceptability of the AVF.

Racial balance is the first. Before the Korean conflict, blacks were underrepresented in the armed forces. Almost all officer positions were filled by whites; blacks were relegated to service functions and often not allowed in combat. Those who served in combat proved themselves valiant, but discrimination in the armed forces reflected the discrimination in society at large.

The military services have striven hard to increase the numbers of black officers, whose ratio to white officers is about the same as the racial balance among college seniors—about one in seven. Much criticism is directed toward the rapid increase of blacks in the enlisted ranks. Charles Moskos and many others have criticized a predominantly black army. Will the country accept an army that is 30 or 40 percent black? In peacetime? In wartime? And black casualty rates that are three or four times or even eight or nine times the representation rate in the society?

A second, sometimes inconsistent criticism of the AVF raises the image of "mercenary soldiers." Senator Sam Nunn and others who are critical of the pay for recruits in the AVF also advocate higher pay for careerists. One could argue, however, that careerists control the armed forces, not recruits. If the primary concern with a mercenary force is that it may become estranged from the values of society and thus threaten the very society it has been formed to protect, then the real concern should be with the career military. An AVF might lead to a much larger career military—too professional, too self-serving, and too different from society. While this is possible, the concern expressed by most critics of the AVF is that it is not as professional, self-reliant, or effective as it should be—that it suffers from the same problems as the society as a whole.

Recruit pay is about at the minimum wage. In a free society, it seems strange to object to paying the established minimum wage to those who are willing to risk life and limb to protect that society. On the contrary, one would expect a society to pay the minimum wage for military service even under a Selective Service draft. It seems patently unfair to levy upon those who are to serve in undesirable and risk-laden tasks an additional "tax" by paying them less than the established minimum wage for such service. Yet the mercenary image of the AVF remains an acceptability problem.

Finally, much criticism has been levied at the ability of volunteers to defend the nation. The "dummy" label has been applied to those who enlist. Clearly, average to below-average scorers on the mental tests are overrepresented in the enlisted ranks of the military, but is that wrong? Officer jobs have been selected as requiring college education or similar experience. Those with considerably below-average test scores are excluded from service (although they were drafted in World War II). While the Army benefits by the leavening effect of college-bound youth and college graduates in its enlisted ranks, will the American people find an Army peopled by youth with average and below-average test scores unacceptable?

The criticism will probably continue as the press finds new instances of drug use, incompetent performance, poor readiness, etc. It will be easy to blame these problems on the quality of the soldiers, i.e., on the AVF. Yet even President Reagan's defense-minded administration has not moved toward a draft. It is unlikely that the acceptance issue will tilt so far as to return to compulsory service, short of clear and present danger to the territorial integrity of the United States or involvement in a shooting war that has nationwide support.

COST

Defense is expensive. Nevertheless, defense costs have declined, as a percentage of the federal budget or the gross national product, and domestic, federal, state, and local expenditures have greatly increased in the past 25 years.[16] Figure 2.1 shows defense costs in relation to other nationwide expenses from 1939 through 1979.

Manpower costs represent about half of military costs, although the specific fraction also depends considerably on the level of nonmanpower procurements. The decision to buy the MX missile system or the B1 bomber will change the

Figure 2.1
Defense Shares of Economic and Budgetary Aggregates

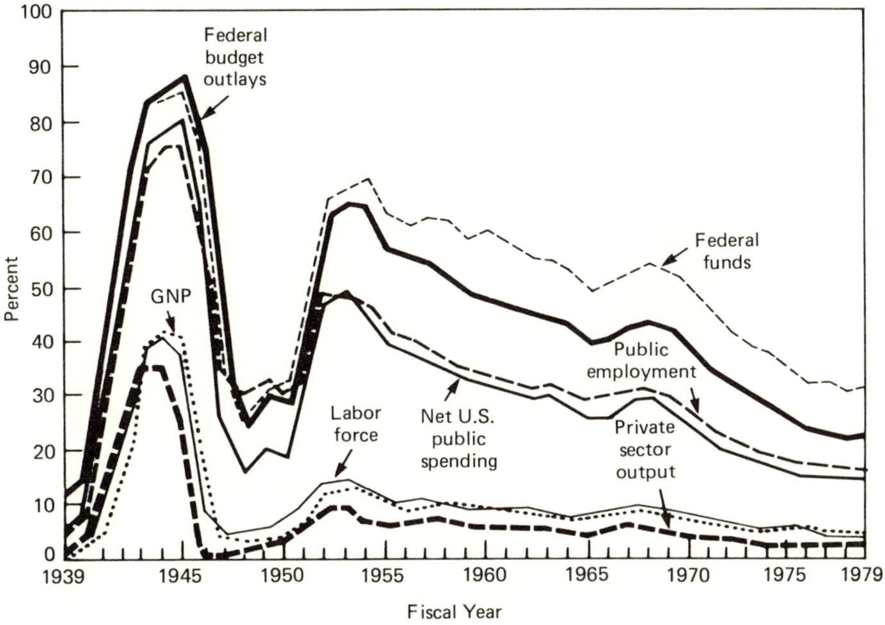

denominator of the equation and thus the fraction. Figure 2.2 shows this directly. The total budget lines have much larger oscillations than the manpower cost line.

If manpower costs are measured in constant 1980 dollars, they reflect the changes in force size. This is shown on Figure 2.3.

Considerable debate has been concerned with the compilation of manpower costs. Military pay and allowances are included, of course, but are retirement benefits? Housing is included, but are hospital operating expenses a cost of doing business or a personnel cost? How about trucks, tanks, and aircraft? They are used to move people and cost more because of human considerations. Carried to its logical conclusion, all costs in the military could be counted as personnel costs. But by convention, manpower costs have been divided as shown in Table 2.3.[17] Using this methodology, manpower costs account for about 60 percent of annual Defense Department outlays, while direct pay for active-duty military personnel makes up about 40 percent of total manpower costs and 20 percent of total defense outlays. Approximately half of the pay goes to first-term personnel.

While manpower costs are high, they were high before the AVF and would likely remain high even if a draft were reenacted. The legitimate question for this chapter is how much the AVF has cost. That is somewhat difficult to answer because societal costs of the draft were never reflected in the budget amounts.[18] In this chapter, only budget costs will be discussed. In that context, what extra money has been spent to have an AVF? It is about what the Gates Commission— the President's Commission on an All-Volunteer Armed Force which in 1970 recommended the AVF—expected (correcting for inflation), although the timing

Figure 2.2
Manpower Costs in Relation to the Total Defense Budget

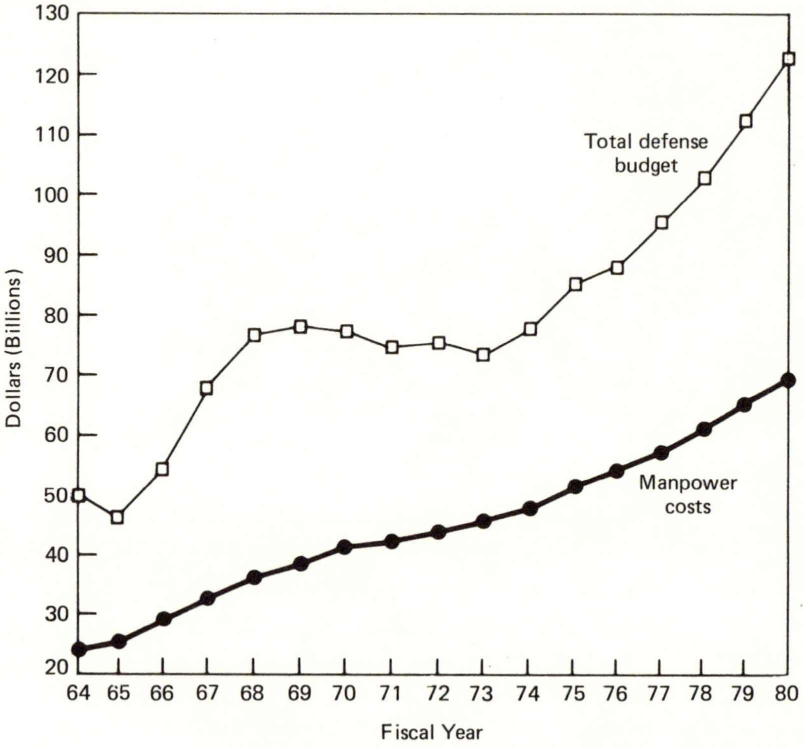

of expenditures is somewhat delayed from the Commission's projected timetable as shown in Figure 2.4.

The General Accounting Office (GAO), in an extensive study of AVF costs conducted in February 1978, attributed to the AVF the cost of items which the Department of Defense attributed to the AVF in testimony.[19] That methodology probably excluded some real costs, but included many costs that likely would have been incurred even without an AVF. For example, housing for career personnel was justified in part on AVF grounds and was included as an AVF cost. On the other hand, certain savings from an AVF were not estimated because they had not yet occurred. For example, G.I. Bill educational benefits had been terminated because the draft ended, but were not counted as savings because they were future savings. The uncounted eventual annual savings is estimated at $1.5 billion per year.[20] The GAO figure probably overstates the actual cost of the AVF. In any case, a cost of about $2 billion per year in 1970 dollars or about $3 billion per year today probably is attributable to an AVF.

This estimate should not be confused with the likely savings of returning to a draft. Many of the costs now attributed to the AVF are part of the basic defense structure of pay, benefits, and facilities and would probably continue even if the

Figure 2.3
Current and Constant Manpower Outlays

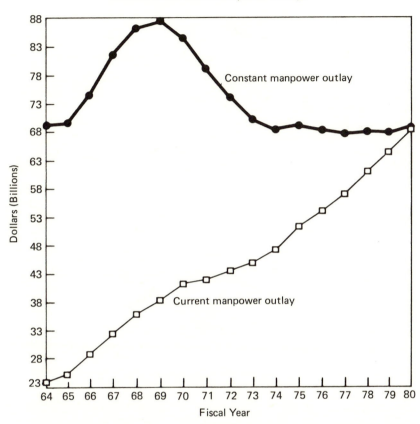

draft were reinstated. In fact, if draftees displaced large numbers of volunteers, new incentives probably would be necessary to attract and hold sufficient careerists to meet the desired experience levels. Congress *could* reenact a G.I. Bill even with an AVF, but it almost surely *would* if the draft were reinstated.

The Department of Defense estimates a possible maximum savings of $0.5 billion in returning to a Selective Service draft.[21] Half a billion dollars represents about $20 per year per person in the United States. Such an amount seems to be a cheap price to avoid the disruption that conscription can create. So far, the American people seem to have been willing to bear the cost.

To the earlier question—has the AVF adequately met America's military manpower requirements in the 1970s—the answer is yes, pretty well. The following paragraphs summarize how well the AVF has met the six evaluation criteria over its first eight years.

1. *Quantity.* The active force has been on strength every year except 1978, and that shortfall was made up the next year. Significant shortfalls have occurred in the reserves, however.

Table 2.3 Military Manpower Costs

	Approximate percent of	
	Manpower costs	Defense outlays
1. Military personnel appropriations: all pay and allowances for active-duty military, including permanent change of station costs, but not training	42	25
2. Defense family housing (excludes civilian pay covered below)	2	1
3. Military retired pay (actual costs to pay current retirees)	15	9
4. Reserve and guard personnel appropriation (excluding civilian costs)	3	2
5. Civilian personnel costs (not a direct appropriation item — civilian costs are included in functional appropriations)	31	19
6. Personnel support costs, including individual training, medical support, recruiting and examination, overseas dependent education, half of base operating support and miscellaneous costs	7	4
Total.	100	60

Figure 2.4
Cost of the All-Volunteer Force
(constant 1970 dollars)

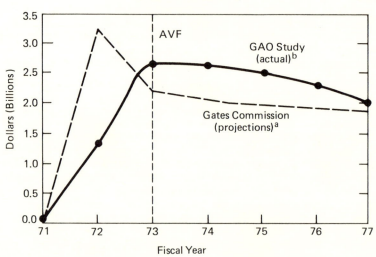

Fiscal Year

[a] Report of the President's Commission on an All-Volunteer
Armed Force, Feb. 1970, adjusted to actual force sizes.
[b] Additional cost of the All-Volunteer Force. GAO. Feb. 1978.

2. *Quality*. The AVF has recruited large numbers of average and below-average youth, but they are trainable and are not very different from the enlisted forces of other armies and the U.S. Army in other peacetime eras. Training in military skills and effective leadership are probably more important than high school diplomas and test scores in determining the effectiveness of an armed force.

3. *Attitude*. Superior attitude—the will to fight under very adverse conditions—often makes the difference between victory and defeat. Attitude is undoubtedly more important than currently used quality measures and is often more important than superior numbers, training, and equipment. Measurements of attitude over the last decade indicate that the AVF appears to be weakest on this criterion. Many studies show the attitude of military personnel to be high near the end of training, but to deteriorate with time in operating or field units. Some garrison troops, especially in Europe, have serious attitude problems manifested in ways ranging from congressional survey responses to drug and alcohol abuse rates. These problems, however, were not caused by the AVF. To the contrary, they were one reason for seeking volunteers, who were expected to be more motivated for peacetime service than draftees. A draft, especially a peacetime draft, does not make patriots, but is likely to build resentment and produce counterproductive behavior. A massive national service program might appear to be more fair than a draft; but compulsory service, with its inevitable make-work and bureaucratic lost-time, is likely to be resented. On balance, even with the identified attitude problems, this criterion favors continuing the AVF over either a draft or national service.

4. *Experience*. By almost any measure the current AVF has more experienced personnel than would be possible under a draft with an armed force of the same size and at about the same cost.

5. *Acceptability*. While the nation is clearly divided over draft-related issues and the armed forces face obvious problems, unhappiness with the racial, mercenary, or educational character of the force does not appear sufficient to crystalize the majority needed to return to peacetime conscription. Perhaps most Americans are ambivalent. They recognize that the AVF is not a cure-all and has some shortcomings, but it is better than the other peacetime alternatives.

6. *Cost*. The AVF costs about $3 billion per year more than would have been spent without it. Nonetheless, a return to conscription would save only about $0.5 billion annually, since many of the costs have been internalized. If anything, salary of military careerists may increase. Labor is expensive. It likely will cost half or more of the defense budget whether there is an AVF or a draft.

On balance one can conclude that the AVF is far from perfect, but most of its problems would not be significantly alleviated by a return to peacetime conscription. America seems to be muddling through, but what of the future? What happens when the effects of "the pill" reach the foxholes? Grade schools are closing and already there are vacant desks in the once-overcrowded secondary schools. How does the AVF look for the rest of the 1980s?

The AVF and Its Alternatives in the 1980s

Assessing the AVF in the 1980s requires considerable speculation. Will there be a major nuclear war or threat of nuclear war? Will there be a conventional confrontation of major proportions? Will U.S. security interests be threatened in the Third World so as to involve us in another limited war? Could real peace break out? Any of these changes in world conditions could result in major changes in the U.S. armed forces.

This chapter assumes that the East-West confrontation will continue within the range of tensions experienced over the last decade, which will result in a military personnel requirement of about two million men and women in uniform. Perhaps there will be an increase of 10 percent if the Reagan expansion is brought to fruition. To evaluate the future of the AVF on these assumptions, let us again use the same six criteria.

QUANTITY

The national training alternatives that require all men (and women) to serve in the military result in too many youth. As Daniel Huck pointed out in his Congressional Budget Office study, the military would have problems managing such large numbers.[22] Experienced personnel now in combat units would have to be reassigned to augmented training units to handle the volume. Current equipment levels would be exhausted just to meet training requirements.

The selective draft alternatives avoid these problems of excess and ensure that desired numbers of personnel are available to all active and reserve units. Strictly from a military personnel planner's perspective, this would be the best class of alternatives and a male-only draft would be the preferred alternative.

The AVF alternatives do not guarantee adequate numbers for all active duty and reserve units. As discussed in the previous section, shortages have occurred especially in reserve combat units. Will supply meet demand through the eighties and nineties? Richard Cooper has developed a supply and demand comparison for youth in the prime recruiting age by using a three-year moving average of 18-year-old men compared to accession requirements for the military.[23] This approach is the best way to compare supply and demand. It is shown in Figure 2.5.

Figure 2.5 shows that supply barely met requirements in the 1950s; but in the

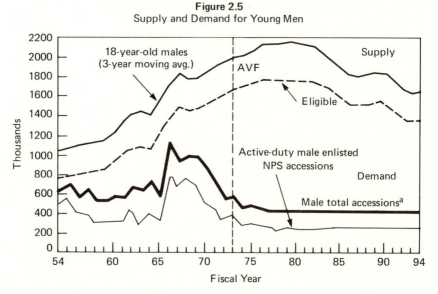

Figure 2.5
Supply and Demand for Young Men

[a]Officer and enlisted, active and reserve.

early 1970s, as the post-Vietnam requirements dropped and supply increased, an AVF became a real possibility. In the 1980s supply will take a significant drop, with demand projected to remain level or increase slightly. While this drop in supply is a concern, note that supply continues to exceed demand by a wide margin.

Figure 2.6 compares the ratio of the total supply and the total demand lines from the previous figure. In the mid-1950s about one out of every 1.5 eligible young men needed to volunteer or be drafted to meet the active and reserve, officer and enlisted military manpower requirements. In the 1960s the ratio was about one out of every two. In the post-Vietnam period the ratio rose rapidly. When the AVF started it was up to one out of every 3.0 and peaked at one out of every 4.4 in 1978. During the 1980s, the ratio tends to drop, reaching a projected low of about one out of every 3.3 youths in the early 1990s. The ratio is expected to rise again to about one of four or slightly more as the children of the baby boom children reach military age. Although the decline in the ratio is of some concern, the ratio is expected to stay above the level of the AVF's early years. Ratios of 1 to 4.0 or 1 to 3.5 are not reasons to return to conscription.

Why did the services have so much trouble meeting AVF manpower requirements in 1978 and 1979, when the ratio was one to five? There were many probable causes for the recruiting problems: unemployment levels were down; federal aid to higher education was up; drug problems and adverse press coverage gave the AVF a bad image. Perhaps most important was the change in relative compensation. After rapid pay increases in the early days of the AVF, Congress in

Figure 2.6
Ratio of 18-Year-Old Military Eligible Males to Total Male Accessions.

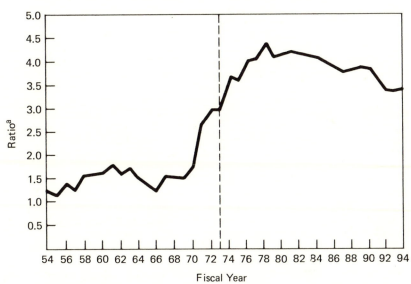

[a]Ratio—Number of military eligibles per male accession.
Note: Total male accessions are active and reserve, officer and enlisted.

the mid-1970s cut back benefits and imposed pay caps. At the same time it raised the civilian minimum wage and increased aid to college students who did not serve in the military. Congress thus placed the military in a disadvantageous recruiting position.

Recently, at Congress's initiative, experiments have been conducted to attract more college-bound youth.[24] Congress has also taken corrective action on military pay. In 1981, for the first time since rates of pay increases for military and federal civilian personnel were linked in 1967, military pay increased by substantially more than civil service general schedule. The current AVF probably can meet recruitment levels through the 1980s and beyond, but with less certainty than with the compulsory service alternatives. The major concern is that congressionally imposed quality restrictions on recruiting may artificially constrain the ability of the services to meet strength, especially the Army.

QUALITY

Accession projections of high school graduates and mental groups being conducted by the Rand Corporation indicate that quality may be more of a problem than quantity.[25] Congress's concern with quality levels has led it to impose quality limits. For FY 1981 Category IV accessions were limited to 25 percent of total enlisted accessions, and the Army was limited to a minimum of 65 percent high school graduates. For FY 1982 no service could recruit more than 25 percent Category IV, and in 1983 no more than 20 percent. If DOD simultaneously readjusts standards for the test norming problems, these combined actions could represent severe recruiting restrictions. But even with the stricter standards, FY 1981 recruiting was much better than required, probably due to the larger pay increases and the recession. Nevertheless, as youth civilian employment prospects rise in the mid-1980s, to meet recruit quality standards will be a serious challenge.

Abandoning the AVF and adopting a universal military training system would introduce other problems. The system would draw in everyone, but selecting and retaining motivated careerists would again become a major problem. Providing meaningful military training to two million (or four million, if women are included) recruits each year would be a monumental task. Not to provide good training could actually reduce fighting capability and thus negate the expected advantages of compulsory service for more college-bound youth with higher test scores.

Returning to a Selective Service draft could produce an ironical result. If the rules that governed the draft before and during the 1970s were reimposed, the military would be prohibited from turning down a minimally qualified volunteer in order to draft a more qualified nonvolunteer. Recruiting in recent years has been relatively selective. The recent congressional actions would make it more selective. The draft could undermine this selective feature and result in increased numbers of minimally qualified recruits who would not be recruited under the AVF. This problem could be avoided only if benefits and pay were severely cut to discourage volunteers, or if minimal entry standards were raised very high. Probably the best way to ensure quality and high performance is to offer benefits and pay that are competitive for the quality of youth desired. Economics does apply to the youth labor market.

The excess of liberal arts college graduates willing to accept officer commissions is evidence of economic factors at work. If the Army's new tank needs college-level personnel, making tank commander an officer position may be a better solution than drafting tank personnel. It has already worked for aircraft pilots, navigators, and flight officers. These economic considerations also work the other way. The services that a few years back could attract engineers and hard science graduates with commissions now are having problems. The reason is not a sudden change in taste, but rather that the entry-level civilian pay for such graduates has risen from less than a second lieutenant's salary to well in excess of a captain's.

The point is that the quality issue can be met in the AVF, if the price is right. This does not attract mercenaries without dedication, but rather many of the same youth who would be drafted. Also it is not really more expensive for society to pay the true cost of recruitment up front. It only seems so because under a draft one does not measure all the costs directly.[26] The conclusion is that in peacetime, a market offering competitive wages for youth with the desired education and test scores can provide adequate quality of voluntary recruits. Under the AVF, in fact, the services may be more selective than under Selective Service.

Higher-than-minimum standards can be retained and requirements can be met at the lowest real cost to the society. Two of the most difficult problems under the AVF, however, are to determine authentic quality requirements and to provide direct funding in the defense budget to meet those requirements. Congress in raising both recruit standards and benefits reflects an understanding of the economics involved and the intention, I believe, to make the AVF provide the appropriate quality of recruits.

ATTITUDE

It is difficult to project future attitudes. During a recognized threat to national survival, such as was experienced in mid-December 1941, public commitment to military measures is high, conscription is accepted, and service to the nation is willingly given. In the latter stages of the Vietnam conflict the opposite was true. It can be projected, however, that volunteers should have the most positive attitudes toward service and conscriptees, the least positive. When one makes his choice, preconditioning helps to rationalize that choice, even if a little complaining is normal. Likewise, when all must serve, service tends to be accepted, like taxes. But when one is selected from the group and forced to serve when most of his peers are not, the potential for serious problems results.

Clearly, a return to a draft or a move to national training would be no panacea for the problems of today's AVF military.[27] It is easy to defend hypotheses that the attitude problems would be more severe if the members of the armed forces had not volunteered for duty under current conditions. Commitment to serve, patriotism, and other desired traits are developed in homes and schools. If anything, a peacetime AVF should have a higher sample of youth strong in these traits than a draft. More important, training in the military and effective leadership after training must reinforce the previous good traits and build commitment where the homes and the schools failed. In the 1980s the armed forces are going to have to work hard to overcome the effects of the "me generation" and to keep the military dedicated and committed regardless of the form of recruitment.

EXPERIENCE

If we adopted compulsory national training, most of the population would gain basic military training and learn the fundamental military skills, providing a very valuable experience pool for the nation. Large segments of the U. S. youth population have never fired a high-caliber rifle or driven a heavy truck or track vehicle, and these are simple, not complex, weapons systems.

Broad-based national training could produce a pool of about four million men or eight million men and women, assuming two years of military service that included training time. Two years can provide sufficient training for most military occupations, but some occupations require much longer. Nuclear submarine personnel, currently on six-year initial enlistments, probably require the longest training; but for a number of other skills as well, two years would be inadequate for training and any meaningful return on that training. A one-year tour would be of limited value except for the most basic military caretaker and service occupations.

While national training could provide the broadest base of experience, it probably would not provide as many people with long-term experience as does the AVF. It certainly would shorten initial enlistments, which now typically run three or four years. The voluntary nature of the initial commitment under the AVF, and the more personal treatment that can result with a training base of about 400,000 instead of two to four million each year, will keep reenlistment potential high.

The experience tradeoff is between a very broad but relatively shallow experience base and a fairly narrow but intensive one. National training alternatives provide the former and the AVF alternatives, the latter. The selective draft alternatives provide a somewhat broader base than the AVF alternatives, although not nearly as broad as national training, and considerably shorter duration of service compared to the AVF. From the perspective of experience, the draft is the worst set of alternatives, but once again, the issue of how *much* experience is needed becomes important.

In wartime, people are sent to combat with as little as thirteen weeks of training. Of course, combat is the most rapid training experience there is, although costly in terms of unnecessary losses among inexperienced troops. The ground combat forces of the Army and Marine Corps tend to prefer more people for a shorter time. On the other hand, the Navy and the Air Force usually are concerned about retaining more of their experienced petty officers, NCOs, and officers, even those in mid-career.

Research and analysis is needed to create a good tradeoff model of breadth versus depth of experience and the effect of experience on the capabilities of the services to perform their wartime mission. Without such a tool, the choice is between one of the extremes or a little of each. Depth of experience gives an armed force more capability in the initial weeks of a major war, while breadth gives staying power in the middle period after mobilization and before new draftees are trained and deployed. If faced with a choice, I would pick depth.

ACCEPTABILITY

A volunteer force would seem to continue to be acceptable in peacetime to the American public, as would a draft in a bona fide national emergency. Use of the draft for a limited war probably would meet considerable resistance, unless it were clear that the American oil supply or some other critical national interest were at risk. National training might be acceptable if it were all-inclusive, of short duration, and perceived as necessary. Such a system seems to work in Switzerland. A make-work national civilian service system probably would suffer from credibility problems. Little or no case, however, can be made for a military mass of millions of partially trained soldiers. The problems with short duration have been mentioned, but whatever else may be said for national training, its extremely high cost probably would keep it from being acceptable.

COST

Manpower is very expensive in the American society and is likely to become even more so throughout the 1980s. Defense manpower will continue to cost a great deal no matter what system we adopt. The future real cost of the armed forces probably is about the same for a draft or an AVF. Budget costs probably would be somewhat higher and hidden costs somewhat lower if the AVF were continued. National training would be the most costly and would require vast sums to train large numbers with little military justification. Expenditures for salaries at the minimum wage would be up to $25 billion per year. By the time additional career personnel, medical and other benefits, equipment and supplies, etc., are added, the annual cost would be several times that figure.

Given the high costs of some alternatives to the AVF and because a draft would realize little if any defense budget savings, it is probable that the nation will be willing to pay the costs of the AVF in the rest of the 1980s.

Conclusions

Both the draft and national training are better than the AVF at maintaining authorized manpower levels. The AVF is meeting authorized levels in the active forces but has fallen short in the reserve components. But national service would provide from five to ten times more people than the armed services can use effectively.

Quality is adequate under the AVF and can be adjusted by changing incentives. Under national training quality would not be a concern. Since all would serve, there would be no shortage of good trainees, though the career force might deteriorate. Under a draft quality could decline, unless pay and benefits were cut back to discourage poorly qualified youth from volunteering, or unless enlistment standards were raised high enough to block their enlistment.

Attitude in the armed forces is not primarily a result of recruiting source. If anything, attitude would probably be worse in a forced system than among volunteers.

Experience is two-dimensional. National training gives broad-based but relatively shallow experience, while the AVF has much more depth of experience. The AVF alternative probably would continue to have much higher reenlistment rates than a conscripted force.

Surveys show that Americans are concerned about the problems in their armed force, but that generally the AVF is being accepted by the American people. Conscription probably is more acceptable than five years ago and would become even more acceptable with the passage of time. National training is probably perceived as more equitable than a selective draft in which only a small percentage would be drafted, but probably is not and would not be viewed as necessary.

While national training has many attractive features, its cost probably is prohibitive. The cost factor narrows the real options to a form of selective draft or a form of AVF. The AVF will cost a little more in the federal budget, and the draft would cost more to the economy as a whole.

I believe that the pressure needed to return to a peacetime draft in the 1980s is not present in the American society today. Mounting world tensions or serious shortfalls in active force strength could change that condition. Recent events around the world, but especially those in the Middle East, have had an effect. A severe curtailment of foreign oil or major Soviet adventurism could change the attitude, as a Pearl Harbor attack on the United States itself certainly would. Short of these eventualities, the armed forces in the 1980s probably will have to make do with a form of volunteer force backed up by some form of draft registration and whatever reserve force can be maintained.

Notes

1. Office of the Assistant Secretary of Defense (Manpower, Reserve Affairs, and Logistics), *America's Volunteers: A Report on the All-Volunteer Armed Force* (Washington, D.C.: Department of Defense, 1978), p. 18.

2. On November 14, 1971, military personnel received a pay increase of 11.6 percent, but recruit pay was doubled from $134.40 per month to $268.50 per month. P.L. 92–192.

3. Richard V. L. Cooper, *Military Manpower and the All-Volunteer Force,* R-1450-ARPA (Santa Monica, Calif.: The Rand Corporation, September 1977), p. 74.

4. *America's Volunteers,* p. 101.

5. Kenneth Coffey discusses the consequences of this shortage in his recent book, *Strategic Implications of the All-Volunteer Force* (Chapel Hill: University of North Carolina Press, 1979).

6. *America's Volunteers,* p. 181.

7. Gerald R. Ford, Presidential Proclamation 4360, FR Doc 75-8628, filed 31 March 1975.

8. An approach comparing actual test scores with minimum scores required was developed by I. M. Greenberg and Jeanne Fites of the Office of the Assistant Secretary of Defense (Manpower and Reserve Affairs) during the early days of the AVF.

9. Robert F. Lockman, "Brief for the Advisory Committee on Manpower Acquisitions Study," CNA memo 801190, Center of Naval Analysis, 19 August 1980; and James S. Thomason, *Rating Assignments to Enhance Retention,* CRC 426, Center of Naval Analysis, February 1980.

10. Office of the Assistant Secretary of Defense (Manpower, Reserve Affairs, and Logistics), *Aptitude Testing of Recruits* (Washington, D.C.: Department of Defense, July 1980).

11. Lockman and Thomason as an example.

12. Robert Sherrod, *Tarawa* (New York: Duell, Sloan and Pearce, 1954), p. 32.

13. Jerry L. Reed, *The Beard Study: An Analysis and Evaluation of the United States Army,* a study prepared for Representative Robin Beard (R.—Tennessee) and published in an appendix to *Hearings on the Status of the All-Volunteer Force,* before the Subcommittee on Manpower and Personnel of the Senate Committee on Armed Services, 20 June 1978. Also, ABC Television Network, "ABC News Closeup . . . The American Army: 'A Shocking State of Readiness,' " 20 April 1978.

14. Charles W. Brown and Charles C. Moskos, "The American Soldier—Will He Fight? A Professional Attitude Analysis," *Military Review* 56, no. 6 (June 1976).

15. Lieutenant General DeWitt C. Smith, Jr., USA, Deputy Chief of Staff of the Army for Personnel, *Hearings on the Status of the All-Volunteer Force,* before the Subcommittee on Manpower and Personnel of the Senate Committee on Armed Services, 20 June 1978.

16. *The United States Budget in Brief, FY 1981,* p. 71.

17. Office of the Assistant Secretary of Defense (Manpower, Reserve Affairs, and Logistics), *Manpower Requirements Report for FY 1980* (Washington, D.C.: Department of Defense, 1979), pp. xiv–8.

18. Richard Cooper discusses in detail the issue of real costs in *Military Manpower and the All-Volunteer Force,* pp. 66-101.

19. U.S. General Accounting Office, *Additional Costs of the All-Volunteer Force,* No. FPCD-78-11, 6 February 1978.

20. Richard L. Eisenman, Mark J. Eitelberg, Agnes C. Purcell, Barry M. Richmond, Curtis L. Wagner III of HumRRO, and Richard W. Hunter of OASD (MRA&L), *Educational Benefits Analysis* (Alexandria, Va.: Human Resources Research Organization

[HumRRO], November 1975). These authors estimated costs at $1,252 million in FY 1975 dollars.

21. *America's Volunteers,* pp. 173–80. See also Kenneth Coffey, "If the Draft Is Restored: Uncertainties, Not Solutions," Chapter 4, this volume.

22. Daniel Huck, *National Service Programs and Their Effects on Military Manpower and Civilian Youth Programs* (Washington, D.C.: Congressional Budget Office, January 1978).

23. Cooper, *Military Manpower and the All-Volunteer Force,* p. 44. See also Richard W. Hunter and Gary R. Nelson, "Eight Years with the All-Volunteer Armed Forces: Assessments and Prospects," in *Military Service in the United States,* edited by Brent Scowcroft (Englewood Cliffs, N.J.: Prentice-Hall, 1982), pp. 80–108.

24. See *Educational Incentives Study,* report requested by the Senate Armed Services Committee and published by the Office of the Assistant Secretary of Defense (Manpower, Reserve Affairs, and Logistics), 9 February 1980.

25. Richard L. Fernandez, *Enlisted Supply Projections FY 79–90* (Santa Monica, Calif.: The Rand Corporation, 1979).

26. See Cooper, *Military Manpower and the All-Volunteer Force,* chap. 5.

27. For further discussion, see David Segal, "Military Organization and Personnel Accession: What Changed with the AVF . . . and What Didn't," Chapter 1, this volume.

3

The Manning of the Force and the Structure of Battle: Part 1—The AVF and the Draft

DAVID H. MARLOWE

Any discussion of whether recruitment for the armed forces should be wholly voluntary and based on a market, or partly nonvoluntary and based on a draft, must begin with a set of premises defining the roles of a military organization. For the discussion to be fruitful, we should disentangle the multiplicity of secondary, social and political roles played by the armed forces from the primary, central role: to engage in and win armed conflicts.

The Primary Function of Armed Forces

In much contemporary public debate, secondary functions overshadow the primary function. For example, a recent issue of *Society* devoted to a discussion of the AVF/conscription controversy focused almost exclusively on issues of class bias and equitable burden sharing.[1] The armed forces have indeed served a number of vital social functions in the past. No one would dispute that military service has offered access to middle-class status and skills to the members of minority groups. It has also provided a mechanism for the employment and training of educationally and academically disadvantaged American youth, has become a model for racial integration, and has served in some ways as a testing ground for the expansion of gender equality in the United States. In many debates about the structuring of the force, these characteristics are given primacy. In other debates, the discussions concern ensuring equity through proportional representation in the force structure (based upon the civil socioeconomic hierarchy). Still other arguments appear to revolve around the unjustness of compulsory and inequitable "taxation"—i.e., loss of time and earning power because of compulsory service, compounded by the unfairness of having one's life involuntarily placed at risk in case of war. Most of these arguments are germane, I believe, only if one does not focus upon two essential questions: (1) What is the ultimate function of an armed force as opposed to its secondary social functions? (2) What is the nature of modern war? Answers to these questions are most often left out of the debate. Many arguments, I believe, evade the bitter realities of resort to armed combat. They are cost-accounted against the balance sheets of peace and not against the potential lost war that could alter the integrity of the nation and its security for decades. An army is a social institution, and one may try to optimize its economic benefits as well as spread service burdens as equitably as possible. It also serves somewhat in the fashion of a vaccine which, if too attentuated, might not provide sufficient resistance to the invading pathogen.

The primary and essential role of the armed forces is to fight and win wars. As Clausewitz put it, "War is thus an act of force to compel our enemy to do our will. [The enemy's fighting forces] must be put in such a condition that they can no longer carry on the fight."[2] This aim holds equally for defensive and aggressive wars, for just and unjust wars, and indeed, whether or not one agrees that armed combat is an "effective" way to pursue policy ends. The injunction to impose our will upon the enemy remains the mandate that the nation has placed upon the military. This does not gainsay the fact that many potential conflicts would not necessarily be fought in response to Clausewitz's injunction; military force can be and is used to attain circumscribed and limited ends as well as to avert dangerous developments. Yet the *ultimate mandate* of a national military establishment remains a "worst-case one" and is based upon forcing the nation's enemies to alter their behavior through armed conflict. The military is assigned a series of tasks—in the form of contingency plans for possible future conflicts—which it is expected to complete successfully. While, in the United States, many would agree with Weigley's view that, contrary to Clausewitz's dictum, war has ceased to be a "continuation of politics by other means [and is instead a] final resort,"[3] the demands made upon the armed forces in that ultimate resort to arms remain inexorable. By treating these realistically probable contingencies as the driving assumptions that underlie force structure, we may be able to clear away some of the confused and confusing detritus of the Vietnam era that has at times obscured the basic functions mandated for the military forces. We shall also be able to reflect upon force structure in terms of the nature of modern war.

A traditional American mode of making war and an American perception of war have, at least since the Civil War, dominated the public vision of armed conflict. The scenario usually begins with an enemy act of aggression. After initial setbacks, a protracted build-up period occurs during which American productive capacity is unleashed and armies are assembled. In this scenario the tempo of warfare provides enough time for the nation to prepare, arm, and then strike back and defeat its enemies. Large standing armies and "forces in being" capable of defeating potential enemies are considered unnecessary, since small standing forces, in conjunction with those of our allies, will slow the enemy until national mobilization goes into effect. A just war precipitated by an act of aggression (such as the firing on Fort Sumter, the sinking of the Maine, unrestricted submarine warfare, Pearl Harbor) has thus been our standard perception, with the justice and righteousness of the American cause always seen as leading to victory. Constabulary actions, such as Korea and Vietnam, were perceived through the same spectacles, at least in their initial phases. In all instances armies were created and expanded, trained, and then committed to the field. The armed forces expanded from 43,656 to 235,785 during the Spanish-American War, from 179,376 to 2,897,167 during World War I, from 458,365 to 12,123,455 during World War II, from 1.5 million to 3.6 million during the Korean conflict, and from 2.6 million to 3.5 million during the Vietnam War.[4]

As Weigley has pointed out, throughout most of American history our political and military leadership "has been vague in [its] descriptions of the political and military necessities for which an American army was intended . . . it was difficult to envision the war and the enemy that the American army would fight."[5] Throughout the fifties and most of the sixties American military doctrine was

shaped toward two complementary ends: a conventional force capable of fighting
limited wars, primarily against perceived surrogates of the Soviet Union; and
strategic forces, delivering nuclear weaponry, designed to deter and if necessary
fight a nuclear war. During much of this period U.S. conventional forces in
Europe were viewed as a tripwire. Their essential function was not to fight and
defeat Soviet forces in conventional battle in the event of an assault upon Western
Europe, but rather, when attacked, to serve as the trigger for massive nuclear
retaliation.

From the late sixties through the seventies, however, American military policy
was reformulated in the doctrine of one-and-a-half-war capability. The "half-war"
represents a limited conflict in an area of vital strategic concern other than the
North American continent and Central or Western Europe, e.g., the Middle East,
Africa, or Latin America. The major war for which the military must be prepared
is a high-intensity, highly lethal, conventional or conventional/tactical nuclear war
fought in response to a Soviet assault upon Western Europe. The most significant
change that has taken place involves the availability of time. In the scenario in
which U.S. forces must now be prepared to operate, time is no longer seen as on
our side. The official U.S. Army Field Manual *100-5: Operations* austerely states:

> The United States could find itself in a short intense war—the outcome of
> which may be dictated by the results of initial combat. This circumstance is
> unprecedented: we are an Army historically unprepared for its first battle.
> We are accustomed to victory wrought with the weight of material and
> population brought to bear after the onset of hostilities. Today the U.S. Army
> must, above all else, *prepare to win the first battle of the next war.*[6]

The war is conceived as being of comparatively short duration, from a few
weeks to three or four months. It will be characterized by intense and fluid battles
involving almost continuous day and night combat. Its resolution would, in what
can loosely be called the "best case," result in acceptance of whatever new status
such combat imposed upon the participants. This might include anything from
Soviet domination of Europe to a return to the status quo following the rebuff,
repulsion, and significant destruction of Soviet invading forces. In the worst case
the inability of the conventional forces to achieve their tactical goals could lead to
the use of both theater and strategic nuclear weapons. There remains, as well, the
possibility of such a conflict devolving into a conventional war of attrition.[7]

Most commentators agree that this conventional war would represent a significant departure from wars of the past, particularly those that have conditioned the
vision of war held by most Americans. Our image has been drawn from World
Wars I and II and the Korean and Vietnam conflicts, as depicted in motion
pictures, newsreels, documentaries, and television coverage. This vision implies
a geographic and temporal structure to war and battle. There is a "front," a
narrow crustlike area in which almost all the actual fighting occurs. The front
moves forward and backward, and combatants move forward and backward with
it. A few miles at most behind the front are all the military support systems,
intermingled with civilians, comparatively safe except for occasional harassment
by stray aircraft or shells. Actual combat exists in the socially and psychologically
discrete strip that Army acronymists formerly designated the MLR (Main Line of
Resistance) or FEBA (the Forward Edge of the Battle Area). This is the universe
of a thousand war movies, of "M.A.S.H.," and of the Vietnam War coverage,
where combat exists in the "boondocks," far away from the cities and canton-
ments. Indeed, one could argue that the disruption of that division between
narrow front and wide rear converted the U.S. forces' sweeping tactical victory in

the Tet Offensive of 1968 into a psychological defeat.[8] Much of the contemporary debate over the AVF and a draft draws its inspiration from the literary, sanitized, and bowdlerized images of battle and the language of war, much of it from World War I, that have become part of English speech and metaphor.[9] Few are aware of the changed demands that new technology and expanded lethality have made upon combat and those who participate in it.

Soviet military doctrine calls for a war against NATO forces that will be one of great movement and combat intensity, involving almost continuous engagement with the enemy. Soviet military analysts normally consider two possibilities for war with the West. The first is what Soviet strategists describe as "conventional war," a war extensively utilizing tactical nuclear weapons combined with continuous, echeloned assault against the enemy. The second is a nonnuclear variant also predicated upon continuous, echeloned assault. In both cases immense volumes of fire are anticipated, using weaponry—rockets, missiles, extended-range artillery—and tactics that will greatly extend the zone of lethality. The war will be keyed to rapid movement, deep penetration, and engagements between opposing maneuvering forces that will take place on a highly fluid battleground extending for hundreds of kilometers in length and width. Soviet forces will attack continuously, subjecting the enemy to nine to twelve or more pulses of combat within each 24-hour period. (For comparison, it should be noted that extremely heavy combat in World War II seldom involved more than three or four pulses of combat a day.) In battle of this sort the very terms *front, rear, combatant,* and *noncombatant* lose their meaning in the vast and fluid zone in which battle takes place.[10]

The "conventional variant" of Soviet military plans is best described by Col. A. A. Siderenko of the Frunze Military Academy in his book, *The Offensive:*

> Having nuclear weapons and long range means for delivering them to the targets as well as highly mobile troops, the attacker can now destroy the defensive simultaneously throughout its entire depth, dependably and in a short time with their skillful use. . . . The resoluteness of the goals and the increased capabilities for their attainment make for the great spatial scope of the offensive. The front, depth, and rate of the offensive will increase in comparison with the last war. The conduct of the offensive will not depend upon the time of year, day or weather conditions. . . . The offensive will be conducted continuously until the complete defeat of the enemy, day and night and in any weather; the action of troops at night will become a regular phenomenon.[11]

The world has already had a glimpse of the nonnuclear variant of Siderenko's mode of warfare in the 1973 Arab-Israeli conflict. Both Egyptian and Syrian forces operated in terms of Soviet offensive doctrine. Assault against Israeli forces was echeloned and continuous. The initial Egyptian attack involved, in echelon, five infantry, three mechanized, and two armored divisions with more than 2,000 tanks and the same number of guns. More than 10,000 shells were fired in the first minute of attack.[12] Munitions were used at rates far surpassing those of any previous conflict. The psychological and physical stresses upon troops were immense and unremitting during the initial two-week period of heavy combat. Ten percent of all Israeli casualties were neuro-psychiatric combat reactions (transitory situational breakdown in response to the extreme stresses and intensity of combat), a high figure for combat of such short duration. Arab losses to stress are presumed to have been equivalent, particularly following the shift of the offensive to the Israelis. Psychiatric and physical casualties were generated in much higher numbers than would have been anticipated from previous wars among combat support and combat service support troops who came under regular interdictory fire from long-range rocketry and artillery.[13]

Survival and success on such a battlefield require highly trained and highly competent soldiers in highly cohesive military units. The Israeli defense forces make a point of assigning their more highly skilled, higher-IQ personnel to the combat arms on the thesis that intelligence is a requisite to survival and success on the complex, ambiguous, and rapidly changing modern battlefield. The Soviet forces strive for the same end:

> Today's soldier, no matter where he serves, deals with complicated war technology. To master this technology and learn to use it in its greatest capacity in battle are not easy tasks. But, in spite of the comparatively short period of obligatory service, military personnel successfully master the technology and weapons. This is a result of the considerably high educational level of Soviet soldiers. . . . At present almost 100% of soldiers have completed the eighth grade, and almost 80% have secondary or higher education.[14]

Quality and Performance

Studies carried out in past wars have consistently indicated a significant relationship between intelligence, education, and performance in combat. As *The American Soldier* noted, "The better educated, the men with the highest AGCT scores and highest mechanical aptitude tend to get the better performance rating."[15] These findings were replicated in the Human Research and Resources Organization (HumRRO—an Army human performance analysis group) "Fighter" studies carried out during the Korean conflict. Successful fighters—that is, successful combat soldiers—tended to be more intelligent, healthier, more socially mature and emotionally stable, and more rapid and accurate in performing manual and physical tasks. Conversely, it was noted that those who were low in intelligence tended to make poor fighters.[16]

Despite the increases in the quality of recruits in 1981–82, the marketplace is an intermittent and unsure source of the quality of soldier needed in future wars. The high-intensity battlefield differs widely from past ones in the premium that it places upon intelligence, complex skills, and individual initiative. These factors were important in past wars, but were not critical to overall military success. They may well be so today. Because of the threat posed by nuclear weapons and massive use of indirect-fire conventional munitions, as well as by air operations, the battlefield has expanded. Small groups are now faced with responsibilities formerly allocated to much larger maneuver elements. In the Civil War, the infantryman was responsible for action within a fighting area no more than four square meters in size; in a land war in Europe, this area is expanded to 4000 square meters and more.[17] Battalions of 800–900 men will have operational responsibilities almost as great as those accorded to divisions (15,000 men) in World War II, and companies (200 plus) will have the responsibilities of battalions. The combination of action in small groups (fire teams, antitank teams), isolation and decentralization, highly complex new weapons, plus higher casualties than in previous conflicts, will require highly skilled soldiers who are quick learners and highly adaptable: individuals who have mastered tasks other than their own primary skills and who are capable of exerting leadership and maintaining organization when leaders become casualties. Intelligence, rapid learning, and the ability to make quick judgments are thus imperatives for survival and success.

The same qualities will be demanded of combat support and combat service support troops to maintain and repair more and more complex weaponry. The Arab-Israeli conflict of 1973 demonstrated, for example, that the role played by tank repair personnel in salvaging and restoring material for combat was critical to success in battle. Service and support troops should ideally be multi-skilled, capable of operating under great stress and on their own initiative, with minimal direction and maximal improvisational skill.

Past research by HumRRO on individuals in combat support schools has demonstrated that a soldier's AFQT score was more significantly related to reading and the other skill abilities than was education, particularly high school graduation.[18] In the twelve years since the HumRRO studies, the quality of military personnel, particularly since the introduction of the AVF, has been compressed within a narrower range heavily biased toward the lower AFQT equivalent ranges, especially in the U.S. Army. While *means* have not changed radically, range has, as shown in Table 3.1's breakdown of non-prior-service male accessions.

Table 3.1   Mental Aptitudes of Non-Prior-Service Male Accessions

					Fiscal year				
	1972	1973	1974	1975	1976	FY7T	1977	1978	1979[a]
Mental categories (percent)									
I	3.9	3.2	1.9	2.6	4.7	4.6	3.3	3.0	2.7
II	28.5	26.8	22.8	24.9	24.3	25.3	17.1	16.8	14.6
III-A	22.9	24.3	23.4	25.2	21.5	17.5	20.0	23.5	21.9
III-B	27.3	29.0	32.5	36.1	41.2	42.8	49.5	44.5	51.7
IV	17.4	16.7	19.4	11.2	8.3	9.8	10.1	12.2	9.1
Mean mental aptitude (AFQT percentile)									
Army	53.5	53.6	49.0	53.1	53.6		48.7	49.2	
Other services	55.4	56.7	58.9	59.8	62.4		62.1	61.0	

[a]Through April.

Source: Human Resources Development Directorate, *Human Readiness Report Number 5*, ODCSPER (Washington, D.C.: Department of the Army, 1979).

(This breakdown actually understates the decline of upper-level personnel, since it has recently been established that misnorming of tests led, in the late 1970s, to the admission of higher numbers of mental Category IVs than is reflected in these numbers. In FY 1979, the non-prior-service cohort was almost 50 percent mental Category IV.)

While some would argue that the shifts in mental category distribution are somewhat compensated for by the high proportions of high school graduates currently in the service, high school graduation no longer denotes the level of skill mastery that it did in the fifties and sixties. Thus, in 1977, more than 60 percent of combat arms and more than 70 percent of all other first-term personnel had at least twelve years of schooling (i.e., were high school graduates). Yet during the same period, it was estimated that only 31 percent of Army recruits could read at the eleventh grade level, while 25 percent read at the fifth grade level or lower.[19]

While additional training and education are provided in the military, the dynamics of retention and reenlistment do not bode well for maintaining and developing an NCO corps able to deal easily with the complex technologies and skills of the modern battlefield. Higher rates of reenlistment tend to be biased toward mental Categories III and IV. Thus, in FY 78, 28.8 percent of personnel in Categories I and II eligible to reenlist did so. The reenlistment rates for Categories III and IV, however, were 37.2 percent and 43.9 percent. The same pattern holds for career soldiers.[20]

In response to this change in the basic skills of new personnel, the Army restructured its technical training programs, switching to more simply compre-hended teaching styles and narrowing the range of skills required for training in many military occupational specialties (MOSs). This, interacting with the in-creased complexity of weaponry and equipment, has led to a proliferation of more and more specialized MOSs as well as to deep concern, expressed more and more often in the media, that the military lacks personnel skilled enough to operate and maintain its equipment in a period of heavy commitment.

A 1980 report stated that only 2 percent of 371 tank turret and artillery repairmen passed the Army's Skill Qualification Test, and only 14 percent of 1574 artillerymen passed.[21] It was also reported that 90 percent of nuclear weapons technicians, 86 percent of artillery crewmen, 77 percent of computer program-mers, 89 percent of tracked vehicle mechanics, and 82 percent of Hawk surface-to-air-missile crewmen failed their Skill Qualification Tests.[22] Equally poor per-formance has been reported for numerous combat and combat support and service specialties, as well as for U.S. forces in NATO maneuvers and tests. It is equally disheartening to note that the highest technology repair and maintenance MOSs also currently have the highest attrition rates during training. It seems doubtful that attempts to shift to "black box" and self-diagnostic equipment can compensate for present personnel difficulties. In a modern, high-technology army actual weaponry represents only one component within a series of complex and integrated systems, involving in each infantry division hundreds of computers and thousands of sophisticated electronic and other devices. The effectiveness of most weaponry is almost entirely dependent upon the operational status of such equipment. In a conflict involving continuous operations, success in battle could be as dependent upon the maintenance of night vision devices as upon the maintenance of weapons.

Thus the interaction of an influx of less qualified and skilled personnel, the narrowing of training and MOS responsibility, and the increasing complexity of weapons and support systems operates to lessen the capability of the current force to survive in high-intensity combat. A force containing many narrowly skilled individuals who are unable to generalize and perform well in areas analogous to the ones in which they were trained is potentially a *brittle* force. It may be too dependent upon its lower echelon leaders and team and crew chiefs, individuals likely to become early casualties of battle. As Canter has pointed out, in this context, non-prior-service accessions in FY 1977 (a comparatively good year for accessions quality compared to FYs 1978–1980) peaked at mental Category III-B; this represents a percentile range of 31 to 49 in military aptitude by standard testing. This should be contrasted with the projection that equipment designs entering and expected to enter the inventory of the ground forces are estimated to "call for median aptitude manning in the 60–70 percentile range."[23] A plethora of personnel unable to generalize from their basic skills, or to improvise under conditions of extreme stress and hardship, and overly dependent upon a few well-trained specialists is at greater risk of defeat for want of the proverbial horse-shoe nail.

Unit Cohesion

Studies carried out in World War II demonstrated that the performance of military units is, in part, governed by the soldiers' perception of the unit and its members. As measured by the relationship between the perceptions of unit members in rifle companies prior to combat and the ratio of nonbattle to battle casualties during combat (a long-accepted indirect measure of unit performance), a significant connection exists between pre-combat attitudes and combat performance. Confidence in combat, skill, stamina, and willingness for combat were reinforced by pride in the company and a sense of mutual trust between officers, noncommissioned officers, and lower-ranking personnel.[24] One of the very real problems within the present AVF involves the attenuation of both the ties among unit members and the esteem in which soldiers hold each other. While much has been written on the erosion and loss of trust of enlisted personnel in officers and NCOs, little has been written about the complementary erosion of respect and trust of officers and NCOs for enlisted personnel, and between lower-ranking enlisted personnel.

In field observations carried out in 1978 by the author and members of the Department of Military Psychiatry, WRAIR, at a basic-training center, drill sergeants and others viewed a substantial proportion of new trainees with contempt, characterizing them as "incompetent," "untrainable," and incapable of becoming soldiers. Many asserted that 20 to 50 percent of the trainees should be washed out immediately. Little about these assessments could be classified as racist. They were heard from both black and white noncommissioned officers; in fact a number felt that the largest proportion (in respect to overall racial representation) of the best trainees were black. The assertions made did not fit into the usual patterns of drill sergeant cant of the fifties and sixties. In those periods the assertion would have been closer to, "They give me incompetent trash to turn into soldiers and I turn almost all of them into soldiers. It's destroying me, but I do my job." Here the view presented was, "They give me incompetent trash; I do my best and have to pass through people whom I would never want with me on the battlefield. My job is meaningless."

These training center attitudes were reflected throughout much of the Army. Human Readiness Report No. 5 in 1979 indicated concern on the part of combat unit officers over the competence of junior NCOs and junior soldiers. This concern is complemented by a steady reciprocal decline in trust of leaders by lower-ranking soldiers. Other observers have noted this pattern of mutual distrust and doubt about competence, ability, and concern,[25] which is underlined by declining perceptions of morale and combat readiness.[26] These responses, when compared to the World War II findings, lead to speculation about the ability of military units whose leaders and members doubt their own unit's competence and skill.

It is important to point out that for many members of the Army, as evidenced weekly in the columns of the *Army Times,* the AVF itself has become both explanation and metaphor for all the difficulties and problems faced by the force in discharging its missions. Most often, commentators writing about this symbolic role played by the AVF tend to view it as the Army's excuse for avoiding the changes needed to correct shortcomings inherent within its structure and policies. To a certain extent, this is indeed true. The AVF and the "personnel ability" issue *are* used as displaced symbols that allow other problems to remain uncorrected. We should recognize, however, that many of the problems are real and that the AVF has also come to symbolize aspects of the Army's relationship to the wider society. The draft was a token of the commitment of American society to the military and to the kind of force required to accomplish the goals and missions that the nation mandated. In the Army of the forties, fifties, and early sixties, the draftee symbolized society's implication in the military. The junior enlisted man could be anyone's son or brother and did not symbolically represent a special social or demographic category. Draftees were not viewed as simply the sweepings from the rubbish heaps of society's incompetents and unemployables nor, during the draft period, could volunteers be so viewed since many of them enlisted, particularly for support and service positions, in response to draft pressures. The termination of the draft within the context of a wide social rejection of the armed forces following the Vietnam conflict could only damage the military's self-image and self-esteem. The Army was left in both a symbolic and a real sense to the unemployables, the undereducated, the less competent, and minorities. This sense of abandonment has, I would suggest, affected the Army's sense of its ability to do its job and is what lies behind the oft-repeated sentiment of officers and senior NCOs that only the return of the draft can save the Army. In good part, it is a response to real questions about the ability and competence of military personnel; it is also a response to a very real symbolic issue regarding perceived national support. As one drill sergeant put it, "If this is what the American people give us, we don't deserve to win the next war." A perceived lack of support, as *The American Soldier* and other studies have demonstrated, directly affects morale and performance in battle.

Personnel ability affects group cohesion, and cohesion at squad, platoon, and company level is one of the most critical factors involved in the maintenance of troops in successful combat performance. Cohesion is founded upon many things but among the most important are trust and confidence by soldiers in each other and in their immediate superiors, i.e., the horizontal bonding between lower-ranking soldiers and the vertical bonds between NCOs and junior officers. Herbert Spiegel, a psychiatrist, observed in the Tunisian campaign in World War II:

> If abstract ideas—hate or desire to kill—did not serve as strong motivating forces, then what did serve them in that critical time? What enabled them to attack, and attack, and attack week after week in mud, rain, dust, and heat until the enemy was smashed? It seemed to me that the drive was more a positive than a negative one. It was love more than hate. Love manifested by 1) regard for their comrades who shared the same dangers, 2) respect for their platoon leader or company commander who led them wisely and backed them with everything at his command, 3) concern for their reputation with their commander and leaders, and 4) an urge to contribute to the task and success of their group and unit.[27]

Military units that are not cohesive are at grave risk for both performance disruption in combat and for the rapid psychological breakdown of their personnel. High-intensity ground warfare produces high psychiatric casualty rates, based upon the experience of past wars. The more cohesive the unit, however, the lower the anticipated rate of breakdown in battle. As A. J. Glass, the leading authority on combat psychiatry, puts it:

> Available epidemiological data indicated that the mental illness of troops in warfare, exclusive of psychotic disorders, is more significantly related to circumstances of the combat situation than to any personality attributes or characteristics of any individuals who are exposed to battle stress. Pertinent combat circumstances include the intensity and duration of battle which can be measured by the battle casualty rate and the days of continuous action. However, of equal importance in determining the frequency of psychiatric cases are less measurable elements of battle; to wit, the degree of support given the individual by buddies, group cohesiveness, and leaders. These less tangible influences explain the marked differences that may occur in combat effectiveness and the frequency of psychiatric cases among units which are exposed to the same intensity and duration of battle.[28]

As Little, Moskos, and others have demonstrated, the perception of competence is also of great importance in group bonding.[29] Soldiers must trust the abilities of their fellows to do their jobs if they are to believe in their own survival and their own ability to perform their tasks. An army that questions the abilities of its members is disadvantaged when it must meet the first shock of combat. Green troops, not welded together by confidence and competence, stand at the greatest risk of poor performance and psychological breakdown, while soldiers of low mental ability have often demonstrated greater difficulties in establishing strong and effective primary group relationships.

Conclusions

The demands and rapidity of modern war dictate that highly trained and competent reserve forces be available for almost immediate deployment in support of the active force as well as to expand and man the training base if a wider build-up of forces is required. A minimum of six months in both training center and initial unit assignment is needed to produce a competent combat soldier, one well trained and sufficiently knowledgeable to fight effectively, endure, survive, and win on the modern battlefield. Only combat-ready reserve forces can be counted upon to play such a role in the initial months of a main force war. By the time newly conscripted armies are raised and prepared for battle, the odds are high that the conflict will have been decided. It is generally agreed that since the introduction of the AVF, both the quantity and quality of U.S. reserve forces have fallen to a dangerous low.

If the kinds of factors outlined above lead us, as it does me, to accept the premise that a return to some form of compulsory service is necessary to man a force capable of achieving success in its missions, the major questions are: Who shall serve? And why? Let us take the why first. It is obvious that the Army's primary need is for soldiers of average and above-average intelligence, abilities, skills, and potentialities. At present, such a force cannot be obtained through the marketplace, and it is questionable that any first-term personnel mix that approaches the optimal could ever be obtained through voluntary enlistment. Enlisted service in the military, particularly in the ground forces, has never been viewed as desirable by the American middle-class male, nor as a preferred alternative to civil employment by the skilled working-class male—a fact borne out by the pattern of enlistment in the AVF. Only a Selective Service System would lead to the certain acquisition of higher-aptitude individuals. Again, if the national mandate is to win the battles that the nation anticipates the military might fight, then that mandate, and not equitable distribution of the burden of service, should ultimately define the characteristics of soldiers to be taken into the force. Arguments about equity of service impress me as germane only in peacetime and in respect to outdated conceptions of the nature of war. Among other considerations, an armed force requires a high level of predictability and continuity in terms of personnel quality. Any All-Volunteer Force is susceptible to extreme fluctuations in personnel quality in response to the vagaries of the marketplace. Years of severe recession, like 1981, result in completed recruitment quotas and higher-quality personnel. When the civilian economy prospers, however, both numbers and quality of personnel decline. Jobs that require high intellectual and military aptitude and that may be critical to maintaining technological advantage over the "enemy" are thus subject to unpredictable fluctuations in manning and effectiveness. The readiness of the force to perform its mandated missions ceases to be predictable beyond the comparatively short-term period constrained by each annual recruiting and retention cycle. The much longer cycles of weapons development and acquisition are not assured the predictability of quality of manpower composition nor the necessary levels of aptitude. Marketplace expedients that may work during periods of moderate-to-severe economic recession may well fail during periods of prosperity since few economic incentives have proven capable of attracting better educated, higher mental category youth. War is not an equal opportunity employer; the stakes are appreciably different in a conflict characterized by a short initial period that will define victory or defeat, and whose potential is escalation into a strategic thermonuclear exchange. Victory in war goes to the smarter, better armed, and better trained force. I find it strange that we continue to cost-account the personnel needs of the armed forces almost entirely in terms of costs during peacetime. A military force, like any other institution designed to deal with future contingencies—a dam for flood control or an insurance policy, for example—must be cost-accounted in terms of the consequences that flow from its ability or inability to meet those contingencies. The cost of a conscriptee's service should, I believe, be balanced not only against the lost time from the individual's life or the economic disparity between two years of military as opposed to civilian earnings, but also against the consequences to the individual and society in the event of a lost war. The accounting must then include the potential costs of profound political, social, and/or economic change. The death of a way of life is perhaps difficult for the econometrician to model, but it is the probable result of our military force's inability to do its job in the battle scenario we face today. To demand or expect success from a force that might not possess the capabilities to achieve it and which might well be condemned to destruction and slaughter by its own limitations would be, I believe, a grave moral responsibility for the nation at large.

Wisdom would seem to indicate a return to a Selective Service System to provide a force capable of achieving the ends that the nation has mandated. To provide less is to condemn the force and possibly the nation, as well, to possible disaster and destruction. The face of war and the demands of the battlefield have changed, and those changes, rather than images of the past or wishes for the present, should drive the personnel structure of the armed forces.

Notes

1. M. Useem, "The Rise and Fall of the Volunteer Army," *Society* 18, no. 3 (1981).
2. Karl von Clausewitz, *On War* (Princeton, N.J.: Princeton University Press, 1976), p. 75.

3. Russell F. Weigley, *The American Way of War* (New York: Macmillan, 1973), p. 475ff.

4. Bureau of the Census, *Historical Statistics of the United States: Colonial Times to 1970,* vol. II (Washington, D.C.: Government Printing Office, 1976).

5. Russell F. Weigley, *Towards an American Army* (New York: Columbia University Press, 1962), p. 250.

6. Army Headquarters, *Field Manual 100-5: Operations* (Washington, D.C.: Department of the Army, 1976), p. 11.

7. See, for example, Kenneth J. Coffey, *Strategic Implications of the All Volunteer Force* (Chapel Hill: University of North Carolina Press, 1979).

8. Peter Braestrup, *Big Story* (Garden City, N.Y.: Anchor Books, 1978).

9. See, for example, Paul Fussell, *The Great War and Modern Memory* (New York: Oxford University Press, 1975).

10. See Y. Novikov and F. Sverdlow, *Maneouvre in Modern Land Warfare* (Moscow: Progress Publishers, 1972); and J. D. Douglas, Jr., *The Soviet Theater Nuclear Offensive* (Washington, D.C.: Government Printing Office, 1975).

11. A. A. Siderenko, *The Offensive,* Moscow, 1970, in Soviet Military Thought Ser. No. 1 (Washington, D.C.: Government Printing Office, n.d.), p. 57.

12. Chaim Herzog, *The War of Atonement* (Boston: Little, Brown, 1976), p. 159.

13. I. Levav, H. Greenfield, and E. Baruch, "Psychiatric Combat Reactions During the Yom Kippur War," *American Journal of Psychiatry* 136, no. 15 (May 1979).

14. V. Drosdov and A. Korkeshkin, *The Soviet Soldier* (Moscow: Progress Publishers, 1980), pp. 94-95.

15. Samuel Stouffer, Arthur A. Lumsdaine, Marion H. Lumsdaine, Robin M. Williams, Jr., M. Brewster Smith, Irving Janis, Shirley A. Star, and Leonard Cottrell, Jr., *The American Soldier: Combat and Its Aftermath,* vol. 2 (Princeton, N.J.: Princeton University Press, 1949), p. 37.

16. Robert L. Egbert, Tom Meeland, Victor B. Clive, Edward W. Forgy, Martin W. Spickler, and Charles Brown, *Fighter 1: An Analysis of Combat Fighters and Non Fighters,* HumRRO Tech. Report 44 (Washington, D.C.: George Washington University, 1957).

17. T. N. DuPuy, *The Evolution of Weapons and Warfare* (Indianapolis: Bobbs-Merrill, 1980), p. 309.

18. E. K. Montague and Morris Showel, *A Review of Combat Support Training,* HumRRO Tech. Report 69-19, Alexandria, Va., 1969, p. 10.

19. Coffey, *Strategic Implications,* p. 61.

20. Human Resources Development Directorate, *Human Readiness Report;* see also J. Fialka, "Can the U.S. Army Fight?" *Washington Star,* 14–19 December 1980.

21. These figures are from Seth Cropsey, "Women in Combat," *The Public Interest* 61 (Fall 1980): 73.

22. Jack Anderson, "G.I.'s Get Poor Marks From European Allies," *Washington Post,* 8 April 1981.

23. R. Canter, "Organization, Management and the Volunteer Force: Policy and Research Issues," paper presented at Security Issues Symposium, Army Strategic Environment 1985–2000, U.S. Army War College, Carlisle, Pa., April 1978 (mimeo), USARIBSS, Alexandria, Va.

24. Stouffer et al., *The American Soldier,* p. 105ff.

25. R. Manning and L. Ingraham, personal communications.

26. Human Resources Development Directorate, *Human Readiness Report.*

27. H. X. Spiegel, "Psychiatric Observations in the Tunisian Campaign," *American Journal of Psychiatry* 101, no. 3 (1944): 381.

28. Albert J. Glass, "Observations Upon the Epidemiology of Mental Illness of Troops During Warfare," in *Symposium on Preventive and Social Psychiatry,* Walter Reed Army Institute of Research, National Research Council (Washington, D.C.: Government Printing Office, 1957), p. 197.

29. Roger W. Little, "Collective Solidarity and Combat Role Performance" (Ph.D. dissertation, Michigan State University, 1955); Charles C. Moskos, *The American Enlisted Man* (New York: Russell Sage Foundation, 1970).

4

If the Draft Is Restored: Uncertainties, Not Solutions

KENNETH J. COFFEY

Prior to the current recession and the resulting improvements in recruiting and retention, the All-Volunteer Force (AVF) had come on hard times, and an increasing barrage of testimony and media comments had highlighted its manpower problems.* We heard of recruiting shortfalls in the active forces and massive manning-level deficits in the Selected Reserve and the Individual Ready Reserve. We read of too many low-quality recruits who were unable to master the complex demands of ever-more sophisticated equipment, and extraordinarily high enlistment rates of black Americans with the resulting prospect of disproportionate minority casualties in time of war.

We were told of major shortages of technically trained NCOs who are needed to maintain equipment and train recruits, and of overall shortcomings in weapons development and procurement programs, strategic mobility and war reserve capabilities. Experts told us that many of these problems could be attributed to the absence of a draft and to the high manpower costs associated with attracting volunteers in the open marketplace. And at the same time, we sensed a growing belief in the Congress and countryside that a draft-supported force would be the most sensible course of action for the nation to follow for the remainder of the 1980s.

Was this belief justified, or would a new draft result in as-yet unrecognized pitfalls? This question must be addressed before a defensible position on the value of restoring conscription can be reached. Whereas the current good times in armed forces recruiting and retention have reduced AVF manpower problems, the expected improvements in youth employment opportunities and other factors portend a return to the manpower problems of the late 1970s and renewed interest in restoring conscription.

The purpose of this chapter is to provide insights into this issue by challenging the assumption that a restoration of the draft would necessarily ameliorate the expected AVF manpower and manpower-related problems. First to be discussed is the need for actual or perceived fairness in draft policies and the likelihood of achieving this objective. Then, as a basis for discussing three different possible

---

* Opinions expressed are entirely the responsibility of the author and do not represent the view of the General Accounting Office.

draftee-volunteer mixes, the recruiting results for the Army during fiscal year 1979 are documented, followed by a discussion of the size and composition of conscript and volunteer groups. The quality of recruits and their racial balance are shown to be functions of the size of draft calls and the mental category standard for volunteering. Then, the possible cost savings of different options are considered. Finally, conclusions are offered. The discussion will illustrate the uncertainties—rather than the solutions—associated with a return to the draft. It is hoped that the discussion also will provoke further reasoned public debate on the issue.

The Need for Equity in Draft Policies

The actual and the perceived degree to which the involuntary military service burden would be shared by the youth population is a key factor in judging the likelihood that a draft could be restored and sustained. This concern for fairness was one of the major reasons the draft of the Vietnam War years became unacceptable, and military manpower experts have come to a definite consensus that equity of service—or at least the appearance of equity—remains an essential ingredient for restoring the draft.[1]

There can be little doubt, however, that in reality the burden of involuntary service would be shared by only a limited segment. Two aspects of this issue merit further discussion: (a) the degree to which the involuntary service burden would be spread among all segments of the youth population; and (b) the proportion of the eligible youth who would serve.

The degree to which the eligible cohorts would be representative of the entire youth population would be determined by deferment, exemption, and disqualification policies and practices. At one extreme, if the armed forces allowed the conscription of those who met the most liberal World War II standards, up to 75 percent of the eligible youth population would be represented. Much more likely, however, is a combination of deferment and exemption policies and high disqualification rates that would limit draft calls to those in groups representing no more than 50 percent of the population.

Young men were drafted into the military in all but one year in the 33 years between 1940 and 1973, and during this period the participation of youth never exceeded the 75-percent level of World War II. To a great degree, at least during the 1950s, 1960s, and early 1970s, this was explained by the granting of a variety of deferments and exemptions which excused or indefinitely postponed the eligibility of many youths with high levels of family income and education. For the most part, such policies were initiated because of decisions to encourage scientific training in the youth population and to provide cheap, college-trained labor for community services.

Since those days, however, much has changed, and today little evidence can be offered to excuse youth from service on these grounds. Thus, if the draft were resumed, the only remaining categories of deferments and exemptions would probably be family hardship and conscientious objection, the two categories that draft reformers of the early 1970s considered inviolable.

To qualify for a hardship deferment, a young man or woman would have to be providing care for his or her family that could not reasonably be assumed by others. Since few youths have such responsibilities, if a draft were restored, the number excused from military service for reasons of family hardship would be very small. Conscientious objection might be more significant. Although the number of applications for CO status from 1940 through the mid-1960s was small, it grew dramatically during the Vietnam War years. Indeed, from 1966 to 1972, almost as many men were applying for CO status as were being inducted. It would be unreasonable, however, to expect that such intense emotions as generated by the Vietnam War would be present in a future draft era.

Nevertheless, because of the turmoil of the Vietnam War period and the broadening of CO eligibility by several Supreme Court decisions, the number of young people seeking CO status would probably be higher than in the pre-Vietnam War years, albeit still at levels that would not hamper the ability of the draft to meet military manpower needs. It also would be likely that the types of youths seeking CO status would resemble those of the Vietnam War era—namely, white youth from better colleges and universities with a small sprinkling of blacks and traditional COs from the peace churches (Mennonites, Brethren, Quakers, etc.).

While the impact of CO decisions on equity would be significant, the strongest reason why the involuntary service burden of a restored draft would not be spread throughout the full youth cohort would be the unwillingness of the armed forces to accept youths with minimal qualifications. Such disqualifications were high during the Vietnam War, when avoiding the draft became a form of high art, if not science. Yet, even during the years of peace which preceded and followed the Vietnam experience, large numbers of youth were rejected.

The highest peacetime rate of disqualification was achieved in 1964, when slightly more than one-half of those examined were rejected at the preinduction review, and a further one out of ten of those who passed the preinduction review was disqualified at the induction exam. In total, 57 out of every 100 men were rejected.[2] During the Vietnam War era, the rejection rates reached higher levels, largely as a result of the sophistication of draft-avoidance programs and the anti-draft sympathies of many examining officials. At its extreme, during 1971, 63 out of every 100 men were rejected.[3]

The rejection levels for 1964 and 1971 (and other years) were influenced by armed forces decisions to limit the number of "low-quality" recruits, as measured by their scores on the standard written entrance examination.[4] Although the results of this test offer no direct relationship to future performance, they are rough predictors of training success and are used in the absence of more valid predictors. Candidates who score in the lowest 10th through 30th percentiles (the so-called mental Category IV personnel) are only marginally acceptable for enlistment, and the AVF has limited the number of such youths, particularly if they have not completed high school. But because of supply and demand factors, the armed forces have not been able to avoid the enlistment of all mental Category IV candidates. Bernard Karpinos has noted, however, that the proportion of the Category IV pool of enlistment candidates declared eligible for enlistment has varied greatly over time.[5]

The following sections discuss three possible scenarios of inductions for the Army under a restored draft. The highest level, postulated on our third scenario, would be a yearly draft call of up to 105,700. Higher calls could be imagined by adding 50,000 or so additional conscripts for the Navy, Air Force, and Marines and providing additional personnel for Selected Reserve units. At the extreme, a form of universal military or civilian training could be implemented for several hundred thousand youths who then would be "on call" as members of the Individual Ready Reserve. Yearly draft calls of up to 500,000 or so are thus conceivable, but the use of the draft for any purpose beyond improving the manning level and quality of the active Army would be very unlikely.

Whether or not the draft was used only for the active Army, or extended to the extreme just mentioned, it is clear that only a minority of the nearly two million young men (or women) who each year turn eighteen would be needed for service.

In sum, even if we returned to the lottery draft policies of the early 1970s, the military service burden would be concentrated on only a limited segment of the youth population, and only a small minority of this segment would be called upon to serve. It will be a very hard task to convince lawmakers and the American public of the necessity for a draft when so few and such an unrepresentative few would be called. Further, as will next be discussed, if the quality or education standards for conscripts are tightened to raise overall quality levels or more closely to approach national racial distribution norms, the burden of military service would be placed on an even smaller portion of the youth cohorts.

A Basis for Comparison

The recruiting results of the Army during FY 1979 provide a good basis for discussing the probable impact of a return to a draft. (I am assuming that a draft would be used primarily for the Army and could significantly change the Army's manning levels, quality of recruits, and racial representation.)

During FY 1979, the Army recruited 129,000 non-prior-service recruits, 17,000 of whom were women. Of the 129,000, only 9 percent were initially classified in mental Category IV. Sixty-four percent of the recruits were high school graduates. Because the Army was unwilling to take additional non-high-school graduates, who were applying for enlistment in large numbers (particularly those who scored in Category IV), a recruiting shortfall of some 16,000 resulted.

The relative success that leaders believed had been achieved by the Army in its recruiting of "high-quality" youths in FY 1979 was abruptly challenged in 1980 when the Pentagon admitted that their methods of determining recruit quality were providing misleading data. The errors—caused by mistakes in norming the test results to the standard reference population—were particularly evident in the ranking of applicants into mental categories.

Whereas the four services for FY 1979 initially reported that they had recruited only 5 percent Category IVs, a recalculation using the correct norming guidelines showed that 30 percent of the recruits were so categorized. The most significant change occurred in the Army. The 9 percent Category IVs initially reported became, under the correct norming procedures, 46 percent, the highest proportion of Category IV personnel in Army recruit groups since the entry testing program was begun in World War II.[6] (For FY 1980, the proportion of Category IVs climbed to 52 percent.)[7] Table 4.1 shows the FY 1979 Army recruitment enlistees divided into mental categories.

As these data illustrate, 64 percent of the Army enlistees during FY 1979 were high school diploma graduates. The rates for black and white enlistees differed, however. Sixty-one percent of the white enlistees, compared to 70 percent of black enlistees, had high school diplomas. The proportion of whites in mental Category IV, however, was considerably lower than that of blacks. Whereas blacks overall made up 37 percent of the Army total, they made up 51 percent of the Category IVs. In contrast, white enlistees made up 60 percent of the Army total, but only 43 percent of the Category IVs. What would have been the results for the Army if they had both used the renormed test and applied their then-current entry standards to the FY 1979 recruit group?

During FY 1979, when the Army was using the misnormed test, their minimum

Table 4.1   Distribution of Non-Prior-Service (male and female) Enlistees by Mental
             Categories (using renormed criteria), U.S. Army, FY 1979

| | High school diploma graduates | | | |
	White	Black	Other	Total
Mental Category I	2,100	67	35	2,200
Mental Category II	13,600	1,700	400	15,500
Mental Category III-A	8,100	3,000	400	11,500
Mental Category III-B	9,500	7,400	700	17,600
Mental Category IV	12,900	21,300	1,700	35,900
	46,200	33,467	3,235	82,700

| | Non-high school diploma graduates | | | |
	White	Black	Other	Total
Mental Category I	200	14	5	219
Mental Category II	3,800	400	100	4,300
Mental Category III-A	4,600	1,100	200	5,900
Mental Category III-B	8,600	3,400	600	12,600
Mental Category IV	12,700	9,200	1,500	23,500
	29,900	14,114	2,405	46,519

entry standards blocked the enlistment of any non-high-school graduates in mental Category IV and limited entry of high school graduates to those who scored in the upper three-fourths of the category. If these standards had been applied to the Army's 1979 group after corrections were made for the misnorming, several changes would have become evident. First, one-fourth of the Army's input, or 32,500 recruits, would have been ineligible for entry. This shortfall, on top of the already recorded shortfall of 16,000, would have left the Army 48,500 below its desired goal of 145,000 non-prior-service recruits. Second, almost one-half, or nearly 15,000, of the 32,500 ineligible recruits would have been black.

Since the discovery of the test misnorming, some have questioned whether the Army should discharge recruits who would have failed to meet the renormed standards. Such actions, however, would have significantly reduced national defense capabilities, and they were never seriously considered. Nevertheless, now that the Department of Defense Authorization Act of 1981 prohibits the Army from recruiting more than 25 percent mental Category IVs in Fiscal Year 1982 and 20 percent in following years, the Army will have to find ways significantly to reduce its intake of Category IV recruits.

It should be noted that there were no shortfalls in the Army recruitment in FYs 1980 and 1981. FY 1981 was particularly successful: the Army recruited 101 percent of its objective, and the number of recruits scoring average or above on the enlistment test and the percentage of high school graduates showed significant improvements.[8] Yet by 1985–1986, as the number of males turning eighteen diminishes further and as civilian economic opportunities for youth improve, quality of recruits may begin to drop and shortfalls may reoccur. Thus, it is useful to use the Army's FY 1979 recruiting figures to imagine a draft's impact on the composition of the force and the possible variations as we vary the conscript-volunteer mixture under a draft.

Impact of Volunteer Policies on Draft Calls and Recruit Quality

The size of yearly draft groups depends upon (a) the policies adopted by the armed forces in regard to volunteering for service; and (b) the extent to which the draft is used to induct youths in the other active forces or in the reserves. For the purposes of this discussion, however, it has been assumed that the draft would be used only for the Army. As noted earlier, during FY 1979 the Army would have liked to recruit a goal of 145,000 higher-quality youths. Using this 145,000 goal, then, varying sizes of conscript groups can be established by postulating that differing numbers of the men and women recruited by the Army in 1979 would have been denied entry in a draft scenario. Thus, if no enlistments were denied, the yearly draft calls (or draft-induced enlistments) would have totaled only 16,000, the 1979 shortfall; if enlistments were denied to all mental Category IVs, except for those high school graduates in the upper half of the category, the yearly draft calls (or draft-induced enlistments) would have risen to 57,000; if Category III-B's (candidates who score in the 31st through 47th percentiles) and all remaining Category IVs were denied entry, the yearly draft calls (or draft-induced enlistments) would have risen to 105,700.

The quality of entering recruit groups could be improved slightly over those of the AVF years if volunteering for service were restricted to individuals in the higher mental categories and educational levels, and if draftees were then used to bring the yearly recruit totals up to desired levels. In addressing this issue, the probable quality levels of draftees is a necessary ingredient, since the limitations on deferments and exemptions and the legal restriction against inducting mental Category V personnel (the lowest 9 percent on the entrance test) provide rough boundaries of the target group. Within this group, quality parameters are defined by the World War II reference population. (If the World War II reference population data are no longer valid, results substantially different from those on the following pages could occur.)

The degree to which public policy would support exclusion of individuals in the lower mental categories from induction would, of course, influence overall recruit quality levels. While the services would prefer inductees with higher educational and quality rankings, it is doubtful that the political leadership could support major departures from historical precedents. Since some mental Category IVs were disqualified for military service, particularly during the years of peace between the Korean and the Vietnam wars, a policy excluding Category IVs would appear to be possible; a draft that excluded only those in the lower half of Category IV (the 10th through 19th percentile) would be a more realistic possibility and is assumed for purposes of this discussion. We are postulating, therefore, that conscript groups will be comprised of 10 percent Category Is, 35 percent Category IIs, 42 percent Category IIIs, and 13 percent Category IVs (rather than the 26 percent Category IVs that would be found in a group excluding only Category V personnel).[9]

As noted earlier, the Army's recruiting record during 1979 can be used to determine the probable effect of a draft on overall recruit quality levels. Three scenarios are offered: (A) conscripts are used only to supplement volunteer recruiting shortfalls; (B) enlistments of Category IV personnel are limited to high

Table 4.2 Change in Quality Distribution of Entering Personnel Under Three Draft
           Scenarios

	Volunteers		Conscripts		Total	
Scenario A: 16,000 conscripts [a]	Num.	%	Num.	%	Num.	%
Mental Category I	2,400	2	1,600	10	4,000	3
Mental Category II	19,800	15	5,600	35	25,400	17
Mental Category III	47,600	37	6,700	42	54,300	38
Mental Category IV	59,400	46	2,100	13	61,500	42
	129,200		16,000		145,200	
Scenario B: 57,000 conscripts [b]						
Mental Category I	2,400	3	5,600	10	8,000	5
Mental Category II	19,800	23	20,000	35	39,800	27
Mental Category III	47,600	54	24,000	42	71,600	50
Mental Category IV	18,000	20	7,400	13	25,400	18
	87,800		57,000		144,800	
Scenario C: 105,700 conscripts [c]						
Mental Category I	2,400	6	10,600	10	12,800	9
Mental Category II	19,800	50	37,000	35	56,900	39
Mental Category III	17,400	44	44,400	42	61,900	43
Mental Category IV	—	—	13,700	13	13,800	9
	39,600		105,700		145,400	

[a] No restrictions on volunteer enlistments
[b] No enlistments from Category IV without high school diploma; enlistments from Category IV reduced to 18,000
[c] No enlistments from Category IV or bottom half of Category III; enlistments from Category III reduced to 17,400

school graduates in the upper half of the category; and (C) no Category IV or III-B personnel are enlisted. These scenarios are represented in Table 4.2.

The addition of 41,000 conscripts to the 16,000 in Scenario A creates a marked improvement in the overall quality of the recruit group in Scenario B. Mental Category IVs have been decreased from 42 percent to 18 percent; Category Is and IIs have been increased to 32 percent from 20 percent. At the same time, however, the profile of the group still would be somewhat below that of the reference population.

In Scenario C, raising the draft totals to 105,700 while at the same time limiting volunteer enlistments to mental Categories I–III-A would also cause a marked improvement in overall quality. Category IVs would be decreased from 18 percent to only 9 percent; Categories I and II would be increased from 32 percent to 48 percent. Further, in contrast to Scenarios A and B, the overall recruit quality levels would be higher than that of the reference population, though only slightly so.

In terms of planning possible future draft policies, then, it is clear that limiting volunteer recruiting in the Army to those with higher qualifications would have a positive impact on the overall quality of recruit groups, and that continuing the policies in effect for volunteers during FY 1979 would have an adverse impact. Because of the complexities of this issue, sophisticated and flexible management by Army leaders would be needed. Whether such rational management philosophies could be followed would depend on the willingness of the American people and their political leaders to enforce conscription for some youths while denying entry to others who would have met past entry standards.

Impact of the Draft on Black Recruits

The number of blacks in Army recruit groups also would be affected by a return to the draft. As with the quality factor, the degree of change would depend upon the size of draft calls and the restrictions placed on volunteer recruiting.

Blacks made up 37 percent of the Army's enlisted non-prior-service recruits in FY 1979. Had a draft been in effect, it is likely blacks would have made up less than 37 percent of the conscript group and the overall black representational level would have been less.

Although current data for predicting the black content of conscript groups is lacking, for purposes of this discussion it will be postulated that (a) each conscript group would contain 12 percent blacks (the proportion of blacks in the youth cohort), and (b) the mental category distribution pattern of the black recruits would reflect that of the World War II reference population, the rates used earlier to reflect the overall quality distribution of conscripts. Again, however, because of the uncertainty of this data, caution should be used.

As in the previous discussion on quality, the recruiting record of the Army during FY 1979 can be used to determine the probable consequences of a return to a draft for black representation and mental category levels. The same three scenarios are offered in Table 4.3.

As Scenario A in Table 4.3 illustrates, the conscription of 1,700 blacks to supplement those voluntarily enlisting would reduce the proportion of Category IVs while increasing the proportion of Category Is and IIs. At the same time, the proportion of blacks among the new accessions would be reduced from 37 percent to 34 percent. Because of the large number of black Category IVs in the Army's FY 1979 recruit group, limiting enlistments of Category IVs in Scenario B would have a marked effect. Indeed, by increasing the draft calls from 16,000 to 57,000, the proportion of black Category IVs is reduced from 62 percent to 33 percent. At the same time, the proportion of Category Is and IIs more than doubles. Further, the overall proportion of blacks in the total number of accessions is reduced to 24 percent.

In Scenario C, limiting enlistments to black and white candidates who scored in mental Categories I–III-A and then filling the recruit ranks with 105,700 draftees would have a marked effect on both black representation and quality levels. Black Category IVs would be reduced from 33 percent to 9 percent. Black Category Is and IIs would almost triple. At the same time, the overall proportion of blacks in the 145,400 persons entering the Army would be reduced to 13 percent, a level roughly equal to that of the black youths in the general population.

As shown in Table 4.3, limiting the eligibility of such recruits would raise quality while lowering overall black levels. A similar argument, though less strong, can be made for the Navy, Marine Corps, and Air Force, whose proportions of blacks are less than those of the Army and whose quality distributions are

Table 4.3   Change in Proportion of Entering Black Personnel Under Three Draft Scenarios

	Black volunteers		Black conscripts		Black totals	
Scenario A: 16,000 conscripts[a]	Num.	%	Num.	%	Num.	%
Mental Category I	100	1	150	8	250	1
Mental Category II	2,100	4	500	28	2,600	6
Mental Category III	14,900	31	650	34	15,550	31
Mental Category IV	30,500	64	400	21	30,900	62
	47,600		1,700		49,300	
Scenario B: 57,000 conscripts[b]						
Mental Category I	100	1	700	10	800	2
Mental Category II	2,100	8	2,400	35	4,500	13
Mental Category III	14,900	53	2,900	42	17,800	51
Mental Category IV	10,700	38	900	13	11,600	33
	27,800		6,900		34,700	
Scenario C: 105,700 conscripts[c]						
Mental Category I	100	2	1,300	10	1,400	7
Mental Category II	2,100	33	4,500	35	6,600	34
Mental Category III	4,100	65	5,500	42	9,600	50
Mental Category IV	—	—	1,700	13	1,700	9
	6,300		13,000		19,300	

[a] No restrictions on volunteer enlistments
[b] No enlistments from Category IV without high school diploma; enlistments from Category IV reduced to 18,000
[c] No enlistments from Category IV or bottom half of Category III; enlistments from Category III reduced to 17,400

closer to the norm.[10] By limiting eligibility, however, many young men and women who desire to serve and would have met the quality entry standards of past years would be denied entry. Though some would urge the implementation of such policies as a means of achieving a more racially balanced force, they could well be unacceptable to the American people. A draft to fill gaps in the ranks of the armed forces is one thing, while using draftees to replace willing volunteers is quite another; and the level to which tradeoffs could be made would depend more on public and political emotions than on pragmatic military manpower planning.

Restoration of the Draft and Possible Cost Savings

Mounting concerns over service manpower costs have focused memories on the $21-a-month conscripts of 1940 and the potentials for significant cost savings in a return to the draft. Such expectations, of course, are far from realistic. While scenarios can be offered in which some cost savings could accrue, other scenarios—ones just as probable—can be offered in which a return to the draft would actually be more expensive. Whether cost-saving or cost-increasing, however, it is clear that a restoration of the draft would not change the status quo of manpower expenditures to any significant degree.

The extent to which budgetary savings could be realized would depend upon several decisions: (a) the size of draft calls, (b) the extent to which pay and allowances for conscripts could be reduced below that of current volunteer levels, (c) the extent to which pay and allowances for volunteers also could be reduced, and (d) possible reductions in related volunteer recruiting expenditures.

At the extreme, pay and allowances reductions could be targeted at all youth in their first term of service, defined as the first three years for discussion purposes. Recognizing that attrition reduces the size of each year group by about 10 percent each year, and using information recently developed by the Department of Defense on the costs of individual service personnel, an overall cost estimate for all first-termers can be developed (see Table 4.4).[11]

Table 4.4　Size and Cost of First-Term Force, FY 1979

Cohort group	Entry size	Size at end of FY 1979	Individual cost	Total cost (billions)
FY 1977	395,000	277,000 (30% loss)	(E-3) $9,590	$2.7
FY 1978	332,000	266,000 (20% loss)	(E-2) $8,857	$2.4
FY 1979	316,000	285,000 (10% loss)	(E-1) $7,992	$2.28
Total	1,043,000	828,000		$7.38

As these figures illustrate, although the target population for any possible reductions in pay and allowances is quite large, its rate of pay is not, even under the current "high manpower cost" era of the All-Volunteer Force. Consequently, the potential for cost savings by making adjustments in the rates appears to be minimal. The amounts that could be saved, however, would depend to a large extent on the numbers of new recruits subject to the lower rates.

The 11.75 percent pay raise granted to all service personnel by Congress in late 1980 was thought to restore most of the parity with civilian wages that had been lost between 1975 and 1979. Yet even with this raise, concerns remain that the services fail to pay a "living wage." As a reasonable guideline for purposes of discussion, it is postulated that reductions of up to 20 percent in the pay and allowances of first-termers would be supported by the Congress, while fully recognizing the hidden or "conscription tax" costs to society of such a position.

If such a reduction was applied only to conscripts, while volunteers retained higher pay rates, the amounts saved would be directly related to the size of draft calls. With an average saving for each conscript of only $1,763 at the 20-percent reduction rate, draft calls of the sizes discussed in earlier sections (16,000, 57,000, and 105,700) would save from $67 million to $446 million. If the reductions were extended to all accessions, the total savings would reach $1.5 billion. A reduction in the recruiting force, advertising, and the elimination of some volunteer enlistment incentives could raise this amount to about $2 billion.

At the other extreme, however, cost increases could result. Because of the two-year term of conscript service (shorter than the average term of volunteers), there would be more people in initial and skill training and fewer in operating units. As a result, there would be strong pressure from military leaders to restore the manning levels of the units. And with a draft-supported force, with more personnel in training, this could be done only by increasing the overall size of the forces—a very expensive undertaking.

Whether cost-saving or cost-adding, however, it is clear that a return to the draft would not alter to more than a small degree the more than $76 billion currently expended for defense manpower.

Conclusion

It would be misleading to use these data and conclusions as the basis for policy decisions or other actions, with the exception of more research. More detailed data would be needed (particularly on the likely characteristics of conscript groups), and much more work would have to be done to determine the characteristics of volunteer and conscript groups under different model mixes. But regardless of the degree of refinement brought to this analysis, certain truths outlined in this chapter would remain.

First, a return to the draft would solve many of the major manpower problems of the Army (but not all) and would most likely prompt enough additional volunteers to eliminate the numerical shortfalls in the other active forces and the Selected Reserve units. The increased flow of young people no longer in the active forces who had lingering reserve service obligations would be large enough to raise the number of Individual Reservists to an adequate level.

Second, the degree to which the services could adjust the size and quality requirements of accepted volunteers without reducing public support below an acceptable level could not be determined in advance. Consequently, we would not know to what extent a draft would counter the expressed concerns over the quality and racial make-up of the Army's recruit groups.

Third, there would be no guarantee that cost savings would result from a return to the draft. Added costs also could be the final result. At either extreme, however, the amounts would be relatively low.

Fourth, the degree to which the public would support a return to the draft cannot be accurately estimated, for it would depend upon many variables that include the size of draft calls, the composition of the conscript groups, and the limitations, if any, on volunteer recruiting. The perceptions of need for a strong military also would be a major factor.

Fifth, a draft would make no significant difference to quality and racial representation unless the services were willing and able to restrict volunteer recruiting of lower-quality personnel while at the same time limiting draft liability to those with more desired characteristics. Obviously, the case for such restrictions would be far less compelling than that for using the draft only to fill unmanned units, and the level of public support would be less.

Finally, there can be little doubt that a draft inducting only a small and unrepresentative proportion of the almost four million men and women who each year reach induction age would not satisfy the many citizens who could accept a draft as equitable only if large numbers of conscripts were needed.

In the 1950s, draft calls reached levels more than double the highest level postulated in this chapter, the induction of women was not acceptable, and the number of 18-year-old males was only half of today's level. The vast majority of eligible candidates were exposed to the draft and many served. In the 1980s, however, a similar participation rate would be impossible to attain, within the confines of our overall peacetime military manpower needs and the constraints of our defense budgets. We could, of course, deny entry to those volunteers outside the draft age group; we could even deny entry to all volunteers and have a totally conscript-supported force. Alternatively, we could cut conscript terms of service so that many more youths would serve, or we could extend conscription to civilian service programs, such as the Peace Corps, reforestation, and disaster relief efforts.

Even if such actions were taken, however, and most of them would not be in the best interests of providing strong armed forces, the majority of youth still would not participate, and public acceptance of the draft would remain uncertain. This uncertainty is the greatest dilemma facing restoration of the draft.

Although specific manpower problems can be identified, and the potential for solving some of them can be seen, we have no assurance that the type and scope of draft needed to overcome the problems would be acceptable to the electorate. More than likely, this could be determined only by the trial and error of restoring a draft without specific parameters for its implementation, which could result in severe societal disruption and little improvement in the armed forces.

Would this degree of uncertainty be worth the potential gains of a return to the draft? Little can be offered in support and much can be offered in opposition. If serious consideration is to be given to restoring the draft, therefore, a serious and informed public debate must provide national leaders with clear justification and objectives. Failing this, expecting the restoration of conscription to eliminate many of the current manpower problems will only detract from the efforts needed now within the All-Volunteer Force to address and overcome them.

Notes

1. The high level of combat casualties among draftees in Vietnam—particularly among minorities—focused public attention on the equity or fairness issue. Although draft officials for many years had justified their various deferments and exemptions as necessary for the national good, such policies became unacceptable. Consequently, major deferment and exemption programs, such as deferments for occupation and college studies, were ended, and the powers of the local draft boards were severely restricted. For a fuller discussion of this draft-reform era of the late 1960s and early 1970s, see Kenneth J. Coffey, *Strategic Implications of the All-Volunteer Force* (Chapel Hill: University of North Carolina Press, 1979), pp. 22-51.

2. Selective Service System, *Annual Report of the Director of Selective Service, 1964* (Washington, D.C.: Government Printing Office, 1965), pp. 61-64.

3. During 1972 and into 1973, when draft calls were small and youths were on notice that the draft was ending, the rejection rates reached substantially higher levels. In January 1973, the last month of large examination groups, fully 65 percent were disqualified at the preinduction review. As no formal draft calls were issued in 1973, however, few individuals ever entered the service. See Selective Service System, *Semi-Annual Report of the Director of Selective Service for the Period January 1, 1973, to June 30, 1973* (Washington, D.C.: Government Printing Office, 1973), pp. 51-52.

4. The grouping of entry test scores into five mental categories has taken place since World War II, and the distribution of service personnel in World War II is used today as the reference population. Thus, if an applicant scores in the top 8 percent (percentile range 93–100), he is classified as a mental Category I. Category IIs represent 28 percent and have percentile scores of 65 to 92. Category IIIs represent 34 percent and have percentile scores

of 31 to 64. Category IVs represent 21 percent and have percentile scores of 10 to 30. Finally, for the 9 percent who score in the 1st to 9th percentiles, Category V has been established. Category Vs are ineligible for enlistment or drafting.

5. Bernard D. Karpinos, "AFQT Historical Data (1958-1972)," special report prepared for the Office of the Assistant Secretary of Defense (Manpower and Reserve Affairs) by HumRRO, July 1975, p. 21.

6. During the 1950s and 1960s, the proportion of Category IV enlistees ranged from a low of 17 percent in 1960, to 28 percent in 1968, to 44 percent in 1952, during the height of the Korean War build-up period.

7. Overall during 1980, the renormed statistics showed that 33 percent of all Department of Defense accessions scored in mental Category IV. In addition to the 52 percent rate for the Army, the rate for the Navy was 17 percent; for the Marine Corps, 27 percent; and for the Air Force, 10 percent. Regardless of branch of service, there was little difference in the proportions of men and women and high school graduates and non-high-school graduates who scored in Category IV. There was a substantial difference, however, in the proportions of blacks and whites who scored in Category IV. In the Army, 40 percent of white recruits scored in Category IV; 76 percent of the black recruits were so ranked.

8. See News Release No. 528-81, Office of the Assistant Secretary of Defense (Public Affairs), Washington, D.C., 17 November 1981.

9. These figures are reached by taking the World War II reference population, and then recalculating the percentages in each category after excluding half the Category IVs and all the Category Vs.

10. 16 percent of the enlistees in the Air Force during FY 1979 were black, the lowest rate among the four active services. In the Selected Reserve, the rates ranged from 10 percent in the Navy reserve to 37 percent in the Army reserve. Of all the active and reserve components, the Navy reserve in 1979 was the only one with a black enlistment rate below that of the national average.

11. The amounts cited are service averages. The rates for each service vary. Essentially, the rates are averages for all personnel in a grade and include cost elements for basic, incentive, and special pay as well as certain personnel-related allowances and expenses. See Office of the Assistant Secretary of Defense (Comptroller), "Average Cost of Military and Civilian Manpower in the Department of Defense," August 1980, pp. 15-16.

Part II
Political Obligation

5

The Obligations of Citizens and the Justification of Conscription

A. JOHN SIMMONS

The Obligation to Serve

Most defenses of the military draft offered in contemporary debates must be understood as having conditional form. When conscription is defended in terms of efficiency (on grounds of cost or the resulting quality of personnel, for instance), the conclusion must be read as incorporating a *ceteris paribus* clause: if there are no *other* relevant differences between possible policies, then conscription is preferable (on grounds of efficiency). Similarly, when it is argued that the draft has advantages in terms of fairness (for instance, by distributing burdens more evenly across racial or economic groups), this fact (if indeed it is a fact) has only conditional weight in determining conclusions about the justifiability of the draft. Just as it is possible to pursue efficiently a desirable end by indefensible means, it is possible to distribute burdens fairly that ought not to be distributed at all. An unconditional moral justification or rejection of conscription would deal not only with its efficiency or distributive fairness, but also with more basic moral characteristics of policies of compulsory military service. For example, such policies involve institutionalized forms of coercion, coercion not in response to (or to prevent) transgressions, but in response to birth and continued residence in the territories of the state. And because the efficiency and fairness of coercive interference seem never to legitimate it (a corporate executive may not simply force other persons to work in his plant, no matter how scrupulously he selects them), appeals to efficiency and fairness in defending the draft may seem pointless.

Such appeals seem more weighty, however, and the contest between conscription and alternative policies seems more equal, when two further considerations are kept in mind. First, the practicable alternatives to the coercive policy of conscription may carry heavy moral costs as well. Reliance on unpaid volunteers to man the armed forces would be disastrous. And the employment of paid volunteers, while it involves no actual coercion, does use "compelling offers" to lure the disadvantaged into a dangerous and restrictive occupation.[1] Serious difficulties may then also be involved in the moral justification of noncoercive policies of manpower procurement. But more central to the defense of conscription, and inevitably appealed to by its defenders, is the claim that each (male) citizen has a moral duty or obligation to serve in the military; with this claim courts, legislators, and laymen routinely begin (and often end) their case for the draft.[2] The obligation to serve is viewed as one of the obligations attached to the role of citizen, others being obligations to pay taxes, to obey other kinds of laws (at least within certain limits), and possibly to "bear his fair share . . . in any other joint work necessary to the interest of the society of which he enjoys the protection."[3]

If obligatory military service is a component of each citizen's political obligations, the moral justification of the draft of course seems much more promising. What was condemned as coercive interference can be viewed instead as the enforcement of a moral obligation owed to the state. The moral distance between the compelling offers that create an All-Volunteer Force and the enforced obligations of the draft is diminished, and considerations of fairness and efficiency again begin to look significant. The entire justificatory program for the draft, then, seems to turn on these central claims about political obligations. I will focus my attention on these claims by examining the contention that there is a community-wide obligation or duty to serve in the military and by discussing the moral justification of conscription.

To reduce the discussion to the size of a chapter, I will make several preliminary points and simplifying assumptions. I will assume, first, that if there is an obligation or duty to serve in the military, this obligation is a species of some more inclusive type of obligation—that is, that if we have the obligation, we have it for reasons that are familiar as the grounds of other, nonmilitary obligations as well. Thus, the obligation to serve might be a promissory or consensual obligation, or the result of receiving benefits, or might be entailed by a more general duty to support just institutions or promote the general welfare, for instance.[4] Second, I will suppose that the moral requirement to serve in the military must belong to one of the three classes of moral requirement: (1) a requirement generated by some voluntary performance or forbearance (for example, by entering voluntarily into some special transaction or relationship, as in the making of a promise); (2) a requirement binding on all persons regardless of their special performances (such as the "natural duties" not to lie to or assault others); or (3) a requirement based in some special, but not necessarily voluntary, relationship (for instance, parent-child or benefactor-beneficiary relationships). All moral requirements, I maintain, fall into one of these three groups, including any obligation to military service.[5] Now I will try to present here some brief and very general points which suggest that it is extremely unlikely that any widely shared moral requirement to serve in the military falls in either class (1) or class (2).[6] My intention is to motivate the special attention that I will give to class (3) requirements later in this essay.

Let us examine first the moral requirements grounded in voluntary performances or forbearances (class 1). These are, first, obligations arising from promises, contracts, and the giving of consent (tacit or express). But this class will also include obligations of fairness or fair play, which arise when persons voluntarily enter into mutual undertakings or cooperative projects. Voluntary participation in a cooperative scheme, even if no actual promise or deliberate commitment is involved, may ground obligations to do one's share within that scheme, by way of reciprocation for the sacrifices made by others. However familiar such obligations may be in everyday life, it seems clear that no widespread obligation to serve in the military (or to perform any other "duties of citizenship") could be of this sort. The suggestion that all or most citizens freely consent or promise (even tacitly) to serve in the military cannot be taken seriously. Naturalized citizens are virtually the only nonofficeholders who expressly consent to anything in the political sphere, and genuine choice situations that would provide opportunities for native-born citizens to give binding consent are all but unheard of in modern political communities. As philosophers since Hume have argued, wherever emigration is the only viable option to performing the duties of citizenship, free consent to those duties will be unusual; continued residence in a country need not, and routinely does not, occur in response to any fairly presented choice.[7] Neither does it seem plausible to characterize the average citizen as voluntarily participating in some ongoing political cooperative scheme with his fellow citizens, and as bound by considerations of fairness to serve in the military. While some persons surely can be taken to be voluntary participants in a fairly strong sense, many others clearly cannot—the poor, the alienated, and those who are trapped, oppressed, and denied genuine opportunities for a decent life.[8] But the political participation of the vast majority of citizens is neither fully voluntary (or informed) nor simply coerced. Instead it consists of making the best of a situation to which there are no options worth considering. Participation of this sort will not ground obligations of the kind discussed above;[9] thus, very few citizens will be bound by class (1) moral requirements to serve in the military.

It seems equally unlikely that there will be a community-wide moral duty to serve that would fall in my second class of moral requirements. These requirements (the natural duties) are not based in any special transactions, relationships, or performances, but arise because of the moral character of the required action or forbearance.[10] I am bound not to murder, for instance, not because of anything I have done (such as promising not to), but because of the moral significance of murder.[11] Similarly, duties not to steal or lie, to give aid to those in need, or to promote justice are shared by all persons, regardless of their voluntary acts. It is hard to accept the claim that there is a duty of this sort to serve in the military, for two reasons. First, because these duties are binding on all persons, the content of any such duty will be general. Our duties will bind us, say, to give aid to anyone who is in need or to refrain from stealing *simpliciter* (or under normal conditions); they will not bind us only with respect to particular persons, institutions, or sets of institutions. By making a promise or entering into some other special relationship I can establish a moral tie between myself and some particular party. But the natural duties, not being grounded in special transactions, lack this kind of "particularity."[12] This creates problems for any attempt to characterize our duty to serve in the military as a natural duty, for such a duty could not bind us to service in any particular state (specifically, our state of citizenship). If, for instance, the duty to serve were conceived as part of a natural duty to support just governments,[13] we would be bound to support not only our own just government, but any other as well. And I assume that a natural duty to serve in the military of all just nations is not one we ought to accept as genuine. What needs to be explained is why a government's being *ours* grounds special moral ties to *it,* such as the requirements to pay taxes to it, obey its laws, and serve in its military. We can understand why our government's being just might establish a moral bond to support it, but not why this would establish a bond to support it *over* other just governments. Of course, a government's being ours routinely has consequences that do seem morally relevant: we receive significant benefits from our government that we do not get from any other, and this may seem sufficient to ground a moral bond. That moral bond, however, would be a requirement falling in my third class. What cannot be shown is that there are any candidates for a natural duty (a requirement in my second class) that would bind us to serve in the military of our own country, without (implausibly) binding us to serve in other countries as well. Since, then, we are seeking an account of a moral duty or obligation that binds citizens to the performance of their traditional "duties of citizenship," the natural duties seem unlikely to provide an account of the sort we seek.

The natural duties appear unpromising in the role under consideration for a second reason. Some of the natural duties are negative duties (requiring only forbearances) and as such can be strict or "perfect" duties (that is, allowing virtually no discretion or options, requiring scrupulous forbearance). The duties not to assault, murder, lie, defraud, steal, and so on are of this sort. These negative duties, however, seem to have no direct relevance to our problem of a duty to serve in the military. The positive natural duties (those requiring positive action and not mere forbearance), on the other hand, are less strict ("imperfect"). We are not required, for instance, to give aid to those in need or to promote justice when doing so would cost us our lives or reduce us to beggary; such performances are clearly supererogatory. The positive natural duties allow a certain discretion in performance, requiring that we perform only when the costs of doing so are kept within reasonable limits. (Otherwise, of course, the demands made upon us by these duties would consume the whole of our lives.) But these positive natural duties would be precisely the ones at issue were there a natural duty to serve in the military (and to perform the other functions of citizens). And there is very real doubt whether the price of citizenship, when it includes military service (e.g., to carry out foreign police actions), constitutes a cost within reasonable limits. The risk of death and disability, the cost in years and economic opportunities lost, may well be such that military service could not be part of the content of a positive natural duty. Similarly, and perhaps more important, the absence of any substantial realm of discretion allowed by government in the performance of "duties of citizenship" suggests that in requiring performance the government cannot be enforcing an imperfect natural duty.

I hope these quick and sketchy arguments will persuade the reader that we have no moral duty or obligation to serve in our country's military that is either a class (1) or class (2) requirement. This would leave us free to deal exclusively with class (3) moral requirements and would allow some hope of reaching a conclusion about the existence of an obligation to serve. Whether or not the reader is persuaded, however, the remainder of the essay should serve some useful purpose. I will, in the following section, proceed to examine the possibilities for giving a class (3) account of the obligation to military service. This, I take it, is of some independent interest, regardless of the force of my objections to class (1) and (2) accounts. Finally, in the last section, I will discuss the relevance of both positive and negative claims about the existence of an obligation to serve to an overall moral justification of conscription, thus returning to the questions raised in the opening pages of this essay.

Obligations and Nonvoluntary Relationships

I have suggested that we reject any class (1) account of the obligation to serve on grounds of realism—the voluntary relationships necessary to ground class (1) moral requirements simply are not in sufficient evidence to support such an account. Class (2) accounts were rejected because of their failure to establish any special tie between the citizen and the country in which he is a citizen. In light of these arguments, a class (3) account must look promising, for class (3) requirements *are* grounded in some special relationship (and so establish a special bond) but do *not* require voluntary performances for the generation of an obligation.

More important, perhaps, a class (3) account seems to capture the spirit of the most familiar answers to questions about political obligation. The reason we are obligated to serve our government (or "country"), many argue, is that it so effectively serves us. It provides numerous and substantial benefits at low cost, and it is the duty of those who benefit from the labors of others to reciprocate. Thus, in the earliest recorded account of political obligation (Plato's *Crito*), Socrates argues for political obligations both as reciprocation for benefits provided and as that which is due a "parent" (to which the state is likened). Here the appeal is to two special relationships (benefactor-beneficiary, parent-child), neither of which need be entered voluntarily, and both of which are ordinarily taken to ground special obligations. Similarly, the well-known consent theory of Locke's *Second Treatise* is in fact only a "front" for Locke's view that those who enjoy the benefits of government are bound to repay them.[14] As A. C. Ewing writes:

> The obligation to one's country or state is more analogous to the obligation to our parents than it is to a business relation. Here also the debt is not incurred deliberately . . . and here also it seems to depend, mainly at least, on uncovenanted benefits conferred on us.[15]

Similar views have been suggested by W. D. Ross and (more recently) by J. P. Plamenatz, Jeffrie Murphy, and Elizabeth Anscombe.[16] I will concentrate here on the parent-child and benefactor-beneficiary relationships, as these seem most likely to be illuminating for our purposes. There are undoubtedly other nonvoluntary relationships that ground obligations (for instance, there are commonly supposed to be other kinds of familial obligations), but I will assume that these are not relevant to possible obligations to serve in the military.

Let me begin by asking why so many have found filial obligations to be analogous to political obligations. First, of course, is the fact that both states and parents provide "uncovenanted benefits." But is there any point in comparing the state to a parent rather than to an unrelated benefactor? Are the obligations we owe our parents different from those we would owe a nonparent who benefited us as extensively as a parent? We might suppose that important differences would arise from the fact that the benefits provided by parents are essential benefits that the child cannot provide for himself and there are (routinely) ties of love and friendship between parents and their children. The analogy between state and parent might seem to be strengthened by noting that the benefits provided by government also are essential (they keep life from being nasty, brutish, and short), and would be difficult for individuals to provide for themselves;[17] and there are (routinely) ties of loyalty and concern between citizens and their states. Perhaps, then, the analogy is a solid one, and it would be worth examining what children do owe their parents, as a possible way of seeing whether citizens do owe military service to their states.

It will be conceded by most that very young children have no moral obligations, to their parents or to anyone else. Where the capacities necessary for minimal levels of moral responsibility are absent, so are moral requirements. As Locke would say, the child is born to, not with, a set of rights and duties. Nor do the child's obligations fall upon him like a moral avalanche at some threshold of maturity. Rather, his obligations grow and extend as his rational powers, self-control, and awareness of the needs of others develop. Thus, the child may have some of the duties of an adult before he has others, since he may grasp the point of some moral prohibitions more readily than others (perhaps property violations, for instance, are more difficult conceptually than more direct kinds of harmful behavior). And the child will owe the obligations and duties to his parents that he owes to others.

He may also have obligations toward his parents that he does not have toward others. Popular candidates are the obligation to obey his parents (at least as long as he is a minor) and the obligation to repay the sacrifices made on his behalf when his parents are in need (after he is self-supporting). It is also commonly supposed that special obligations arise from familial ties of love. Let me deal briefly with each of these.

Children, I contend, never owe obligations of obedience to their parents, given normal family relations—e.g., excluding special contracts to obey, etc. Young children do not, because they owe no obligations to anyone; mature children do not, because they have the same rights and obligations as adults.[18] Children in their middle years, of course, cannot be accounted for as easily, but I think it a mistake to ascribe to them obligations of obedience to their parents. A child, of whatever age, clearly does not always act wrongly (even prima facie wrongly) by disobeying parental commands or by breaking parental rules, which may be pernicious or arbitrary. A child does no wrong in refusing to obey his tough father's command to beat up every child in his class, or in reading an assigned book in school against his parents' wishes. He has not failed to discharge a moral obligation when he does not meet his parents' 8:00 P.M. curfew (which may be perfectly in line with what other parents impose). Children certainly do act wrongly in many instances while disobeying their parents. Excessive drinking, use of dangerous drugs, and lack of respect for the property and rights of others may all be both wrong and prohibited by most parents. But if they are wrong it is for the same reasons that they are wrong for adults; other things will be wrong for children for the same reasons that they would be wrong for a sensitive or confused adult. The wrongness is never, however, a function of the parental command or rule having been disobeyed.

An acceptable position seems to me to be this: to the extent that children have moral obligations at all, their obligations are to do those things that are obligatory for adults of similar capacities, not to do what they are told to do by their parents. As long as they need their parents' help, of course, they may be "obliged" prudentially to obey all sorts of family rules, good, bad, and indifferent. And children will often want to please their parents by obeying, especially where the parents are loving and reasonable in their demands. Parents, on the other hand, do owe special obligations of care and attention to their children. These may be grounded in the voluntary acceptance of responsibility that sometimes accompanies procreation, but we bear special responsibilities as well for even the accidental or unwanted consequences of our actions.[19] Parents have rights also, rights possessed simply in virtue of their parenthood, and which are part of the "package" that comes with these special responsibilities. The rights in question, however, are not rights to be obeyed, held against their children, but are rather rights not to have the functions of parenthood usurped by others, rights which are held "in rem" (against the world at large).[20] These rights may be easily forfeited by abandonment, neglect, or abuse (in short, by the failure to fulfill the obligations of parenthood). Certain kinds of demands made upon children by their parents are within the parents' rights to make. Some of these demands are made rightly by parents. But children are not morally obligated to fulfill any of these demands simply on the grounds that their parents have made them.

Even if the analogy between the child-parent and citizen-state relationships is sound, then, attempts to model our political obligations (including the obligation to obey the state's command to serve in the military) on the obligations children have to obey their parents will fail. But there may be more (or, rather, less) to filial obligations than an obligation to obey. Certain kinds of special consideration or requital of benefits may be due a parent, even if obedience is not. An obvious way to make a case for these more limited obligations is through the idea of obligatory reciprocation for parental sacrifices. But many who have written on the subject have felt that obligations of reciprocation are either not the whole of filial obligations or are not even a part of them.[21] Filial obligations, they maintain, arise (either "as well" or "solely") from the love, friendship, or personal intimacy of the parent-child relationship. Jane English writes that "the filial obligations of grown children are a result of friendship, rather than owed for services rendered."[22] Where the "love relationship" between parents and their children ceases to exist, she argues, so do the obligations of children toward their parents. This seems to me wrong, as does the suggestion that special moral obligations arise out of "mutual caring." I will try to present a more plausible position.

The central claim of the position I wish to reject is that moral obligations are generated by mutual caring (love, friendship, etc.). On that account, a necessary condition for my having obligations to you (a loved one, say) is my continued caring; obligations cease when the feelings (on either part) that define the relationship cease. But if obligations arose in this way from mutual caring, part of the point of moral obligations would be defeated, for they would no longer be assurances of future behavior on which we could count and around which we could organize our lives. Love and friendship can grow cold and die in puzzling ways and in ways over which those who have the feelings normally have no firm control. Further, after feelings have died the point of ascribing moral obligations comes most clearly into focus. Where love or friendship flourishes, individuals give of themselves without any feeling of obligation or moral compulsion (one might say that talk of obligations cheapens such relationships). But where love ends for one party, the other may be left with frustrated expectations, lost opportunities, and a life structured in a fashion now rendered pointless. There may have been substantial sacrifices, financial or otherwise. To suggest that, when my child feels love toward me, he has moral obligations to consider my interests specially but that, when his heart hardens, he has none, seems to me extremely implausible. What point can obligations have where they can be ended by hardening one's heart? Surely the answer is that any filial obligations arise not from mutual caring, but from some other ground. The moral component of the parent-child relationship is independent of the child's loving feelings (though not entirely independent of parental love). Indeed, a child who must give to his parents out of a sense of duty has almost certainly failed to love them fully. (Of course, the child may still have duties toward his parents even if he never acts out of a sense of duty. This, I think, is the situation in the ideal parent-child relationship). If mutual caring is not a ground of moral obligation, as I have argued, this defeats yet another potential line of argument for the existence of an obligation to military service. For it will no longer be persuasive to argue by analogy that the citizen has an obligation to serve that is grounded in his feelings of loyalty or devotion to country.

I return finally to the idea with which we began—that filial obligations are a kind of obligation of reciprocation, and that our obligation to serve in the military may be analogous on these grounds alone. Even on this point, however, it is not easy to make a case for widespread filial obligations (and analogous widespread political obligations). The obvious point that bears on the moral significance of parental provision of benefits is that it is often the parents' duty or responsibility to provide them. The care, attention, and healthy environment that a good parent gives his children can hardly be compared with a gift from some unrelated individual. But that it is a parent's duty to benefit his child does not show, by itself, that no obligation to reciprocate is owed by the child. Sometimes duty-meeting beneficial action requires reciprocation, sometimes it does not. If you are drowning and I ruin my new suit or incur some injury while saving you, few would maintain that you owe me nothing. Perhaps paying for the suit or tending to the injury would be appropriate as a return; if serious risk were involved, perhaps more of a return would be fitting (if it were possible and agreeable to the benefactor). But what is clearly true is that I did no more than my duty in saving you. Had I ignored your plight (perhaps out of concern for my suit), I would have been open to the most severe moral condemnation. There are, then, familiar cases in which the provision of benefits that it is our duty to provide nonetheless grounds obligations to reciprocate. There are obviously other kinds of cases in which it does not.[23] If I have a duty to pay you $10 (which I borrowed from you), you are not bound to reciprocate when I give you the $10. Which of these kinds of cases resembles that in which parents benefit their children (as they are duty-bound to do)? Any resemblance must surely be to the second case, for what is striking about the benefits parents provide is that the parents have themselves *created* the needs these benefits satisfy (by creating the child who has them). Parents not only have a duty to care for their children but are (normally) morally responsible for the necessity of caring for them. It is as if, instead of just pulling you from the water, I had first pushed you in (accidentally or intentionally), making me responsible for your need. In such a case, it is far less convincing to claim that anything is owed me as benefactor; and by analogy it is unconvincing to insist that filial obligations arise from parental benefaction.

More, then, than simply caring for a child and seeing that its needs are met will be necessary for the generation of filial obligations. Perhaps extraordinary sacrifices by parents will make a difference;[24] certainly nonbiological parents (or, say, victims of rape), who have voluntarily taken on a child's care without being morally responsible for its existence, will be owed more by their children than biological parents. Even the "gift" of firm but loving guidance, so seldom and with such great difficulty given by parents but so crucial to the child's psychological well-being and potential for happiness, may (in conjunction with more routine benefits) ground special filial obligations. This seems to me to be the proper explanation of the relevance of love to the moral component of the parent-child relationship. Genuine parental love, understood here as a deep emotional commitment to a painstaking and disciplined pursuit of the child's long-term happiness, is so difficult to give fully and wisely that it may count as the kind of benefit that is not simply a straightforward requirement of parental responsibility. If this is so, then filial obligations may be generated by the parent's loving care (though, as mentioned above, in the ideal parent-child relationship the child will not be motivated by any sense of duty or obligation). These obligations will not be grounded in a relationship of mutual caring, but love will be important to their generation.

My conclusion is that children do not, simply as a matter of course, have special obligations of consideration toward their parents. (These arise only in family situations that exhibit further important characteristics.) It would be unfortunate, then, if defenders of a citizen's alleged obligation to serve in the military attempted to demonstrate the generality of this obligation by analogy with "widespread" filial obligations. The requirements of special loving care or extraordinary sacrifice that might ground filial obligations are surely not in evidence in the relations between state and citizen; the features of the parent-child relationship most important to the creation of special obligations, in other words, are simply not mirrored in normal citizen-state relationship. Perhaps, then, those who would argue for political obligations on the strength of the analogy with familial relations have simply missed the mark, as, for instance, philosophers in the Lockean tradition have long argued.[25]

We began with an effort to find some nonvoluntary special relationship in which individuals might find themselves, a relationship which nonetheless grounded special obligations for them; thus we hoped to avoid the problems of realism and particularity discussed earlier. Comparisons with the nonvoluntary position "child" seemed not to advance our case very far. But we have not yet considered situations of simple benefaction, independent of family relations. If, as my arguments seem to suggest, we may owe more to unrelated benefactors than we owe to our parents, perhaps we may owe obligations of simple reciprocation to our state, which we would not seem to owe when we try to characterize the state as a kind of parent. The state, after all, is not (as a parent is) responsible for the creation of the needs it satisfies. Will this alter our position substantially? The answer again seems to me to be no.[26]

Though we may have obligations to repay benefits even when we have not voluntarily accepted the benefits, strict conditions of other sorts must be met for this to come about. Not just any receipt of benefits obligates us to reciprocate (as we can easily see when we consider benefits that are forced upon us against our wills, or benefactors who are hopelessly inept and bothersome in their efforts). Now, the state may be in certain ways inept in its provision of benefits, and those benefits may be forced on some citizens against their wills. But let us suppose that, for the most part at least, citizens do not regard themselves as ill-used in the processes that lead to their receipt of the benefits a government supplies. Can we derive from this a moral obligation to reciprocate by serving in the military when service is demanded?

Of several relevant points, and the most important for our purposes here, we must consider the content of an obligation of reciprocation. What we owe a benefactor is almost never determined with any precision by the context, but varies with our capabilities, the benefactor's needs, and the value of and sacrifice involved in providing the benefit. What we certainly do not owe a benefactor is whatever he demands as repayment. Of course, our reciprocation should be at least as responsive to the benefactor's needs as the benefit he provided was to ours. But this does not mean that he is empowered to specify which of his needs we will consider or to what extent we will satisfy it. The best guide to discharging such an obligation is only a very vague sense of what constitutes a fitting return. Put in another way, obligations of reciprocation are not "content-specific" in the way that, for example, a contractual obligation is.

These facts seem sufficient to sink any attempt to defend a "reciprocation account" of the obligation to serve in the military (or, more generally, a "recipro-cation account" of political obligation). Even if we are obligated to reciprocate for the benefits we receive from government, we are not obligated to reciprocate in all (or perhaps any) of the ways that governments demand. We are not morally required to serve in the military, to obey every law, or to pay precisely the amount of tax imposed on us simply because we are told to do so. The government, as benefactor, has no special claim to dictate the content of our obligation or to pass final judgment on what constitutes a fitting return (govern-ments have needs, for instance, other than military service). And when we recall that the tax load of most citizens in modern democracies is indeed substantial, it is not at all clear that the price government requires us to pay is not grossly out of proportion with the benefits it supplies. When we add to this the observation that the special efforts and sacrifices involved in extending the benefits of government to one additional citizen are miniscule, it is hard to believe that each of us is bound to give up freedom, years of our lives, economic opportunities, and possibly life or limb in the military, all in reciprocation for benefits that our tax dollars have already purchased.

However far we may be bound to reciprocate, then, it seems clear that this obligation falls far short of morally required military service. Indeed, it seems to me unlikely that we have any obligations to repay the benefits of government at all. If I am right, then the most promising, class (3) accounts of the moral obligation to serve must fail. In conjunction with my earlier claims, the conclusion is clear: citizens generally have no moral obligation or duty to serve in the military. Nor should this conclusion be particularly surprising. The ideal of the citizen-soldier dates from times when states were very different than they are now, when the models of participatory scheme and parent-child relationship had considerably more relevance to political philosophy than they do today.[27]

Enforcing Obligations and Infringing Rights

If there is no moral obligation to serve for most citizens, attempted justifications of conscription will be considerably hampered. The defender of conscription must then find some alternative justification for a basically coercive policy. In the absence of a moral obligation to serve, an All-Volunteer Force seems almost certain to emerge as the most defensible military policy. For regardless of the "economic compulsion" at work in many voluntary enlistments, there is little doubt that volunteering does create an obligation to serve which may legitimate the coercive practices of the military. I anticipate, however, that some readers will remain unconvinced by my argument that there is no obligation to serve in the military. And because it will be useful as well in understanding attempted moral justifications of conscription, I will very briefly consider what seem to be the consequences for such a justification of both negative and affirmative answers to our question about the existence of an obligation to serve.

Let us suppose, first, that I am mistaken, and that there are in fact community-wide (or at least widely held) political obligations, one of which is the moral obligation to serve in the military. Many apparently feel that the existence of such an obligation would serve, by itself, to justify conscription, but this is not obvious because the connection between obligation and justified coercion is not a simple one. That Jones owes a moral obligation to you (or to someone else), I maintain, does not entail that you are justified in doing whatever is necessary to force Jones to discharge his obligation (and may not entail that you are justified in using coercion at all). Much of the body of philosophical literature on obligation and coercion grows out of John Stuart Mill's classic analyses. Mill maintains that when we say that a man has a moral obligation (or that it is morally right for him to do something, which is Mill's equivalent), we mean in part that he ought to be compelled to discharge it. Mill thus appears to be prepared to claim that the use of at least some coercion is always justified in the enforcement of obligations.[28] More recently, similar claims have been common. H. L. A. Hart commits himself to the position that if I owe you an obligation, you have a "moral justification for limiting [my] freedom."[29] Kurt Baier holds that one of the distinctive things about moral obligations is that it is justifiable to "ensure" that individuals fulfill their obligations;[30] and David Richards writes that "to say that a rule is obligatory is to say that coercion is thought to be justified, in the last resort, to get people to do what the rule requires."[31]

This view is misleading in its simplicity, in ways that affect our interest in the possible justification of conscription (and in ways that do not).[32] One point that needs to be clarified for our purposes is the nature of the "justification of coercion" that an obligation's existence allegedly entails. It is not true that whenever someone has an obligation someone (or everyone) else is morally justified in forcing performance. Just as it can be morally wrong to discharge an obligation, it can be wrong to force another to discharge his obligation. The kinds of conflicts that motivated W. D. Ross's account of prima facie moral require-ments are particularly clear examples of this point: it would be wrong for me to ignore the drowning man in order to discharge my obligation to meet you for lunch, and it would be wrong of you to force me to discharge my obligation to you. The only kind of justification of coercion that could possibly follow from the existence of an obligation is a prima facie justification (or justification ceteris paribus), and this mere presumption of a justification could be defeated by any number of countervailing moral considerations. (I will not pause here to discuss the very real possibility that many obligations do not involve even a prima facie justification of coercion. Coercion is, after all, a serious business.)[33]

Even the very limited points made thus far affect the justifiability of conscrip-tion. Even if citizens did have a moral obligation to serve in the military, the state would not be justified in enforcing this obligation (through conscription) under many conceivable circumstances. Some of these circumstances involve obliga-tions that outweigh the obligation to serve and are in fact recognized in current practice: the obligation to support dependent family members and the obligations of religious and moral conscience are (or have been) recognized as having overriding importance (and making state enforcement of the obligation to serve indefensible). Similar cases involve nonobligatory services rendered to society. Those who contribute, and will continue to contribute, to the well-being of others and to the diminishment of suffering often ought not to be forced to serve in the military; their importance to society, even though it is not required by any moral obligation, will have moral weight far greater than their obligation to serve as soldiers. Members of any group or profession may fill this role, although certain doctors, exceptional religious or political leaders, social workers, and those who contribute centrally to other essential services seem likely to be the best candi-dates. Many other circumstances in which state enforcement of the obligation to military service is illegitimate are not (and by their nature will never be) recog-nized in actual practice. These are cases in which the conscript is to be used for morally unacceptable purposes. The state may not legitimately enforce obliga-tions by conscription against those who will be employed in unjust or otherwise indefensible wars, police actions, or domestic control. Here the moral obligations a citizen is under to resist conscription will never be recognized by the state, but will be no less real for that. Where it is wrong to serve it cannot be right to force service.

Lest it seem that in spite of these limits to the state's legitimate enforcement of obligations there will still be numerous and routine cases of justified conscription, I would remind the reader of the kind of obligation the state would be enforcing. If there are any widespread obligations to military service (and I have argued that there are not), they will be obligations of the sort least likely to be legitimately enforceable in routine cases. For they cannot be obligations that flow from deliberate commitments (the facts of political life do not include widespread acts of this sort), nor can the failure to serve in the military be seen as directly and clearly injurious to others (and so be morally wrong in the ways that murder and assault are). But these are the kinds of obligations that most clearly justify enforcement. If there is any obligation to serve, it is almost certainly the kind of obligation that includes a wide realm of discretion in time and manner of performance. The state's requirement of prompt compliance to a specific set of demands cannot be viewed as the enforcement (let alone justifiable enforcement) of an obligation of that sort.

Assume now that there is no general obligation to serve, and that each citizen has a moral right not to be coerced by government to serve. Is defensible conscription out of the question in this case? It is not, for just as obligations sometimes ought not to be discharged, so rights may sometimes be legitimately infringed. I do not act wrongly in taking your car without permission (and so violating your property rights) or failing to deliver the product I sold you (violating your contractual rights), if these acts and omissions are necessary to save someone from great and unmerited harm. Our rights may sometimes be infringed in the performance of important duties or to prevent extremely unhappy occurrences. Similarly, we are often not justified in exercising our rights; sometimes we ought not to press moral claims (in the case of positive rights) and should allow others to interfere where we have (negative) rights that they not interfere.

The relevance of these points to the justification of conscription is again readily apparent. Even if citizens have no obligation to serve, certain kinds of social and military emergencies may still make conscription morally justifiable; even if citizens have a moral right not to be conscripted, they may be justifiably conscripted. But because conscription violates many people's rights, and extensively so (causing prolonged loss of liberty and opportunity, and risk of death), justifying emergencies must be very real and very serious indeed. Emergencies of this sort will, of course, also affect the justifiability of conscription favorably if citizens do have an obligation to serve. In either instance, the seriousness of the emergency will throw a corresponding moral weight on the side of legitimating conscription.[35]

It is hard to specify with any precision what constitutes a serious emergency, but the emergencies I have in mind will involve a high probability of significant loss of life or liberty. Natural disasters, epidemics, and civil disturbances may sometimes qualify, although they are unlikely to justify wholesale military conscription. Threat of invasion by a foreign power may also qualify and will routinely justify more coercive interference in the lives of citizens. The imminent overthrow of a government (from within or without), however, which will almost always be counted as an emergency by those in power, will in fact be an emergency serious enough to justify conscription only if the costs (in terms of life and liberty) of overthrow outweigh those of continuation. The continuation of the government might constitute the actual emergency.

Further, not only domestic emergencies may serve to justify conscription, although they seem to be the justifying circumstances most often mentioned in discussions of these points.[35] Foreign crises and suffering must carry the same moral weight as those at home, if we are not blinded by moral parochialism.[36] Only the existence of a special moral tie to our own state (which I have denied) could justify conscription for special attention to domestic emergencies while ignoring emergencies of similar importance abroad. Of course, conscription (and military involvement generally) may not (and very often will not) affect the course of an emergency sufficiently to justify the extensive violation of rights that conscription involves. In that case, neither the seriousness of the emergency nor the probable suffering should be weighed against the cost of conscription; rather, the probability and extent of beneficial effects of conscription must be balanced against the infringed rights and other costs. For instance, even if we judged the conflicts in Korea and Vietnam to have constituted genuine and serious emergencies,[37] the prospects for their successful resolution through foreign intervention were so limited that the probable benefits of conscripting for such intervention could not have outweighed the costs. And because the prospects for successful resolution of foreign emergencies through intervention will generally be far worse than those for overcoming domestic emergencies, conscription to combat domestic emergencies (such as invasion) will have a much higher likelihood of being justified (even though domestic emergency has no special moral priority over foreign emergency).

Responding to an emergency by conscripting may involve moral costs beyond the massive infringement of rights directly associated with conscription. The rights of innocent persons who have not been conscripted but against whom the conscripts are used may also be infringed, and here the wrongness or injustice of a government's cause again bears on the justifiability of conscription. Where conscription, even if it is to avoid dire consequences, nonetheless is for the purpose of aggressing against innocent persons, the magnitude of the emergency involved must be staggering. Aggressive war to protect vital national interests and to avoid domestic disturbances—for instance, to seize needed oil supplies, occupy needed additional living space, or expropriate food-producing territories for a starving nation—involves serious infringement of foreign rights. If such a war is fought through conscription, it will also involve serious infringement of domestic rights. This combination of moral costs (not to mention the possibility of triggering other, greater evils) is unlikely ever to be outweighed by the probable avoidance of suffering that the war would produce. Conscription in wartime will be justifiable only where the war itself is justifiable (and not always then).

But this makes the case for occasional conscription look better than it really is. For in order to be justified the benefits of conscription must not only outweigh its costs, but the policy of conscription must be the morally best approach to reaping those benefits; and conscription must be far enough better in this way than the next best alternative policy that its higher probability for success outweighs the infringed rights which it, but not the alternative policy, involves. But this means that because an All-Volunteer Force involves no overt infringements of rights (and only minimal moral costs of other sorts), conscription to counter emergencies would have to improve the probability of success (over reliance on volunteers) sufficiently to outweigh the massive violation of rights it produces. The difference between the effectiveness of an All-Volunteer Force and a conscripted force could be that great only if the All-Volunteer Force suffered virtual collapse. So even if conscription might otherwise be defensible, it would almost certainly be unjustifiable in virtue of the moral superiority of alternative policies.

But suppose that enlistment or the quality of recruits was so low that the All-Volunteer Force was in fact unable to perform with even minimal competence. And might we not construe the increasing imbalance of military power in the world as itself constituting a military emergency for the United States? There is, of course, no red alert imminence of invasion or nuclear attack, but by the time there was such a concrete emergency, conscription could not possibly be of any use in countering it. We can no longer call out the Minute Men to save the nation. Might we not, then, conscript a force that would be capable of meeting emergencies when they arose? I believe that such a course would be morally unjustifiable, for the same reason that the state is not justified in conscripting a force of citizens to watch and wait for nonmilitary emergencies before there is any concrete indication that they will occur. The loss of liberty and infringed rights such policies involve cannot be justified by the probability of diminished suffering that the existence of such a force involves. The responsibility of government in a modern democracy is not to conscript against an "inevitable" emergency; it is rather to work to make service attractive, to make clear to citizens the value (if any) of a strong deterrent force, and to leave the results to the voluntary decisions of the people whose nation it is.[38]

Notes

1. How convincing such arguments seem will turn on our more general evaluation of free markets. See Jules Coleman, "Liberalism, Unfair Advantage, and the Volunteer Armed Forces," Chapter 7, this volume.

2. See Hugo Bedau's discussion in Part I of "Military Service and Moral Obligation," in *Philosophy and Political Action,* edited by Virginia Held, Kai Nielsen, and Charles Parsons (New York: Oxford University Press, 1972).

3. John Stuart Mill, *On Liberty,* chap. 1.

4. What the obligation to serve will not be is its own type, where the principle of obligation covers military service and no other moral obligations. This rules out of consideration the claim that it is self-evident that we have an obligation to military service, and requires the giving of recognizably moral reasons in defense of obligation claims.

5. The distinction between (1) and (2), of course, corresponds to that drawn by H. L. A. Hart, John Rawls, and others. For Rawls, (1) and (2) are "obligations" and "natural duties" (*A Theory of Justice* [Cambridge, Mass.: Harvard University Press, 1971], section 19). The third class does not fit neatly into the Rawlsian classification, but Hart had earlier distinguished between the special rights that correlate with class (3) and other requirements in "Are There Any Natural Rights?," *Philosophical Review* 64 (1955): 186-87.

6. For a more careful and detailed account of these arguments, I regret that I must refer the reader to other work. See my *Moral Principles and Political Obligations* (Princeton, N.J.: Princeton University Press, 1979). For the arguments concerning class (1) requirements, see especially chaps. 3–5; in connection with class (2) requirements, see chaps. 2 and 6.

7. David Hume, "Of the Original Contract." For a dissenting view, see Harry Beran, "In Defense of the Consent Theory of Political Obligation and Authority," *Ethics* 87 (1977).

8. And, of course, these very worst candidates for voluntary participants are called first to military service.

9. All of these arguments are by now familiar. See, for instance, Rawls, *A Theory of Justice,* chap. 6; and M. B. E. Smith, "Is There a Prima Facie Obligation to Obey the Law?," *Yale Law Journal* 82 (1973). For more recent arguments against the voluntarist account of political obligation, see note 6 and Rolf Sartorius, "Political Authority and Political Obligation," *Virginia Law Review* 67 (1981).

10. Hart, "Are There Any Natural Rights?," p. 179.

11. My meeting you for lunch, as I promised, on the other hand, is not obligatory for me because meeting you for lunch is an especially good thing to do. It is obligatory simply because it was promised, and may be of quite neutral character independent of the promise.

12. For a more extensive discussion of the problem of particularity, see my *Moral Principles and Political Obligations,* chap. 2.

13. I choose this example, of course, because of its relevance to the prominent theory of this sort offered by Rawls.

14. Simmons, *Moral Principles and Political Obligations,* chap. 4.

15. A. C. Ewing, *The Individual, the State, and World Government* (New York: Macmillian, 1947), p. 218.

16. W. D. Ross, *The Right and the Good* (London: Oxford University Press, 1967), p. 27; J. P. Plamenatz, *Consent, Freedom, and Political Obligation* (New York: Oxford University Press, 1968), p. 24; Jeffrie Murphy, "In Defense of Obligation," in *Nomos XII: Political and Legal Obligation,* edited by J. R. Pennock and J. W. Chapman (New York: Atherton, 1970),

pp. 42–43; Elizabeth Anscombe, "On the Source of the Authority of the State," *Ratio* 20 (1978): 16–18.

17. For comments on this line of argument, see my "Voluntarism and Political Associations," *Virginia Law Review* 67 (1981).

18. See A. D. Woozley, *Law and Obedience: The Arguments of Plato's Crito* (London: Duckworth, 1979), p. 67. The remainder of chap. 4 of Woozley's work is also relevant to the points under discussion.

19. We can, I think, easily imagine bizarre science fiction or religious stories in which a child was the result of no one's voluntary actions. In such a case, the biological parents would, I believe, have no duties to their child beyond that of giving aid to anyone who needs it.

20. Sartorius, "Political Authority and Political Obligation."

21. A. I. Melden, for instance, holds the former view (in *Rights and Persons* [Berkeley: University of California Press, 1977], pp. 67–68); while Jane English maintains the latter (in "What Do Grown Children Owe Their Parents?," in *Having Children,* edited by Onora O'Neill and William Ruddick [New York: Oxford University Press, 1979]).

22. English, "What Do Grown Children Owe Their Parents?," p. 354.

23. See my more detailed discussion of these problems in *Moral Principles and Political Obligations,* pp. 179–83.

24. English, implausibly I think, denies this, contending that "the quantity of parental sacrifice is not relevant in determining what duties the grown child has" ("What Do Grown Children Owe Their Parents?," p. 354).

25. I assume that by now it will be clear that the mere biological relation of childhood cannot, by itself, ground obligations, and that, by analogy, mere citizenship cannot ground political obligations. Biological parents are surely owed nothing by children they abandon at birth, and states are owed nothing by citizens who benefit not at all from their policies. This point ties in with my insistence that any obligation to serve in the military must be a species of some more inclusive type of obligation.

26. See my *Moral Principles and Political Obligations,* chap. 7., for a fuller development of this claim.

27. Michael Walzer, "Political Alienation and Military Service," in *Obligations: Essays on Disobedience, War, and Citizenship* (New York: Simon & Schuster, 1970), p. 99; and Bedau, "Military Service and Moral Obligation," pp.147–48.

28. John Stuart Mill, *Utilitarianism,* chap. 5, paragraph 14.

29. Hart, "Are There Any Natural Rights?," p. 178. Hart's actual discussion concerns rights rather than obligations, but his views on their correlation entail the position I attribute to him.

30. Kurt Baier, "Moral Obligation," *American Philosophical Quarterly* 3 (1966): 223.

31. David A. J. Richards, *A Theory of Reasons for Action* (London: Oxford University Press, 1971), p. 98.

32. One problem I will not discuss here concerns who is justified in enforcing obligations (if anyone is). I will assume that if the obligation to serve in the military is owed to the state, then the state is justified (if anyone is) in enforcing it. What happens when the state enforces obligations not owed directly to it is more confusing and is, of course, at issue in resolving problems concerning the Lockean "executive right" or "right of all to punish." See Locke, *Second Treatise of Government,* chap. 2, paragraphs 7–13; Robert Nozick, *Anarchy, State, and Utopia* (New York: Basic Books, 1974), chap. 6; A. John Simmons, "Inalienable Rights and Locke's *Second Treatise,*" forthcoming in a collection on rights, edited by H. Miller and W. Williams.

33. This appears to be Nozick's position, at least in his attack on Hart *(Anarchy, State, and Utopia,* pp. 91–93).

34. Nonpolitical duties may seem to favor conscription in emergencies as well—e.g., our duty to help those in need. But we should remember that such duties are neither owed to the government (making government enforcement questionable), nor do they bind us to specific performances (making the government's specific demands inappropriate). Yet I am sure that many individuals have been moved to volunteer for military service out of the sense of a duty to help; clear cases might be (many of) those Americans who served in British, Russian, and Chinese units during World War II.

35. For instance, in Walzer, "Political Alienation and Military Service," pp. 117–18, and Bedau, "Military Service and Moral Obligation," pp. 157–58.

36. This point is recognized by Rawls *(A Theory of Justice,* p. 380).

37. I do not think that a case can be made that either instance was a genuine and serious emergency. The probable loss of life and liberty seemed at least as great in responding to the emergency as in ignoring it (not even counting those who died because of the intervention), and the qualities of the governments preserved were not such as to make them worth preserving on independent grounds.

38. Many of the views expressed here grew out of the enjoyable discussions of conscription I had with Captain George Higgens, Instructor at the United States Military Academy.

6

Individual Rights and Political-Military Obligations

ALAN GEWIRTH

Should any person in a society like ours be subject to military conscription? This question involves many complex issues, ranging from the grounds of political obligation to the present and future conditions of United States–Soviet relations. I cannot, of course, deal with all these issues here. Elsewhere I have discussed some of the chief considerations bearing on political obligation as it derives from the supreme principle of morality, and I shall summarize these in what follows.[1] I shall begin, however, with a brief presentation of certain leading ideas about the justification of military conscription in the light of the considerations just mentioned, and I shall then go on to provide some of the needed elucidations and qualifications.

Military Conscription and Ethical Individualism

One of the main issues in justifying military conscription may be put as follows. The primary justification of the political authority possessed by states and governments is that they secure or protect certain important rights of individual persons. But military service removes or endangers the objects of two of the most basic of these rights: life and liberty. Conscripts may lose their lives in combat, and their freedom is severely restricted when they are subjected to military duty. It would seem to follow, then, that a state cannot be justified in imposing the requirement of military service on any of its citizens, for such a requirement removes or endangers the very objects whose protection constitutes the primary justification of the state's authority.

It may be contended that this conclusion does not follow, for there are many areas where the state justifiably limits persons' possession of objects it is designed to protect. For example, one justification of the state's authority is that it protects the right to property; but still it justifiably imposes taxes, which remove from persons some of their property, in order to be able to carry on its necessary functions. Similarly, it may be held that the state can justifiably impose military conscription, even though this removes much liberty and may endanger life, insofar as this is needed to preserve the state and thereby to help it carry on its necessary functions.

This reply is inadequate. For, apart from all other questions about the justifiability of taxation, we must note that the objects removed by taxation are far less important for the fundamental rights of persons than the objects removed or threatened by military conscription. We may, of course, regard taxation as a "conscripting" of property, or conscription as a "taxing" of life and liberty. But these verbal maneuvers do not affect the main point, which bears on the benefits persons receive from the state's protecting their rights. While it may be rational for a person to give up some of his property if this enables him to keep the rest securely and to acquire more, it is not in any comparable way rational for him to give up or to endanger his life. And it is also the extensiveness of the loss of liberty in military service, the drastic subjection to military orders and regimentation, that distinguishes the conscript's lot from that of the taxpayer.

One premise of these remarks should be made explicit. I am here, so far, assuming ethical individualism. This is not to be understood, however, in the perhaps more usual sense that the individual's judgment or conscience is to be the decisive source or criterion for determining what is morally right and wrong.[2] By "ethical individualism" I mean to refer to ends or values rather than to epistemic or decisional sources. It is the goods and rights of individuals that constitute the primary criterion or end of moral rightness. Thus the state or society itself is to be viewed as instrumental, not final: it is a means to protect the rights of individuals, rather than an end or good in itself. Hence, the preservation of the state or nation is valuable and worthy only insofar as this benefits its individual members. The problem we have been considering is how the state, as but a means to an end, can justifiably act to remove or endanger the end itself.

Another way to put part of this point is to say that distributive criteria must take priority over aggregative or collective criteria. What is morally right must be assayed primarily by reference to the rights of each person taken severally, rather than by reference to the good of the collective whole or the summation or maximization of goods. In this way, the primary moral principle must be a deontological one of distributive justice, rather than an aggregative or collectivist principle, such as utilitarianism or organicism. Aggregative or collective goods may be justifiably invoked only as means to distributive goods. Hence, again, it seems impossible to justify military conscription with its drastic subordination of distributive to collective goods.

I shall subsequently present several qualifications of the point just made. But, remaining for now within the ethical individualism so far sketched, we can see the severe difficulty it poses for the question of justifying military conscription. If the state exists to protect the rights of individuals, how can it be justified in removing or threatening those very rights? It is easy to dispose of many answers. For example, it may be said that military conscription does not remove rights but only the objects of the rights: not, for example, the right to liberty but only liberty itself. But this distinction, while perhaps plausible in some contexts, is here an empty one. Rights, after all, have objects, they are rights to something; and if these objects are removed, then the right too is infringed. It is no comfort at all to assure someone who is about to be killed that he still has the *right* to life; all he is about to lose is life itself. Another inadequate answer is that the ethical individualism upheld here would make legal punishment impossible. How can the state justifiably send someone to prison and thereby deprive him of his freedom if one of its main justifications is its protection of the right to freedom? The answer is that the criminal's loss of freedom has an entirely different basis from the conscript's. The criminal has violated some other person's rights, and punishment is justified as a way of redressing the balance of mutual nonaggression that the criminal has voluntarily disrupted. No such fault can be attributed to the conscript as such, so that his being deprived of freedom lacks any comparable justification. It will be noted that the ground here adduced for punishment is retributive and distributive rather than utilitarian or aggregative.

Other suggestions for the justification of military conscription run parallel to the justification of political obligation and incur comparable difficulties. It may be said, for example, that military conscription is justified if it is needed for the common good. But this raises the questions of what is meant by "common good" and whether, in any of its meanings, it can rightly override the rights of individuals. For present purposes, we may distinguish two main meanings. First, "common good" may be interpreted aggregatively or collectively to mean the good either of many individuals summed together or of the community taken as a whole having a value distinct from that of its individual members. In either case, to say that the common good so interpreted may override the basic goods of some individuals is to uphold a collectivist sacrifice of the few to the many or the "whole." On this view, it would be justified to enslave the few if this would lead to more overall good. There is no adequate basis for thus preferring the whole to the part or even for attributing value to the aggregate or collective whole as against its individual members.

Second, "common good" may be interpreted distributively or individualistically so that it refers to goods that are common to—equally held by—each of the individual members of some group or community. But if it is said that military conscription is justified because it promotes the common good in this distributive sense, the question still remains of how the relevant goods are equally common both to all the nonconscripted members of society and to the conscripted individuals who thereby lose some of their most basic goods. The common good taken distributively cannot justify coercively sacrificing the goods of some persons for the sake of others.

Another familiar group of proposed justifications for military conscription is that individuals owe services to the state in return for the benefits they receive from it. Under this heading come such familiar concepts as "fair play" and "gratitude." The criticisms of these accounts are perhaps equally familiar.[3] First, if individuals have no choice but to receive certain benefits, then it is implausible that they owe any services in return. Second, it may be questioned whether the benefits received are so great as to justify losing liberty and possibly life. Third, there is the problem of drastically unequal benefits. It may be questioned whether any services are owed by those who live impoverished, degraded lives in squalid ghettoes.

Finally, conscription may be defended by appeal to one or another version of contractualism, either in the ideal form upheld by John Rawls or in the empirical form found in various theories of consent. All these versions have severe difficulties that disqualify them as theories either of morality in general or of social justice or political obligation.[4] And these difficulties apply even more strongly to the problem of military conscription.

The Primacy of Moral Obligation

Where, then, does this leave us? Must we conclude that military conscription cannot be morally justified at all?

Such a conclusion would be premature. The difficulties discussed above have arisen because the problem has not been pushed back far enough. The problem of military conscription requires for its adequate answer a solution of the problem of political obligation: Why are persons morally obligated to obey the laws of some state or government? For military conscription is imposed by the laws of a state; hence, although the solution of the problem of political obligation may not be a sufficient condition of the solution of the problem of justifying military conscription, it is at least a necessary condition. And the solution of the problem of political obligation, in turn, requires an understanding of the basic principles of morality, since the problem is about the moral justification of persons' political bonds. On these principles, I shall recur to some of the considerations mentioned in my opening paragraph.

To begin with, we must note the primacy of moral obligation. This primacy is suggested by the very concept of a morality, but ultimately it requires detailed justificatory argument. A morality is a set of categorically obligatory requirements for action that are addressed at least in part to every actual or prospective agent, and that are concerned with furthering the interests, especially the most important interests, of persons or recipients other than or in addition to the agent or the speaker. It will be noted that this definition combines two kinds of considerations: formal and material. The *formal* consideration is that moral requirements are categorically obligatory and are addressed at least in part to every agent. The requirements are categorically obligatory in that compliance with them is mandatory for every person addressed by them regardless of whether he wants to accept them or their results and regardless also of the requirements of any other institutions, such as law or etiquette, whose obligatoriness may itself be doubtful or variable. Ultimately, what is categorically obligatory is the whole system of morality as deriving from its supreme principle, so that while one moral requirement may be overridden by another, it may not be overridden by any nonmoral requirement, nor can its normative bindingness be escaped simply by shifting one's inclinations, opinions, or ideals.

This formal consideration, taken by itself, still leaves open three main questions, two of which involve the material consideration in the above definition of morality. One question is the proof or justification of the claim for the categorical obligatoriness of morality. I call this the *authoritative question* of moral philosophy. One of the most famous ways of expressing it is to ask: Why should one be moral? In particular, why should moral requirements take precedence over all other practical requirements, including political and legal ones? The other two questions bear on the specific contents to which this claim attaches. In the definition of morality just given, these contents were presented in general terms, as being "concerned with furthering the interests, especially the most important interests, of persons other than or in addition to the agent or the speaker." So the second question is: What are the "most important interests" of persons? And the third is: *Which* persons should have their most important interests furthered or favorably considered in action? I call these latter two questions, respectively, the *substantive question* and the *distributive question* of moral philosophy, and both bear on the *material* considerations that are combined with the formal one in the definition of morality presented above.

In my book *Reason and Morality,* I have given detailed arguments for certain answers to each of these three questions. The general basis of the answers consists in a certain supreme principle of morality which prescribes fulfillment of the conditions that are needed by every prospective purposive agent if he is to be able to act either at all or with some chance of success in achieving his purposes. The principle says to every agent that just as, in acting, he acts in accord with his own rights to agency, so too ought he to act in accord with his recipients' rights to agency. This "ought," when fully spelled out, specifies all the moral obligations owed by individuals to one another in their various personal transactions. The principle has a rigorously rational foundation both for the material reason that it is grounded in the necessary conditions of human action and for the formal reason that denial or violation of the principle involves self-contradiction on the part of the agent.

I have elsewhere indicated somewhat more explicitly how these considerations provide answers to each of the three central questions of moral philosophy. The substantive and distributive questions are answered by showing that every agent must act in accord with the rights of his recipients to the necessary goods or conditions of action, consisting in freedom and well-being. The recipients in question are other prospective purposive agents, whose specific range may vary in different interpersonal and more broadly institutional contexts. It has been shown that every prospective purposive agent has equally the generic rights, i.e., rights to the generic features of action which constitute the necessary goods of agency, viz. freedom and well-being. Thus the substantive and distributive answers uphold an equality of generic rights among all actual or prospective agents. The authoritative question of moral philosophy is answered in two ways: formally and materially. The formal answer is that the answers just indicated to the substantive and distributive questions are necessarily true, in that any agent who rejects or denies them is caught in a contradiction. Hence, for any agent's position to be rationally justified, he logically must accept the principle that embodies these answers. The appeal to consistency constitutes a culminating structural argument for the normative necessity of accepting this supreme moral principle, for it shows that the indicated substantive and distributive answers are so conclusive that logical inconsistency results from rejecting them.

The material answer to the authoritative question refers to the specific contents of the answer to the substantive question. These contents consist in the most important goods or interests of persons, namely, the generic features of all action. Hence, the substantive answer applies to every agent in all his interpersonal actions, so that it takes precedence over any more specific requirements or conditions of particular kinds of actions or institutions.

The moral principle that grounds these three answers to the distributive, substantive, and authoritative questions of moral philosophy is the following precept, addressed to every actual or prospective agent: *Act in accord with the generic rights of your recipients as well as of yourself.* I call this the Principle of Generic Consistency *(PGC)* because it combines the formal consideration of consistency with the material consideration of the generic features and rights of action.[5] Compliance with this principle is categorically obligatory for every agent for the reasons just indicated in connection with the authoritative question. The *PGC* is a principle of the equality of generic rights in that it requires of every agent that he give equal favorable consideration to the rights of each of his recipients to freedom and well-being as well as to his own generic rights. As will be indicated below, in many contexts the effectuation of this equality requires a system of institutional rules.

We are now in a position to see how the *PGC,* as the supreme principle of morality, imposes certain qualifications on the ethical individualism from which I began. First, this individualism must be egalitarian: all persons must have equal rights to the necessary goods of action. Second, these rights entail certain correlative duties or obligations on the part of all prospective purposive agents, so that the right to freedom which was one of the chief components of the initial ethical individualism must also accommodate various restrictions on freedom. These restrictions or duties, moreover, are positive as well as negative. The generic rights of each purposive agent entail not only the negative duty of all other agents to refrain from interfering with any agent's having the necessary goods of action, but also the positive duty to help persons have or maintain these goods when they cannot do so by their own efforts and when they can be helped at no comparable cost to the agent. Thus, ethical individualism as justified by the *PGC* must be sharply distinguished from egoism. What the *PGC* justifies is a whole system of mutually supportive rights and duties. This system is similar to the "common good" in the distributive meaning distinguished above, but it adds to it the requirement of mutuality, whereby persons not only must refrain from removing from others any of the necessary goods of action, but also must help others to obtain those goods when they cannot obtain them by their own efforts. The latter duty often requires a context of institutional rules.

The Justification of Political Obligation

From the above delineation of the form and content of moral obligation, comprised in the *PGC* as the principle of the answers to the three main questions of moral philosophy, there follows a corresponding mandatoriness for political obligation. To see how this is so, we must note that the *PGC* not only applies *directly* to the actions of individual agents in noninstitutional contexts, but also applies *indirectly* to the actions of agents that occur within, or are objects of, social rules and institutions. In these indirect applications, the *PGC*'s requirements are imposed in the first instance not on the actions of individual agents but rather on social rules and institutions, which must conform to the *PGC*. The requirements of these rules and institutions are then imposed in turn on the actions of individuals subject to them. Thus the *PGC* is here applied to the actions of individual persons only through the mediation of social rules. These rules are morally justified, and the persons who act according to them fulfill their moral obligations, when the rules express or serve to protect or foster the equal freedom and well-being of the persons subject to them.

When social rules and institutions are in this way justified by the *PGC*, their requirements take precedence over the direct applications of the *PGC*. For example, when the umpire in a baseball game declares the batter out, the latter must leave the batter's box, thus experiencing coercion rather than freedom; when the judge sentences the criminal to prison or to a fine, the latter must undergo these losses of well-being and freedom. Such transactions occur in contexts structured by institutional rules; hence, the requirements of such rules, insofar as they are morally justified by the *PGC*, take priority over those of its noninstitutional contexts.

The social rules and institutions that are justified in this way by the *PGC* include three kinds or aspects of political institutions. First, the *minimal state,* consisting in the criminal law and the institutional arrangements for establishing and enforcing it, is justified by the most basic part of the *PGC*'s well-being component. For the rules of the criminal law are instrumentally justified by the *PGC* in that they uphold in certain ways the rights of all persons to such basic components of well-being as life, liberty, and physical integrity, as well as such other important goods as reputation and privacy.

Second, the *supportive state* is also instrumentally justified by the *PGC*, but in a dynamic rather than in a static way. For, unlike the criminal law, it tries not to correct or prevent a disruption of an antecedent situation of mutual nonharm, but rather tries to move toward a new situation in which equality of well-being is attained or more closely approximated. Under this heading come various provisions for welfare, education, and other goods relieving severe needs or promoting equality of opportunity. The supportive state's arrangements also include a general context of order that protects and extends well-being through uniform rules that provide for predictability and for impartial resolution of conflicts of interest. Thus, the supportive state protects the right to well-being by providing various public goods that improve persons' capabilities for action and productive work, and by supplying basic goods, such as food and housing, to those persons who cannot obtain them by their own efforts.

Third, the *democratic state* is procedurally justified by the freedom component of the *PGC*. For in such a state specific laws and officials are determined by the method of consent consisting in the equal distribution of the civil liberties in the political process. The democratic state also upholds the civil liberties in all other phases of social action.

These three kinds of state, then, are each justified by the *PGC*, either instrumentally or procedurally. Now, as we have seen, compliance with the *PGC*, and thus acceptance of the moral obligations it imposes, is categorically obligatory for all actual or prospective agents. Hence, since the kinds of state just delineated are themselves justified by the *PGC*, the moral obligations that derive from the supreme principle of morality are also owed to such states by persons living within their territory, so that there is a moral obligation to obey and support them. In this way, political obligation emerges as a species of moral obligation.

The argument to this conclusion may be put somewhat more formally as follows. It has been shown that every prospective agent morally ought to act in accord with the generic rights of all other prospective agents as well as of himself. But obedience to and support of the state and its laws that fulfill the *PGC*'s requirements are conceptually or causally necessary for such action. For such a state serves to protect the generic rights of all persons within its jurisdiction and to bring it about, in various direct or indirect ways, that persons act in accord with one another's generic rights. Therefore, every purposive agent morally ought to obey and support such a state and its laws that obtain within the territory in which he lives.

It will have been noted that in the above discussion I have used the phrases "moral obligation" and "morally ought" without distinguishing between them. This synonymy is based on the categorical obligatoriness that attaches to moral requirements; I shall have something more to say on this below. But at this point it may be helpful to indicate a connected point about the relation between "moral obligation" and "political (or legal) obligation." It is sometimes held that these are two distinct and parallel types of obligation.[6] But this is a mistake. The point that has emerged from my above argument is that "Because it is the law" does not, as such, indicate a sufficient ground of obligation; to be sufficient, the law in question must satisfy the institutional requirements of the *PGC* as embodied in the minimal, supportive, and democratic state. From this it follows that moral obligation and political or legal obligation are not parallel modes of obligation, since the latter must derive its justificatory ground from the former. And, for the same reason, they are not even distinct modes of obligation, since political obligation, in order to be genuinely obligatory, must be a mode or species of moral obligation.

The PGC and Alternative Doctrines of Political Obligation

I have now briefly given my answer to the problem of how the obligation to obey and support the laws of some state can be morally justified. It will be noted that only some states can meet the conditions of this justification. It must also be noted that the justification I have given leaves open many questions that require further scrutiny. I have justified the institutions of the state and its laws by their serving to protect or secure the rights of persons, the equal distribution of which is required by the supreme principle of morality. This argument assumes that for the fulfillment of this moral function there should be only one state within a given territory, or at least one state possessing sovereignty. The argument, while leaving open how extensive this territory should be, is compatible both with the existence of historically determinate states embodying various traditions and loyalties and with the formation of new states.

In addition to such historical relativity, it must be recognized that different states may vary in the degrees to which they achieve the protection of rights prescribed by the *PGC*. If a minimal state does not equally protect all its members from crime, to what extent does it deserve obedience? What if the minimal state is not, in addition, supportive, because *(a)* it does not provide an adequate context of rules that remove disorder and resolve conflicts of interest or *(b)* it does not promote equality of well-being among all its members? What if a minimal or a supportive state is not also democratic, or if a democratic state is not also supportive?

Such questions show that a full answer to the problem of political obligation requires a principled establishment of priorities that take adequate account both of the moral requirements or grounds that underlie political obligation and of historical contexts and possibilities. One important criterion for such priorities, deriving from the *PGC*, is that of the degrees of necessity for action. One moral right takes precedence over another insofar as the good that is the object of the former right is more necessary for action than is the good that is the object of the latter right. This is why, for example, the right not to be lied to must give way to the right not to be murdered when these two rights are in conflict. Similarly, one may hold that when the conditions of a minimal state are in conflict with the conditions of a democratic state, the former conditions should take precedence because a situation where there is unrestricted bloodshed and wanton killing is more deleterious to the necessary conditions of action than is a situation where the civil liberties are restricted. It must be emphasized, however, as is tragically shown by the current situation in parts of Latin America and elsewhere, that if such applications of the criterion of necessity for action are to be rationally justified, the conflict between the two sets of conditions must not be caused or exacerbated by the authorities themselves, nor can the suppression of democracy be justified by appeals to tradition or to conceptions of propriety.

These difficulties in applying the criterion of political obligation still leave firm, however, its basis or ground in the generic rights of persons as these are upheld by the *PGC*. It may help to clarify further the principle's rights-based justification of political obligation if I contrast it briefly with two other kinds of doctrine about political obligation, which I shall call *affirmative* and *negative*. These doctrines hold, respectively, that moral justifications of political obligation can, and cannot, be given. I have already briefly considered the affirmative doctrines, but I shall now look at them again in the light of the justification I have presented here.

There are at least five respects in which the *PGC*'s rights-based justification of political obligation differs from justification models based on gratitude, fair play, consent, or other criteria. First, when the *PGC* provides that political obligation is justified by the state's protecting basic rights to freedom and well-being, this justification is not necessarily, or only, backward-looking or retrospective; it may also be forward-looking or prospective. For the justification is based not merely on the fact that the state has protected basic rights in the past and so "deserves" support or obedience in the future; it is also, and primarily, based on the fact that such support is needed in order to enable the state to continue to protect basic rights.

Now, there is a contrast here with the justification based on gratitude. For gratitude is owed only for *past* benefits received. Such a retrospective criterion, however, obscures the fact that there would be no political obligation to obey some law if the law in its *present* or *future* operations did not protect rights. The same contrast obtains if political obligation is held to be justified by the duty of fair play where this is construed as assuming equal burdens for *past* equal benefits accepted.

Second, the *PGC*'s rights-based justification of political obligation is not comparative or relative as is the justification based on fair play. According to the latter, political obligation is contingent on some persons' first accepting certain restrictions or burdens in order to receive certain benefits which also accrue to other persons, especially the so-called "public goods"; these latter persons are then held to be obligated to take on their fair share of the restrictions or burdens in return for the benefits received. But there still remain the questions of whether the latter persons wish to receive these benefits and whether they might not receive them in ways other than those arranged for by the first group of persons. In addition, the stringency or necessity of political obligation is hardly accounted for when the obligation is made contingent on some initial group's acceptance of benefits.

In contrast, the *PGC*'s rights-based justification of political obligation refers directly to each person's having the moral duty to obey rules or laws that are themselves justified by their being instrumental to the protection of the generic rights for all persons. There is indeed a complementary duty of fairness, in that each person not only must obey the laws but also must accept the particular applications of the laws to himself when he comes under their specific provisions. But this comparative duty is derivative from and thus posterior to the rights-based obligation to obey the laws in the first instance.

A third important contrast is that the *PGC*'s rights-based justification of political obligation does not appeal to any presumed optional or voluntary consent. It does not say that persons have obligations to obey the state and its laws because they have voluntarily accepted its benefits and have therefore tacitly consented to its having authority over themselves. The arguments for such voluntary acceptance and tacit consent are weak.[7] Rather, the rights-based justification refers to the state's being needed to protect basic and other rights. Since the argument of the *PGC* establishes that moral obligation is based on practical adherence to and support of the rights to freedom and well-being for all prospective purposive agents, the state's being needed to assure such adherence and support provides a sufficient basis for the moral obligation to obey the state and its laws.

A fourth important contrast is that the *PGC*'s rights-based justification of political obligation refers to *necessary* goods, not contingent ones. The objects of the rights whose protection justifies political obligation are the goods whose possession by agents is the proximate necessary condition of their being able to act either at all or with some chance of success in achieving their purposes. This necessity of the objects explicates and connects with the necessity of the obligation. It is because effective possession of the generic rights is necessary for action that obedience to the state which protects these rights is a necessary moral obligation. In doctrines of political obligation based on consent, gratitude, or fair play, on the other hand, this necessity of the obligation is left unexplained because its grounding in the necessary goods of action is not provided for.

A fifth contrast, finally, is that the *PGC*'s justification of political obligation is grounded in or derived from a moral principle which is inherently rational in that violation or denial of it commits one to self-contradiction. Because of this, political obligation itself emerges as inherently rational and categorically obligatory insofar as the laws and states to which the obligation is owed fulfill the *PGC*'s requirements. The other ways of justifying political obligation, by contrast, can appeal to no such rationality; they ultimately rest either on the vagaries of utilitarian calculation or on intuitions that, because they admit the possibility of rival intuitions, are characterized by arbitrariness and merely assertive dogmatism rather than by any rational finality.

Negative Doctrines of Political Obligation

In contrast to the affirmative doctrines which hold that political obligation can be morally justified, there are negative doctrines which deny this possibility. I shall briefly consider two such doctrines. Each is based on a kind of separatism between morality and politics. One version I shall call *nonmoral separatism*. The exponent of this position concedes that morally justified precepts must be complied with, but he maintains that proper understanding of the problem of political obligation requires abstraction from any moral justification of political authority. Thus he insists that, so far as this problem is concerned, the laws must be viewed as nonmoral. The problem as he conceives it is whether anyone "has a duty to obey the laws of the state *simply because they are the laws*."[8] This "simply because" is designed to present "the laws" as entities that fulfill only the most general positivist criteria, without regard for any moral specification of contents or procedures.

It is no wonder, then, that such a philosopher fails to solve his "problem." Since laws may be egregiously evil in their contents or dictatorially imposed, to demand a justification of a moral duty or obligation of obedience to all laws simply as such is to guarantee failure. This guarantee is compounded when the demand is accompanied by a requirement of individual "autonomy" that exalts freedom of decision with no specification of the content of the decisions that deserve acceptance. In contrast to such nonmoral separatism, the *PGC*'s justification of political obligation requires that the laws have a certain moral content derived from the supreme principle of morality.

A second negative doctrine is based on what I shall call *moral separatism*. The upholder of this doctrine does grant a certain moral content to the laws, but he maintains that, even when the laws have this content, there follows no moral obligation to obey them. He obtains this negative result by construing the word "obligation" as it occurs in "political obligation" in a very restrictive way, so that it is far from coextensive with the whole moral "ought," especially in its categorical, all-things-considered import. In this more specific sense, "obligation" comprises only those moral requirements that derive from voluntary transactions engaged in by agents and that are owed to specific persons.[9]

Now, I do not deny that the word "obligation" is sometimes used in this more restricted sense. But it is also used in more extensive senses, including the categorical or conclusive "ought." If, however, political obligation is confined to "obligation" in the restricted sense, then it is quite understandable that the philosopher who uses only this sense has failed to find an adequate basis for political obligation. For voluntary transactions related to specific persons are unable to provide sufficient grounds for the full scope of political bonds where these are viewed as mandatory for all persons within a given state. Such mandatoriness and universality cannot be accounted for by contingent, voluntary, specific relations or transactions among persons designated by such restricted criteria.

In the system I have outlined above, on the other hand, political obligation derives from the *PGC,* compliance with which is itself morally obligatory in the full-blooded, all-things-considered sense for all actual or prospective agents, because of the logical connection of the generic rights with the necessary goods of action. Since compliance with the *PGC* is categorically obligatory, so too is compliance with the minimal, supportive, and democratic state, since such a state functions for the moral end of securing the *PGC*-based rights of all persons to the necessary goods of action. In this way, political obligation is justified as a species of moral obligation, since the state is internally instrumental to achieving the purpose of the supreme principle of morality.

This position has no difficulty in meeting the "particularity requirement" according to which political obligation must "bind an individual to one *particular* political community, set of political institutions, etc." It has been contended that when, as in my doctrine, political obligation is made to depend on the just quality of a government, "it does not follow that there is anything *special* about this obligation. I am equally constrained by the same moral bond to support every other just government. Thus, the obligation in question would not bind me to any particular political authority in the way we want."[10]

The main reply to this contention is given by a consideration that has already been stated briefly, above. Political obligation is the obligation to obey and support a state and its laws that obtain within the territory in which one lives. There are, then, two conditions, each necessary and jointly sufficient, for some person's having the obligation to obey the laws of some state. First, the state must embody the minimal, supportive, and democratic requirements imposed by the *PGC*, although this condition may be affected by the variabilities and priorities noted above. Second, the person must live within the state's territory. (This latter condition also assumes that there is only one state as a sovereign unit, within each politically relevant territory.)

The point of the latter condition is a practical one deriving from the general justification for the existence of states. I have emphasized, in this justification, the moral, rights-securing functions of the state. But these moral functions do not exist in a physical vacuum, in some purely spiritual fashion. On the contrary, they must operate in relation to persons who are physically present in a specific physical area. If there were a world-state, this area would, of course, comprise the whole inhabited earth (and perhaps other planets, if interplanetary travel is developed). But in any case, a state's jurisdiction, with the correlative political obligation, applies within the specific territory in which persons regularly reside. Thus the problem of political obligation is not merely: Why should one obey the laws of any state? but rather: Why should one obey the laws of the territorially circumscribed state in which one lives? Or, alternatively: What is the justification for there being states that claim authority over the persons living within their respective particular territories?

This territorial aspect of political obligation removes the point of questions that might otherwise be raised against the *PGC*'s justification of political obligation.

For example, if some person A lives in state X, which is minimal but not supportive, should he obey the laws of state X or of state Y, which is supportive as well as minimal? Obviously, as long as he lives in state X, it is to its laws that he is obligated. The persons in state X do indeed have moral rights to a supportive state as well, so long as state X is capable of being supportive; and state X is less justified in claiming their obedience than is state Y in claiming the obedience of *its* members. In this way, the *PGC* indicates the goals toward which all states should strive. Nevertheless, the obligation of state X's inhabitants is to obey *its* laws, not those of some other state.

It must also be kept in mind, however, that the minimal state consists primarily in institutions that establish and enforce the criminal law, whose contents are largely the same as the most basic requirements of the *PGC*. Since the minimal state as justified by the *PGC* protects the most basic moral rights for all persons, obedience to it is indeed incumbent on everyone. The moral requirements here at issue are universal in their obligatoriness, not particular, so that the concomitant political obligations are likewise universal in that they are had by all persons. Thus, when citizen A of state X violates the criminal law in state Y, he is rightly subject to state Y's jurisdiction, because the diversities or particularities of nation-states are accidental to the universal applicability of the law in question. At the same time, however, it is because A has committed the violation within the territory of state Y that he is subject to its jurisdiction.

What if state Y has no criminal law that makes A's action punishable? Suppose, for example, A has killed B, a member of a severely oppressed class in state Y. In such a case, state Y is not entitled to obedience from the members of this class at least, for it is not even a minimal state in relation to them. And there is good ground for A's being punished when he returns to state X.

The universality to which I have just referred is not antithetical to the existence of more particularized legal requirements. Just as, in the natural-law tradition, positive law comprises various specifications or particularizations of the universal requirements of natural law, so too in my doctrine there are such relations of positive laws to the *PGC*. Because of the diverse needs of particular times and places, the positive laws of one state may embody different requirements from those of another state without thereby being opposed to the general requirements of justice as propounded in the *PGC*. With the qualification just noted, the jurisdiction of states and the political obligations of citizens are territorially circumscribed; whatever the future prospects of a world-state may be, at the present time and in the foreseeable future the practical needs of persons involve their living within distinct states, and it is their laws that persons are morally obligated to obey as the particularized versions of the general moral requirements contained in the *PGC*.

It is a fallacy to assume that the general obligation to obey the *PGC* is incompatible with particular obligations to obey different laws in distinct states. For this assumption confuses the universality of the *validity* of the principle of morality with the particularity of the *political instrument* for effectuating this principle. Such an assumption is as unwarranted as the parallel idea that the existence of rules of justice that are incumbent on all states is antithetical to the existence of particular, territorially circumscribed sovereign states. As political thinkers at least since Bodin have emphasized, the sovereignty of any state must be limited by the general principles of justice. Hence, the criteria of political obligation may embody universal requirements of justice without violating the "particularity requirement."

Ethical Universalism and Distributive Consequentialism

Let us now return to the question of military conscription. It will be recalled that the question with which I began was whether military conscription can justifiably be imposed on persons in a society like ours. I shall here assume that our society meets the conditions of the minimal, supportive, and democratic state.

Any attempt at even a qualified affirmative answer to this question must take account of the ethical individualist argument presented at the beginning of this chapter. We have already seen how the *PGC,* because of its indirect applications to social rules and institutions, provides certain qualifications of ethical individualism, as initially sketched above. These applications entail that individual rights, including those of life and liberty, do not have the absolute status that my initial argument seemed to ascribe to them. What the *PGC* makes primary, rather, is the whole mutually supportive system of equal rights to freedom and well-being. Sacrifices in the way of military service for the defense of this system are justified if and only if the system cannot be maintained without them. And if the sacrifices are indeed necessary for this purpose, then, in accordance with the *PGC*'s equality of generic rights, they must be imposed as impartially as possible with a view to the indicated objective.

Despite my earlier remarks made solely within the context of an unreconstructed ethical individualism, there is indeed a parallel between taxation and conscription, despite the much greater sacrifices imposed by the latter. I initially characterized taxation as justified to the individual taxpayer by a cost-benefit calculation in which the costs of taxes were outweighed by the benefits he personally derived from them. Such an analysis would fail to justify military conscription to most of the individuals subject to it. Viewed in the perspective of the *PGC,* however, taxation is justified more adequately by the contribution it makes, although in a more restricted way than conscription, to the whole mutually supportive system of the equality of generic rights.

The general point may be put as follows. The *PGC* imposes obligations on every prospective purposive agent to respect the generic rights of other persons to freedom and well-being. This respect entails obeying and supporting the territorially circumscribed sociopolitical system that fosters and protects these rights for all persons within that territory. In cases of conflict, however, it is the egalitarian-universalist system that takes priority. This subordination of ethical individualism to a certain kind of ethical corporatism may be analyzed into three stages, two of which I have briefly mentioned above. First, in justifying both moral and political obligations, the *PGC* already justifies restrictions on the freedom of individuals, since obligations set limits on freedom. Thus, each person has duties toward other persons correlative with his rights against other persons. Second, the *PGC* embodies not only a purely individualist requirement but also a certain relational or comparative one, since it upholds not merely the generic rights of individuals per se, but also an equality of generic rights between all agents and recipients. Third, the *PGC* upholds this equality not only in transactions between individuals but also in the system, including especially the state, that exists to protect this equality. In this way, the requirements of the state take precedence over the freedom and well-being of individuals in cases of conflict. But it must be emphasized not only that such conflicts must be avoided whenever possible, but also that this priority obtains only when conflicts are indeed genuine and unavoidable, and that the state in question must fulfill the requirements of the *PGC* as embodying the equality of generic rights in a social order or system of mutually supportive rights. The state must in this way protect and support the equality of generic rights for all persons within its territorial jurisdiction.

It follows from these considerations that the generic rights of individuals are not absolute; they are subordinate to the equality of generic rights and to the system that protects this equality. For this very reason, however, a justified state must infringe the rights of individuals as little as possible, and then only when this is needed for preserving and supporting the system as a whole. But the system as a whole exists only for the sake of the equal rights of all its individual members. There is thus a continuum between the ethical individualism described above and the *PGC*'s ethical corporatism. For the latter is distributive, not collective; it extends the generic rights to all persons equally and provides the institutional, systematic framework for the equality of generic rights. In this way, the *PGC* supports the values of community and sociality as well as those of individuality and rational autonomy.

The corporate requirements of the *PGC*'s institutional applications can be further clarified by contrasting them with utilitarianism. As we saw above, utilitarianism's requirement that utility be maximized overall may impose severe sacrifices on the few for the sake of the many. How does this differ from the sacrifices that the *PGC* may impose on individuals in the name of the social values embodied in the minimal, supportive, and democratic state?

There are at least three important differences.[11] First, by virtue of the equality of generic rights, whatever sacrifices the *PGC* may impose regarding the objects of rights must be allocated equally so far as possible. This stands in contrast to an efficiency calculus that looks only to the maximizing of certain outcomes without regard for their possibly differential impacts on individuals. Second, the *PGC*'s sacrifices must be imposed only for the sake of the generic rights, i.e., the rights to the *necessary* goods of action. This stands in contrast to utilitarianism's concern with goods in general. Although utilitarians sometimes try to show how goods may be weighed in terms of importance, these attempts have incurred notorious difficulties. Third, the *PGC*'s sacrifices are imposed not to maximize utility indiscriminately, but only to support the equal rights of individuals. The *PGC*'s instrumentalism, whereby the state is justified as securing the equality of generic rights, is internal rather than external: the state as means to an end must embody so far as possible the distributive egalitarianism of the end itself.[12] Hence, unlike utilitarianism, the *PGC* cannot justify sacrificing the necessary goods of individuals to the end of maximizing utility. Both the *PGC*'s means and its ends must embody respect for the equality of generic rights.

Another way to put this point about the *PGC*'s instrumentalism is as follows. Part of the *PGC*'s institutional requirements, like the whole of utilitarianism's, are consequentialist in that the moral rightness of social rules and institutions is assayed by their producing certain consequences. Nevertheless, the two types of consequentialism are quite different. It is a mistake to assume, as is often done, that all consequentialism is aggregative in a utilitarian or some other good-maximizing way.[13] There may also be a *distributive consequentialism,* where the consequences that serve as criterion of the moral rightness of social rules and institutions are assayed not by how much nonmoral good they produce but rather by their promotion of distributive justice. The *PGC*'s institutional applications to the minimal, supportive, and democratic state are of this distributive-consequentialist sort, since such a state is justified by its being internally instrumental to securing an equality of generic rights among all its members. But the limits imposed by the internal character of this instrumentalism must be emphasized.

The primary aim is that all persons equally have the necessary conditions of action.

An important effect of this difference is that the *PGC*'s consequentialism, unlike that of utilitarianism, cannot be used to violate the equal rights of persons in order to maximize utility overall. The distributive, egalitarian character of the relevant consequences prohibits any such unjust mode of practice or argument.

Military Conscription versus Voluntary Military Service

It follows from these premises that military conscription can be morally justified, but only when the equality of generic rights embodied in a morally justified state can be protected in no other way. It is not the case, then, that a state's fulfilling the minimal, supportive, and democratic requirements of the *PGC* is itself a sufficient condition of the moral justifiability of a law it may propound requiring military conscription. Such a law would need a further, independent justificatory scrutiny to check whether military conscription is indeed necessary for protecting the state. But if the answer is affirmative, then the rights protected by the state require legally prescribed duties of individuals to help maintain that protection. Otherwise, a volunteer army is preferable, because of its greater fulfillment of the right to freedom.

A counterargument in favor of (universal) conscription over a volunteer military force may be based on the analogy with taxation, mentioned above. Taxes are a burden in support of the state that are allocated among all eligible citizens in proportion to their ability to pay. Why shouldn't a similar fair, universal procedure be used for staffing the military forces? There are at least two answers. One is that few persons are likely to voluntarily give the money needed for all the purposes served by tax revenues, especially when they think that relatively few other persons will contribute. Nor does the tax situation offer compensating factors of the sort that can serve to attract suitable volunteers for the military forces, since the financial, educational, and other emoluments invoked for the latter purpose would presumably be already within the reach of possible voluntary taxpayers.

The other answer is that military duties are much more specific than the diffuse purposes for which taxes must be used. Hence, while a general, nonselective procedure must be used to raise taxes, a more selective approach, of the sort embodied in a voluntary military force, is feasible for staffing the military. Thus, while equality of sacrifice is indeed desirable, it could be balanced by providing monetary and other incentives similar to those used to procure workers in other socially necessary but potentially hazardous occupations, such as in the mines and chemical industries.[14] Hence, except in conditions where a voluntary system can quite clearly not serve the nation's military needs, it is preferable.

A second important counterargument for military conscription is that since the purpose of military service is the protection of the whole society, all its members who are capable of such service ought to perform it or ought at least to be subject to the requirement of performing it when needed. The objection continues that the policy of using a volunteer force equates military service with other types of "careers," and thus obliterates the deep moral distinctions between services essential to the survival of one's society and other occupations, and between tasks that threaten one's very life and other far less dangerous functions.

It is more plausible, however, to regard the distinctions emphasized by these objections as differences of degree rather than of kind. Farming, mining, and many other tasks are also vital to the survival of one's society; and if these tasks cannot be performed in some society because of natural limitations of the territory, then other tasks must be performed when possible in order to provide exchange for the needed goods. Yet none of these tasks demands conscription. In addition, as was already mentioned, other socially needed tasks besides military service may also be life-threatening. The case remains, then, that a voluntary system of military service is preferable to conscription unless the evidence is quite clear that such a system cannot serve the nation's military needs, themselves estimated on as accurate a basis as possible.

The restrictions just indicated direct attention, of course, to a host of empirical facts and probabilities. I do not have the space here to go into the requisite scrutiny of Soviet intentions and capabilities and their comparison with those of the United States and its allies. Nor can I now examine the extent to which the United States fulfills the requirements of the *PGC*. I wish to emphasize, however, that when phrases like "national defense" and "national security" are used in discussing military requirements, the justified use of such phrases must refer back to the moral conditions of the *PGC*. As I noted above, states and societies may satisfy these conditions in varying degrees. It is because and insofar as the sociopolitical system of the United States meets this test that it is worthy of support, including the drastic kind of support embodied in military service.

Notes

1. Alan Gewirth, *Reason and Morality* (Chicago: University of Chicago Press, 1978), especially pp. 290–327. I have also previously discussed the problem of political obligation in "Obligation: Political, Legal, Moral," *Nomos XII: Political and Legal Obligation,* edited by J. Roland Pennock and John W. Chapman (New York: Atherton Press, 1970), pp. 55–88; and "Political Justice," in *Social Justice,* edited by Richard B. Brandt (Englewood Cliffs, N.J.: Prentice-Hall, 1962), pp. 128 ff.

2. See Steven Lukes, *Individualism* (Oxford: Basil Blackwell, 1973), pp. 101–6.

3. For a good recent discussion of some of these answers, see A. John Simmons, *Moral Principles and Political Obligations* (Princeton, N.J.: Princeton University Press, 1979), chaps. 5–7.

4. See Gewirth, *Reason and Morality,* pp. 18, 19–20, 108–9; "Political Justice," pp. 130–37. See also the excellent discussion of theories of consent in Simmons, *Moral Principles and Political Obligations,* chaps. 3, 4.

5. The *PGC* has a structure similar to that of the Golden Rule and Kant's categorical imperative. Unlike the latter, however, the *PGC* directly incorporates material components (the generic rights) and not only the formal requirement of universalizability. I have discussed the *PGC's* differences from the Golden Rule in *Reason and Morality,* pp. 164–71, and in "The Golden Rule Rationalized," *Midwest Studies in Philosophy* 3 (1978): 133–47. The Golden Rule says that an agent should act toward others as he would want them to act toward himself, so that the criterion of the rightness of actions consists in the agent's wishes for himself *qua* recipient. But these wishes may be opposed both to his recipients' wishes for themselves and to justified social rules. According to the *PGC,* on the other hand, the criterion of the rightness of actions consists in respect for the generic rights that are common to all agents and their recipients; the objects of these rights are the necessary conditions of action, so that they cannot vary from one person to another.

6. See, for example, H. L. A. Hart, "Legal and Moral Obligations," in *Essays in Moral Philosophy,* edited by A. I. Melden (Seattle: University of Washington Press, 1958), pp. 83 ff., and *The Concept of Law* (Oxford: Clarendon Press, 1961), pp. 163 ff.

7. See texts cited above, note 4.

8. Robert Paul Wolff, *In Defense of Anarchism* (New York: Harper & Row, 1970), p. 18 (emphasis in original).

9. See Simmons, *Moral Principles and Political Obligations,* pp. 14–15. Simmons also

uses "political obligation" in an expanded sense to include "duties" as well as "obligations" narrowly conceived; see pp. 12, 30–31, 37. This expansion, however, does not help him to avoid his negative conclusion, for at least two reasons. First, he still distinguishes moral obligation in this expanded sense from the moral "ought" where the latter signifies conclusive, all-things-considered moral requirements; see chap. 8, *passim.* Second, when he discusses the "natural duty of justice" as a basis of persons' political bonds, the "duty" he adduces is grounded not in persons' rights to the *necessary* goods of action, but rather in seemingly arbitrary goods, as in his example of an "Institute for the Advancement of Philosophers" dedicated only to certain *contingent,* dispensable goods; see pp. 148 ff.

10. Simmons, *Moral Principles and Political Obligations.* Both quotes are from p. 31. In both cases the emphases are in the original. Simmons makes this point with particular reference to military service in Chapter 5, this volume.

11. I have discussed these points more fully in "Can Utilitarianism Justify Any Moral Rights?," *Nomos XXIV: Ethics, Economics, and the Law,* edited by J. Roland Pennock and John W. Chapman (New York: New York University Press, 1982), pp. 158–93; reprinted in Alan Gewirth, *Human Rights: Essays on Justification and Applications* (Chicago: University of Chicago Press, 1982), pp. 143–62.

12. On the distinction between internal and external instrumentalism, see Gewirth, *Reason and Morality,* pp. 296–99.

13. For a recent example of this mistaken assumption, see Germain Grisez, "Against Consequentialism," *American Journal of Jurisprudence* 23 (1978): 24 ff.

14. Some of the moral problems of such incentives are discussed in Alan Gewirth, "Human Rights and the Prevention of Cancer," *American Philosophical Quarterly* 17 (1980): 117–25; reprinted in Gewirth, *Human Rights* (see above, n. 11), pp. 181–96.

Part III

Who Should Serve?
Distributive Fairness and
Conscientious Objection

7

Liberalism, Unfair Advantage, and the Volunteer Armed Forces

JULES L. COLEMAN

The ranks of the American military have always been unrepresentative in terms of social class.[1] This lack of representativeness has seemingly been magnified by the all-volunteer policy. Nonwhites now make up 42 percent of the enlisted ranks in the Army, and the skew toward enlistments from the lower economic classes is greater now than it ever has been.[2] This lack of racial and class balance, especially in the Army, is the source of several objections to the current all-volunteer policy for staffing the services. One argument is that the all-volunteer policy is really conscription through poverty; or that it unfairly excuses the privileged from military service while placing the burden on minorities and the poor.[3]

The standard response to this criticism is that the objection is misplaced: all those who currently serve in the military enlist *voluntarily*; no one is forced against his will to bear the burden of service. This fact—that service is a result of voluntary agreements—removes the basis for moral objection to the enlistment results of present policy.[4]

This standard response, while pertinent, will not fully allay the moral concerns of those who object to the All-Volunteer Force (AVF) on grounds of its unrepresentativeness. Nor does it address the fear that the "voluntariness" of enlistment is a veneer masking a reality of economic coercion; and that even if the ranks are composed of poor and minorities who really enlist voluntarily, the voluntary nature of their agreements may not suffice to make the resulting profile of the military morally unobjectionable.

This chapter addresses the question of whether there exists a moral basis for objection to the AVF, even if all enlistments are voluntary. It argues against the view that we cannot morally object to agreements made voluntarily and in full knowledge of their consequences. While the absence of more attractive alternatives may be insufficient to render a choice involuntary, choices made against the background of limited options can reflect a general weakness in an individual's bargaining strength. Where the disparity in bargaining strength between parties to an agreement is great enough, we may speak of one party having an "unfair advantage." Agreements that involve one individual's taking an unfair advantage of another's relative bargaining weakness may be morally objectionable even if the agreement between them is a fully voluntary one.

This chapter outlines a conceptual and normative framework for understanding and evaluating the claim that an agreement is objectionable because it involves unfair advantage-taking.[5] The framework is then applied in an effort to explain the source of the liberal's uneasiness regarding the current scheme of staffing the military, that the AVF takes unfair advantage of society's "underclass." The chapter does not directly address the legitimacy or the ultimate force of the objection; instead, on the assumption that the objection or a variation of it contains at least a grain of truth, it concludes with a discussion of various measures that might be taken to alleviate the problem.

I. Traditional Sources of Objection to Agreements

The traditional view is that an agreement between two or more individuals may be subject to moral objection on any of four grounds.[6] These are: *(a)* the consent of one or more of the parties is not fully or sufficiently voluntary; *(b)* the outcome of the agreement does not improve the welfare of the parties to it; *(c)* the outcome results in an undesirable distribution of wealth or holdings; or *(d)* it adversely and wrongly affects the interests of third parties. If A and B contract, their agreement will be morally objectionable if, for example, B held a gun to A's head in order to secure his consent; or if A or B or both were mistaken in perceiving the exchange as being to the advantage of each; or if some desirable distribution of wealth will be grossly upset by the exchange; or if the agreement between A and B wrongly injures C (who is not party to the exchange, but whose interests are adversely affected by it). The received view is that an exchange that is: *(a)* fully voluntary, *(b)* Pareto superior,[7] and has *(c)* no undesirable wealth-redistributive effects and *(d)* no other adverse third-party effects is justifiable, as is its outcome. The claim is not that any of these conditions (other than perhaps *a*) is a necessary condition of a justifiable exchange. Rather, it is that taken together these four conditions are jointly sufficient for consensual arrangements to justify their outcomes.[8]

None of these conditions placed on permissible agreements speaks directly or adequately to a concern for the relative bargaining positions of the parties. This is unfortunate for two reasons. First, it is easy to demonstrate formally (and to illustrate informally) that were we to make certain standard assumptions in economics—for example, rationality, the absence of nontrivial transaction costs, and cooperative behavior between (or among) negotiating parties—what an individual can rationally expect to secure from a bargain is determined by his relative initial bargaining position.

Second, at times we object morally to agreements reached voluntarily precisely because, though voluntary, the arrangement reached takes an unfair advantage of the bargaining weakness of one of the parties to it. I will discuss each of these points in turn.

II. Bargaining Strength and Expected Payoff

Suppose that A and B are given the opportunity to play a "bargaining game." The game is that if they reach an accord about how to do so, they can share $100; otherwise each receives nothing. Assume first that A and B are of equal relative bargaining strength. A would like to pocket the full $100; so would B. For either to receive the $100 payoff the other would have to be willing to accept nothing. Neither A's nor B's dream of a full payoff can reach fruition provided both are even minimally self-interested. Instead, on the assumption that both A and B are rational maximizers of their expected utilities, the "solution" to the bargaining game is exactly what one would expect: an even (50–50) split. Being of equal strength, each would veto a payoff in which the other party secured more than he did.

If, however, we suppose that A and B are of disparate strengths and that the utilities each assigns to possible outcomes reflects this feature of their relative starting points, the same game, played under the same conditions, has a different solution. Suppose, for example, that A is very well-to-do and that B is nearly impoverished. In playing this game, A may be willing to take a shot at winning it all—or nearly all—on the grounds that he does not need the money as much. On the other hand, B may be willing to accept a lesser payoff simply because he does not want to chance failing to cash in on the opportunity the game provides for him to increase his wealth. The utilities A and B assign to the possible outcomes reflect this feature of their background positions and the interest each has in securing a particular payoff. To make the exposition easier, assume that A assigns utilities to outcomes just as he did in the previous game; B, however, assigns relatively high utilities to every positive outcome. If each wants to maximize his expected utility, A can reasonably expect to receive a payoff in excess of $50, and B a payoff less than $50. What exact payoff it is rational for A and B to expect to receive will depend on the precise utilities each assigns to the various outcomes. Nevertheless, on the assumption that A is not altruistic regarding B's lesser lot in life, it is natural—according to the axioms of bargaining theory—for A to expect to receive more from playing the game than B can, simply because he, A, already has more than B. Perhaps this is the source of the conventional wisdom that "the rich get richer."

The example is couched entirely in terms of what it would be rational for individuals of various relative bargaining strengths *to expect* from playing a particular bargaining game. What each party *actually* secures from a bargain depends on a wide range of factors excluded from the example, including knowledge of the other party's relative strength, bargaining skills (the "poker face"), and luck. The example is developed only to illustrate the important connection between one's initial bargaining position and what one can rationally expect to receive from entering into negotiations with others of disparate relative strengths.[9]

To put the example in terms of the relationship between starting points and expected, rather than actual, outcomes does not detract from its force. For if we assume that the parties to an agreement are rational maximizers of their expected utility, and that transactions between them are (nearly) costless, the claim that the outcomes of voluntary agreements which make both parties better off and which have no adverse third-party effects are therefore free from objection is just the claim that there are no moral grounds for objecting to continually redistributing wealth and other resources according to already existing patterns of advantages and liabilities. In other words, if what you and I already have defines our relative bargaining strengths, and if our relative strengths determine what is rational for us to expect to secure from our mutual negotiations, and if we are both rational maximizers of our expected utility, then what we should expect to secure from our negotiations—luck and transaction costs aside—is entirely a function of what we already have. This is the Bargaining Theory "Theory of Justice": to each according to his initial advantage—or "threat value."

If the process of free exchange is supposed to impart justification on the redistributive outcomes of agreements—which, after all, is a central component in conventional liberal doctrine—something more has to be said about the confines within which already existing patterns of advantages may legitimately determine outcomes. In other words, what sorts of constraints are warranted, if any, on bargaining advantages and/or on the way in which individuals may exploit advantages?

III. Having and Taking Unfair Advantage

In our example neither A nor B needs to have known anything about the other's relative bargaining position in order for his own position to determine the expected outcome. In other words, each may assign utilities to possible payoffs in ignorance of his own relative strength; in the example we gave, each does. For all B knows A may be in the same boat as he is. The same can be said of A. This feature of the example is important for the following reason: if the agreement concluded between A and B in which A secures more than B just because A already has more than B is objectionable, the source of the objection cannot be that A has *taken* unfair advantage of B. To be sure, A has an advantage with respect to B, which may or may not constitute an unfair one. Moreover, A benefits from the advantage he has. Still, there is no sense in which he has exploited or (more neutrally) employed his advantage for his benefit. Any objection, then, is that the outcome results from unfair starting points; and to rectify matters we would want to do something about equalizing the starting points.

This sort of case differs from other cases in which an individual takes or exploits an advantage of his. This difference points to an important fact about our judgments of fairness and unfairness: the difference between *taking* advantage and *having* an advantage. Thus, our judgments about situations of advantage are capable of far more complexity than may be first noticed. A person may *have* an advantage, legitimate or illegitimate, which he does not use or exploit. For example, a boxer with superior speed may elect not to capitalize on this advantage by dancing away but may elect instead to slug it out.

On the other hand, the boxer may *take* advantage of his speed to dance and confuse his opponent. In this case the advantage possessed by the boxer is not illegitimate, and it is not unfair for him to exploit it. On the other hand, if one boxer is forced to fight with a hand tied behind his back, then the other boxer has an unfair advantage, and if he presses his advantage, unfairly capitalizes on it.

In other cases someone may have a legitimate advantage over another but may capitalize on it in unfair or illegitimate ways. A manager or foreman, for example, might threaten to use his legitimate power of promotion or dismissal to extort or coerce sexual favors from a subordinate. Indeed, there may also be occasions on which one has an illegitimate or unfair advantage over another and may *fairly* or legitimately exploit it.

As we saw in discussing the bargaining game between A and B, an individual may possess and benefit from an advantage though he makes no effort to capitalize on it; or in some instances, in spite of his best efforts to avoid doing so. In order to *take* advantage, an individual must be aware of his advantage, seek to capitalize on it, and succeed in doing so. The primary conceptual difference between benefiting from one's advantage and taking advantage of one's advantage concerns the actor's knowledge, intentions, and the role he plays in the causal network between his advantage and the subsequent gain.

In short, we may make separate judgments about the fairness or unfairness of having an advantage, of benefiting from an advantage one has, and of exploiting an advantage one has. Situations of advantage often call for multiple or complex judgments.

In negotiations one sort of advantage may be superior bargaining strength. This sort of advantage is especially important since, as we noted, what an individual can naturally expect to secure from negotiations depends in large part on his relative bargaining strength.

IV. Bargaining Strength

An agreement consists of three components: (a) the background conditions; (b) the rules, procedures, and common practices governing the formation and consummation of an agreement, i.e., the agreement process; and (c) the outcome of the negotiation. The background conditions include those states of affairs that might affect the capacity of the negotiating parties to strike a bargain both in a particular case and in general. Included within this category are the relative wealth of the parties, alternatives open to them should they fail to reach agreement, and their cognitive capacities, as well as the extent to which each has knowledge of facts relevant to both the substance of the bargain and the bargaining process. The second category includes those practices and procedures that specify the ground-rules for negotiating agreements in a particular context; for example, rules pertaining to disclosure of information, as well as to prohibitions (if any) against the use of coercion, force, or fraud in securing an agreement. Within the third category are the effects on the wealth, satisfactions, and entitlements of the parties to the negotiation and others affected by it, as well as the effects on the capacity of first and third parties to negotiate successfully in the future.

An individual's *bargaining strength* or advantage—his "threat value"—is a function of the background conditions and the rules, practices, and procedures governing agreement formation. If A has information material to the exchange that B does not possess, A is at an advantage with respect to B. This background advantage can be equalized or mitigated by requiring full disclosure in forming an agreement. Other sorts of informational advantages (for example, knowledge of the conditions of a product) can be eliminated by the imposition of nonwaivable warranties. Labor negotiations present additional examples of a manner in which both background conditions and the process of agreement formation determine bargaining strength. An employer might have a background advantage in that in the event of a strike he might be able to substitute nonunion workers for his union employees. In other circumstances, the employees may have the background advantage—as do police and firefighters. The possibility of rampant crime and raging fires should the police and firemen go on strike gives them a bargaining advantage. In both cases the background advantage can be nullified by rules governing the contractual or bargaining process. In the first case, the employer may be prohibited from using nonunion workers; in the second, the police and firefighters may be prohibited by law (as they often are) from striking. In general, distortions in background strength are rectified—when they are corrected at all—by rules governing the formation of agreements.

V. Unfair Advantage, Voluntariness, and Wealth

We have so far a tentative account of the elements that constitute a person's bargaining strength as well as an account of the ways in which bargaining strength determines expected outcomes, and a crude taxonomy of the various sorts of moral assessments we make regarding the fairness or unfairness of an advantage-taking and of an advantage taken. We have, in short, at least the broad outlines of a conceptual framework within which we can locate the charge that certain exchanges, bargains, or agreements are objectionable because they involve unacceptable forms of advantage-taking. We have not specified precisely what makes an advantage taken or an advantage-taking unfair or impermissible.[10] Prior to reaching that question we must take up the more basic objection that everything we might want to say about unfair advantage-taking can be put in terms of one or more of the traditional grounds for objection to agreements noted in Section I.

It might be argued that when we object to an exchange as involving either unfair advantage-taking or the taking of an unfair advantage we mean to say that the agreement is really not a fully or sufficiently voluntary one; or we mean to object to the fact that it is the expected outcome of an unfair distribution of wealth.[11] In this view, there is no normative independence in the allegation that an exchange involves unfair advantage-taking, or that its results are determined by a pattern of unfair advantage.

Can every claim that an agreement is objectionable because it involves unfair advantage-taking be reduced to the claim that the consent of one of the parties to it was insufficiently voluntary? The notion of voluntariness is elastic; it can be used in a very expansive way, as it is when we talk about a perfectly voluntary choice. In that sense, anything less than complete information, rationality, and total freedom from external or internal pressures contributes to a choice being less than fully voluntary. When the concept of voluntariness is used in this way, the absence of complete voluntariness no longer can be considered a bar to enforcing an agreement or to holding a person liable since few, if any, actions are fully voluntary in this sense. Often, one party's advantage consists in his having access to information the other party does not have; or in his being less pressured to make a deal in virtue of greater options open to him. Since full information and the absence of external pressure are necessary for an act to be fully voluntary on this expansive view of voluntariness, there is a sense in which we can capture the criticism involved in unfair advantage-taking within the voluntariness umbrella.[12]

Nevertheless, there are two reasons, one analytic, the other normative, for separating unfair advantage-taking from involuntariness as a grounds for finding fault in agreements. Reconsider the original bargaining game we discussed. B's lack of economic strength relative to A reduces the options open to him, weakens his bargaining position, and increases the likelihood that he will accept considerably less than will A—simply because he *has* considerably less than A. He no doubt would have held out for a better split were he better off. It does not follow, however, that the agreement A and B reach is not voluntary in any meaningful sense. It was the deal, given the circumstances, B wanted to make.

Consider a case in which a decision appears to be fully voluntary although it may involve an element of unfair advantage-taking. You are a landlord and I am a prospective tenant in an area in which desirable housing units are scarce, the demand for them high, and their cost astronomical. Suppose no legal rules require you to disclose the condition of your apartment or to warranty its "habitability." You have information regarding the condition of your unit which you are not required to reveal to me and, given the market in rental units, information I am unlikely to be able to extract from you. If I demand it from you, you will simply rent to someone who makes no such demand. I cannot demand similar information or a warranty of fitness from any landlord for similar reasons—unless, that is, I am prepared to pay a much higher price. Suppose I know all this, have scouted all the neighborhoods and decided that no matter which apartment I lease I'll be taking a risk, but that I'd much prefer to take the risk living in your neighborhood than in any other. Nevertheless, you have information which, if I had it, might well make a difference in what I do. Moreover, your bargaining advantage is precisely what enables you to keep this information from me.[13] The advantage, however, does not imply that my decision is involuntary, or that I would not want the courts to enforce its terms, or to give legal effect in other ways to it. I see no reason for thinking that the lease agreement we reach is not a voluntary one.

The normative reason for separating involuntariness from unfair advantage concerns the sort of institutional response that provides the most appropriate remedy to agreements that suffer from either kind of fault. When A's consent to an agreement is involuntary, the normal institutional response is to refuse to enforce the terms of the agreement against A, or to refuse in other ways to recognize or give legal effect to his decision. In contrast, in many cases of unfair advantage-taking the party taken advantage of does not want the appropriate legal authorities to refuse to recognize the agreement and enforce its terms. Certainly that is the case in both of the examples we just considered. It may be unfair for B to receive only a $25 payoff rather than an even split from playing the game we described. Still, I suspect the last thing B wants is for the person who devised the game to realize the injustice and refuse to dole out the agreed-upon split. And the last thing I want is for an authority in the housing department to refuse to permit me to reach the agreement I did with you simply because it was unjust of you to take advantage of me. If the person who devised the bargaining game doesn't like the way background weaknesses can be exploited to produce unfair outcomes, he should do something about rectifying the way in which initial advantages can dominate; and if the housing authority objects to the advantage landlords can take over tenants in tight markets, it should do something about loosening the market. In both cases, the appropriate remedy is to nullify or correct for the advantage; it is *not* to refuse to enforce or otherwise recognize the terms of the agreements reached. The latter is, however, the typical response when a choice is involuntary and therefore not one for which individuals can rightly be held responsible.

Because the number of options open to someone is often connected to one's wealth, it may be tempting to reduce the bargaining strength constraint on exchanges to the wealth-distributional one. In other words, it may be claimed that what one is objecting to in inequities in bargaining strength is really that the parties come from disparate economic positions.

Although economic well-being enhances one's options, alternative courses of conduct are only one of many features of an individual's bargaining strength. Equally, if not more, important are informational disparities as well as differences in cognitive capacities. Manufacturers, quite apart from their success or failure in the marketplace, possess information that individual consumers—regardless of their wealth—cannot gather on their own. Members of the police and fire union(s) may be individually and collectively less well off than the municipality (which represents the general population) with whom they negotiate labor agreements. Nevertheless, they have in their capacity to strike (in the absence of a rule prohibiting them from doing so) a bargaining chip that is not wealth-distributionally related. And certain individuals possess talents and abilities that constitute, for want of a better phrase, "natural" bargaining advantages that are not wealth-dependent.

I admit the existence of a sense of the term "wealth" in which *any* advantage a person might have can constitute part of his wealth. In that sense any unfairness in outcome which results from an advantage is wealth-related. But this way of thinking of unfair advantage puts the cart before the horse, since the reason these advantages are thought of as related to wealth distribution is that they can be capitalized upon in ways that enhance an individual's wealth. The advantages, in other words, are not themselves wealth-dependent; one's wealth, however, may depend on having them.[14]

VI. Is Absolute Equity of Bargaining Strength Necessary?

The importance of disparities in bargaining strength to the justifiability of the outcome of an exchange depends on what is at stake in the bargain. For example, if the purpose of the bargain is to reach an accord on the principles of justice (on the first principles or rules formulated to guide action and determine legitimate or right conduct)—as in the social contract theory of justice developed by John Rawls[15]—then absolute equity in bargaining position is required. The outcome of the bargain will reflect initial bargaining positions, what the individuals to the bargain already have; and whether what they already have should as a matter of justice figure in the justifiability of outcomes is presumably among the issues the principles of justice will be designed to address. (While there may be no way actually of eliminating existing holdings, talents, and capacities, we can correct for the advantages each creates by not permitting them to figure in one's choice of first principles. By placing individuals behind a veil of ignorance Rawls effectively restricts the role such advantages can create in determining the outcome.) Negotiations over more ordinary matters are less likely to require absolute equity in relative bargaining positions. This is not to say that considerations of bargaining strength never enter considerations regarding the justifiability or legitimacy of day-to-day transactions. Indeed, one way of understanding concern over monopolies and monopoly pricing is in terms of the limitations on bargaining alternatives they create. Regulation of the prices charged by efficient monopolies, like utilities, can then be understood as a way of correcting for the bargaining advantages monopolies maintain.

VII. Bargaining Strength and Liberalism

The importance of disparities in bargaining to the justifiability of the outcomes of exchanges also depends on one's other, deeper commitments in political philosophy. Suppose we accept for the time being the overworked distinction between "historical" and "patterned" theories of justice. According to a patterned theorist, a formula exists at any given time for the just distribution of wealth in society. The prevailing distribution can be measured against the formula and evaluated accordingly. In historical theories, no magical formula exists; instead, justice in holdings or wealth depends on justice in the practices of acquisition and transfer of wealth. A distribution—whatever it ends up looking like—will be just provided the rules of acquisition and transfer are followed.

If you are a proponent of a patterned view of justice, you will determine when an advantage in bargaining strength is unfair by analyzing various initial conditions under which voluntary exchanges undertaken are likely to lead toward or away from the desired pattern. For example, if you are an egalitarian, you are unlikely to accept bargaining advantages that help to make the rich richer—as in our bargaining game involving parties of vastly different economic strength. You are likely to favor rules requiring full disclosure and others imposing implicit warranties of fitness, since they tend to equalize differences in access to information. The central point is that you would look to the likely outcomes of the exchanges and argue back from them to appropriate constraints on relative bargaining strength.

If, instead, you are a proponent of an historical approach to justice, e.g., libertarianism, in your opinion whether an exchange is justified does not depend on its outcome, but on whether the exchange is voluntary. If the worry about unequal bargaining strengths cannot be reduced to a concern for whether or not the exchange is voluntary, considerations of relative bargaining strengths are actually irrelevant to the moral assessment of exchange. In this view the consensual component of an exchange *alone* imparts justification to its outcome.

Any libertarian theory worth taking seriously must provide an account of how the exercise of freedom or autonomy in the context of giving consent or reaching an accord imparts justification on the outcome of exchanges. We can distinguish between "thin" and "thick" forms of libertarianism. According to the thin theory, voluntary consent is a necessary condition of a just transfer of resources, because securing the consent of the parties to a transfer is the only way to ensure that neither party's rights have been violated. According to the thick theory, voluntary consent is important because of its connection to more fundamental goals of self-actualization, self-realization, self-worth, and self-respect.

The thin theory takes individuals having certain rights as primary, and voluntary exchange as the only way to ensure that these rights not be violated. These more basic rights, presumably to one's property or resources (broadly speaking), are violated by nonvoluntary transfers *only* if included among the rights one has is the right not to have others use or take one's resources without one's permission. Otherwise it would not follow that a nonvoluntary transfer necessarily involved a right violation.[16]

For the thin theorist, the only constraints legitimately imposed on exchanges have to do with whether or not an agreement is voluntary, as well as limitations on permissible third-party effects. Coercion, either through force or fraud, negates an exchange and therefore fails to justify its redistributive effects; similarly, coercive third-party effects are impermissible. Thin theorists are primarily concerned with physical and other kinds of force and with certain uses to which one party might put an advantage it has with respect to pertinent information (fraud). For example, the kind of concern the thin libertarian might have about current military recruiting would focus on possible fraudulent misrepresentation on the part of recruiters, which would undermine the informed consent of the recruit. In general, then, the thin theorist probably does not recognize unfair advantage-taking—except insofar as involuntariness of an exchange can be viewed as a kind of unfair disadvantage[17]—as an independent grounds for objecting to agreements. In one sense even the thin theorist is concerned with equity in bargaining position: all parties to the agreement must be equally uncoerced. This may just be another way of saying for the libertarian that the agreement is voluntary on both sides.

In the thick theory, the justificatory force of voluntary consent derives from its connection to individual values, such as self-worth, self-respect, and the actualization of one's potential. The values of self-worth, self-respect, and actualization to which the exercise of liberty is said to be connected have a special place in our political morality. But if they do, then the exercise of liberty has justificatory import *to the extent to which it promotes these goods for everyone*. There is no sense to the view that one individual's self-worth is more valuable than another's, for this is simply the view that one person is *intrinsically* more valuable than another. In order for the liberty of which the libertarian speaks so fondly to bear the weight of moral justification, its exercise must be meaningful and actual, not empty and only theoretically possible. To be free to perform an action in the sense of there existing no rules against doing so is hardly conducive to individual development, when, for lack of capacity, skill, resources, or the like, one is literally unable to do so. The impoverished are free to attend college in this sense; no rules prohibit them from doing so. Still, it is hard to see how this freedom will lead to anything other than frustration and a sense of inadequacy.

Once he admits that the justificatory force of freedom or of volitional conduct depends on its connection to the capacity of individuals meaningfully to exercise it, the libertarian must pay heed to those features of their existence brought by the individuals to choice and exchange situations. These include, for example, the state of their financial, physical, and emotional well-being and the set of alternative actions genuinely open to them—in other words, components of the individuals' bargaining position. If the exercise of freedom is supposed to impart justification on its outcomes, then it cannot do so without regard to the conditions under which people exercise their freedom.

Certain libertarians and conventional liberals are committed to a concern for constraints on bargaining strengths as a condition for warranting free exchange, but for different reasons. The patterned theorist is concerned with disparities in bargaining strength to the extent that such differences are likely to contribute to unacceptable departures from desirable patterns of holdings. He argues from the desired pattern to appropriate constraints. In contrast, because he is basically unconcerned with patterns of holdings, the libertarian relies on the manner or process of their genesis as justification for them. This, in his view, shifts justificatory focus from outcomes to processes: in particular, to freedom of exchange. But to ignore the very powerful objection that by themselves the resulting patterns can indict the process as unworthy, the libertarian must root the exercise of freedom in a deeper, more powerful moral theory of the individual, or in a prior theory of rights. Having done so, he cannot escape concern for the meaningful exercise of freedom which, in turn, will lead to a view about the initial conditions that must be satisfied before the exercise of freedom can carry the moral force the libertarian assigns to it. These initial conditions—which will include limitations on the extent to which divergent threat values may determine outcomes—will derive not from a theory of desired outcomes, but from an account of the conditions necessary for the exercise of freedom to be meaningful to an individual.

VIII. Unfair Advantage and the AVF

Let us now apply the ideas about agreements and their conditions to the current policy of staffing the military services. What appears to trouble nearly everyone is that the AVF is disproportionately composed of youths from the underclass. For some, this is objectionable because it raises quality problems; for others, the problem is that the burdens of military service are not dispensed equally. For still others, this feature of the AVF suggests a lack of volition on the part of recruits. But for the liberal, the problem is not that poor youths are compelled to enlist; he may concede the voluntariness of their enlistments. Rather, it is that their alternatives to enlistment are few and that what is so unattractive to nearly everyone else appears to be attractive to them. Because the set of alternatives open to an individual helps to comprise his relative bargaining strength, the source of this objection to the AVF is really that it takes advantage of, or exploits, the relative bargaining weakness of the underclass.

In light of the conceptual framework developed in the earlier sections, is this how the liberal should put his objection? Does the all-volunteer policy *take* advantage of the economic weakness of the underclass, i.e., does it meet the conditions laid out in Section III? Or does the all-volunteer policy merely *benefit* from the weakness of the underclass in the way A benefited from his bargaining strength over B? Does it matter which way the liberal puts his objection to the all-volunteer policy?

It might. We might well think worse of someone who benefits from deliberately exploiting an unfair advantage than of one who benefits from an unfair advantage although he did not seek to capitalize on it. Certainly, it would seem appropriate to assign responsibility and blame differently in the two instances. Nevertheless, the liberal may find the outcomes of the all-volunteer policy morally unattractive whether the outcome is a taking-advantage or a mere benefiting from advantage.

If the situation is morally undesirable, how might we make it better? Some possible or suggested remedies are (a) reintroduce a draft, (b) refuse to permit or otherwise recognize contractual agreements by members of the underclass to serve in the military, (c) weaken the bargaining position of others vis-à-vis the underclass, (d) strengthen the bargaining position of the disadvantaged (or exploited) group, and (e) make military service more attractive generally.

Each of these approaches raises problems. Reintroducing the draft would do nothing to enhance the bargaining strength of the underclass. Indeed, it would present an irony. In other circumstances the government usually comes to the aid of the disadvantaged group by enacting legislation, such as minimum wage, maximum hours, and safety regulations, which corrects for the advantages of employers by removing certain items from negotiation. In the case of the AVF, hovering in the background of voluntary enlistments is the threat that the legislature will reinstate the draft. The mere threat of a draft further reduces the bargaining strength of potential enlistees, since its availability weakens the capability of potential enlistees to hold out for higher salaries or better terms of enlistment.

Refusing to permit or otherwise give legal effect to enlistment contracts involving the underclass on the grounds that their terms reflect an unfair disparity in bargaining strength would only worsen the lot of the disadvantaged group in two ways. First, it would refuse to recognize a bargain that the enlistee views as in his best interest. Second, it would reduce further the range of options available to the underclass. If the objection to the AVF is that it takes unfair advantage of the fact that likely enlistees have too few legitimate options, and are therefore in an extremely weak bargaining position, we do little to rectify matters by eliminating one of their more attractive available employment opportunities.

Instead of refusing to permit or recognize unfair bargains, we might consider rectifying the conditions which lead to them. We could do this either by enhancing the bargaining position of the least well-off, or by minimizing the bargaining advantages of the better-off. Both approaches would affect the capacity of either group to negotiate with the government. Recently, Ken Coffey has advocated taking the latter approach.[18] Coffey believes that short of reinstating a draft, our military personnel problems could be alleviated by imposing a tax on individuals (of military age) who forgo military service in favor of more lucrative and otherwise more desirable means of employment. The tax would be imposed on the difference between the pay individuals would receive in the military and what they in fact receive in their chosen profession. First, it would reduce the disparity in income by decreasing the after-tax income of nonmilitary service. Second, proceeds from the tax would go (in part) to increasing military pay, thus further closing the gap between civilian and military employment. The desired effect of this proposal is to make military employment more attractive to potential "quality" recruits. An individual of military age would either volunteer for the armed forces or pay dearly for the right not to.

Coffey's approach does little to aid the situation of the least well-off who are unable to pay the tax in order to avoid service. Moreover, if what troubles us about the AVF is that it takes unfair advantage of the disparity in bargaining strengths between recruits and the military, we are unlikely to applaud measures designed to create more extreme bargaining distortions. The Coffey approach simply puts more people in the same boat the poor already occupy. It does this by nullifying the advantages they have in virtue of their larger set of desirable alternatives, so that for ever-increasing numbers of people there is at the margin no substantial difference between military and civilian employment. The obvious effect is to create an expanded weaker class, all of whom share the same disadvantages in negotiating a desirable agreement.

Instead of weakening the bargaining position of the middle class vis-à-vis the lower class—which does absolutely nothing to enhance anyone's bargaining position vis-à-vis the government—we might attempt to strengthen the bargaining position of the least well-off. It is probably as hard to object to such a policy as it is to come out against trimming fat from the budget.

One way of increasing the bargaining strength of the least well-off is to provide whatever is necessary to increase their options in life. This would require dramatic institutional changes. Moreover, as the bargaining position of the underclass was strengthened, the desirability of military service would likely decrease, thus making it significantly more difficult to staff the military within current budgetary constraints. One is struck by the fact that as the underclass options increase, they no longer find military service desirable. It's hard to imagine more striking evidence of the fact that those who do join (by and large) do so precisely because they have so few other options. And the bargains they reach cannot help but reflect the weakness of their bargaining position.

As an alternative to the remedies so far considered, we could nullify the government's bargaining advantage by requiring it to act as if it were trying to recruit from the middle class. The government would ask itself what it would take to attract middle-class recruits and then offer this package to all actual recruits. Actual recruits would gain the surplus between what it would have taken to secure their enlistment (for those everywhere, but at the margin this will be less than they receive) and what in fact they are paid. This approach does not enhance the general bargaining position of the poor; instead it prohibits the government from negotiating from its threat advantage. By doing so, it nullifies much of the government's advantage during labor negotiations.

The problem with this approach is that if military service is made more attractive to the middle class, middle-class enlistment will rise and lower-class enlistment will fall as a consequence. In the end such a proposal might further reduce the range of desirable employment opportunities open to the poor. It looks as if the poor must accept being taken advantage of—and they may well be prepared to do so. But consider one variation on this last approach.

We might restrict the percentage of middle-class recruits. In effect what we would have done is to locate the "equilibrium" price for middle-class recruits, thus ensuring that the pool of possible recruits is greater than the demand; then we would choose among the pool of interested parties according to some principle that guarantees representation by socio-economic mix at wages that do not take advantage of the weaker bargaining position of the underclass. There will be some reduction in lower-class enlistments, but this may be the price we have to pay to ensure that *all* underclass enlistees are not taken advantage of.

Notes

1. See the essays in the symposium "The Rise and Fall of the Volunteer Army," *Society* 18 (March/April 1981): 28-60, especially Michael Useem, "Conscription and Class," pp. 28-30; David R. Segal, "How Equal is 'Equity'?", pp. 31-33; and Neil Fligstein, "Militarism, Not Service," pp. 43-44.

2. See Segal, "How Equal is 'Equity'?"; and Charles Moskos, "Making the All-Volunteer Force Work: A National Service Approach," *Foreign Affairs* 60 (Fall 1981): 17-34.

3. See Moskos, "Making the All-Volunteer Force Work"; and Joseph Califano, "Playing the Draft Card," *The Washington Post,* 27 January 1970, B7.

4. See Richard W. Hunter, "Military Discrimination," *Society* 18 (March/April 1981): 47.

5. This essay is addressed to an audience not necessarily trained in philosophy nor familiar with the formal techniques of game theory. I have tried therefore to avoid discussing in too much detail many of the philosophic issues closely connected to the notion of unfair bargains, including coercion, voluntariness, paternalism. This is not to say that I have entirely ignored these issues. Rather, I have tried to say as little controversial about them as I can in the hope that by doing so I can get the main point across in a way that the likely reader of this volume will find helpful and sensible, if not always convincing. For similar reasons I have relegated formal and technical discussions to footnotes.

6. On voluntariness as a condition of justification, see Robert Nozick, *Anarchy, State, and Utopia* (New York: Basic Books, 1974); with regard to the other conditions, see Guido Calabresi and Philip Bobbitt, *Tragic Choices* (New York: W. W. Norton & Company, 1978).

7. One state of affairs T is Pareto superior to another S provided that in going from S to T no one's welfare diminishes, and the welfare of at least one person is improved. To say that an exchange constitutes a Pareto improvement is just to say that no party to it prefers the previous state of affairs to that which comes about in virtue of the exchange, and at least one person prefers the new state of affairs to the former one.

8. A distinction exists between the claim that a state of affairs is just and that it is justifiable: justice being one element in an assessment of the "on balance" justifiability of an action or state of affairs. Some forms of libertarianism, what I call "thin" theories, are concerned with whether an exchange is just only, not with whether its redistributive effects are justifiable on balance. See the discussion in Section VII.

9. We can formulate the "rational" expectation because a determinate outcome can be derived from a game in which no other factor is present except the utility assignments of the players over the different outcome. The determinate outcome is derived mechanically. This can be seen by setting out formally the structure of the bargaining game. Let $T_1, T_2, T_3 \ldots$ T_n represent the set of possible trades; and let T^* represent the status quo, i.e., the state in which no bargain has as yet been made. With each trade we can associate a particular utility measure for A and B derived from each's ordinal ranking of the various possible trades. So for each T, there exists a pair of utilities, u and v, which represent the utility of that particular trade for A and B respectively. Because the set of possible trades may be ranked ordinally, A's and B's utility functions may be indexed numerically. Moreover, as long as the goods to be traded are finitely divisible—if divisible at all—there will be a finite number of possible trades between them. Figure 7.1 represents the set of possible trades between A and B.

T^* represents the starting point or status quo; and (u^*, v^*) represents the utilities for A and B respectively of being at T^*. The most desirable trade (most preferred state) for A is represented by p. At p, A is furthest from the origin; his utility is therefore maximized. The most desirable trade for B is represented by q, since at that point his utility is maximized. Going from T^* to q would make A worse off than he is now; going from T^* to p would have a similar impact on B. Neither point is achievable if we assume each party will veto trades that are not in his self-interest.

Formally, the solution requires a function that operates on what we call the bargaining game $S(u^*, v^*)$—that game which has the starting point $T^*(u^*, v^*)$—which will produce a unique point (u^o, v^o). Such a function must satisfy four assumptions: (a) invariance of utility functions, (b) Pareto optimality, (c) independence of irrelevant alternatives, and (d) symmetry.

Only one function satisfies these conditions: the Nash formula. The Nash formula for

Figure 7.1

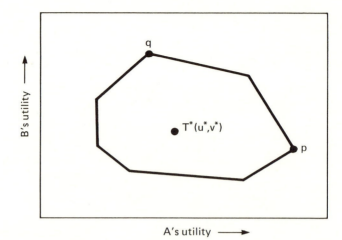

solving the bargaining game [S(u*, v*)] is obtained by inverting the utility transformations on (u_o, v_o). The point (u_n, v_o) is a point in the bargaining game [S(u_o, v_o)]. The game [S(u_o, v_o] is obtained by transforming the game [S(u*, v*)] into a game in which (u*, v*) have the values (0, 0). In short, the new game [S(u_o, v_o)] is just the game [S(u*, v*)] in which the status quo is (0, 0): where the value to both parties of staying where they are is zero. All states of affairs that are better for A (or for B) can then be expressed by increasing positive integers greater than zero.

Take a simple bargaining problem to see how the solution is derived. Suppose that A and B are in a bargaining situation. The game is that they can share $100 if they agree; otherwise each receives nothing. This bargaining game is represented in Figure 7.2.

Prior to the game A and B are presumed to be at the origin; each is at a point of zero utility. A, of course, would like B to agree to give him, A, the $100. B would like to have A do the same for him. Every point from the origin constitutes a Pareto improvement. The effect of transforming the original game into this one has been to make every possible move between A and B one which would have been represented as a move to the northeast in the original game [S(u*, v*)]. If utilities are linear with money, and if the preference of both A and B is to maximize their respective utilities, the Nash solution to this game is the obvious one, (50, 50), as shown in Table 7.1. The Nash solution is said to be fair in that it is the result rational bargainers of *equal economic* strength could expect.

Table 7.1

Payoffs		Utilities		Utility products
A	B	A	B	
$ 0	100	.00	1.00	.000
25	75	.25	.75	.1875
50	50	.50	.50	.250
75	25	.75	.25	.1875
100	0	1.00	.00	.000

Figure 7.2

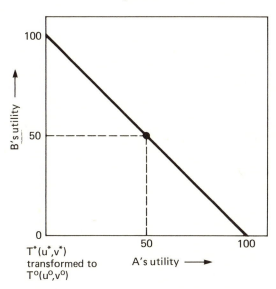

T*(u*,v*)
transformed to
T⁰(u⁰,v⁰)

Table 7.2

Payoffs		Utilities		Utility products
A	B	A	B	
$ 0	100	.00	1.00	.000
25	75	.25	.98	.245
50	50	.50	.90	.450
75	25	.75	.73	.540
100	0	1.00	.00	.000

Luce and Raiffa consider a case in which the initial economic positions of the bargainers are far from equal. Suppose that A and B are once again in a situation in which if they agree they can share $100; otherwise they receive nothing. Unlike the previous example, in this case while both A and B desire to maximize their respective utilities, A is significantly better off economically than B. Once again we transform the game into another in which the status quo is zero utility for both A and B. Although the utility of no deal is zero for both A and B, making some sort of deal is more urgent for B than for A. Their respective utility functions can be expected to reflect the disparity in their initial strengths, and therefore in the value to each of certain payoff pairs. Table 7.2 represents a partial ordering of utilities, payoffs, and outcomes of utility transformations.

The utility functions in Table 7.2 are easily explained. Any payoff is valuable to B since he has a significantly greater need than does A. The same is not true for A. Under these conditions the Nash—or *fair*—solution is (75, 25).

10. In fact we won't. The most interesting attempt to do so—but which fails neverthe-less—is to be found in Anthony T. Kronman, "Contract Law and Distributive Justice," *Yale Law Journal* 89 (1980): 472.

11. It does not seem plausible that one could reduce the objection to the failure of the Pareto condition or of the third-party–effects condition. The kinds of agreements one finds questionable may easily satisfy both conditions.

12. Joel Feinberg has developed the most complicated and extensive criterion of volun-tariness as a condition of responsibility. See his book-length manuscript, "The Moral Limits of the Criminal Law" (unpublished).

13. Note one problem with trying to correct for this unfair advantage in an apparently plausible way: that is, by requiring full disclosure. Full disclosure requirements may raise housing costs, since gathering the pertinent information is costly. This cost, in the housing market we are imagining, would be passed on to tenants, thus pricing out of the market those individuals at the margin who might have been willing to take the risk at the lower cost. Thus, by correcting for the disadvantage in this way, the courts may put certain individuals in an even tighter spot for securing housing at an affordable price.

14. This is the sense in which Kronman talks about advantages being related to one's wealth, and the way in which courts enforcing contracts that result from one party's advantage over the other are concerned with matters of *distributive justice*. Kronman is able to reach that ironic conclusion about contract laws precisely because he thinks of one's advantages in terms of *distributive* attributes that affect one's wealth. Whenever the court permits an agreement that involves an advantage taken, it sanctions something that one considers the province of distributive justice.

Another way of expressing skepticism about objections based on advantage-taking is not to try to reduce the objection to some other objection, but to try to rule it out of court on the grounds that it is impossible to specify when the fact that A has an unfair advantage over B, or unfairly takes advantage of B, is supposed to count as an objection to whatever agreement A and B reach.

The question of whether and when inequality of bargaining strength constitutes a compelling objection to an agreement is really no different from similar questions regarding the more settled bases for objecting to exchanges. For it does not follow from the fact that an exchange adversely affects one or more of the parties to it (or some other individual) that it should not be enforced, or even that it is objectionable. Nevertheless, under certain conditions adverse third-party effects—as in the case of a husband's assigning his wages to the detriment of his family—suffice to bar enforcement. The existence of third-party effects sometimes suffices to bar a contract's enforcement, but more often does not. And though contracts or clauses within contracts that impose "unconscionable" burdens will not be enforced, the vast majority of exchanges that do not work to the benefit of all concerned are enforceable. One explanation of the enforceability of contracts that are not welfare-maximizing is that they are freely consented to. Indeed, some commentators have tried (unsuccessfully in my view) to explain the legal doctrine of unconscionability—the refusal to enforce clauses or agreements that seem grossly unfair—on the grounds that a party agreeing to such a clause could not possibly have done so freely. (See Richard Epstein, "Unconscionability: A Critical Reappraisal," *Journal of Law and Economics* 18 [1975]: 293-311). The unfairness of the bargain is, in this view, used as evidence of fraud or duress and indirectly as proof of the involuntariness of the consent. Efforts along these lines are motivated largely by the belief that if anything can count as a sufficient bar to an exchange, the exchange must not have been freely agreed to. But even here, the question arises whether involuntariness of an exchange is *always* sufficient to nullify it. For it is clear that many "forced exchanges" are *not* objectionable. For example, a municipality's condemning private property (e.g., a private residence) for a public use (e.g., construction of a highway) is often justifiable provided the landowner is fully compensated at the fair market value for his property. Recent efforts to justify takings on the grounds that (in our example) by accepting compensation *ex post* the landowner *gives his consent* to the exchange, thereby making it "unforced," are rooted in the mistaken belief that exchanges are justifiable only if they are consented to. (See Richard Posner, "The Ethical and Political Basis of the Efficiency Norm in Common Law Adjudication," *Hofstra Law Review* 8 [1980]: 487.) Once we abandon that view, it becomes clear that for all the grounds upon which one could lodge a complaint against an exchange, the questions of under what conditions does the failure to satisfy any one of them suffice to nullify the exchange or to doubt the justifiability of its outcome arises. (See Jules Coleman, "The Normative Basis of Economic Analysis," *Stanford Law Review,* forthcoming.) The concern one has over whether there exists an unfairness in the relative bargaining strengths of the parties is, in this important regard, no different.

15. John Rawls, *A Theory of Justice* (Cambridge: Harvard University Press, 1971).

16. Indeed, as I understand it, the requirement of voluntariness in transfer boils down to a claim about what it means, on the libertarian view, to have or own property. Voluntariness is *necessary* for a non-right-invading transfer only if having property entails the right not to have others take, use, or otherwise control it in any way. If that right is not part of what it means to have property, it will not follow that a forced transfer of property necessarily violates any of the property-holder's rights. But then what looked like an independent criterion of *justness in transfer* is really just another way of stating what the definition of property for a libertarian is.

17. Kronman holds this view in "Contract Law and Distributive Justice."

18. Ken Coffey, "You Won't Enlist? Then Ante Up," *The Washington Star,* 15 March 1981.

8

The Rationality of Military Service

ADRIAN M. S. PIPER

The aim of this discussion is twofold.* First, I shall scrutinize certain prevailing rationales for enlisting for military service and show that these justifications are inadequate to meet the military's recruiting needs. Larger numbers of enlistees who are fully equipped, both in technical skills and morale, for combat readiness are in great demand, but the arguments used to recruit potential enlistees are self-defeating. I shall show how and why they attract volunteers who are rendered singularly unfit to meet these demands by those very arguments themselves.

I shall also suggest that these justifications are deficient in failing to satisfy certain elementary conditions that any adequate justification for action must satisfy, and that this second deficiency at least partly explains the first. Thus my second aim will be to adumbrate briefly these unsatisfied conditions and to show how careful attention to them can change our thinking about who should serve in the military and why.

Two rationales for military service will be described. I shall argue that their deficiencies, both in logic and in strategy, arise out of a misleading conception of what rational justification consists in. An alternative model of rational justification and two arguments in its defense will follow, and the model will be applied to the questions: Who should serve in the military? Why? And under what conditions? I shall conclude that advantaged Americans rationally ought to enlist in the military for patriotic as well as self-interested reasons and that these reasons would equally justify their conscription.

I. Two Justifications for Military Enlistment

Two sorts of considerations are typically proffered in favor of military service. The first group mentions that one's country must be prepared to repel the threat of invasion; that its institutions, values, and way of life must be defended vigilantly; and that its allies and/or its essential economic interests in other countries must be protected. These considerations presuppose that the country in question, its institutions, values, way of life, political and economic interests, and so on, are worth protecting. Let us refer to them as *patriotic considerations*.

A second group of considerations frequently cited refers to the specialized

* I am indebted to the CASH Collective (University of Michigan), Robert Fullinwider, Allan Gibbard, and Peter Railton for helpful comments on sections of earlier drafts of this essay.

technical training offered by military service; the range of professional and career opportunities available; the chance to see unfamiliar parts of the world; the opportunity to gain the training that builds endurance, self-reliance, and self-discipline; and so on. These considerations have been invoked frequently in military recruiting; they appeal to features of military life that certain individuals may find personally attractive or rewarding. We can refer to these as *self-interested considerations*.

These two kinds of considerations are often addressed to different audiences. Patriotic considerations are commonly invoked by and addressed to policymakers and to those whose support can be expected to make an impact on the formation and enforcement of social policy: representatives of business and government whose economic, political, or diplomatic interests would be advanced by military defense; their constituents; and the large segment of the American public whose ways of life are sufficiently valuable to them that they feel an allegiance to the institutions that promote them and to the values and standards embodied by such institutions.

Patriotic considerations are addressed less frequently to those who are to be convinced to enlist in the All-Volunteer Force itself. To those young men and women who are adjudged to be most capable of making a contribution to this country's welfare through their military defense of it (rather than, say, through their technical or professional skills within the civilian sector, their roles as parents, or their anticipated roles as educated and productive citizens upon completion of their civilian education), appeal is more often made to self-interested considerations. These considerations represent military life as the most attractive option available for pursuing personal aspirations.

Patriotic and self-interested considerations *may* not be mutually exclusive. Some individuals may hold strong convictions both that (a) this country, its civilian institutions, and the civilian ways of life they offer are worth defending; and that (b) time spent in the military is a more attractive option for personal and professional advancement than any available in the civilian sector. Both considerations might be compatible, for example, under the more general presumption that the career and personal opportunities offered through military service embody the same liberal-democratic values embodied in the civilian institutions of this country and are to be comparably evaluated. This presumption regards the military way of life merely as one among many others, all equally advanced by liberal-democratic institutions, and all providing equal opportunity for the pursuit of individual aspirations.

This general presumption is surely false. The military is not an "equal opportunity employer" in *this* sense. It requires of a potential enlistee, in exchange for the personal and professional opportunities it offers, a readiness to risk his or her life and safety in the event of a war—a war, moreover, about whose purpose or significance he or she may have serious doubts. In addition, it requires an abdication of personal autonomy to military superiors whose primary commitment is to winning a current or anticipated war, rather than to protecting his or her life or ensuring its comfort. The primary activity of a peacetime military is the achievement and maintenance of combat readiness, and personal career goals and aspirations are perforce sacrificed to this end.[1] Equal opportunity to advance one's life prospects in the military is purchased by sacrificing the right to autonomous self-preservation, in the service of ends whose worth one may have reason to question. Civilian recipients of the benefits of liberal-democratic institutions are not expected to pay this price.

These facts seem to differentiate military service from superficially comparable high-risk jobs in the civilian sector, such as fireman, coal miner, or construction worker. These jobs one can quit if one believes that the risk to life is not worth the goal to be achieved. But it is not easy to withdraw from the military, in the event of war, without incurring a court martial or dishonorable discharge, or the shame and dishonor that attend a refusal to defend one's country in times of need.

Perhaps, however, these considerations do not in fact distinguish military service from apparently comparable civilian jobs. It may be argued that economic need or social disadvantage forces workers in high-risk civilian occupations to retain their jobs and to abdicate autonomous self-preservation for the sake of controversial ends, just as the threat of military discipline or social disapprobation forces enlistees to retain theirs. To the extent that the comparison holds, the same reservations about the general presumption apply as well to these high-risk civilian occupations. We may certainly question whether any such employment is compatible with liberal-democratic institutions that purport to offer equal opportunity for improving one's life prospects, when the price of equal opportunity in these cases is a readiness to abdicate those life prospects in order to promote ends of controversial worth. In this discussion, however, we will be concerned only with military service.

Alternately, both patriotic and self-interested considerations might appeal to individuals who are personally attracted to the glory and honor attendant upon successful military service, precisely because of strong underlying patriotic feelings. These patriotic feelings, and the identification of their personal interests with those of their country, can be an important source of self-esteem for individuals who may encounter frustration in other areas of life. Such feelings may arise as well from a deeply internalized disposition to regard oneself as part of a larger group and to respond naturally to its imperatives, independent of the compensatory benefits of doing so. Individuals for whom this is true do not form the primary targets of recruitment efforts, and so I ignore them in the following remarks but will return to them in Section IV.

We are left, then, with some interesting asymmetries. Patriotic considerations, on the one hand, are addressed to those whose interest in the military defense of civilian institutions is greatest, but whose availability for actual military service is comparatively small. Self-interested considerations, on the other hand, are addressed to those whose interest in the military defense of civilian institutions in their current form is comparatively small, but whose availability for actual military service is greatest. It is noteworthy that patriotic considerations are not generally invoked to justify military service to a potential enlistee, and in the same way self-interested considerations are held in abeyance when attempting to justify increases in military spending in congressional debate: no congressperson would be convinced that we should increase spending for the production of land missiles, or raise the pay scale of the average NCO, to provide career opportunities or technical training to those who were unable to find comparable training in the civilian sector. In both cases, the explanation for the silence is the same: the missing considerations would be irrelevant, unconvincing, and counterproductive to the party in question. So it appears that the most persuasive justification for undertaking military service depends almost entirely on the audience to whom the justification is addressed.

But this relativism is not as neutral as it may first appear; patriotic and self-interested considerations are not, in fact, equally veridical as representations of the actual purpose and function of the military. It is not true that the function of the military in providing training, experience, and career opportunities to otherwise disadvantaged Americans is just as central or important as its function in providing military defense. The real reason for staffing and training the military is to ensure the readiness and capability for defending the country and its important economic and political interests against attack. The personal and professional benefits proffered function as inducements to enlist for individuals whose interest in military life otherwise would be minimal. With respect to the actual purpose and function of the military, then, self-interested considerations are subordinate to patriotic ones. With respect to the enterprise of persuading individuals to enlist in the military, however, patriotic considerations are subordinate to self-interested ones.

We now see that something is patently wrong, for the enterprise of persuasion seems to require misrepresenting the realities of military life: to obscure the real point of being in the military—i.e., an unconditional readiness for military defense—to convince individuals to join it.[2] This carries the disturbing implication that it would be a tactical error to represent the true conditions and purpose of military life to those who must be induced to serve, for this representation would fail to convince many potential enlistees to do so.

II. Two Models of Rationality

This conclusion may not seem obvious to one who subscribes to the prevailing model of rational action as the maximally efficient achievement of one's ends, whatever they are, given the constraints on information available: call this the *model of means-rationality*. On this model, that the self-interested justification of military service depends upon omitting certain facts about military life does not impair its rationality. If, given the information *available* to an agent, military service advances that agent's most important ends more efficiently than any other alternative, it is rationally justified. Thus military service as a means to career advancement would be justified for an agent from whom certain facts were withheld that suggested that his or her interests would be better advanced through organized protest against education and employment inequity in the civilian sector. The rationality of withholding certain information can in turn be shown by demonstrating this tactic to be a necessary means to the end of military recruitment, and this in turn to be a necessary means to the end of military defense.

But note that those to whom the self-interested considerations are intended to justify enlistment are not those to whom the need for military manpower supposedly justifies the tactical use of such considerations in recruitment efforts. Rather, potential enlistees are persuaded to join by a set of self-interested considerations which themselves must be justified by other, partly patriotic and partly tactical, ones that undermine them (i.e., that defense of our country requires discipline, a large degree of personal discomfort, and the sacrifice of personal ambition of a kind that cannot be revealed fully to potential soldiers before their enlistment) and which are therefore proffered not to potential recruits themselves, but to other interested parties. But it cannot be rational for me to enlist in the military if the ultimate patriotic and tactical reasons why I should could not convince me to do so. Such reasons may or may not justify my forcible induction, but they cannot justify my *volunteering* to join. To claim that it is rational to obscure the real point and character of military life in order to get individuals to enlist strongly suggests that it would be irrational for them to volunteer were that information made available to them.

These observations suggest three intuitive criteria of rationality that the model of means-rationality fails to satisfy. One is that if an action is rational for me to perform, then (if I am cognitively and psychologically normal) it must be possible for you fully to justify that action *to me*. More generally, if it is rational for some group—say, of potential enlistees—to undertake some action, then it must be possible, at least in theory, *for that group* to recognize all the considerations that justify that action as persuasive reasons for them to perform the action. Let us refer to this as the *social viability* criterion. (We shall return to it later in amplified form in Section V.) One implication is that if those targeted by the services as potential enlistees could not be convinced to join by the full patriotic and tactical justification for doing so, then it is irrational for that group to enlist, and the military might do better to target a different group.

A second criterion given short shrift by the model of means-rationality is that the justification of a rational action must depend upon a realistic conception of the action's circumstances. It should invoke relevant considerations and facts recognizable as true by well-informed parties, and should exclude recognizable falsehoods, distortions, or omissions. This criterion too will be spelled out more fully in Section V as the *realism* criterion. One of its immediate implications is that the self-interested considerations favoring enlistment by themselves fail to constitute a rational justification to the target audience. For the persuasive power of the self-interested justification depends largely upon the irrationality or ignorance of potential enlistees, and on the ability of recruitment officers to paint an appealing picture of military life that fails adequately to depict the facts.

A third criterion of rationality largely neglected by the model of means-rationality is what we shall refer to as the *consistency* criterion: the full justification of a rational action must not invoke inconsistent norms. If military preparedness requires enlisted soldiers to sacrifice personal career aspirations, then one cannot invoke the norms both of military preparedness *and* of the satisfaction of personal career ambitions as reasons for enlistment, for they are inconsistent. We will group these three criteria under the rubric of the model of *end-rationality,* for reasons that will become clearer as we proceed.

The first requirement, of social viability, says that the full justification of a rational action must be recognizably rational to the agent who is to perform it. This means that it will not do to bifurcate that justification, offering the self-interested considerations to potential enlistees and the patriotic and tactical considerations to recruitment officers and interested representatives and senators. If volunteering for the military is rational for a potential enlistee, he or she should have access to *all* the reasons why it is rational. Yet the second requirement, that of realism, says that the full justification of a rational action cannot depend upon recognizable omissions, distortions, or falsifications. This means that if the self-interested part of the justification is vulnerable to this charge, this is prima facie evidence for calling its rationality into question. And since the third requirement, of consistency, requires that a rational justification not appeal to inconsistent norms, then if the self-interested norms are inconsistent with the patriotic and tactical ones, one set of norms must be dropped. So if the self-interested justification for enlistment proves to be irrational in the ways already suggested, there is a strong prima facie case for using some other argument to persuade individuals to enlist in the military, or for dropping the putative appeal to reason altogether.

These last two alternatives may be equally justified by the same considerations, i.e., the patriotic ones. For if there *is* a non-self-interested, rational justification for enlisting, the same justification could be invoked to support the military conscription of those individuals who failed to recognize its rationality for them, and the patriotic justification just may have this potential. If it is rational for some individuals to serve in the military for patriotic and non-self-interested reasons, then there may be circumstances (e.g., a national emergency, a serious threat to the interests or security of the country) under which it would be rational to force them to serve. Nevertheless, the plausibility of this thesis requires disposing of certain immediate objections, in the next two sections.

III. *Not All Desired Ends Are Rational*

One such objection runs as follows. The thesis implies that one may have good reason to accept military conscription if military enlistment is rationally justified, but one cannot bring oneself to do what one recognizes as rationally justified. To this it might be objected that one cannot have sufficiently good reason to do something if, when all the facts are in and one is fully ambulatory, one is not *motivated* to do it. The objection assimilates the concept of having a sufficient reason to do something to that of there being sufficient cause for something's occurring. It supposes that reasons are always causes and that a consideration that strongly favors some course of action must automatically motivate one to perform it. But this supposition is in turn based on the further mistaken supposition that one important class of causes of action, namely desires, are always reasons for action. The objection assumes that any good (or sufficient) justification for doing something must include as a reason that performing the action will satisfy some desire of the agent. Therefore, it is concluded, there can be no sufficiently good reason for doing something that does not motivate the agent to do it.

It is not true, however, that the presence of a desire to do or achieve something always provides a prima facie reason for doing or achieving it. The supposition that it does depends upon the further controversial assumption that the pursuit of self-interest is inherently rational. The reasoning appears to be that since the self has a prima facie self-directed interest in satisfying its desires, and since the self-directed interests of the self take rational precedence over any other interests, any such interest of the self in satisfying one of its desires has a rational claim to fulfillment.

But it is not obvious that the self-interests of the self take precedence over all other interests, e.g., of the larger community or the nation. Certainly they may in the view of any arbitrarily selected self, particularly if its psychology is individualistically inclined. But whence comes the authority of this point of view over others? To conclude that it is rational for any self to give precedence to the pursuit of its self-interests would be to beg the question of whether or not the pursuit of self-interest is, in fact, inherently rational.

To require, as the social viability criterion does, that a rational action be fully justifiable to the agent who is to perform it is not to require that appeal be made to some self-interest of the agent in order to justify its performance. To show me that it would be rational for me to enlist in the Army does not necessarily require a demonstration that some self-interest of mine would be served by doing so. If I am strongly enough committed to my country, or feel sufficiently hostile toward its enemies, it may be rational for me to enlist even if my self-interest must be sacrificed, as long as the three suggested criteria of rationality are met.

If the reasons given for a rationally justified action need not include an appeal to the pursuit of self-interest, and if desires hold a prima facie claim to satisfaction because they fulfill self-interest, then the presence of a desire is not necessarily a reason for satisfying it. Of course other arguments may favor the satisfaction of a desire—based, for example, on the independent worth of the end desired. But not just any desired end will constitute a prima facie reason for action, simply in

virtue of being a desire the agent wants to satisfy. Thus some desired ends are
irrational, even if they satisfy the constraints on the model of means-rationality.

Major Kurtz's desire for absolute and divine dominion in *Apocalypse Now*
seems to illustrate such a case. It is hard to imagine a rational justification of his
actions, much less how it would resolve the normative inconsistencies between
his desire for absolute dominion and control, and the slaughter of those over
whom he had control; or between his desire for absolute reverence and submission from his subjects, and his fear of their revenge or rebellion. Kurtz may have
attained his ultimate desired end, and perhaps even in the most efficient way
possible, given the information available to him. But this does not make his desire
rational.

Hence if one's desires are irrational, there may be *no* connection between what
one has good reason to do—i.e., what it is rational for one to do—and what one is
motivated to do. What it is rational for one to do may be completely independent
of the actual ends one happens to desire. So it does not follow from the fact that
one is not motivated to join the military that one has no sufficiently good reason to
do so. That one lacks motivation to enlist may show no more than that one's
motivations are not necessarily determined by rational considerations—an observation that scarcely needs belaboring.

IV. Not All Rational Ends Must Be Objects of Desire

Military recruitment policymakers seem to suppose that most individuals can be
persuaded to enlist in the All-Volunteer Force only by a demonstration that
military service is the most efficient means of satisfying their desires for training
and education, travel, and career opportunities. Such policymakers presuppose
the model of means-rationality. It has already been suggested that this model is
deficient on at least two counts: first, it validates as rational a justification of
military service that depends upon omitting certain information that would, in all
probability, alter an agent's choice if it were made available; and second, it
supposes that any instrumentally efficacious action is rational, regardless of the
ends it promotes, although ends like those of Major Kurtz call this supposition
into question as well.

But even more problematic, the model of means-rationality assumes that an
action can be justified to a fully rational and autonomous individual only by
demonstrating that it promotes the efficient satisfaction of *some* desire the agent
has.[3] For even if the end one happens to have is rational in the suggested sense, it
is not obvious that one must have a *desire* for such an end in order to recognize
that end as rationally justified for one to pursue. It is easy to imagine cases in
which I adopt and pursue ends, not because I have a desire for those ends, but
because they instantiate normative principles or values to which I am deeply
committed.

Thus, for example, I may regularly wait for the green light when crossing the
street. I do so intentionally, deliberately, and consciously, but not because I have
any occurrent *desire* to do so. Indeed, no consequences of importance to me at all
may turn on whether or not I cross at the green (suppose no traffic is to be seen). I
cross at the green out of an internalized disposition to conform to the norm that
one ought to cross at the green, not in between.

Another example: I may contribute time or money to Amnesty International, in
order to help restore the civil rights of certain political prisoners. But not because
I want to, nor even from any benevolent desire to increase the well-being of the
prisoners involved. Indeed, their convictions and attitudes toward life may

represent values I deplore and would actively discourage if they were in the position to promulgate them. Nevertheless, I may find their torture or imprisonment morally unacceptable, regardless of my desires with respect to them, and act to prevent it out of sheer moral indignation that their civil rights are being abridged. These feelings constitute a motivationally effective state. But they need not make me *want* to aid them. They may simply make me do so.

In neither case is an intervening desire required to explain my behavior. All that is required is a motivationally effective disposition to conform to normative principles—of public behavior or of the inalienability of individual civil rights—which is deeply enough felt to motivate certain responses under certain circumstances.

These examples are both mundane cases in which I perform rational actions intentionally, but without any necessarily concomitant desire for their ends. There are others: must I *desire* to brush my teeth every morning in order to do so? Or to say "Hello" each time I answer the phone in order to say it? Evidently not. I just do these things reflexively.

These actions, and others like them, are also relatively unproblematic from the point of view of motivation. Typically, the process of human socialization includes instilling a broad range of normative social dispositions to action deeply enough so that the mere recognition of the kind of behavior required under particular circumstances elicits that behavior more or less automatically. Deeply instilled dispositions to such behavior shape our character, not by motivating us to *want* to do a certain act, but by motivating us to *do* it.

This is not to argue that there are no individual desires. Desires express important aspects of personality. Rather it is to argue, first, that individual desires are not the only kind of motives to action; second, that for most people in most situations, they are not even predominant. Third, it is to suggest that even where such desires are present, they are usually determined by prior, deeply instilled social norms to which they conform.

It may be observed that it is often much easier for us to act immediately on the recognition that one ought to, e.g., cross at the green, or say "Hello" when answering the phone, than it is to respond reflexively to the recognition that it is appropriate to, for example, help those in need even at some personal cost, or to respect those whose values, lifestyle, or appearance differ radically from one's own. But it seems to me that this fact reflects the social inefficacy of those institutions that attempt to instill moral norms, and the social efficacy of those that implicitly oppose or undermine them. This may also mean that some moral norms are not realistic requirements to impose on human behavior. But these differences do not reflect any qualitative difference between norms of conventional behavior and moral norms that would force us to the conclusion that desires are motivationally necessary in the latter case, but not in the former. For individuals often do perform moral actions naturally and reflexively, even when this conflicts with their desires or interests. If the structure of our social institutions encouraged a wholehearted commitment to moral norms of behavior to the extent to which it encourages a wholehearted commitment to norms of etiquette and conventional social behavior, there is little reason to doubt that our response to the recognition of what is appropriate would be as immediate and reflexive in both cases.

Thus to stipulate some desire or interest that necessarily intervenes between the recognition of what it is appropriate to do and the resulting action seems both counterintuitive, from the point of view of commonsense introspection, and methodologically messy. It seems that the stipulation of such a desire as necessary in all cases is based on the self-fulfilling hypothesis that a desire must have been present in order for one to act at all: i.e., that action not motivated by the self-directed interest in satisfying one's desires is a conceptual impossibility. But if my performing the action makes it true *by definition* that I desired its end, and yet I find no evidence of such a desire when I examine my own motives, then the concept of a necessarily motivating desire must be relegated to the explanatory status of a "theoretical entity" that does no explanatory work at all.

Hence views that suppose us to need a *desire* to conform to motivationally effective social norms in order to conform to them are equally mistaken. If the norm of concern for others is motivationally effective, then to perceive that someone is in need of help, support, or comfort is to be motivationally disposed to help, support, or comfort him or her, regardless of any desires or inclinations one may have.

Given the workings of actual social institutions, military service is not necessarily of a piece with the cases just enumerated, but it may be. In West Germany, for example, all able-bodied young men are required to serve for two years in the Deutsche Bundeswehr directly upon completion of high school or professional training. This is an effective and stable social practice of relatively long standing that has a high degree of acceptance in West German society. This practice can be rationally justified by invoking circumstantial considerations concerning Germany's recent history, its geographical location, the nature of its diplomatic relations with Eastern Bloc countries, and so on. And often, young prospective soldiers will invoke such considerations *exclusively,* in order to explain their compliance with this stable social convention. They will make no mention of their desire to defend the fatherland, or of their interest in avoiding imprisonment for draft evasion, or of their desire to avoid social disapproval.

The correct inference, it seems to me, is that they are motivated to serve in the Bundeswehr by a deeply instilled, wholehearted *commitment to the principle* of active readiness to come to West Germany's defense, if it should be necessary, quite independent of any desires or interests; and that this commitment is realized by fulfilling the requirement of military service. To insist that some desire or interest must be present to explain their behavior (or, more implausibly, their commitment to this principle) is to beg the question of whether it is necessary to postulate the existence of such a desire or interest in the first place. In the cases just discussed, it seems clear that a deeply instilled commitment to principle plus a set of appropriate beliefs and perceptions of the given circumstances suffice to do the job.

V. Outline of a Model of End-Rationality

The conclusions of the two preceding sections lend support to the suggested model of end-rationality proposed in Section II.[4] If desires are not, in fact, necessary variables in a rational justification of action, we are free to appeal exclusively to the more general normative considerations we actually do invoke in determining an action's rationality, irrespective of the desires we happen to have: its value in our scheme of ethical convictions, how it affects individuals and groups to whom we are loyal or opposed, its pragmatic worth in realizing ends to which we are committed, general facts about how the world works, and so on. We are free, moreover, to examine critically those general normative considerations according to the criteria we actually use in ascertaining their rational status: how psychologically palatable the considerations would be to the agents involved, the degree to which the considerations demonstrate a realistic grasp of the situation, and whether the considerations are consistent with our other beliefs and values. That is to say, we are now in a better position to make use of the suggested criteria of the model of end-rationality earlier introduced.

Consider some features of the conventional practice of justifying an action. First one attempts to persuade another that some action is worth undertaking. This feature calls attention to the intersubjective character of rational justification: assuming we are both cognitively and psychologically normal, the aim of my behavior is to obtain your agreement that my (or your, or an) action is worthwhile. I attempt to make my action rationally intelligible to you by citing the final end at which the action aims and demonstrating that this action is the best way of achieving that end: the most efficient, perhaps, or the most honorable, or the least socially disruptive. But the success of this enterprise requires that you and I agree on the value of such things as efficiency, the preservation of virtue, or the minimizing of social disruption. Most important, it requires that we agree that the final end itself is worth achieving. No matter how eloquently I argue that pursuing a career in research dermatology is the most efficient, honorable, and socially harmonious way of discovering a method of turning my skin permanently green, you will fail to be convinced of the rationality of my behavior if you have trouble accepting the notion of having permanently green skin as a worthwhile final end.

This shows that ends of action embody different values, some of which are intersubjectively shared and some of which are not. Having permanently green skin or absolute divine dominion over one's social environment are among those idiosyncratic ends that fail to justify actions taken to achieve them because they do not embody intelligible and intersubjectively shared values, and because it is hard to imagine a human community that might share them. The general point can be expressed by describing ends of actions as instantiating social norms. By a *norm* I mean a principle, practice, ideal, value, or convention, with its attendant beliefs. Anything that has normative force, i.e., that can be translated into a recommendation or prescription for action, will count as a norm in this broad sense. This characterization of a norm makes it clear that norms can always be understood as *rules* of action. Hence I will often speak of normative *principles* or *practices*. My claims will apply equally, ceteris paribus, to ideals, values, aspirations, etc., unless otherwise indicated.[5]

An end *instantiates* a norm if the norm can be invoked by the agent to explain why the end is worth pursuing. We may say that the norm *explicates* the values, beliefs, and expectations that are implicit in the end. For example, suppose I aspire to be a lieutenant general in the U.S. Army. The end *instantiates* the norms that military service is an honorable occupation, that the role of lieutenant general is crucial in the testing of military strategy, that one's first duty is to defend one's country, that self-interest should be made to coincide with patriotic duty as far as possible, and so on. These norms *explicate* as *values* military service, self-discipline, honor, military strategy, patriotism, the coincidence of duty and self-interest, the defense of one's country, and so on. They also explicate the *beliefs* and *expectations* that as lieutenant general one can have a significant impact on military strategy, that women who aspire to become lieutenant generals stand a reasonable chance of doing so, that one's personal career choice will have an effect on the defense of one's country, that one will be due to receive honor for one's military service, and so on. Together with such beliefs and expectations, these values can be translated into recommendations or prescriptions to realize them under certain circumstances; this is what shows them to be norms. The task is now to explain what a *rational* norm is. The three criteria of end-rationality explicated earlier are intended to answer this question.

First, a rational norm is one whose values, beliefs, and expectations are socially viable. A *socially viable* norm is one that *could be* operative within the community of human beings whose behavior it is supposed to regulate. It need not be in fact, but it must closely enough express the dispositions and capacities that characterize human beings so that it could be adopted and practiced by a human community under some material human circumstances. Thus it must be psychologically palatable to those agents in the sense described in Section II.

An example of a norm that would *not* be socially viable in this sense, presumably, would be one that required members of a human community to spend each day in research devoted to the enterprise of turning their skin green as a final end, or communicating solely in barks, grunts, and squeaks, or hoarding useless rubbish. Some seriously advanced and believed moral norms may be of this kind as well, e.g., Christian norms of extreme self-denial. These norms would not be socially viable because human beings are not characteristically disposed to do such things. And the material circumstances of human existence do not naturally favor the development of such dispositions.

One reason for requiring that a rational norm be socially viable depends on the argument made in Section IV, that it is part of the process of socialization to internalize many social practices so deeply that they become dispositional traits of character. It was claimed that one's awareness of social circumstances of various kinds then evokes these dispositional responses almost automatically, without the necessary intervention of a desire on the part of the agent.

Clearly, human beings are not infinitely malleable, and we could not internalize just *any* norm or practice indifferently. Perhaps some idiosyncratic individuals could be trained, for example, to obliterate themselves for extended periods of time à la Howard Hughes, or everything else in their environment à la Major Kurtz. But one way of imposing constraints on our conception of the broad range of dispositions and capacities that characterize human beings is to require that the behavior or desire in question conform closely enough to human capacities that it *could* be instilled as part of the process of socialization into some human community, so that one's commitment to it could indeed motivate one to action. A practice that refused to adapt to the limitations of human physiology and psychology in this way could hardly be rational for human beings to act on. Thus the requirement of social viability ensures that the norm in question could be motivationally effective in the way that our conventions of dress, hygiene, and socially acceptable behavior are.

Social viability alone, however, does not exhaust the criteria a norm must meet in order to count as rational. We can imagine cases in which bizarre but socially viable norms arise, say, through the ingestion of hallucinogenic drugs, or through the covert inculcation of irrational ideological beliefs, or in other suspect ways. In such cases—Jonestown, Guyana, is an example—it makes sense to describe a whole community as irrational.

A norm must satisfy two further criteria in order to count as rational. First, it must be internally consistent within a system of such norms, i.e., logically consistent with all the other norms a fully rational and autonomous member of a human community adopts. This is important because logical consistency is an obvious, necessary (though insufficient) condition of rational justification. If I attempt to persuade you to join the military on the grounds that we all have a duty to defend our country, but refuse to join myself because military life is too risky and distasteful, you have good reason to suspect me of holding mutually inconsistent norms, and therefore to question my rationality or sincerity.

But even the combination of social viability and internal consistency does not suffice to identify a norm as rational. The ritual of sacrificing a calf to the gods in order to propitiate their wrath and thereby ensure victory in battle was both socially viable for human beings and also internally coherent within a certain historical and cultural setting. But if a group of Pentagon generals in present-day Washington, D.C., practiced this ritual, we would have good reason to call them irrational. Their behavior would seem to ignore salient features of the present-day environment that reveal such behavior as highly inappropriate. We would describe them as, at the very least, "out of touch with reality." That the norms an action instantiates seem to lack a veridical awareness of the surrounding environment is good grounds for refusing to call that action rational.

Thus the third (and for purposes of this discussion, final) criterion that a rational norm must satisfy is that it must be *realistic*.[6] That is, a rational norm must explicate values, beliefs, and expectations that can be interpreted as socially adaptive to some veridically perceived material and social environment. More precisely, the values and expectations explicated by a rational norm must be such that they could be explained *as though* they were valid inductive inferences from a series of trial-and-error attempts to adapt human needs and dispositions to the veridically perceived constraints and resources of the social and material environment.

A *rational action,* then, is one whose ends are rationally intelligible to suitably placed others and which therefore justify the action in question. An end is rationally intelligible if it instantiates norms whose values, beliefs, and expectations are socially viable, internally coherent, and could have arisen from a realistic conception of the surrounding environment. Hence a rational action is one that can be justified with reference to the circumstances of its performance. If an action aspires to realize normative values that are recognizably worth achieving, that are consistent with other values one may have, and that are appropriate to the constraints and resources inherent in the action's environment, that action is rational.[7]

VI. Self-Interest and Military Enlistment

To see how the suggested conception of end-rationality might work in practice, reconsider the self-interested justification originally cited in favor of enlisting in the All-Volunteer Force. The self-interested justification for joining the military depicts it as a means to education and technical training, career advancement, and personal development superior to the means available in the civilian sector. Let us provisionally describe individuals for whom this is true as *disadvantaged Americans,* reserving for later a discussion of why this terminology is apt.

It is true that military service may offer training in technical professional areas that is unavailable to disadvantaged Americans in the civilian sector, and that this training may brighten one's future prospects considerably in later civilian life. Moreover, the military contains a hierarchy through which one can advance just as far, in theory, as in a large civilian corporation. These and other such personal benefits of military service help to close the gap between the perceived social predicament of many disadvantaged Americans and that vision of the United States which forms the foundation of a wholehearted patriotic commitment to it. The more one feels like a valued and productive member of society, the more one feels able and entitled to take advantage of available social opportunities, and the more one will value the institutions and way of life that make them available. In this way military service may complete the integration of disadvantaged Americans into American society as productive, self-respecting, and patriotic citizens.

By ameliorating the deplorable social conditions of which most civilian institutions have apparently washed their hands, military service may have further positive consequences for society at large.

Before we discuss the value of this particular consequence, the self-interested justification must be considered on its own merits. Only when these merits have been determined will it become clear whether or not this particular consequence is, in fact, a positive one.

Relative to the self-interested justification addressed to potential enlistees, the end of enlisting in the military instantiates the following *norm* (among others):

(A) Military service is valuable as a way of promoting individual interests.

(A), in turn, explicates the following *values:*

    (i) Military service is worthwhile as an instrumental or subordinate end;
    (ii) The promotion of individual interests is worthwhile as a final end.

(A) also explicates the *expectations* that

    (iii) Military service will, in fact, promote individual interests;
    (iv) The individual interests promoted by military service will be recognized as having social worth and be treated accordingly.

This list of values and expectations explicated by (A) does not aim to be exhaustive. It will be sufficient for purposes of illustration if application of the model of end-rationality to some of the assumptions contained in the self-interested justification of military service yields rather different conclusions from those of the prevailing model of means-rationality, but conclusions that make an equal claim to plausibility. A norm's *degree* of rationality can then be calibrated by the number and importance of its values, expectations, and beliefs that satisfy or violate the suggested criteria of rationality.

One assumption that comes under immediate fire is the expectation expressed in (A.iii). (A.iii) seems to violate the second criterion of rationality, that a norm must be logically consistent within a system of rational norms, and hence (A) violates it as well. (A.iii) seems to violate the second criterion because it is inconsistent with the following norm (which I shall assume to be unproblematic for purposes of argument):

(B) Military service is a valuable means for promoting the national interest,

which itself includes the expectation that

    (i) Military service will, in fact, promote the national interest.

Of course this is not to claim that the promotion of individual interests is always inconsistent with promoting the national interest. But unfortunately, the invisible hand is incapable of providing a stable organizational structure within the military, given its overriding purpose. When promoting the national interest requires the enlisted ranks to be prepared to sacrifice self-interest for the defense of their country—as it does in the military context—(A.iii) is inconsistent with (B.i).

One may object that for enlistees to be *prepared* to sacrifice individual interests does not automatically entail that they must *in fact* sacrifice individual interests; and that, in particular, in a peacetime force the probability of having to mobilize for active combat is low enough to warrant taking the risk to obtain the personal and professional benefits that the military has to offer.

This objection seems to be misplaced, on three counts. First, it has already been pointed out (in Section I) that having to be *prepared* to risk one's life in military combat is a major concession that the military exacts from enlistees in exchange for the promise of training, professional advancement, travel, etc. It is hard to see why disadvantaged Americans should have to pay this price for social and professional opportunities that are freely available to most civilians. They already have had to forfeit the more equitable distribution of social and economic resources that our sense of justice seems to demand, in order merely to obtain that relative paucity of resources with which they must in fact make do. They thereby have had to accept considerably reduced prospects of personal, social, and intellectual development without which the formation of long-range plans and aspirations is difficult, and the effective utilization of resources in the service of those plans and aspirations even more so. These sacrifices have conferred upon other, more fortunate Americans correspondingly larger shares of social and economic resources. These, in turn, have better equipped them to take advantage of the social and professional opportunities our civilian institutions purport to offer all American citizens equally. Thus the sacrifices of disadvantaged Americans have had as a consequence that more advantaged, better equipped citizens will be more overridingly able and disposed to utilize those "equal" social and professional opportunities in the service of their own goals. Disadvantaged Americans have paid this price merely to have access—however remote—to these "equal" opportunities at all. It is hard to see why they should be prepared to risk their lives to obtain them as well. But if there is no further reason why disadvantaged Americans should have to pay this price for social and career opportunities to which others have free access, then it is irrational to exact it from them.[8]

Second, the basic requirement of a peacetime military, that troops achieve and maintain readiness for active combat mobilization, is given greater urgency by the very real possibility of conflict outbreaks in a number of unstable areas where the interests of the United States are vulnerable (of which the Persian Gulf area, Eastern Europe, and El Salvador are only the most sensitive at the moment). These circumstances reduce considerably the probability of pursuing without uninterruption any career-oriented course of training. Under these circumstances, it is far from obvious that the training and career opportunities promised by the Army—and we should remember that it promises only the *opportunities,* not the actual training or career—are worth the risks involved.

Third, we have already seen that even under present, peacetime conditions, the military's attempt to approximate civilian training and employment institutions as additional incentives for enlistment has failed.[9] It does not seem possible to maintain the necessary degree of military discipline, uniformity, and commitment and at the same time to fulfill the promises of individual advancement that characterize civilian prospects in a liberal-democratic society. It seems to be a hard truth that military service, whether in peacetime or in war, requires subordination of individual interests to the national interest. That is, military preparedness requires, to a large extent, the actual sacrifice of self-interest; therefore the expectations that

(A.iii) Military service will, in fact, promote individual interests

and that

(B.i) Military service will, in fact, promote the national interest

are incompatible. The same considerations strongly suggest that (A.iii) is unrealistic as well. And if (A.iii) is irrational on these grounds, so is (A.iv).

It might be argued that military service can be shown to serve the individual interests of disadvantaged Americans, in a wider sense. For although disadvantaged Americans often have little cause for optimism about their life prospects in the civilian sector, they would be even worse off were this country to be invaded or defeated in war. This fact, it is claimed, gives them a self-interested motive for defending their country through military service.[10]

But this conclusion does not follow. That is, it does not follow from the fact—if it is a fact—that disadvantaged Americans are better off in the civilian sector under this set of social and political institutions than they would be under any realistic alternative that they therefore have good reason to defend militarily this set of institutions. Perhaps they may have good reason to prefer to see this set of institutions defended or preserved by *someone*. But they have good reason to defend it *themselves* only if they are sufficiently better off that they are willing to risk the possibility of death or injury to maintain their current situation. This is not, in fact, the case. Apparently, some disadvantaged Americans *are* willing to risk death or injury in order to improve their current situations (although I have suggested that this is ultimately irrational); that is, they prefer to take that risk *rather than* remain where they are. But the conclusion in question requires that disadvantaged Americans choose to take that risk *in order to* remain where they are; and this would presuppose a far greater attachment to their current situation in the civilian sector than they have any reason to hold. Hence, even if they are better off in civilian life than they would be under any alternative arrangements, it is by no means obvious that they are sufficiently better off to make these institutions worth risking their lives to defend. This must be shown, not presupposed. So the enlarged conception of the self-interests of disadvantaged Americans is no more successful in justifying their military enlistment than was the original one. (A.iii) remains irrational.

Next consider (A.ii). The rationality of (A.ii) is questionable because it seems so clearly to be an unrealistic response to the social and material environment of the military. It is hard to imagine attempting to promote the above individual interests as socially adaptive behavior, given the constraints and resources inherent in the military environment. The concerted attempt to inculcate uniformity, discipline, obedience to and respect for authority, a sense of mission, and a collective identity through the conditions of basic training and the rigors of military life, plus the emphasis on personal sacrifice and readiness to fight, combine not only to make the promotion of those interests practically difficult, but also to diminish the actual value of promoting individual interests under those conditions. Appeals to the promotion of individual interests are addressed to recruitable but self-interested civilians. Actual military life attempts to extinguish both the force of such appeals and the prominence of self-interested motivations in the psychology of the soldier.

It is easy to see why this must be so. The constraints and functions of military defense require the subordination of self-interest to the other considerations already described. A military whose primary commitment was to the college education, professional training, or personal enrichment of its soldiers would fail to be identifiable as a military institution at all. This suggests that (A.ii) is not only unrealistic, but lacks social viability as well.

Thus some of the most important values and expectations contained in (A) are irrational, and this makes (A) itself irrational. Let us describe such a norm, when invoked in the attempt to justify action, as a *pseudojustification*.

One may accept this conclusion but nevertheless attempt to justify rationally the self-interested pseudojustification itself as a necessary means to the end of military recruitment, and this in turn as a necessary means to the end of military defense, as does the means-rational tactical argument described in Section II. Thus the end of deploying the self-interested pseudojustification instantiates the following norm:

   (C) (A) is the best available means of promoting military enlistment, which in turn is necessary for military defense.

(C) explicates the following *values:*

   (i) The self-interested pseudojustification is a valuable means to the end of increasing military enlistment;
   (ii) Increasing military enlistment is valuable as a further instrumental end in order to increase our capacity for military defense.

(C) also explicates the *expectations* that

   (iii) The self-interested pseudojustification will, in fact, increase military enlistment;
   (iv) The increased military enlistment resulting from the promulgation of (A) will, in fact, increase our capacity for military defense.

Let us begin by examining (C.i), that the self-interested pseudojustification is the best available strategy for recruiting an All-Volunteer Force. Now, it has already been observed that recruitment efforts are addressed to those disadvantaged Americans for whom even meager advances in personal and career prospects in the Army are preferable to those available in the civilian sector. This requires that these individuals view dimly their prospects for individual advancement in the civilian sector, i.e., the opportunities there are remote for completing their education or obtaining a higher one, for skill or career training, and for employment in a satisfying job promising individual achievement, financial security, and advances in professional status. For these individuals, the civilian institutions of this country offer no attractive or realistic opportunities for improving their overall life prospects, and this is why military service can be made to seem attractive. This is also why it is apposite to think of them as disadvantaged Americans.

A few moments' reflection indicates that (C.i) is not socially viable because it could not be adopted by that segment of the community to whom the self-interested pseudojustification was originally addressed. Potential military enlistees could not be expected to acquiesce in advance to being duped in order to get them into the military; the very idea is incoherent. In particular, disadvantaged Americans can hardly be expected to accept the proposition that they must be deceived about where their individual interests lie in order to seduce them into an environment that does not, in fact, serve their individual interests at all. For either they have motivationally effective patriotic dispositions, in which case they would reject the assumption that such deception is necessary; or else they are moved by the above-described individual interests, in which case they would reject the claim that they should be herded into an environment that does not serve them.[11]

Now consider (C.iv). (C.iv) is unrealistic, if "military enlistment" is understood to refer to that activity whose policies are purported to justify the self-interested pseudojustification. For as we have already seen, (A) is designed to appeal to disadvantaged Americans; for whom military service most often represents their last chance to complete or obtain further education. Thus these recruits enter the military with educational disadvantages and inadequately developed intellectual skills that they are led to expect the military to ameliorate.[12] They are understandably disappointed and demoralized when these expectations are left unsatisfied.

The failure of the military to deliver on its promise of remedial or higher education and training results in a force that is inadequately prepared to handle the highly complex weaponry of today's military.[13] This, in turn, reduces considerably the readiness level of active combat units to mobilize rapidly and engage in active combat with any degree of confidence in the outcome.[14] These facts indicate that the expectation expressed in (C.iv) is unrealistic. And if (C.iv) is unrealistic, then it is equally unrealistic to view this brand of recruitment as a valuable, important, or essential means of military defense (C.ii). Hence (C) is irrational: the self-interested pseudojustification is no more rational as a means to military defense than it is as a reason for disadvantaged Americans to enlist in the military.

Is there any reason at all for disadvantaged Americans to enlist? Perhaps there is. For recall the *patriotic* justification in support of military enlistment, i.e., that

(D) The present civilian institutions of the United States should be defended against attack.

Upon reflection, however, it would seem that (D) is neither internally consistent nor socially viable. For it has already been observed that many disadvantaged Americans seek their fortunes in the AVF because they correctly regard civilian institutions as inadequate and unresponsive to their personal and professional aspirations. They enlist because they are dissatisfied and disappointed with the current state and functioning of civilian institutions and find no reason to continue to participate in them. But if this description more or less correctly identifies the conscious alienation of many enlistees from civilian institutions, then it would be inconsistent for them to adopt *both* (D) and the norm that

(E) The present civilian institutions of the United States should be radically reformed.

(D) and (E) are inconsistent because any concerted attempt to conform to (E)— through organizing, consciousness-raising, protest-marching, striking, passive resistance, civil disobedience, etc.—involves some form of attack on civilian institutions. It requires that alienated, discouraged, or disillusioned citizens refuse to continue to participate in the institutional process by which they are demoralized. It requires that they refuse to adjust downward the expectations generated by those very institutions to conform to their de facto inadequacies, and instead take active steps to adjust upward the quality and functioning of those institutions to conform to those expectations.

Certainly it seems possible that these institutions could be attacked on one front, through internal reform, and simultaneously defended on another, from external threats to their existence, and hence that (D) and (E) are compatible. But the distinction between internal and external fronts is not clear enough to justify this possibility. It is not implausible to suppose that the Army as well as the National Guard might be called upon to quell a strike or protest of sufficient magnitude, nor to suppose that, say, patriotic American businesspeople might ally themselves with international commercial concerns in order to effect changes in the structure of American political and economic institutions. And so it appears that one cannot adopt both (D) and (E), upon pain of inconsistency.

In fact, it is unlikely that those enlistees whose sentiments about the current conditions of American civilian institutions are expressed by (E) could be supposed to adopt (D) as a norm.[15] Those for whom the military's career development-oriented recruitment campaign has the greatest appeal tend to enlist for reasons of self-betterment; they are motivated not to defend civilian institutions, but rather to reject them. This is the sense in which (D) fails to be socially viable. Thus if there *is* any good reason for disadvantaged Americans to enlist in the military, we have yet to learn what it is.

VII. Patriotism and Military Conscription

If disadvantaged Americans have no rational justification for enlisting in the service, for whom might the patriotic justification contained in (D) prove rationally compelling? I shall argue that advantaged Americans would be rationally justified in enlisting, for patriotic as well as self-interested reasons; and therefore the failure to recognize the rationality of so doing would justify their conscription.

Let us begin by considering a qualified version of (D):

(F) The present civilian institutions of the United States should be defended by advantaged Americans.

(F) explicates the following *values:*

(i) The present civilian institutions of the United States are worth defending for advantaged Americans;
(ii) Advantaged Americans should defend them.

(F) also explicates the *expectation* that

(iii) Advantaged Americans can, in fact, successfully defend these institutions.

First consider (F.i), which certainly appears to be socially viable. Disadvantaged Americans may concur in the observation that advantaged Americans have been the prime beneficiaries of civilian institutions and so have good reason to view them as valuable. Similarly advantaged Americans themselves will conclude that the particular ways of life, benefits, and opportunities that make their lives individually worth living depend upon the particular social and political institutions that make these things possible. They need not hesitate, therefore, to extend the same worth they ascribe to their individual life circumstances to the institutions that provide them. Clearly, ascribing a positive value to American civilian institutions is consistent with taking a critical and highly qualified attitude toward them.

Second, (F.i) is realistic. It could have been formulated as an adaptive and veridical response to the salient features of the American social and material environment. For advantaged Americans, this would require little more than a disinterested survey of the resources and constraints on the achievement of individual ends that characterize this environment and an informed comparison with possible alternative institutions. Of course the conclusions of such a survey would be to a certain degree self-fulfilling. Since this environment determines, almost uniquely, the valued ends that advantaged Americans tend to adopt, it stands to reason that they would find this environment best suited to their achievement.

But it would be wrong to suppose that these hypotheses apply only to egoistic or personal ends. Precisely such institutionalized values as individual rights and liberties, autonomy, self-fulfillment, and so on encourage many reflective advantaged Americans to be dissatisfied with the current capacity of American civilian institutions to improve the lot of the less advantaged so as more adequately to reflect these values. But to voice such a criticism within the constraints of these institutions, and to work, similarly within these constraints, for their improvement, seems clearly to presuppose the view of institutionalized norms and procedures described in Section IV. And just as clearly, the estimated worth of such institutionalized procedures reflects on the worth of the institutions that generate them.

Hence, advantaged Americans themselves have good reason to find American civilian institutions worth defending. For disadvantaged Americans the realistic formulation of (F.i) requires merely a disinterested survey of the conditions and attitudes of advantaged Americans. This conclusion strongly suggests that (F.i) is not only socially viable, but also realistic. In the absence of any strong arguments to show that (F.i) is inconsistent within an advantaged agent's system of norms, we are justified in supposing that (F.i) is rational.

Next consider (F.ii). It has already been argued that disadvantaged Americans rationally ought not to defend these institutions. On what *realistic* basis can it be argued that advantaged Americans ought to?

First, (F.ii) is realistic because advantaged Americans have the strongest de facto commitment to the institutions and values that characterize this country. They also have obtained sufficient benefits from it so as to bring to its defense a large variety of needed skills and resources, including intellectual skills, professional and technical training, and a broad understanding of the purpose and function of the rigors and necessities of military life. Above all, as the major beneficiaries of American values and institutions, advantaged Americans are in the position to contribute the most concrete and well-grounded appreciation of those values and institutions as well *worth* defending, for they would have the most to lose from their demise. These considerations suggest the realism of (F.iii) as well.

To these arguments three objections might be raised. First, it might be claimed that the norm that

> (G) Advantaged Americans should be exposed to the possibility of combat and risk of death

is inconsistent with (B) and (B.i), in particular. For it is in the national interest to preserve and protect them as well as the institutions they uphold. If it were not for our doctors, lawyers, parents, judges, professors, politicians, psychiatrists, corporate businesspeople, engineers, and scientists, the quality of American society would deteriorate considerably.

Yet it is logically inconsistent to claim, on the one hand, that the United States is eminently worth defending because of its plethora of valuable human resources, and on the other, that the business of defense is not important enough to entrust to those best able to do the job, nor to those with the greatest interest in seeing the job well done. To view military defense as the highest social priority, while worrying that those to whom military defense is entrusted are too immature to adjust to military discipline, are incapable of operating complex military equipment or of rapid mobilization in case of a national emergency, or lack sufficient patriotism, is to overlook the obvious. This is that if this country really is worth defending because of the high level of human resources it has nurtured, then an adequate and successful military defense of it requires mobilizing those same resources on its behalf. Hence (G) is prima facie consistent with other norms we have rational grounds for accepting.

Second, it might be claimed that (F.ii) is not socially viable and hence not realistic, since advantaged Americans personally stand to lose too much by being exposed to the risk of military combat to be willing to undertake military service. It is instead in their interest to let other, less advantaged Americans do the fighting and dying, so that they themselves may continue to enjoy the social and economic benefits they have received.

First, the general conclusion does not follow. That is, it does not follow from the fact that a norm is socially nonviable that it is therefore unrealistic (for example, a norm prescribing free-rider behavior might be realistic, but could not be socially viable). Second, it is not true that (F.ii) is not socially viable. It has already been argued (in Section IV) that what one is rationally committed to doing may well be independent of what one has a desire to do, or a personal interest in doing. It has also been suggested (in Section III) that it is not necessarily rational to pursue self-interest. If we are entitled to assume that most human beings at least try to behave as rationally as they can, then if we can marshal persuasive reasons why advantaged Americans rationally ought to be the first to defend their country, there is no reason to suppose *in advance* that such individuals could not be moved to do so, just because a sacrifice of self-interest or personal gratification would be required. It would be sad indeed if the patriotic justification for military service turned out to be nothing but a rationalization for self-interested and cowardly impulses that advantaged Americans could scarcely justify to themselves, much less to others. On this controversial question of the psychology of advantaged Americans, let us be unpleasantly surprised if we must, rather than unduly pessimistic when we needn't be.

Third, the norm on which this objection is based,

(H) Other, less advantaged citizens should risk their lives in defense of the right of advantaged Americans to continue enjoying the social benefits and opportunities which disadvantaged Americans lack,

is not socially viable, for the same reasons that (C.i) was not. The norm cannot be made viable without circumscribing the social community so as to exclude those members of the community on whom the burden of defense is to be placed. And as we have seen, there are no coherent or realistic grounds for this policy.

Finally, it might be argued that even if these considerations support the rationality of (F.ii), they do not even begin to establish the realism of (F.iii), and hence fail to establish the rationality of (F). For in fact it is not correct to claim that advantaged Americans can participate in military defense in any full-blooded sense, if they are sufficiently persuaded by the two preceding objections that they lack all motivation to do so. If advantaged Americans strongly prefer enjoying the benefits and opportunities of American civilian institutions to defending them, or believe that it is not in the national interest for them to risk their lives in its defense, then in a certain sense they may be thought to be incapable of moving themselves to its defense.

But of course the sense of "can" in which it is relevant to inquire whether (F.iii) is realistic has to do with the capacities, skills, and training such individuals would contribute to military defense, and not with their motivation. And in this relevant sense of "can," it becomes more difficult to doubt that (F.iii) is, indeed, realistic.

Furthermore, it has already been suggested that it is not obvious that self-interested but irrational considerations of the kind just described would predominate as motivationally effective in all cases. If any group can be expected to recognize their rational obligation to defend their country, one would certainly hope and expect that advantaged Americans might do so.

Of course it is possible—or perhaps even likely—that self-interested considerations might weaken advantaged Americans' commitment to rational behavior, and thus render them insensitive to the rationality of the proposal that they should be the first to undertake the military defense of their country. If this turned out to be true, patriotic considerations would rationally justify subjecting them to military conscription.

The necessity of putting into practice such a policy might increase our sensitivity to the actual stakes involved in war and reduce somewhat the bellicose enthusiasm of our leaders for waging it.

Notes

1. "Much of the dissatisfaction that exists among volunteers is based on the lack of adequate information to prepare the new enlistee for military life. The major piece of information missing is: the U.S. Army is a military organization with the specific mission of fighting. . . . In many instances the jobs assigned to soldiers may be boring, demeaning, or repetitious. A spirit of dedication and sacrifice is expected from all soldiers. This spirit of sacrifice and dedication combined with proper discipline is essential for wartime service when it is imperative that soldiers unswervingly perform their duties." From J. L. Reed, "An Analysis and Evaluation of the United States Army (*The Beard Study*)," appendix to *Status of the All-Volunteer Armed Force,* Hearing Before the Subcommittee on Manpower and Personnel, Committee on Armed Services, United States Senate, 95th Congress, 2nd Session, 20 June 1978 (Washington, D.C.: Government Printing Office, 1978), pp. 254–55. Subsequently referred to as *The Beard Study.*

"Even though the majority of enlistees had or were learning and practicing with equipment and language of combat, few seem to have given any serious thought as to how they would feel or behave given the need to enter a combat situation" (David Gottlieb, *Babes in Arms: Youth in the Army* [Beverly Hills, Calif.: Sage Publications, 1980], p. 77).

2. "Army recruiting is focussed on appealing to enlistees on the basis of employment, travel, and a chance for a college education. . . . overstressing these incentives has created a flow of individuals into the service with high expectations that Army life will be an 8-to-5 job with weekends off, 30 days paid vacation and a life-style comparable to that which might be available in the private sector of U.S. society. My interviews with junior enlisted personnel have indicated that an overwhelmingly large number feel frustrated by not getting the college education that they believe was promised to them. They also feel that the Army was going to be just another job and are very disappointed after experiencing military life. . . . When I interviewed recruiters I found that they are under great pressure to meet quotas and readily admit to using any technique to 'sell' individuals on enlisting in the Army" (*The Beard Study,* pp. 135–36; see also 157–59, 165–66, 209–12).

3. See, for example, Philippa Foot, "Reasons for Action and Desire," *Proceedings of the Aristotelian Society,* Supp. Vol. 44 (1972): 189-210; and "Morality as a System of Hypothetical Imperatives," *Philosophical Review* 81 (1972): 305-16.

4. The topic of this section is a large one, for which I can do scarcely more here than indicate, very roughly, the outline of my own views. For a fuller treatment, see my "A New Model of Rationality" (Ph.D. dissertation, Harvard University, 1981).

5. Hence I include both so-called "consequentialist" and so-called "deontological" prescriptions for action under the rubric of a norm (for reasons that are clarified in "A Distinction Without a Difference," *Midwest Studies in Philosophy, Vol. VII: Social and Political Philosophy* [Minneapolis: University of Minnesota Press, 1982]). In that discussion I neglected to speculate upon the sense of freedom from moral regulations and prohibitions one might experience upon adopting a consequentialist stance, after having been raised in an environment highly structured by such regulations and prohibitions; and the sense of security and certitude one might experience upon adopting a deontological stance, having come from an environment in which moral regulations and prohibitions were ineffective, ambiguous, or altogether absent. For the overly conscientious, consequentialism may be a liberation; for the intemperate or undisciplined, deontologism may be a refuge.

6. Other, commonsense criteria of rational norms, i.e., that they should allow one to

achieve more rather than fewer of one's valued ends, that they should permit a hierarchical ranking of ends, and so on, can be accommodated easily to this account.

7. It may be noticed that this conception of rational action makes no mention of the efficient achievement of ends, nor of their maximization. This is because both of these are instrumental ends, i.e., means for realizing final ends, that may but do not necessarily satisfy the criteria just enumerated.

8. It may be protested that no one is exacting or extorting anything from anyone. For we are considering only voluntarily undertaken military service, not military conscription. And disadvantaged Americans may rationally choose to pursue opportunities and benefits where they are available, whether in the military or anywhere else. But whether and to what extent the decision of a disadvantaged American to undertake military service can be viewed correctly as a choice, when the alternatives are between service in the military and considerably fewer prospects than most others have in the civilian sector, is surely controversial. And if the decision to undertake military service is not, properly speaking, a choice, it is a fortiori not a *rational* choice. I am indebted to Charles Tilley for valuable discussions on this topic. See, further, Jules Coleman, "Liberalism, Unfair Advantage, and the Volunteer Armed Forces," Chapter 7, this volume.

9. See notes 1 and 2.

10. I am indebted to Allan Gibbard and Thomas Holt for insisting on the importance of this point.

11. Of course we could envision a social community in which a large segment was trained from infancy to be highly specialized warriors, and programmed to believe that the best life of all consisted in military combat and risking one's life for the sake of military honor; and that the best death of all was on the battlefield. We could imagine the rest of the community collaborating in the perpetuation of this ideology among the warrior class in order that they would *in fact* risk their lives in defense of the rest of the community's right to continue enjoying its social benefits. But it is much harder to imagine successfully perpetuating (C.i) itself among the warrior class and continuing to receive its compliance. To inform soldiers that they were being deceived and used solely to defend benefits that other citizens enjoyed, but to which they themselves had no access, would be to invite rebellion. This means that those who did the fighting would have to be excluded from the community that adopted (C.i).

12. See *The Beard Study*, p. 137.

13. Ibid., pp. 137-38, 140.

14. Ibid., p. 212; and Gottlieb, *Babes in Arms*, p. 94.

15. The remarks contained in this paragraph are based upon informal interviews with enlisted soldiers in Heidelberg, West Germany, in the winter of 1978.

9

Conscientious Objection to Military Service

JAMES F. CHILDRESS

One major reason for the shift to the All-Volunteer Force was the vigorous opposition in the 1960s and early 1970s to conscription into service in a war widely perceived to be unjustified.[1] To receive an exemption from military service as a conscientious objector at that time, a person had to conform to or fulfill the following requirement:

> Section 6 (j) Conscientious Objectors.—Nothing contained in this title shall be construed to require any person to be subject to combatant training and service in the armed forces of the United States *who, by reason of religious training and belief, is conscientiously opposed to participation in war in any form. As used in this subsection, the term "religious training and belief" does not include essentially political, sociological, or philosophical views, or a merely personal moral code.* Any person claiming exemption from combatant training and service because of such conscientious objections whose claim is sustained by the local board shall, if he is inducted into the armed forces under this title, be assigned to noncombatant service [or] such civilian work . . . as the local board . . . may deem appropriate [Military Selective Service Act, 1967].

Three major criteria determined who could be exempted under this section: (a) conscientiousness, (b) pacifism, and (c) religious training and belief. Widespread opposition to the war in Vietnam generated pressure to break down the second and third criteria. Under a steady stream of judicial interpretation, which will be discussed later, the religious requirement, for all practical purposes, was washed away. But despite several challenges, the requirement of pacifism remained intact. As society considers the possibility of restoring a draft for military service, it is important to determine *whether* conscientious objectors should be exempted from military service and *who* should be counted as conscientious objectors. I will address the first question very briefly in order to concentrate on the *scope* of the conscientious objector provision, particularly whether objectors to particular wars should be exempted along with objectors to all wars. (Hereinafter "CO" will be used for "conscientious objection" and "conscientious objector.")

Two points about my perspective may be useful. First, it is important and necessary to deal with penultimate questions, even when we cannot resolve ultimate questions. Thus I will not try to determine whether the state or conscience should be granted final authority but, rather, what our public policy ought to be toward conscientious objectors to military service. Should we exempt them from some public responsibilities in order to protect them from the sanction of conscience?

Second, I will concentrate on three principles that frequently come into conflict in this area of public policy: (1) respect for persons and their consciences, (2) fairness in procedures and in the distribution of burdens in the society, and (3) utility—the production of a net balance of good over bad consequences. I will not here defend these principles, which can be supported in various ways, but will assume them in part because of their frequent invocation in public, legislative, and judicial debates about conscription and conscientious objection.[2]

Exemption of Conscientious Objectors from Military Service

Although there are good reasons for exempting at least some conscientious objectors from military service, it is difficult to claim a constitutional right for such an exemption. In debates about the Bill of Rights in 1789, James Madison proposed a clause to the Second Amendment: "but no person religiously scrupulous of bearing arms shall be compelled to bear arms in person."[3] His proposal was not accepted. In the absence of such a clause, but also in the absence of a clear necessity to determine the issue, the Supreme Court has frequently observed that exemption of COs from military service is a privilege, a matter of legislative grace.[4] What Congress gives, Congress may, of course, take away. Nevertheless, it may not attach unconstitutional conditions to its privileges.[5]

Pragmatic reasons for exemption of COs are not unimportant, for instance, the difficulty or even impossibility of making adequate soldiers out of people who are conscientiously opposed to fighting. In addition, it would be very difficult politically to abolish a privilege that has been in existence for so long. Attempts to eliminate it would provoke vigorous opposition not only from the historic peace churches (Mennonites, Brethren, and Quakers), who were the earliest beneficiaries of this privilege, but also from many other religious and secular groups.[6]

Principled grounds for exemption of COs include respect for conscience and fairness. It is at least prima facie wrong to force a person to act against his conscience, although it may sometimes be justified and even necessary. And it is unfair to conscientious persons to give them the "hard choice"of obedience to the law or criminal classification, when this can be avoided. In our tradition and our vision of the free society, "in the forum of conscience, duty to a moral power higher than the state has always been maintained." In addition, the "value of conscientious action" to the community has been recognized by legislators and courts as well as by others.[7]

Arguments against exemption of COs usually appeal to the unfairness of exempting some people from military service when others have to serve. For this reason, exemption of COs from combatant service is also conjoined with the requirement of either noncombatant service or alternative service for an equal period of time, to distribute some of the burdens of conscription more fairly and equitably. The CO has to spend an equal amount of time in service, and his life plan (e.g., career and family) is disrupted just as is another draftee's. Of course, the risks of injury and death are not equalized. Because COs for the most part are not exposed to such risks, it might even be fair for them to serve for longer periods of time or at less pay.

Consequentialist arguments against an exemption for at least some COs sound hollow in view of our society's successful policies in the past. At the very least these policies have been successful in protecting many consciences without any apparent damage to the country's military security. Nevertheless, it is appropriate to ask whether a policy of exemption can be maintained without detrimental effects when the criteria of CO are broadened. Thus, the questions of exemption of COs and the scope of that exemption merge. As I have indicated, arguments based on principles of respect for persons and fairness support a policy of exempting (some) COs from military duties, even though fairness may also justify and even require the imposition of some other burdens such as noncombatant or alternative service. But consideration of possible or probable consequences may make exemption for a broad range of COs difficult, if not impossible.

Scope of Policies Toward Conscientious Objectors: Religious Training and Belief

Exemption of COs from military service in the United States has generally been limited to religious pacifists. Civil War and World War I exemptions were limited to members of "peace churches." The Selective Service Act of 1917 exempted from combatant duty registrants who were

> found by a local board to be a member of any well-recognized religious sect or organization organized and existing May 18, 1917, and whose then existing creed or principles forbid its members to participate in war in any form, and whose religious convictions are against war or participation therein in accordance with the creed or principles of said religious organizations.

The actual administration of the law was more liberal, for the Secretary of War, under whose authority all COs served, ordered that "personal scruples against war" be counted as sufficient for conscientious objection.[8]

While the Selective Training and Service Act of 1940 did not require church membership, COs had to be opposed to participation in war in any form "by reason of religious training and belief," a criterion subject to widely different interpretations. This criterion was interpreted in broader and broader ways as it moved up the different levels of appeal. Its ambiguity also troubled the federal courts. Some defined it as equivalent to conscience, however informed, while others restricted it to theistic beliefs.[9] In 1948 Congress tried to resolve these conflicting interpretations by sharpening the statute:

> Religious training and belief in this connection means an individual's belief in a relation to a Supreme Being involving duties superior to those arising from any human relation, but does not include essentially political, sociological, or philosophical views or a merely personal moral code.

In a major decision, *United States* v. *Seeger,* 380 U.S. 163 (1965), the Supreme Court held that Congress "was merely clarifying the meaning of religious training and belief so as to embrace all religion," including such modern interpretations as Paul Tillich's and John Robinson's as well as the Ethical Culture Movement. Thus, according to the Court, the conscription act did not discriminate between forms of religious expression. But the Court went on to construct a test of belief "in a relation to a Supreme Being":

> whether a given belief that is sincere and meaningful occupies a place in the life of its possessor parallel to that filled by the orthodox belief in God by one who clearly qualifies for the exemption.

According to this "parallel belief" test, what is relevant is not the *content* of the belief, but its *place* or *role* or *function* in the believer's life. It is not necessary to affirm theism.

In 1968 Congress deleted the "Supreme Being" clause, but retained the clause that excluded "essentially political, sociological, or philosophical views or a merely personal moral code" as grounds for exemption. In *Welsh* v. *United States,* 398 U.S. 340 (1970), decided under the pre-1968 language because of the date of origin of the case, the Supreme Court held that what is necessary for a registrant's conscientious objection to all war to be "religious" within the meaning of the statute is that

> this opposition to war stem from the registrant's moral, ethical, or religious beliefs about what is right and wrong and that these beliefs be held with the *strength* of traditional religious convictions. . . . If an individual *deeply and sincerely holds beliefs which are purely ethical or moral in source and content* but which nevertheless impose upon him a *duty of conscience* to refrain from participating in any war at any time, those beliefs certainly occupy in the life of that individual "a place parallel to that filled by . . . God" in traditionally religious persons. Because his beliefs function as a religion in his life, such an individual is as much entitled to a "religious" conscientious objector exemption under #6 (j) as is someone who derives his conscientious opposition to war from traditional religious convictions. [The CO provision] exempts from military service all those whose consciences, spurred by deeply held moral, ethical, or religious beliefs, would give them no rest or peace if they allowed themselves to become a part of the instrument of war [emphasis added].

Its exclusionary clause does not rule out COs whose pacifism "is founded to a substantial extent upon considerations of public policy." It does, however, rule out

> those whose beliefs are not deeply held and those whose objection to war *does not rest at all* upon moral, ethical, or religious principle but instead *rests solely upon* considerations of policy, pragmatism, or expediency [emphasis added].

Obviously the Court avoided facing the constitutional question whether this CO exemption violated the Establishment Clause of the First Amendment. Indeed, Justice Harlan, who concurred in the result but filed a separate opinion, contended that while *Seeger* was "a remarkable feat of judicial surgery" because it removed the theistic requirement of the statute, *Welsh* performed "a lobotomy." The *Welsh* decision reinterpreted the statute in order to salvage its constitutionality.

Future legislation should, in my opinion, affirm the conclusions of *Seeger* and *Welsh* but should state those conclusions in "nonreligious" terms. The criterion of "religious training and belief," now rendered almost completely vacuous, should be stated merely as a criterion of moral, ethical, or religious conscientious objection. Respect for conscience should not be limited to respect for "religious" conscience, however liberally defined. The place, function, centrality, and intensity of the belief in the registrant's life are important for defining both conscientious objection and its moral, ethical, or religious bases. How moral, ethical, and religious bases might be distinguished from other bases, such as political ones, will be considered in relation to conscientious objection to participation in a particular war.

Absolute Pacifism and Selective Conscientious Objection

Another question of *scope* concerns the range of opposition to participation in war. Should exemption from military service be granted only to those who are conscientiously opposed to participation in any war, or should it also be extended to those who are conscientiously opposed to participation in a particular war? So far our government has recognized only universal or absolute conscientious objectors (hereafter called UCOs), i.e., those who are pacifists. While pacifism has various meanings, I will define it narrowly as opposition to participation in *any* war; an absolute pacifist is one who is opposed to his participation in all wars. Obviously, this is a minimal definition, for most pacifists are also opposed to war and not only to their own participation in it. Likewise, for this discussion the selective conscientious objector (SCO) is opposed to his participation in a particular war but not necessarily in all wars.

Since 1940 conscription legislation has exempted only COs who are opposed to "participation in war in any form," a phrase that also appeared in the 1917 legislation. Although some interpreters have held that "in any form" modifies "participation" rather than "war," such an interpretation makes no sense, because a CO might oppose only combatant duties while being willing to perform noncombatant duties (e.g., service as a medic). Before the war in Vietnam the requirement of absolute pacifism received little attention, despite the centrality of the just-war tradition in the Roman Catholic and major Protestant denominations, probably in part because it was assumed that government officials, rather than citizens, determine whether or not a particular war is just. Unfortunately, discussions of SCO in the 1960s and early 1970s suffered greatly from their entanglement with the issue of the war in Vietnam; the policy questions are independent of that particular context, however much it may have stimulated interest in them.

The Supreme Court has consistently upheld this legislative requirement of absolute pacifism for exemption from military service, even while occasionally stretching its meaning. One major challenge came from the Jehovah's Witnesses, who over time have created the most difficulties for the Selective Service System. They are not strict pacifists. They are not only willing to use force to defend themselves, their families, and their faith; they are also willing to fight in some wars, namely, theocratic wars, such as the battle of Armageddon that Jehovah will conduct. Before 1955 the Justice Department determined that Jehovah's Witnesses claiming exemption from military service solely on the basis of the movement's beliefs would not be recognized as conscientious objectors because they were not "conscientiously opposed to participation in war in any form." In *Sicurella* v. *United States,* 348 U.S. 385 (1955), the Supreme Court held that Congress "had in mind shooting wars when it referred to participating in war in any form—actual military conflicts between nations of the earth in any form— actual military conflicts between nations of the earth in our time." It also noted that Jehovah had not commanded such a war since Biblical times and that no such command was expected in the immediate future. In effect, the Court gave Jehovah's Witnesses the benefit of the doubt.

During the Vietnam era, Black Muslims were frequently denied exemption from military service because they indicated that their religion would permit them to fight in some wars—for example, if the United States gave them territory to defend. Thus, the government argued that their objection to the war in Vietnam was political rather than religious, and selective rather than universal. In Muhammed Ali's case, the government did not question the religious basis of his opposition or his sincerity, but his pacifism. In such cases, the defense usually argued that the Black Muslims are similar to the Jehovah's Witnesses in all respects relevant for conscientious objector classification.[10]

Apart from these exceptions, SCOs have not been recognized.[11] Whether they should be included in any future exemptions for COs depends on several factors. At the risk of some oversimplifications, I will consider the main arguments for and against exemptions for SCOs under three headings: the nature of SCO claims, fairness and respect for persons, and consequences. To a great extent, the last two depend on the first.

THE NATURE OF SCO CLAIMS

The National Advisory Commission on Selective Service's 1967 report to the president offered a major argument against exemption for SCOs:

> So-called selective pacifism is *essentially a political* question of support or nonsupport of a war and cannot be judged in terms of special moral imperatives. Political opposition to a particular war should be expressed through recognized democratic processes and should claim no special right of exemption from democratic decisions [emphasis added].[12]

If this argument were sound, it would provide important premises for the arguments that invoke the principles of respect for persons, fairness, and utility. But there are reasons for thinking that it rests on several confusions. In trying to determine whether SCO is essentially political, rather than moral, we are interested in the distinction between "moral" and "nonmoral" (e.g., political and legal), rather than the distinction between "moral" and "immoral." The first distinction concerns the classification of judgments and reasons; the second concerns their evaluation.

Consider the following reasons a draftee might offer for holding that his participation in a particular war would violate his conscience:

1. All wars are wrong.
2. Our aims in this war are unjust.
3. The evil effects of this particular war will probably outweigh its good effects.
4. This war is wrong because we are directly killing noncombatants.

Reason 1 represents the UCO, who rejects participation in any war. Reasons 2 through 4 represent possible claims by an objector to a particular war. Are reasons 2 through 4 essentially political rather than moral?

Several reasons for characterizing SCO as essentially political may be rejected without further discussion. The SCO's qualified judgment about war, the complexity of his reasons, and his appeal to the facts of the situation in no way make his position less "moral" than the UCO's.

The *subject matter* of all four judgments is a governmental policy: war. Thus, we cannot appeal to the subject matter in order to distinguish "political" from "moral." In terms of subject matter, UCOs are just as political as SCOs, for all of them alike make a negative judgment about a governmental policy.

Some opponents would respond that SCO is essentially political not because it is a judgment about government policy, but because it is a judgment about *one's own government's policy*.[13] While the UCO condemns all governments for their policies of war, the SCO offers a special condemnation of his own government. It is logically possible for the SCO to hold that both belligerents are waging an unjust war (e.g., two powers are seeking to expand their territorial influence). Nevertheless, in many cases (perhaps most) the SCO will hold that his own government's policies are unjust. This stance does not, however, render his position essentially political rather than moral.

In order to see why it is not possible to characterize SCOs as essentially political simply because they make a judgment about governmental policy, it is useful, as Alan Gewirth suggests, to distinguish the *subject matter* about which judgments are made from the *nature* of those judgments.[14] An agent may make moral, or political, or other judgments about political matters. Suppose we criticize a president who vetoes a bill. We might criticize his political act because we believe it is unwise for him to alienate a powerful lobby that could help him be reelected, or because we believe it is unjust. While the subject matter of the judgments is a political act, the two judgments are different and have different grounds, one political and one moral.

In the last several years, philosophers have devoted considerable attention to the (metaethical) distinction between moral and nonmoral judgments. They have proposed several criteria of moral judgments. The first three are formal: a moral judgment must be (a) prescriptive, (b) overriding, and (c) universalizable. The first and second criteria relate very closely to the place, function, centrality, and intensity of belief that the Supreme Court has emphasized in analyzing CO. And it is clear that the SCO's judgment may be both prescriptive and overriding for him. According to the third criterion, to be moral a judgment must be consistent from case to case; that is, the agent must judge relevantly similar cases in a similar way. Suppose the SCO holds that he is conscientiously opposed to participation in war X but not in war Y. According to the third criterion, his opposition may count as moral if he identifies relevant dissimilarities such as the injustice of X and the justice of Y. A fourth criterion focuses on material content, usually the welfare of others. According to this criterion, a judgment is not moral unless it makes some reference to the welfare of others. Any of the positions 2 through 4 offered by the SCO may satisfy this criterion and count as moral in contrast to political.[15]

Some critics of SCO have held that consideration of the consequences of a war (as in position 3) is political. They tend to view consequentialist reasons as political and deontological reasons (which hold that there are some standards of right and wrong independent of an act's consequences) as moral. But this distinction between consequentialist and deontological reasoning will not enable us to differentiate political judgments from moral judgments or even to distinguish SCOs from UCOs. It rather indicates *two types of moral reasoning* in political and other activities. Even if a government's policies and opponents' judgments are based on consequentialist considerations, they are not necessarily political, rather than moral.

It is not even possible to distinguish UCOs and SCOs in terms of their mode of moral reasoning. While much pacifism is deontological (e.g., the historic peace churches), pacifism may be based on judgments about the *effects* of *all* wars (e.g., they produce more evil than good).[16] Conversely, SCOs often oppose a particular war not because of its consequences, but because of its violation of principles of right conduct.

Traditional just-war theory draws an important distinction between *jus ad bellum* (the right to go to war) and *jus in bello* (right conduct within war). The former includes such considerations of ends and consequences as just cause and proportionality—considerations appealed to by positions 2 and 3. The latter includes such constraints on conduct as prohibition of treachery and direct attacks on noncombatants. For example, position 4 holds that "This war is wrong because we are directly killing noncombatants." The SCO may object to a particular war because it contravenes *jus ad bellum* and/or *jus in bello*. Either may be a *moral* objection.[17]

In addition, either may be expressed in a conscientious conviction, a "can't help." An agent who appeals to his conscience as a motive for his conduct claims that if he acted against certain moral convictions, he would experience a severe personal sanction: guilt and/or shame and a loss of integrity, wholeness, and unity in the self.[18] John Rohr has argued that SCO is not a " 'can't help,' but is based on arguments that are constitutional, political, and historical—as well as moral or religious."[19] But this experience of conscience, this "can't help," may be the outcome of extended deliberation. It is not limited to intuitionists who hear voices of conscience or to fideists who hear the voice of God. It may result from a complex application of several principles to a set of circumstances. The possibility that the war itself may change, or that the agent's interpretation of the facts may change, in no way alters the moral or conscientious nature of his opposition to the war.

FAIRNESS AND RESPECT FOR PERSONS

If a sharp distinction exists between the grounds of SCO and UCO, such that SCO is political and UCO is moral, then neither the principle of respect for persons nor the principle of fairness would strongly support exemption for SCOs. But if, as I have argued, *both* SCO and UCO may be moral, as well as conscientious, these principles support exemption for SCOs as well as UCOs.

First, at the very least, fairness (or formal justice) requires treating similar cases in a similar way. If both the UCO and the SCO are conscientiously opposed to participation in a war for moral or religious reasons, they seem relevantly similar. To exclude the SCO because of the *content* (such as just war theory) or the *scope* (such as viewing killing in some wars as justified) of his moral principles appears unjust.[20] Neither the content nor the scope of his principles requires that they be labeled as political rather than moral. As an SCO on moral grounds, he seems entitled to treatment similar to the UCO's. To exempt the UCO while forcing the SCO to serve is to put the SCO at an unfair disadvantage. Others have argued that a policy restricting exemption to UCOs discriminates against citizens in the "mainstream" of Jewish, Christian, and humanist thought and practice in the West. It affords legal recognition to a "minority" or "sectarian" position (pacifism) while excluding the "consensus" position (just-war theory).[21]

Second, exclusion of the SCO is a denial of equal respect. If respect for persons requires respect for conscientious objection, it cannot be extended to UCOs and denied to SCOs simply because SCOs appeal to principles of just war rather than pacifism. The difference in content or scope does not constitute a warrant for disrespect to SCOs.

But whether these principles are decisive for public policy will depend in part on prediction and assessment of the consequences of broad and narrow policies. Indeed, the difficulties of *fairly* administering the SCO exemption are alleged to create some of its worst consequences.

CONSEQUENTIALIST ARGUMENTS

In *Gillette* v. *United States* (401 U.S. 437 [1971]) the Supreme Court held that Congress had valid, neutral, secular reasons to exempt the UCO but not the SCO from military service. The government had offered two lines of argument: *(a)* the nature of SCO claims—SCO is basically political—and *(b)* fairness—the administration of SCO would be erratic, uneven, and even unfair. The Court rejected the first line of argument, at least in its narrow sense, emphasizing that SCO may be "rooted in religion and conscience" whatever other judgments are involved. But the Court did hold that the nature of SCO, in conjunction with the fairness argument, may be held to support the statutory restriction to UCO: bad consequences might arise if SCOs were exempted from military service because such an exemption cannot be fairly administered in view of the "uncertain dimensions" and "indeterminate scope" of the claims of SCOs.

> Real dangers . . . might arise if an exemption were made available that in its nature could not be administered fairly and uniformly over the run of relevant fact situations. Should it be thought that those who go to war are chosen unfairly or capriciously, then a mood of bitterness and cynicism might corrode the spirit of public service and the values of willing performance of a citizen's duties that are the very heart of free government. . . . In light of these valid concerns, we conclude that it is supportable for Congress to have decided that the objector to all war—to all killing in war—has a claim that is distinct enough and intense enough to justify special status, while the objector to a particular war does not.[22]

The Court's analysis of policies was undertaken to determine whether Congress had a neutral, secular justification for drawing the lines as it did; in the presence of such a justification, the Court could hold that exclusion of SCOs did not violate either the Establishment Clause or the Free Exercise Clause. But the Court did not imply that Congress "would have acted irrationally or unreasonably had it decided to exempt those who object to particular wars."

Let us consider the debate about consequences more carefully. Although proponents sometimes appeal to the positive consequences of a policy of exempting SCOs, for the most part they try to show that the consequences feared by critics are not that probable or terrible, or that they are outweighed by good consequences or relevant principles. Many of the consequentialist arguments against SCO exemption point to possibilities (what could happen) rather than to probabilities (what probably would happen) if SCO were recognized. And yet public policy regarding SCO should be based on probable positive and negative consequences, not mere possibilities. For example, the report of the majority of the National Advisory Commission on Selective Service, used by the Supreme Court in *Gillette,* held that "legal recognition of selective pacifism *could* open the doors to a general theory of selective disobedience to law, which *could* quickly tear down the fabric of government" and *"could* be disruptive to the morale and effectiveness of the Armed Forces."[23] We need to determine the probability of such consequences as well as to assess them.

Selective disobedience to law. At least two important responses are possible to the claim that legal exemption of SCOs could lead to selective disobedience to law. First, if this wedge argument holds for SCO, it also holds for UCO. Whether the request for an exemption from a law is absolute or selective has no bearing on "selective disobedience to law." Consider opposition to the payment of a particular tax, the example used by the National Advisory Commission. Many UCOs also oppose the payment of taxes that support the military system, and they, as well as some objectors to the war in Vietnam, refused to pay part of their income taxes and the telephone tax surcharge.

Second, this wedge argument holds for neither SCO nor UCO. There are important dissimilarities between the legal recognition of SCO (and UCO) and "selective disobedience to law." In the one case, the government accepts certain reasons for exemption from legal duties; in the other, individuals or groups disobey established legal requirements. And it is not clear why legal recognition of certain reasons for exemption from military service would contribute to disobedience. Indeed, legal recognition of SCO would reduce the number of criminal acts in one area by decriminalizing acts of refusing to participate in a particular war. SCOs would not have to go underground or into exile. In addition, without their "examples" of disobedience, disobedience to law might decline.

Perhaps opponents of SCO do not really fear "selective disobedience to law." They may instead believe that if society recognized the SCO's claim to exemption from military service, it would be hard-pressed to deny other conscientious claims for exemption, for example, from particular taxes. But several distinctions are relevant. One is between service and obedience or subjection. In the range of positive duties that the state might impose, a few are clear examples of service (e.g., jury duty and military service). Individuals selected for these duties are the law's instruments; they carry out the law. Some have contended that refusal of service is not a nullification of the law, although disobedience might be.[24] Thus the government need not treat conscientious refusals of service and conscientious disobedience in the same way.

Finally, the nature of the service, the kinds of action required, may also be important. The society could hold that killing in war is such a distinctive and special kind of action that conscientious scruples to its performance should be respected whether they are universal or selective.

Numbers. One widespread fear is that exemption of SCOs would allow a de facto referendum by which large numbers of citizens who are eligible for a draft could thwart a national policy arrived at democratically. While this fear should not be ignored or dismissed, it may not be determinative. Several points need attention.

First, in contrast to some supporters of SCO, I do not think it is possible to generalize from Britian's lack of serious difficulty with its policy of exempting SCOs, particularly because it was under siege during World War II and fighting for its survival against an enemy widely perceived to be evil.[25] All the British example shows is that exemption of SCOs is sometimes feasible.

Second, the number of SCOs is unpredictable because it depends on the particular war; the number of UCOs is relatively stable and predictable. If the number of SCOs is large because the war is considered by many to be unjust, or because the government cannot make its case stronger, then perhaps the war needs reconsideration.

Third, if, however, the state faces an emergency (a situation of necessity), it may justifiably draft *both* UCOs and SCOs, but it should not distinguish between them if my analysis of the nature of both claims is sound. Instead of denying exemptions for both types of COs, or preferring the UCO over the SCO, a better (in part because fairer) procedure would limit the number of exemptions for conscience, determining by means of a lottery who would be exempted and who would be forced to serve or face criminal penalties. This procedure would also be a fairer way to reduce numbers than by restoring the traditional religious requirement.[26] Of course the number would need to be set in a nonarbitrary and noncapricious way.

Morale and effectiveness of the armed forces. The National Advisory Commission contended that "a legal recognition of selective pacifism could be disruptive to the morale and effectiveness of the Armed Forces."[27] How does the Commission's report support this contention? First, it holds that "a determination of the justness or unjustness of any war could *only* be made within the context of that war itself" (emphasis added). This implies the necessity of waiting until one is an actual participant before one can appraise one's participation. But there is no reason why the SCO cannot make a judgment about *jus ad bellum* and *jus in bello* apart from involvement in that war.

Second, the report somehow supposes that a legal recognition of SCO *requires* that each citizen and soldier determine whether he deems a particular war to be just or unjust. Allegedly this policy would force "upon the individual the necessity" of making that decision and put "a burden heretofore unknown on the man in uniform and even on the brink of combat." But in fact the SCO provision would *permit* individuals to make this determination; it would not *require* them to do so. And even now individual soldiers can be held accountable for "crimes of war," their actions against the "laws of war" (such as killing innocent people), but not for participation in an "unjust" war. Thus, it is not clear why the SCO provision would have "disastrous" results for the individual soldier, his unit, and "the entire military tradition."[28]

It is possible that the morale of the armed forces would suffer if large numbers of persons eligible for the draft or already drafted claimed to be SCOs. It is hard to fight a war that one's fellow citizens oppose as unjust. But little evidence supports the claim that this difficulty would be increased by the exemption of SCOs, even though more people could avoid military service. Indeed, exemption of SCOs could provide a pressure valve and reduce societal protest against an unpopular war.

The most likely source of a negative effect on the morale and effectiveness of the armed forces was emphasized by the Supreme Court: the draftee's sense of unfairness in the distribution of the burdens of military service.[29] A draftee might have moral reservations about a particular war but feel bound by the results of the democratic process to endure service. His own resolve, however, might be weakened if he perceived that the burdens of service were distributed in an erratic and unfair way. And, the Court continued, erratic and unfair distribution could be expected in view of the "indeterminate scope" of SCO. Thus, the Court held, Congress had good reasons (though it would not have acted "irrationally or unreasonably" if it had exempted SCOs) to decide "that the objector to all war—to all killing in war—has a claim that is distinct enough and intense enough to justify special status, while the objector to a particular war does not."

It is difficult to predict with assurance what might occur under a policy of exemption for SCOs. But in view of the important principles involved, the government ought to seek ways to distribute burdens of service equitably while respecting CO, both universal and selective. If a fair administrative procedure cannot be developed, and if the country reaches a state of emergency, universal conscription could, of course, be justified.

Positive consequences of SCO. Some proponents of SCO appeal not only to the principles of respect for persons and fairness and attempt to rebut the consequentialist arguments against SCO; they also appeal to the positive effects of excusing SCOs from military service. One such argument is that legal recognition of SCO would elevate "the level of moral discourse on the uses of force" in the society.[30] Presumably people would reflect on the criteria of justice of and in war. Although few people would dispute the importance of elevating the level of moral discourse about war, such a consequence would have little weight by itself; it is not a very probable result of exemption of SCOs, and it can be sought in other ways. Furthermore, it is more plausible to hold that a policy of recognizing SCOs would not be feasible without an elevation of the society's moral discourse. This elevation is a presupposition rather than a probable consequence of the recognition of SCOs. Without it some of the consequences that opponents fear may indeed occur.

Another argument also focuses on moral education. It holds that principles or rules such as "Never kill in war" are

> almost sure to lead to error through oversimplification; while principles of a more limited scope, while also uncertain, have a far better chance of approximating the truth, if there is one. We do well, therefore, to credit the conscientious man with limited principles, rather than to discredit him because his principles are limited.[31]

This, according to Carl Cohen, is a matter not only of justice, but of wisdom. This argument is risky, however, because it introduces the question of truth and falsity into the determination of whether COs should be excused from social duties. The SCO should be exempted not because his reasons are more likely to be true (because more limited or qualified), but because the principles of respect for persons and fairness support such a policy. (I will return to the question of truth and falsity in the final section.)

In summary, while the positive consequences sometimes adduced for excusing SCOs from military service are tenuous, other arguments are more compelling. First, the principle of respect for persons supports recognition of the conscience of the selective objector as much as of the universal objector. Second, because the UCO and the SCO are relevantly similar in their conscientiousness, it is unfair to excuse the UCO without also excusing the SCO. Both arguments hinge on the nature of the SCO's judgment and reasons. Just as with universal objection, selective objection may be based on religious and moral principles and may be genuinely conscientious. Although the SCO's opposition is more complex and is based, in part, on the facts of a particular war, it is not necessarily political. Finally, most of the negative consequences anticipated by critics of exemption of SCOs from military service are not very probable, and the critics' claims often rest on conceptual confusions. When conjoined with an analysis of the nature of SCO claims, the principles of respect for persons and fairness support governmental efforts to develop a mechanism to obviate the difficulties of administering the SCO provision in a fair and equitable way. But if such efforts fail and serious problems develop for the armed forces, or if the nation faces an emergency in war, the government may be forced to override the claims of COs.

Pragmatic considerations (especially the hopelessness of making an adequate soldier out of the CO) apply to both the UCO and the SCO. Forced military participation of the objector probably would be detrimental to the war effort, and many would choose jail or exile rather than military service, as during the war in Vietnam. Few opponents of SCO ever deal explicitly with this consideration, either (a) because they believe that the negative consequences for the war and for the society of exempting SCOs would outweigh the negative consequences of not exempting them, or (b) because they believe that SCOs are at best political objectors and at worst slackers, whom the threat of imprisonment for noncompliance will make into adequate combatants. I tried to answer (a) in this section and (b) in the discussion of the nature of SCO claims, but I will also touch on (b) in the next section.

Conscientiousness and Sincerity

At least in this century, the third criterion of CO has been conscientiousness. Determination of conscientiousness, or of sincerity in claiming conscientiousness, is easier, of course, if the other two traditional criteria are employed: pacifism, and religious training and belief. Indeed, pacifism and a narrow interpretation of religious training and belief can provide objective tests of CO. Because I have proposed eliminating both of these criteria, determination of conscientiousness hinges on subjective considerations. The task is not to determine the truth or falsity of the beliefs in question, but only to determine that they are truly and deeply held.

Even the "erroneous conscience," based on moral or religious beliefs, merits protection. After all, from the standpoint of the government, UCO represents an "erroneous conscience." An "erroneous conscience" may be mistaken in its moral or religious principles or its interpretation of the factual situation to which it applies its principles. And it may be useful to try to distinguish the factual and moral errors of UCO or SCO, perhaps in order to deny an exemption to the CO whose position presupposes mistakes about factual matters. For example, a SCO may be mistaken in his belief that his country is systematically killing innocent civilians. Even if some factual mistakes may in principle disqualify a CO's position, it is not easy or often even possible to disentangle a position's factual and ethical components. Finally, the primary consideration in conscientiousness is not the truth or falsity of the moral belief (e.g., "I believe that this war is wrong because . . ."), but its sincerity.

Whether a CO policy that emphasizes such subjective considerations can be administered evenly and fairly is, as we have seen, a very important consideration in its adoption. Sorting out the genuine and spurious claims of CO will be a difficult administrative task. In this section, I will not make proposals about procedures (e.g., local boards, appeals boards, and judicial review), which also need careful attention. Instead I will make a few observations about tests of sincerity of CO claims.

Why not accept the potential CO at his word? Why not accept without question his claim to be a CO on moral, ethical, or religious grounds? A major reason is that exemption from military service because of conscience imposes greater burdens on others, some of whom have to serve in the CO's place and to bear greater risks of injury and death. Thus, it is important to have some tests of sincerity because COs gain, or are thought to gain, some advantage over others in not being required to be combatants in military service. And the principle of respect for persons does not require respect for the insincere conscience.

Earlier I contended that, because of the principles of fairness and respect for persons, the government should bear the burden of proof that the class of COs should not be exempted from military service. Nevertheless, the individual who claims to be a member of that class of COs should bear the burden of proof that he really holds the convictions in question and that he holds them deeply and intensely. He should bear the burden of proof because he may be presumed to have an interest in avoiding the risks of injury and death in military service. Sincerity is a threshold question to be answered by the objector, but his burden of proof should not be heavy. He should not have to establish his sincerity beyond a reasonable doubt; to establish that the preponderance of the evidence is on his side should be sufficient.

Requests for exemption from military service can have complex motivations. For example, a person may want both to avoid the risks of injury and death and to avoid participation in what he believes to be immoral killing. But then the question is, how can we determine whether conscientious objection on moral, ethical, or religious grounds is primary or dominant in an objector's motives for requesting exemption from military service? What is the weight or significance of his motive of conscience vis-à-vis his other motives? For example, we might wonder whether his conscience is necessary or sufficient for his opposition to participation in a war. As C.D. Broad has suggested, an objector's conscience may be (a) necessary and sufficient, (b) necessary but not sufficient, (c) sufficient but not necessary, or (d) neither necessary nor sufficient for his opposition to participation in war.[32] Objectors in the last category should not qualify for exemption because conscience does not play a significant role in their action; but objectors in the first category should qualify because, whatever their other motives, they would not have objected to participation if their conscience had not been involved, and their conscience would have driven them to opposition even if other motives (such as fear) had been absent.

But (b) and (c), perhaps the most common, are the most difficult. Suppose conscience is necessary but not sufficient. Both conscience and fear are motives, but neither is strong enough to drive the individual to seek an exemption, while both together are strong enough. Is this conscientious objection? Or suppose that conscience is sufficient but not necessary. In such a case, conscience by itself is strong enough to lead the agent to request an exemption, but fear is also strong enough. Where conscience is sufficient but not necessary, exemption is warranted, but whether exemption is warranted for the person whose conscience is necessary but not sufficient would depend on its centrality and strength in his claim.

Even apart from self-deception and intentional deception of others, a person can rarely be sure that his action is conscientious, as C. D. Broad has insisted, because to determine the necessity and sufficiency of certain motives a person has to ask what he *would do* if certain actual motives such as fear *were* absent. We cannot know the answer to that question with any certainty even when we examine our own conduct, much less the conduct of others. For this reason, Broad argued against the British exemption of COs in World War II and, in another context, contended that the death penalty ought to be applied to COs.[33] Such a penalty would presumably provide a clear and definite test of sincerity. Others have suggested imprisonment, or a severe tax, or even confiscation of the CO's property.[34] Such proposals may help us distinguish those who would have only some "pinpricks" of conscience if they served in the military from those "whose consciences, spurred by deeply held moral, ethical, or religious beliefs, would give them no rest or peace if they allowed themselves to become a part of an instrument of war."[35] But these proposals go too far: it is unfair to impose such hard choices on conscience when they can be avoided. Furthermore, society loses the service that the CO can provide in other ways. Alternative service not only (partially) satisfies the principle of fairness, it also provides one test of sincerity by reducing (though not eliminating) the advantages that the CO might gain.

In addition to such obvious tests as demeanor and credibility, one major test of sincerity is *consistency*. Its application is, of course, easier in the case of the UCO than in the case of the SCO, at least in part because the pacifist's commitments often entail a way of life—a vocation—that reflects his outlook. But even for the UCO certain popular questions are irrelevant to his conscientious objection to participation in war: "what would you do if your grandmother were attacked?" The courts have indicated that such hypothetical questions are irrelevant because they presuppose that pacifism (as objection to participation in war in any form) entails opposition to killing in all settings. For example, a person can be a UCO and still support abortion, euthanasia, and killing in self-defense in some circumstances.[36] Nevertheless, some questions can be useful in determining consistency, such as questions about different wars. Yet consistency cannot be so defined as to rule out "Damascus Road conversions." And, projected into the future, it cannot require absolute certainty about unchangeability.

Most tests focus on the authority, power, or strength of the convictions for the registrant, but some also focus on the *process* by which the convictions were formed. For example, the traditional requirement of "religious training and belief" was usually interpreted to include both "training and belief," not "training *or* belief." Nevertheless, the Court tended to concentrate on "belief," not "training." After *Welsh,* however, a memorandum from the Director of the Selective Service held that to

> find that a registrant's moral and ethical beliefs are against participation in war in any form and are held with the strength of traditional religious convictions, the local board should consider the *nature and history of the process by which he acquired such beliefs.* The registrant must demonstrate that his ethical or moral convictions were gained through training, study, contemplation, or other activity, comparable in rigor and dedication to the processes by which traditional religious convictions are formulated [emphasis added].[37]

Of course, this is one way to hold on to and to interpret the exclusion of a "merely personal moral code." At the same time, the Director of Selective Service indicated that CO claimants should have consulted "wise men." The danger is that the process of conscience-formation will be interpreted in categories that are excessively rationalistic and academic and that favor more articulate and educated applicants.[38]

In conclusion, because of the principles of respect for persons and fairness, as well as practical realities, exemption of some COs is morally appropriate and perhaps even morally (though not constitutionally) mandatory. Such principles also indicate that the scope of the CO exemption should be broad. It should include moral and ethical as well as religious objectors, and selective as well as universal objectors. A major part of my argument established that SCOs may be conscientiously opposed to participation in a particular war on moral, ethical, or religious grounds. Their position and its grounds are not necessarily or merely political. Furthermore, the possible or probable negative consequences of exempting SCOs from military service have been exaggerated. It is possible to devise mechanisms to avoid some of these consequences, and in view of the importance of the principles involved, such mechanisms should be sought, in particular to determine the sincerity of claims of conscientious objection.

Notes

1. See the editorial "How Conscientious Is an Objection?" *Washington Post,* 14 July 1970, Sec. A, p. 14: "An all-volunteer army would obviate the need to judge individual claims of conscience." Others saw conscription as "an impossible choice between conscience and justice" (Michael Walzer, *Obligations* [Cambridge: Harvard University Press, 1970], p. 144).

2. See the discussion of these principles and others in Tom L. Beauchamp and James F. Childress, *Principles of Biomedical Ethics* (New York: Oxford University Press, 1979).

3. *Annals of Congress: The Debates and Proceedings in the United States,* Vol. I (1789), p. 434; reprinted in *Conscience in America: A Documentary History of Conscientious Objection in America, 1757–1967,* edited by Lillian Schlissel (New York: E. P. Dutton, 1968), p. 47.

4. *United States* v. *Macintosh,* 283 U.S. 605 (1931) and *Hamilton* v. *Regents of University of California,* 293 U.S. 245 (1934).

5. *Sherbert* v. *Verner,* 374 U.S. 398 (1963).

6. For the history of conscientious objection in the United States, see Schlissel, ed., *Conscience in America;* and *Conscientious Objection,* Selective Service System Special Monograph No. 11, 2 vols. (Washington, D.C.: Government Printing Office, 1950). See also Richard K. MacMaster with Samuel L. Horst and Robert F. Ulle, *Conscience in Crisis: Mennonites and Other Peace Churches in America, 1739–1789,* Studies in Anabaptist and Mennonite History XX (Scottdale, Pa.: Herald Press, 1979).

7. See *United States* v. *Macintosh,* 283 U.S. 605, 633 (1931) (Hughes, C. J., dissenting); and *Gillette* v. *United States,* 401 U.S. 437 (1971).

8. See Schlissel, ed., *Conscience in America,* pp. 133, 165, and 171 (the last for the president's 1918 Executive Order which recognized "religious or other conscientious scruples").

9. See, for example, the broad definition of the Second Circuit in *United States* v. *Kauten,* 133 F.2d 703 (C.A. 2d Cir. 1943); and the narrow interpretation of the Ninth Circuit in *Berman* v. *United States,* 156 F.2d 377 (1946).

10. *Clay* v. *United States,* 403 U.S. 698 (1971). This case is discussed in Richard J. Regan, S.J., *Private Conscience and Public Law: The American Experience* (New York: Fordham University Press, 1972), p. 31, a valuable study of legal decisions regarding conscience.

11. *Gillette* upheld the constitutionality of the restriction of the exemption to UCOs.

12. Report of the National Advisory Commission on Selective Service, *In Pursuit of Equity: Who Serves When Not All Serve?* (Washington, D.C.: Government Printing Office, 1967), p. 50, hereinafter cited as *In Pursuit of Equity.* See also John A. Rohr, *Prophets Without Honor: Public Policy and the Selective Conscientious Objector* (Nashville: Abingdon Press, 1971).

13. Rohr, *Prophets Without Honor,* pp. 143, 148.

14. Alan Gewirth, "Reasons and Conscience: The Claims of the Selective Conscientious Objector," in *Philosophy, Morality, and International Affairs,* edited by Virginia Held, Sidney Morgenbesser, and Thomas Nagel (New York: Oxford University Press, 1974), p. 99.

15. For a discussion of these formal and material criteria and philosophers who have proposed and opposed them, see James F. Childress, "The Identification of Ethical Principles," *Journal of Religious Ethics* 5 (Spring 1977): 39-68.

16. For a good discussion of the varieties of religious pacifism, see John H. Yoder, *Nevertheless: The Varieties of Religious Pacifism* (Scottdale, Pa.: Herald Press, 1972).

17. Commentators tend to concentrate almost exclusively on one or the other. For example, Alan Gewirth and Carl Cohen tend to characterize SCO in terms of *jus ad bellum,* while Paul Ramsey comes close to advocating recognition only of SCOs who appeal to the standards of *jus in bello* articulated in legal codes, treaties, etc. See Gewirth, "Reasons and Conscience," pp. 89–117; Cohen, "Conscientious Objection," *Ethics* 78 (July 1968): 269-79; and Ramsey, "Selective Conscientious Objection: Warrants and Reservations," in *A Conflict of Loyalties: The Case for Selective Conscientious Objection,* edited by James Finn (New York: Pegasus, 1968), pp. 31-77. For another argument for recognition of objection to war crimes as defined by international law, see Donald A. Peppers, "War Crimes and Induction: A Case for Selective Nonconscientious Objection," *Philosophy & Public Affairs* 3 (Winter 1974): 129-66.

18. For a fuller discussion of these points, see James F. Childress, "Appeals to Conscience," *Ethics* 89, no. 4 (July 1979): 315-35.

19. Rohr, *Prophets Without Honor,* p. 22; see also *In Pursuit of Equity,* p. 50.

20. See Cohen, "Conscientious Objection," pp. 271, 277.

21. *In Pursuit of Equity,* pp. 48-49. This argument, offered by some members of the Commission, was rejected by the majority.

22. Some of the concerns about fairness mentioned by the Supreme Court would also

apply to pacifists. The administration of a provision for UCOs might favor the "more articulate, better educated, or better counseled," and might favor claims more closely connected to conventional religiosity.

23. *In Pursuit of Equity,* p. 50. See the criticisms by Quentin L. Quade, "Selective Conscientious Objection and Political Obligation," in Finn, ed., *A Conflict of Loyalties,* pp. 195-218.

24. See Walzer, *Obligations,* p. 136.

25. For generalizations from the British experience, see Gewirth, "Reasons and Conscience," p. 98; and David Malament, "Selective Conscientious Objection and the *Gillette* Decision," *Philosophy & Public Affairs* 1 (Summer 1972): 383-85. Contrast Quade, "Selective Conscientious Objection and Political Obligation," p. 205. For a discussion of the British experience, see Dennis Hayes, *Challenge of Conscience: The Story of the Conscientious Objectors of 1939–1949* (London: George Allen & Unwin, 1949).

26. Ralph Potter contends that we should restore the religious criterion in order to accommodate SCOs, because he believes that we cannot eliminate the religious requirement and the pacifist requirement at the same time. See Potter, "Conscientious Objection to Particular Wars," in *Religion and the Public Order,* edited by Donald A. Giannella (Ithaca, N.Y.: Cornell University Press, 1968); see also Ramsey, "Selective Conscientious Objection," pp. 31-77. For a defense of a lottery, see John Mansfield, "Conscientious Objection— 1964 Term," in *Religion and the Public Order,* edited by Donald A. Giannella (Chicago: University of Chicago Press, 1966), p. 46, n. 59, and p. 73.

27. *In Pursuit of Equity,* p. 50.

28. Ibid.

29. See *Gillette.*

30. *In Pursuit of Equity,* p. 49 (a minority position). See also Potter, "Conscientious Objection to Particular Wars."

31. Cohen, "Conscientious Objection," p. 277.

32. C. D. Broad, "Conscience and Conscientious Action," in *Moral Concepts,* edited by Joel Feinberg (New York: Oxford University Press, 1970), pp. 74-79.

33. C. D. Broad, "Ought We To Fight for Our Country in the Next War?" *Ethics and the History of Philosophy* (London: Routledge & Kegan Paul, 1952), pp. 232-43.

34. An internal Selective Service report, prepared by Donald Guritz, but not accepted by Selective Service. See George C. Wilson, "Conscientious Objector Problem Seen," *Washington Post,* 27 March 1980, Sec. A, p. 13.

35. *Welsh v. United States,* 398 U.S. 340 (1970).

36. See *Goldstein v. Middendorf,* 535 F. 2d 1339 (1976).

37. The same point and much of the same language appears in the 1980 proposed revisions in the Selective Service Regulations. See Federal Register 44, no. 234 (3 December 1980): 80138.

38. In this discussion, I have concentrated on whether and which COs should be exempted from military service. I have not included conscientious refusals to register for a draft. For an examination of some ethical issues in the government's response to draft evasion, desertion, civil disobedience, and war crimes after they have occurred, see James F. Childress, "The Amnesty Argument," *Cross Currents* 23 (Fall 1973): 310-28.

Part IV
Race and Gender

10

Changing Organizational Structure and the Future of Race Relations in the Military

JOHN SIBLEY BUTLER and

MALCOLM D. HOLMES

Our fundamental thesis is that the changes in military organization adopted for the All-Volunteer Force (AVF) should alter specific patterns of race relations.* Our approach is grounded in a tradition of military organization theory which examines the convergence/divergence of civil-military structures. As background, a brief historical overview is presented to show how the military evolved into a racially egalitarian institution. The second section reviews theories that attempt to explain the rapid transformation of race relations within the military from systematic inequality to the movement toward equality. The final section presents and explores our major thesis. Since most of the racial issues relate to the Army, the analysis applies to the other services with qualifications.

Historical Overview

Historical research reveals that blacks have participated in all American military conflicts.[1] Although this is true, early participation took place within a non-egalitarian military. Table 10.1 presents a classification of major military conflicts by the estimated number of blacks who served, according to whether or not official policy was egalitarian, and according to the absence or presence of a recruit-retain-and-reject policy. The latter refers to the historical pattern of recruiting blacks during times of conflict (usually because of manpower shortages or other forced circumstances), retaining them through the conflict, and systematically rejecting them at the end of the conflict.

About 5,000 blacks participated in the Revolutionary War. Blacks were not, however, originally viewed as a source of manpower. When the war began

*The authors would like to thank Charles C. Moskos, Jr., Robert K. Fullinwider, and Peter G. Brown for comments on an earlier draft of this chapter.

Table 10.1 Major Military Conflicts by Estimated Black Participation, Racial Policy, and Recruit-Retain-and-Reject Experience

Conflict	Estimated black participation	Official policy	RRR experience
Revolutionary War	5,000	nonegalitarian	Yes
Civil War	180,000	nonegalitarian	Yes
World War I	200,000	nonegalitarian	Yes
World War II	900,000	nonegalitarian	Yes
Korea	219,128	toward egalitarianism	No
Vietnam	350,000	egalitarian	No

Note: Racial policy is defined in terms of official segregation vs. official integration (egalitarian vs. nonegalitarian).

General Washington issued four orders forbidding black (both slave and free) enlistment in the Continental Army. Early in the war the British forces offered blacks their freedom if they would join the side of the Crown. When news of the British plans reached General Washington, he issued an order authorizing recruiting officers to accept free blacks.[2]

Although some ranks were integrated, the typical black soldier was a private with no official identity. He was carried on rolls as "a negro man" or a "negro not known." The seven brigades of Washington's army averaged 54 blacks each. Some colonies, such as Rhode Island and Massachusetts, raised all-black battalions. The defeat of the British forces removed the necessity of black troops. They were not allowed to remain in the military (or militia), and slaves who had been promised freedom were sent back to bondage. The ideology of war and the promises of freedom were replaced by the conservatism of the constitutional era.

The Revolutionary War set the systematic pattern of recruit-retain-and-reject that would continue until Korea. When northern blacks during the Civil War responded with enthusiasm to the first call for volunteers, the Secretary of War said, "This department has no intention to call into service any colored soldiers."[3] But because of manpower shortages in 1863, War Department Order G0143 allowed black participation for the first time in the Civil War. The nearly 180,000 blacks who fought on the Union side were formed into separate units designated "United Coloured Troops." These segregated units fought in pivotal battles, won fourteen congressional medals of honor, and played major roles in the liberation of Petersburg and Richmond.[4] During the war the black casualty rate was 40 percent higher than the white rate. All blacks were paid $7.00 a month, while the lowest-ranking white received $13.00 a month.[5] When the war concluded, the War Department took the position that the enlistment of blacks was a "peculiarity of the volunteer service." Blacks were not authorized for utilization for postwar regular service.[6]

When the United States declared war on Germany in World War I, black Americans responded to President Wilson's call to "make the world safe for democracy." At the same time Frank Park, a representative from Georgia, introduced a bill to make it unlawful to appoint blacks to the rank of either noncommissioned or commissioned officer.[7] More than 200,000 blacks served in segregated units, 150,000 in back-breaking stevedore battalions.

More than 900,000 blacks served in the segregated Army of World War II. In the aftermath of that conflict the military began to feel the pressure of civil rights groups for egalitarian policies. During this time, also, the Army began to reexamine the use of black troops. In 1944, Lieutenant General Alvin C. Gillem was charged with establishing a board to study how blacks could be used more efficiently within the Army's traditional segregated structure. The board interviewed approximately 320 white officers, the majority of whom were dead-set against integration. The report, known as the "Gillem Report," was issued in 1945 and concluded that small black units together with larger white units were superior to large black units in all respects—combat readiness, morale, discipline. The report also suggested that the Army should limit black recruitment to 10 percent of the total Army and continue policies of segregation. Five years later, another Army board headed by Lieutenant General S. J. Chamberlin produced essentially the same conclusions.

In 1948 nonegalitarianism received a major blow when President Truman signed Executive Order 9981:

> It is the declared policy of the President of the United States that there shall be equality of treatment and opportunity for all persons in the Armed Forces. This policy shall be put into effect as rapidly as possible, having due regard to the time required to effectuate any necessary changes without impairing efficiency or morale.[8]

Truman also established the Fahy Committee to pursue equal treatment for military personnel. With the guidance of this committee, the Army eliminated the quota system in 1950 and was integrating some training camps when the Korean conflict broke out.

Korea proved to be the final stand for official unequal treatment of blacks in the military. The need for combat soldiers was high. This resulted in bringing blacks out of support units, where they had been concentrated for the most part during the two world wars, and assigning them to combat. Integrated units in combat performed well. As integration in Korea became standard, it was noted that the fighting abilities of blacks and whites did not differ.[9] By May 1951, 20 percent of black soldiers in the Eighth Army were in integrated units, three-fifths of them in combat arms. Thus, although Executive Order 9981 marked the beginning of the demise of sanctioned institutional racism in the Army, the Korean conflict served as the major catalyst.

The aftermath of Korea (sometimes referred to as the Cold War period, lasting from 1952–1965) witnessed a continuing improvement in race relations in the Army up through the middle of the Vietnam War. Although the fighting in Vietnam produced heightened racial conflict, the official policy of the military remained egalitarian. All blacks served in integrated units.

One can see that historically blacks in the military, like those in the civilian sector, were not given the complete opportunity to participate within its institutions on an egalitarian basis. But unlike the civilian sector, the change to egalitarian principles within the military happened almost overnight.

The Integration of the Present-Day Army

In 1966 Charles C. Moskos, Jr., the foremost scholar on race in the military, wrote:

> For the man newly entering the armed forces, it is hard to conceive that the military was one of America's most segregated institutions less than two decades ago. For today color barriers at the formal level are absent through-

out the military establishment. Equal treatment regardless of race is official policy in such non-duty facilities as swimming pools, chapels, barbershops, post exchanges, movie theaters and other more formal aspects of the military.[10]

Moreover, noted Moskos, white personnel are often commanded by black superiors, a situation rarely realized in the civilian sector.

One of the ironies of democracy is that the military, a conservative institution which genuflects before tradition, found itself at the forefront of the experiment of racial equality. Military institutions were the first to take significant steps toward equal treatment of personnel, officially ending de jure segregation more than three years in advance of the landmark 1954 school desegregation decision. For millions of Americans this institution served as their first, and perhaps only, truly integrated/egalitarian experience. Scholars have noted that the post-Korean military, which was directly preceded by a systematically segregated organization, is an excellent example of the ability of different racial groups to adjust to egalitarian practices, although with some strain.[11]

Although racial inequalities have always existed within military institutions (e.g., in assignments, military justice, and promotions),[12] research on black soldiers began to show that they perceived military institutions as more egalitarian than civilian life.[13] This research, along with actual observations of military vs. civilian life,[14] led to a general proposition: when the military is compared to the civilian sector vis-à-vis race relations, the former stands in a much more favorable light.

In order to account for this general proposition, and the rapid transformation in race relations within the military, scholars emphasize the unique characteristics of this organization: its separation from the larger society, and its strict hierarchical structure.

Although the military is a corporate part of society and its social structure, it is a separate entity.[15] Of course, people who enter and adjust to the military bring with them patterns of responses derived from the civilian setting. Thus the very structure of the military and patterns of human association within it will, to some considerable degree, reflect the social patterns and structure of the civil society. Nevertheless, the net effect of becoming a part of military organizations is to be separated from one's former society both physically and, to a certain extent, psychologically. Since the military is self-contained, all the individual's primary needs are met within it. This separation is consciously promoted by command, especially in the case of new recruits, who are restricted to the base during basic training, thus speeding the process of assimilation which finally results in the recruit's finding the satisfaction of his needs within the military organization.

Once the policy of total racial integration and equality had been established, the discontinuity of military institutions with the civilian sector aided the rapid transformation of race relations. Another factor interacting strongly with the separateness of military society to produce the transformation was the bureaucratic hierarchical power structure of the military organization. This structure is highly crystalized. As Max Weber noted, hierarchical organizations are characterized by a distribution of authority coming from a central place in an integrated series of offices. Each office is endowed with specific powers and privileges. Unique to military organizations is the presidential nexus. The president of the country occupies the dual office of chief executive and commander-in-chief of the military. Under him the military hierarchy is composed of clearly identifiable grade classes. Rank is indicated by bars and stripes, which furnish visible symbols so that all will know how to act toward one another. This system is the backbone of military etiquette, and one is subject to penalty if customs (wearing insignia, etc.) are violated. Because of this highly stratified command structure, once the order for integration and movement toward egalitarianism was given by the president, things moved rapidly. Put differently, because of the hierarchical structure, which is patterned on the relationships of command and obedience, decisions regarding race did not have to accommodate the personal desires of military personnel.

The effects of such a structure also had implications for race relations. Given that the military base traditionally was separate from the civilian environment, black and white troops were forced, despite their racial orientations, to live together. This contact eventually produced changes in the perceptions of black and white troops toward each other. But it must be remembered that this contact was originally forced because of the "total institutional" aspect of military organizations.[16] Individuals were regimented, and there was essentially no separation of workplace and residence.

That forced contact produced a reduction in negative racial attitudes is explained by the "contact hypothesis": under certain conditions, the more contact individuals have with other racial groups, the less their negative racial attitudes. The conditions under which the hypothesis is expected to be true are *(a)* when an authority positively sanctions interaction, *(b)* when there are commonly shared goals, *(c)* when the contact is by equal-status individuals, and *(d)* when interaction between individuals is cooperative, prolonged, and covers a wide range of activities. The military provides a setting for all these conditions. Therefore, since the publication of *The American Soldier,* the contact hypothesis has stayed intact within military institutions.[17] The more that black and white soldiers come into contact with each other, the less their negative racial attitudes.

Another consequence of the traditional military structure was that soldiers worked among themselves, separate from civilians and the racial attitudes of the civilian sector. We can hypothesize, then, that the behavior of soldiers comes to resemble the racial (and class) separatism of the larger society as they are removed from the military environment.[18]

A further consequence of the traditional military was its resulting class/race mixture. This mixture was not representative of the larger society, but as one toured military bases, there was always a probability that one could converse with soldiers from all segments of American society, especially in the enlisted ranks.

Thus the special structure of the military service was a major causal factor in the rapid movement of that institution toward egalitarian reality. When compared to the civilian sector, the military was perceived by black soldiers as standing in a more favorable light. Indeed, we can say without reservation that it is the only institution where blacks are present, albeit not always at their civilian percentage, in all levels of the rank structure. In corporate or other institutions within the civilian sector, few (and sometimes no) blacks are located in higher ranks. Blacks tend to be located in lower management jobs and at the very bottom of civilian occupations.

We now turn to an examination of the future of race relations within the military, given the changes in military structure accompanying the All-Volunteer Force.

Race Relations Within the Future AVF

Our contention is that the organizational changes associated with the all-volunteer format should have implications for race relations. Such a proposal is not predicated on approval or disapproval of the All-Volunteer Force. Our goal is simply to analyze the changing nature of military service and its impact on race relations. Our hypothesis is that race relation patterns within the military will become more like those of the civilian sector because of changes associated with the organizational format of the AVF. Put differently, just as factors associated with the pre-AVF caused race relations to diverge from the civilian sector, the organizational outcome of the volunteer military will cause military and civilian race relations to converge. The traditional hierarchical structure of the military should mitigate, but not stop, this convergence.

The convergence/divergence theme has been the theoretical backbone of civil-military relations theory. This theoretical tradition examines the extent to which organizational similarities and differences occur in military and civilian structures. Measures of convergence/divergence include the differences in required skills for those in civilian and military occupations. The general conclusion from this theoretical tradition is that some structures of the military will be divergent (i.e., combat units) and others will be convergent (i.e., technical, administrative, and clerical units).

The military under the all-volunteer format has come to exhibit more closely the ethos of civilian organizations. Although differences between military and civilian organizations will always be apparent, the policy guiding the development of the present force clearly converges with civilian structures on one of the most important variables of civilian organizational life: the development of market-place standards for the recruitment and retention of members. Moskos has characterized this convergence as moving from an *institutional* to an *occupational* format.[19] The former sort of organization is legitimated by norms and values which transcend individual self-interest in favor of a presumed higher good (e.g., service to country). In contrast, individuals who work in occupations place priority on their own self-interest rather than on that of the employing organization. Under the institutional format, members receive compensation in noncash form such as uniforms, food, and housing, which is consistent with the emphasis on uniform organizational experience and goals.[20] An occupation receives its legitimation from marketplace standards, defined as prevailing monetary rewards for equivalent competencies. Under this format the cash-nexus variable creates a negotiation between individual and organizational needs. Reflecting the primacy of the occupational format, the military has moved toward eliminating or making significant changes in such traditional institutional services as subsidies for commissaries, health care for dependents, and the retirement system.

The developing trends associated with the organizational format of the military that will have implications for race relations are *(a)* the "relaxation" of traditional military norms and the increased use of civilian employees, *(b)* the separation of residence and workplace, and *(c)* the changing structure of the racial composition of the enlisted ranks.[21]

TRADITION, RELAXATION, AND CIVILIAN EMPLOYEES

There is no doubt that the advent of the AVF relaxed traditional military norms. Soldiers are no longer required to "make reveille"; "kitchen police" has become less important; the relationship between lower-ranking personnel and noncommissioned officers has been altered. This is true for the basic training experience as well as the everyday experience of troops. Under the traditional military, the NCO was the strong backbone and enforcer of military tradition. With the advent of military contracts and new guidelines for the treatment of lower-ranking enlistees, the authority of NCOs has weakened. Under the occupational format, people who "work for" (volunteer for) the military expect to be treated like employees of any other organization.

The emphasis on group solidarity and commitment is being replaced by a new stress on individuality and a concentration on "me." Coupled with this, civilians are performing many tasks once performed by military personnel. From 1964 to 1978, contract civilians rose from 5.4 percent to 14.5 percent of total defense manpower.[22] How, then, will this metamorphosis in military institutions affect race relations?

We theorize that the more nontraditional military service becomes, the more race relations in the military will resemble those of the larger society. If contract civilians bring with them the racial norms of the larger society, the racial norms of the military should also become transformed. Civilian employees' attitudes are less subject to modification through the structure of the military.

In our recent work, we have examined perceived discrimination within all four services.[23] While previous studies have shown that most blacks perceive some discrimination in the armed forces, these perceptions vary by branch of service. Our data show that black Marines perceive considerably less discrimination, on the average, than those in other services. We attribute this finding to the influence of the Marine Corps' traditional structure on group solidarity and commitment to the Corps. The service that has largely retained the traditional institutional format is seen in the best light by its black members.

On the other hand, in the services where the rigidity of authoritarian command-and-obedience structures has been loosened and traditional communal values downplayed, perceptions of discrimination are higher. This is consistent with the hypothesis that as services become more like civilian organizations, black perceptions of discrimination in the military and in society will become more similar.

SEPARATION OF RESIDENCE AND WORKPLACE

One feature of the traditional military was the contiguity of workplace and residence. This was particularly the case for the enlisted population, who typically shared common living and dining quarters on the base where they worked. In terms of race relations, such an arrangement produced increased informal contact, which often produced better race relations in the workplace. There was also a higher probability that friendships between the races would receive additional "cement." Even between 1965 and 1969, when racial confrontations broke out on military bases, informal networks produced by the common residence softened the incidents' impact.

As informal contact between the races decreases, the effects accounted for by the contact hypothesis should weaken.[24] It has been estimated that currently almost 30 percent of enlistees live off-base in stateside installations. This percentage increases when married enlistees are included. If off-base residence of military personnel follows the racial patterns of housing in America, one can expect that black and white troops will live in separate sectors of the community. Thus blacks and whites within the military increasingly will associate with each other only in the workplace. The racial patterns that characterize civilian life are likely, as a consequence, to emerge within military institutions. Although this phenomenon has always been present within military institutions to some degree, it should become stronger in the future. Thus the demise of communal military housing should have consequences for race relations.

CHANGING RACIAL COMPOSITION

No trend associated with the AVF has received as much attention as the changing racial make-up of the enlisted ranks of the Army. When the Gates Commission (the President's Commission on an All-Volunteer Armed Force) recommended the all-volunteer service, it projected that blacks would not be overrepresented. It was argued that the percentage of blacks in the military would not exceed the percentage of blacks in American society. Between 1972 and 1980, however, the percentage of blacks at the enlisted level in the Army increased from 17.4 percent to 32.2 percent. A lively and important discussion on black composition in the enlisted ranks has resulted.[25] Initial discussion revolved around the legitimacy of questioning the changing racial proportions. Then the discussion turned to specific questions, such as the relationship between racial composition and combat casualties, strategies to curb the growing percentage of blacks, and the general question of service and citizenship.[26] In a real sense, the high percentage of blacks at the enlisted level is an accomplished fact. The question becomes, "What are the implications of this trend for race relations within the organization?" Our research has led us to inquire about the impact of race on organizational commitment and about the changing racial climate which has seen the ascendency of the concept of reverse discrimination.

A clear relationship exists between racial issues and commitment within American society. (By commitment we mean the process linking a person to an occupation, neighborhood, or organization.) We know, for instance, that as the black percentage of a neighborhood increases, white commitment to that neighborhood decreases.[27] The same is true for white commitment to schools as the percentage of blacks increases.[28] The racial make-up of occupations has similarly altered over the years. Given this reality of American life, we must ask similar questions about military institutions. Are military and civilian life likely to converge on the question of race and commitment? Will whites show less commitment to the enlisted ranks because of their racial make-up?

In a previous study, we empirically examined a closely related question. We concentrated on the relationship between commitment intentions to the enlisted ranks of the Army and separatist racial attitudes.[29] We took account of such factors as job satisfaction, education, time in the service, and race. This allowed us to examine the impact of separatist racial attitudes on commitment intentions while controlling for variables that have been excellent predictors of commitment intentions in civilian organizations.[30] The results indicated no conclusive evidence that as a group whites might be "pushed" from the enlisted ranks by their reluctance to participate in a well-integrated organization, If, however, whites hold high separatist racist attitudes (e.g., that blacks and whites should not work together or live together), they are less likely to show commitment intentions to the enlisted ranks. Thus degrees of separatist attitudes may interact strongly with race in allowing one to predict commitment.

If we assume a convergence between the civilian and the military vis-à-vis racial patterns of commitment, we might expect the following developments within the enlisted ranks. Whites may gravitate toward military occupations that have a low percentage of blacks. Thus the organization retains them, but only in specific occupations. This would be similar to the situation where whites attend integrated schools but are in segregated classes. Even today percentages of blacks are high in certain military occupations (e.g., the infantry) and low in other occupations. The volunteerism of the AVF should be expected to create racial trends which resemble those of the civilian sector. We should always keep in mind that race relations were actually "forced" before the all-volunteer military came into effect. Stated another way, the two races did not get to choose their military experience.

Clearly, one of the most significant issues of race relations to emerge within the civilian sector over the last ten years revolves around the concept of "reverse discrimination." Growing out of the affirmative action era, reverse discrimination has been defined as majority group members treating other majority group members unequally so that minority members can receive rewards. Such a conceptualization is designed to capture the fact that minority group members are less likely to be in positions which affect the rewards of the majority. Thus the concept stresses the differential treatment of majority group members on behalf of minority (or female) members.

One of the interesting changes in the rank structure of the enlisted ranks is the increasing percentage of blacks in the higher grades (see Table 10.2). Between 1964 and 1980, the percentage of blacks in grade E9 increased from 3.3 percent to 19 percent. For grade E7, for the same period, the increase was from 7.9 percent to 25.2 percent. Given that blacks will have authority over whites to a significant degree within the enlisted grades, we must ask to what extent issues of reverse discrimination will evolve. Unlike the civilian sector, where the concept refers to majority members discriminating against other majority members on behalf of a minority, in military institutions blacks have significant authority over whites.

Perceptions of reverse discrimination have been examined in military communities.[31] The findings are that perceptions of *discrimination* are the most important element in black evaluations of the racial climate in their communities, and that, likewise, perceptions of *reverse discrimination* are the most important element in white evaluations of the racial climate. The notion of reverse discrimination creates a "rhetorical balance" with the notion of discrimination within military communities. Despite clear evidence that blacks are promoted at a slower pace than whites and experience other inequalities in the military, white perceptions to the contrary nevertheless must be dealt with. Issues of reverse discrimination may become more salient in the years ahead within the AVF.

Table 10.2 Black Enlisted Participation in the Army by Grade and Selected Years

Grade	1964	1972	1980
E-9 (sergeant major)	3.3	8.6	19.0
E-8 (master sergeant)	5.8	14.4	22.9
E-7 (sergeant first class)	7.9	19.9	25.2
E-6 (staff sergeant)	12.2	23.9	22.8
E-5 (sergeant)	14.8	16.9	28.6
E-4 (specialist 4)	12.5	14.1	33.7
E-3 (private 1st class)	11.9	16.7	37.8
E-2 (private)	11.6	18.5	37.9
E-1 (private)	6.4	18.4	37.3
Total enlisted	11.8	17.4	32.2

Source: Charles C. Moskos, Jr., "Symposium: Race and the U.S. Military," *Armed Forces and Society* 6 (Summer 1980): 586–613.

Conclusion

In this chapter's examination of the impact of the changing structure of military organization on race relations, we noted that the structure of military organizations accounted for the rapid change in race relations in the military. We examined trends associated with the All-Volunteer Force and showed how these trends work to weaken the traditional military structures which produced the improvement in racial equality. Our research suggests that as the military becomes more like civilian organizations in structure and ethos, race relations in the services will come more closely to resemble those in society at large. Future investigations will show whether this convergence actually takes place.

Notes

1. A number of excellent books examine black participation in the military. For example, see Benjamin Quarles, *The Negro in the American Revolution* (Chapel Hill: University of North Carolina Press, 1961); Earl Brown, *The Negro and the War* (New York: Harper, 1942).

2. "Black Soldier, A Compendium," Department of Defense USAEUR Race Relations School (1972), p. 1.

3. Richard J. Stillman, *Integration of the Negro in the U.S. Armed Forces* (New York: Frederick Praeger, 1968), p. 9.

4. Dwight W. Hoover, *Understanding Negro History* (Chicago: Quadrangle Books, 1968), p. 270.

5. John Hope Franklin, *From Slavery to Freedom: A History of Negro Americans* (New York: Alfred A. Knopf, 1964).

6. John D. Foner, *The United States Soldier: Between Two Wars* (New York: Humanities Press, 1970), p. 127.

7. Stokely Carmichael and Charles Hamilton, *Black Power: The Politics of Liberation in America* (New York: Vintage Books, 1967), p. 26.

8. John P. Davis, *The Negro Reference Book* (Englewood Cliffs, N.J.: Prentice-Hall, 1971).

9. Charles C. Moskos, Jr., *The American Enlisted Man* (New York: Russell Sage Foundation, 1971).

10. Charles C. Moskos, Jr., "Racial Integration in the Armed Forces," *American Journal of Sociology* 72 (1966): 132-48.

11. Moskos, *The American Enlisted Man.*

12. For example, see John Sibley Butler, "Inequality in the Military: An Examination of Promotion Rates for Black and White Enlisted Men," *American Sociological Review* 41 (October 1976): 807-18; and Butler, "Assessing Black Enlisted Participation in the Army," in *Readings in Institutional Discrimination* (Ft. Leavenworth, Kansas: U.S. Army Command and General Staff College, 1976).

13. For example, see William J. Brink and Louis Harris, *Black and White: A Study of U.S. Racial Attitudes Today* (New York: Simon & Schuster, 1967); and Dale K. Brown and Peter G. Nordlie, *Changes in Black and White Perceptions of the Army's Race Relations/Equal Opportunity Program: 1972–1974* (McLean, Va.: Human Sciences Research, 1975).

14. Moskos, *The American Enlisted Man.*

15. This discussion of military organization is based on the following works: G. Dearborn Spindler, "The Military—A Systematic Analysis," *Social Forces* 27 (1948): 83-88; Felton D. Freeman, "The Army as a Social Structure," *Social Forces* 27 (1948): 78-83; and Moskos, "Racial Integration in the Armed Forces."

16. Erving Goffman, *Asylums* (New York: Doubleday, 1961).

17. Samuel Stouffer, Arthur A. Lumsdaine, Marion H. Lumsdaine, Robin Williams, Jr., M. Brewster Smith, Irving L. Janis, Shirley Star, and Leonard Cottrell, Jr., *The American Soldier,* 2 vols. (Princeton, N.J.: Princeton University Press, 1949); John Sibley Butler and Kenneth L. Wilson, "The American Soldier Revisited: Race and the Military," *Social Science Quarterly* 59 (December 1978): 451-67.

18. Moskos, *The American Enlisted Man,* p. 122.

19. Charles C. Moskos, Jr., "From Institution to Occupation," *Armed Forces and Society* 4 (Fall 1977): 41-50; and "The Enlisted Ranks in the All-Volunteer Army," in *The All-Volunteer Force and American Society,* edited by J. B. Keeley (Charlottesville: University of Virginia Press, 1978).

20. See also David Segal, J. D. Blair, and S. Stephens, "Convergence, Isomorphism and Interdependence at the Civil-Military Interface," *Journal of Political and Military Sociology* 2: 157-72.

21. The specification of trends appears in Moskos, "From Institution to Occupation."

22. Ibid.

23. John Sibley Butler and Malcolm D. Holmes, "Perceived Discrimination and the Military Experience," *Journal of Political and Military Sociology* 9 (Spring 1981): 17-30.

24. Butler and Wilson, "The American Soldier Revisited."

25. See, e.g., Morris Janowitz and Charles C. Moskos, Jr., "Racial Composition in the All-Volunteer Force," *Armed Forces and Society* 1 (Fall 1974): 109-23; and Alvin J. Schexnider and John Sibley Butler, "Race and the All-Volunteer System," *Armed Forces and Society* 2 (May 1976): 431-32.

26. See "Race in the United States Military, a Symposium," *Armed Forces and Society* 6 (Summer 1980): 586-613.

27. R. Farley and K. E. Taeuber, "Population Trends and Residential Segregation since 1960," *Science* (March 1968): 953-56.

28. Michael W. Giles, Everett Cataldo, and Douglas S. Gatlin, "White Flight and Percent Black: The Tipping Point Reexamined," *Social Science Quarterly* 56 (1975): 85-92.

29. John Sibley Butler and Malcolm D. Holmes, "Role Commitment and Racial Factors: Implications for Organizational Research," paper delivered at the 1980 meetings of the American Sociological Association, New York.

30. Commitment intention was operationalized by the following question: "At the present time do you intend to stay in the service for a total of 20 years? (1) Yes (2) No."

31. John Sibley Butler and Kenneth L. Wilson, "Reverse Discrimination, Discrimination and Racism," paper presented at the 1981 meetings of the American Sociological Association.

11

The All-Volunteer Force and Racial Balance

ROBERT K. FULLINWIDER

When the creation of an all-volunteer military was being debated between 1967 and 1971, one frequent objection was that the All-Volunteer Force (AVF) would become largely black.* Such a fear underlay the opposition to the AVF by a group of liberals led by Senator Edward Kennedy, for example.[1] The Gates Commission, whose 1970 report to the president laid the basis for the transition to an all-volunteer system, explicitly addressed this objection. It argued that the racial composition of the armed forces would be little affected by substituting an all-volunteer policy for a mixed policy of conscription and volunteering. In June 1969, the armed forces were 9.5 percent black. By 1980, predicted the Gates Commission, the military would be 14.9 percent black under an all-volunteer system or 14.1 percent black under a mixed system.[2] In fact, by March 1982, the military was 19.9 percent black. This figure, however, obscures the uneven distribution of blacks through the different services and through the ranks. The enlisted ranks of the military are 22.1 percent black (30.4 percent minority), and the principal contributor to this figure is the Army, whose enlisted ranks are 32.9 percent black (41.1 percent minority).[3] This growth in black enlisted personnel in the Army has led to concern and at least one prediction that soon the junior enlisted ranks of the Army would be 45 percent black and the career enlisted force 65 percent black.[4]

Is this racial imbalance in the Army significant? Can there be too many blacks in the military? Two sorts of concerns have been expressed about racial overparticipation in the Army. The first sort wonders whether the racial imbalance may produce harmful or undesirable conditions or states of affairs. It is contended that a disproportionately large population of black enlisted persons could (a) produce a "tipping" effect, causing white volunteering to drop off, (b) exacerbate racial tensions inside the Army, (c) erode public support for the military, (d) raise doubts among both allies and enemies about the reliability of American combat arms, especially with respect to combat in Third World countries, and (e) exacerbate racial tensions in society, especially in case of combat where black casualties ranging from 30 to 40 percent might prove politically indigestible and precipitate domestic crisis.[5]

*I am grateful to Peter French for his trenchant comments on an earlier version of this essay.

The second sort of concern is more directly moral. The all-volunteer policy is charged by many with being exploitive, unjust, and undemocratic because it recruits disproportionate numbers of blacks and minorities. In the words of one congressman,

> the fatal defect in the All-Volunteer Force is that time has proven the current system is not a "volunteer" system at all. The AVF has proven an unjust and inequitable system of economic and racial conscription. A system in which those who have the least in our society are offered the opportunity to be trained to risk all in exchange for the very thing they have been denied by the society they are asked to defend, a job.[6]

To the charge that the AVF is unjust is often added the charge that it ill serves the principles of democracy. One distinguished student of the military contends that "the racial composition of the military raises the question of representativeness and political legitimacy of institutions that are at the core of democratic society."[7] And James Fallows answers the question of representation in this manner: "The military has been an avenue of opportunity for many young blacks. They may well be first-class fighting men. They *do not* represent the nation."[8]

In the following sections I will examine these concerns about the racial imbalance in the military and try to set the criticisms of the AVF in some better perspective, so that their presuppositions and commitments can better be seen.

The AVF as Exploitive

Charges that the all-volunteer policy is "forcing the responsibility for the manning of our military services . . . on the underprivileged segments of our society in totally disproportionate numbers,"[9] that it is "not a volunteer system at all,"[10] and that it amounts to "conscription through poverty"[11] are made with great frequency and doubtless strike a receptive chord in most listeners. But the charges are difficult to evaluate, once we get beyond a gut response, because the critics never make clear what concepts of voluntariness and coercion or what standards of justice stand behind their complaints.

The animus of the critics toward the all-volunteer policy is fueled by what I will call the "dominant image"—a vision of a black youth, without wealth or decent economic prospects, who chooses military service as a way out of poverty. Does this dominant image define a straightforwardly unjust situation? Does the all-volunteer system exploit this youth? What can we say about his choice of military service?

When it is claimed that the all-volunteer system is "not volunteer at all" and that it is "conscription through poverty," the idea being offered is that the black youth is "forced by circumstances" into the military; he has no other options. But these claims are too blunt; they blur important distinctions. On the account of voluntariness given by Aristotle in the *Nichomachean Ethics,* a voluntary action is compatible with "having no choice." Aristotle gives the example of a sea captain who jettisons his cargo in a storm to save the ship. His action was voluntary, although he was in a circumstance where he could do "nothing else."[12] This point about voluntariness comports with our ordinary understanding. Suppose my doctor tells me that I will certainly die soon from a malady unless I have a simple surgical procedure, which offers a 95 percent probability of my living out my natural life. I have no option about what to do, yet my election of surgery is voluntary. Strictly speaking, of course, I do have a choice. What we mean by saying I "have no choice" is that the one option (surgery) is so much better than any other that no reasonable person would choose otherwise.

Likewise, in the dominant image, the black youth has, strictly speaking, the option to endure unemployment or the option to serve in the military. If the first option cor stitutes economic desperation, then the second option seems the only rational course.[13] The black youth, then, acts voluntarily; he chooses the better of a limited set of options. What is wrong is that he is in a situation where military service is his *best* option.

But why is this state of affairs unjust in itself? If we viewed military service as a considerable good, we would view as a happy circumstance that it was available to the young black as an option to unemployment. Why would we find the state of affairs a matter of special complaint? We doubtless believe, of course, that it is desirable for a young person to have many options, not just a few. But if nevertheless he has few in fact, we would not be discomfited if what he faced was a choice between unemployment and a scholarship to a good university.[14] This fact points up, I believe, a basic assumption underlying the criticism of the all-volunteer policy as objectionably exploitive. The assumption is that military service is not a good choice to have, that military service is in itself undesirable (unpleasant, dangerous, perhaps demeaning and morally corrupting).[15] Perhaps some individuals may have a taste for the subordination and regimentation of military life, but for those who do not, such a life ought not to be endured as an alternative to economic deprivation.

If we are to view the situation of the black youth in the dominant image as unjust and the all-volunteer system as exploitive, we must view his life in the enlisted ranks as a net bad. His distaste for military life is not fully compensated. Service is a lesser evil than unemployment, which is why he chooses it; still, it must be a *net* evil. But suppose the services offered a starting salary of $25,000 a year. It would then be difficult to maintain that it was unjust that the black youth's alternative was military service, and harder still to view the all-volunteer policy as exploiting him. Exploitation, at least as we commonly think of it, occurs when we take advantage of someone's weakness to get something from him at less than he otherwise would have demanded. If we took advantage of the black youth's unemployment to offer him military service at wages, say, that were 60 percent of the average wages for unskilled, entry-level civilian jobs, our action *would* seem exploitive. But offering the youth military service at $25,000 does not seem exploitive because we assume he would see the opportunity as a positively desirable one and would choose it in any case.

Or we might view exploitation as taking advantage of someone's weakness to get something from him for less than we *ought* to pay him.[16] Even in this sense most of us will not consider the black youth exploited, since we are likely to consider a starting salary of $25,000 as at least above the threshold of what we *ought* to pay for the rigors and risks of military service.[17]

Since its inception in 1973, the AVF has (with the exception of the period FY 1977–1980) offered a starting compensation package roughly equivalent to civilian entry-level wages for unskilled youth. The critic, in order to sustain his charge of exploitation, must believe that the unemployed black youth would view military life as distinctly less desirable than comparable civilian alternatives. Otherwise the youth, while not having a civilian job as an actual option, would on entering service be electing what was in his eyes an economic equivalent. Or the critic must view military life as objectively less desirable than comparable civilian tasks; otherwise, he would have no reason to believe the military *ought* to pay more than the going wage for civilian work.

Why not think of military work and civilian work as roughly equivalent? Many military jobs are tedious, dirty, and unpleasant, but so are many of the civilian jobs young people must enter. Membership in the military subjects the individual to great regimentation and control.[18] Work in civilian industries, however, may be only marginally less regimenting. A soldier's life is potentially dangerous; in war he may be called upon to fight and die. But the chance for any soldier of there being a war and of his being killed in it may be no greater than of death as a construction worker, a coal miner, a chemical worker, a policeman, or a fire-fighter.

And to balance the bads of military service, are there not goods as well—the goods of service to country, opportunity for self-mastery, and the pride that comes from team accomplishment?

The crux of the matter, I believe, is this. If there were a war, large numbers of blacks might die, and in any case they would die out of proportion to their share of the general population.[19] This prospect deeply troubles the critics of the AVF. Moreover, their concern is not especially eased if they are convinced that black soldiers took full account of and properly discounted the risks when they appraised the economic value of military service and elected to join.[20] For, aside from the collective impact of such deaths on the black community (a matter which I will discuss further below), another feature of military service puts the risks endured by blacks in a special light. When a black chooses a risky civilian job, he takes the risk for himself and his private ends. But when he accepts the risks of military service, he takes the risks for the entire population. Military service is for *our* defense, to serve *our* ends, to protect *our* interests. Once again, it appears that America—as it always has—casts the black into a servile role.

The image of blacks pulling the dirty load for white America is compelling for many and surely must evoke at least a question from all of us about the racial imbalance in the Army. But whether we are to conclude that the image signifies some deeper reality depends upon what we think of military life and what we think it takes to compensate for its rigors and risks. The critics must make very much plainer why there is *no* level of compensation which makes acceptable the risks that blacks assume in military service, or why, if there is a level, the all-volunteer policy fails to achieve it.

Causes of Black Volunteering

In the previous section we discussed whether the dominant image—the image of the black youth whose only way out of joblessness was military service—depicted a situation of exploitation and injustice. If it does, then the critic has a standard against which to measure the all-volunteer system. But a negative evaluation of the AVF won't be derivable from the standard unless we further suppose the dominant image reflects reality. Does it? I imagine many think it is beyond question that the dominant image describes the predominant situation.

Do young blacks view the military as employer of last resort? Do they typically see service as an onerous and unrewarding burden that they would avoid but for their desperation? Do black recruits take no satisfaction from their service? How many black recruits are unemployed at the time they enter service? We can't give definitive answers to these questions because there are insufficient data. But what data there are suggest a mixed picture.

Throughout the 1970s black youth faced a higher unemployment rate than white youth, and even when employed their earnings decreased throughout the decade relative to the earnings of white youth.[21] This means that military pay was increasingly attractive to blacks whether they were employed or not. Undoubtedly, many young blacks turned to the services as a refuge from unemployment.

Nevertheless, for the hard-core unemployed—black high school drop-outs scoring in Categories IV or V—the services proved generally unwelcoming.[22] Except for a period between 1977 and 1980, when recruiting was difficult, the military has tried to exclude those applicants who do not have a high school diploma and especially those who also score poorly on the mental category tests. (The services are precluded by law from admitting those who score in Category V.)

In the primary target group for military recruiting—high school graduates scoring in Categories I–III—unemployment among black youths is still high, but often the prospect facing such a black considering service is not unemployment but unattractive employment alternatives—work at the car wash, at McDonalds, and so on. All he finds available are low-paying jobs that neither lead to advancement nor enable him to finance, out of his earnings, training that will lead to improved opportunities. Against this background, a three-year stint in the Army may look preferable. Even if served in the infantry, which offers little training in skills with civilian carry-over, his tour of service can allow him to amass a college fund of $15,000 while he earns an income competitive with civilian alternatives.[23]

In a 1976 survey, "Monitoring the Future: A Continuing Study of the Lifestyles and Values of Youth," by the Institute for Social Research at the University of Michigan, high school seniors were asked if they expected definitely or probably to serve in the military. Forty-three percent of black males answered yes, twice the percentage of white males. This finding conforms, of course, to the dominant image, but the following answer does not. To the question "suppose you could do what you'd like and nothing stood in your way," 31 percent of the black males said they would choose military service.[24] This answer, to the extent it reflects a general attitude among black youth, challenges the notion that the military is viewed as "employer of last resort."

Military service is often viewed by blacks as a positive alternative to civilian employment. This is accounted for in part by the fact that the AVF has tried to make military life relatively more attractive and economically competitive. It is also accounted for in large measure by the fact that military participation has enjoyed a high prestige in the black community. (This positive attitude is due to a very considerable extent to the perception among blacks that the military is the fairest and least discriminatory institution in America.)[25] Thus, a combination of factors works to generate a high rate of volunteering for military service among blacks.

Regardless of whether or not we think the dominant image needs modifying, the fact that the racial imbalance in the Army is caused by high rates of black *volunteering* is extremely significant in our evaluation of policy. Moreover, the *growth* in rates of black volunteering began in the 1960s, not with the advent of the all-volunteer policy.

We must not forget that we had between 1948 and 1973 a *mixed* conscription/ volunteer system. Throughout the draft period, there were always substantial numbers of "true" volunteers—individuals who were neither conscripts nor "draft-induced" volunteers. By the late 1960s the rate of black "true volunteering" was twice the rate of white.[26] It is more than likely that, had the draft been retained in 1972, the racial profile of the military would have differed little from what it is today.

In 1962, 9 percent of all enlisted accessions were black; in 1972, 15 percent; in 1982, 19 percent. During this same period, the proportion of black high school graduates and blacks in Categories I–III grew considerably. Likewise, the rates at which blacks passed physical entrance exams increased markedly.[27] What has increased since 1962 is not the rate at which eligible blacks volunteer, but the rate at which blacks are eligible to volunteer.

With the reductions in force that followed the end of the Vietnam engagement, draft calls would have been low in the 1970s and a high proportion of accessions would have been volunteers. This fact, combined with the high unemployment among black youth, the positive image of military service in the black community, and the increased eligibility of blacks for enlistment, would have meant the continued growth of black volunteering after 1972 independent of any decision about the all-volunteer policy. If the draft had been retained, it is not unlikely that by the end of the 1970s the Army's enlisted ranks would have approached 30 percent black, no matter what.

If we cannot tolerate the current black-white profile in the enlisted ranks of the Army, then our animus should be directed not toward the all-volunteer system but toward volunteering, period!

This brings us to a consideration of options. What can be done about the racial balance in the Army? By this point in the discussion it should be apparent that calls for a simple return to a draft won't do. To meet its authorized end-strength in 1981, the Army needed to take 136,800 into its enlisted ranks; 137,900 volunteers were in fact enlisted.[28] Thus, if the draft had been reinstated, the draft call for the Army would have been zero. As Kenneth Coffey shows in Chapter 4 of this volume, a draft will make a difference in the racial make-up of the Army only if draft calls are substantial. Under current circumstances, there appear to be only two ways to achieve racial balance. The first is to *increase* the size of the military until needed accessions far outstrip the pool of volunteers; the shortfall would be made up through a representative draft. Given the current supply of volunteers, this strategy could well require a massive growth beyond any imaginable military justification and with severe increases in cost. Moreover, if our concern is that the AVF is "exploiting" blacks because blacks have few economic options, the drawback to this first proposal is that it in no way diminishes the number of blacks who enter military service; it just adds to their number enough whites to make the overall racial profile more balanced.

The second way to change the racial balance is to *suppress* black volunteering. (The resulting decrease in black volunteering would be made up by increased white volunteering or through a draft.) We might try to suppress black volunteering by suppressing volunteering in general. For example, first-term pay could be reduced to $200 a month, or the minimum initial volunteer enlistment could be increased to five years. Such moves might reduce white volunteering even more than black volunteering. Alternatively, we could manipulate standards to selectively diminish black accessions. In any case, volunteering would have to be cut severely if a draft were to be used to make up shortfalls with the expectation that it would have a significant impact on racial balance.

Whatever device we elect to suppress black volunteering, the net effect would be to deny to many young blacks the military opportunities they otherwise would choose. If our concern about the racial make-up of the military has been prompted by a fear that young blacks are being exploited, this outcome seems unattractive. The young blacks whom we worried were being "victimized" by the all-volunteer policy because they were "forced" to choose between service and unemployment are now reduced to one choice: unemployment. Under those circumstances, they might be unable to appreciate how they had been relieved of victimization! If our concern about the all-volunteer policy is injustice to individual blacks who are "coerced" into service, then a more reasonable solution may be one which improves the conditions of their service rather than one which worsens further their limited set of opportunities.[29]

A Representative Military

Independent of whether it is a sign of "exploitation," the racial imbalance in the military has been taken by some to be an affront to the principles of democracy. I quoted James Fallows earlier as saying of the disproportionate number of blacks in the military: "They do not represent the nation." He goes on to claim that the racial imbalance "has destructive spiritual effects in a nation based on the democratic creed."[30] In what sense does democracy require a "representative" military? In what way does the military fail to represent America?

To represent means to "stand for." I think we want the military to "stand for" us in the sense that we want it peopled by soldiers and sailors who understand and value the ends which the military must serve. Our services represent us, in this moral sense, when their members share and endorse the same basic commitments and values reflected in the population at large.[31] An "alien" force would be composed of individuals prepared to fight for pay but who do not understand, value, or subscribe to the goals and aspirations of the culture they protect and the political institutions they defend.

If the racial imbalance in the military signifies a failure of representation in this moral sense, it must be because the black recruits are "aliens." We would have to hold that they are so "alienated" from American society that they choose service *solely* as an economic choice and that they neither possess nor ought to possess any commitment to American institutions and values. If, on the other hand, we view the current military as composed of American youth with American values, what further interest could we have in "representativeness"? Why should we be concerned that the military *mirror* the social, educational, racial, economic, religious, regional, and other demographic patterns found in society as a whole? Simple demographic representation seems to have no value in itself.[32]

It might be argued that the racial imbalance in the military signifies a failure of moral representation not on the grounds that black youth are less attached to American institutions than white youth, but that they have less reason to be. The argument presupposes that those who have the greatest reason to value American institutions should defend them in greatest proportion.[33] The appeal is less to a principle of democracy than to a principle of fairness. On the other hand, fairness may enter the picture from several directions. Although it may be fair that those who have greatest reason to value American institutions serve in greatest proportion, is it fair to deny service to those who want it? Is it fair to discourage service by those who do in fact greatly value American institutions, although we think that they have every reason not to? Until we are given some greater guidance about how the proffered principle of fair service is to be adjusted to other considerations, including other claims of fairness, we cannot say what exactly it would have us do about the all-volunteer system.

We might not be swayed by any of the foregoing moral indictments of the AVF and yet be concerned about racial representativeness. We could believe there is a connection between such representativeness and political tranquility, or military effectiveness, or the welfare of the black community, or all of these. That is to say, although we might not be moved by the direct moral arguments against racial imbalance, we might be moved by the prudential concerns enumerated in the first part of this chapter. Let us, then, turn our attention to these concerns.

Conclusion

The current level of racial imbalance in the Army has not produced "tipping"; race relations in the military are at least as good as they are outside; public support for the military as an institution has been growing in recent years rather than waning; and no evidence indicates that either America's allies or its enemies have changed their behavior because of the number of blacks in the Army. It is, of course, possible that all of this could change. It is possible, further, that American black soldiers could refuse to fight against certain foes. But this possibility is remote as long as the Army treats blacks in its ranks fairly and without discrimination. If black enlistees feel they have full participation in the Army, this will promote their institutional loyalty. In an Army in which they serve well and are well respected for their service, there should be no special concern over their reliability or effectiveness as soldiers.

Moreover, to the extent that blacks are well represented in all ranks and occupations, the fact that in a war there will be (initially) a high proportion of black casualties may be less inflammatory to the black community as a whole. Even though the rate of black casualties will exceed the ratio of blacks to whites in the general population, it will not exceed the ratio of blacks to whites in the Army. Nevertheless, the fear that black casualty rates of 30–40 percent or more will prove to be politically explosive is not a wildly unreasonable fear. It may be that black leaders and congressmen foresee high black casualties as tolerable if blacks are in the Army of their own accord and are fully integrated in all its specialties and ranks,[34] but I do not believe that anyone can safely predict how the black community would actually react in the event. In the emotional climate aroused by combat deaths, attitudes and feelings are subject to volatile shifts and might suddenly crystalize into adamant opposition to the military action, especially under the stimulation of concentrated and graphic television coverage of a highly telegenic issue. Moreover, the political effects of spontaneous but deep opposition by the black community might carry over into the Army itself, creating instability and threatening morale.

The lasting effects of such opposition by the black community are unpredictable but almost certainly undesirable. Even if such opposition did not arise, the collective impact of concentrated casualties could be directly injurious to the black community, robbing it of future leadership and talent. Just as we might want to take steps to see that extensive casualties are not concentrated on a single geographical community, we might similarly want to take steps to see that extensive casualties are not concentrated on a single cultural or ethnic community. Our concern need not be about the fairness to the community of concentrated casualties, but about the effects on the community's stability and functional health.

Many blacks are wary of expressions of concern about the number of blacks in the Army. They view whites as too easily alarmed by black overparticipation, too quick to see problems when blacks cease to be a small, invisible minority. Black commentators are fearful that any "solution" to the "problem" of black overparticipation will come at the expense of blacks.

In fact, *any* effort to make the Army more racially representative must be at the expense of black enlistments, *unless there is to be growth in force size.* Thus, because almost any scheme for getting a more racially balanced Army must diminish the opportunities for blacks to serve, and because white policymakers may well be disposed to magnify the seriousness of problems arising from black overparticipation, it seems reasonable to set a high threshold of proof that racial

imbalance is a problem. Evidence of the deleterious effects of black overparticipation must be strongly persuasive, if not compelling. Speculative scenarios with
merely some degree of plausibility are insufficient as bases for policy change.

On the other hand, we cannot dismiss out of hand the contention that disproportionately large black participation is, or will become, a problem for blacks as well
as whites, for the Army as well as society. If policy changes to achieve balanced
racial representation are needed, the representational aims should be no more
ambitious than absolutely necessary, and the means for realizing the aims should
be as mild as possible in their adverse impact on potential black recruits.

Notes

1. Lawrence M. Baskir and William A. Strauss, *Chance and Circumstance* (New York:
Vintage Books, 1978), p. 237.

2. *The Report of the President's Commission on an All-Volunteer Armed Force* (the
Gates Commission) (New York: Collier Books/Macmillan Co., 1970), pp. 141, 147.

3. The Marine Corps is 21.5 percent black in its enlisted ranks, the Air Force 16.7
percent, and the Navy 12.2 percent. The percentage of black commissioned officers ranges
from 8.6 percent in the Army to 2.7 percent in the Navy. These figures are from printout
DMDC-3035, "Distribution of Active Duty Forces by Service, Rank, Sex and Ethnic
Group" (Office of the Assistant Secretary of Defense for Manpower, Reserve Affairs, and
Logistics, March 1982).

4. The prediction was made by Congressman Robin Beard of Tennessee. His alarm was
somewhat overdone; he made the prediction for 1980. See *Hearings on Military Posture and
H.R. 1872*, Committee on Armed Services, House of Representatives, 96th Congress, 1st
Sess. 14 February–2 April, 1979, Part 5, p. 182.

5. See Morris Janowitz, "Focus on Blacks in the Military," *Focus*, June 1975, p. 3; and
Charles Moskos, "Symposium: Race in the United States Military," *Armed Forces and
Society* 6 (Summer 1980); 587-94, esp. 589.

6. Congressman John Cavanaugh, *Synergist*, Winter 1980, p. 14; reprinted in *Presidential
Commission on National Service and National Commission on Voluntarism*, Hearing
Before the Subcommittee on Child and Human Development, Committee on Labor and
Human Resources, U.S. Senate, 96th Congress, 2nd Sess., 13 March 1980, p. 432.

7. Janowitz, "Focus," p. 3.

8. James Fallows, "The Draft: Why the Country Needs It," *Atlantic* 245 (April 1980): 79;
reprinted in Jason Berger, ed., *The Military Draft* (The Reference Shelf, vol. 53, no. 4 [New
York: H. W. Wilson Co., 1981]), p. 79 (emphasis added). In *National Defense* (New York:
Random House, 1981), Fallows puts his point this way: "They [the soldiers] are white
country boys, blacks and browns from the cities. Taken one by one, the soldiers in the
volunteer force command an outsider's respect. I could not point to more than a dozen or so
of the roughly 150 soldiers I met who would be obvious examples of the 'quality' problem.
Rather, the issue is one of balance. While the soldiers may be, individually, tough,
humorous, and appealing, as a group they clearly come from outside the mainstream of
American life" (pp. 127-28).

9. General William Westmoreland, interviewed in *U.S. News & World Report* 88 (May
17, 1980); reprinted in Berger, ed., *The Military Draft*, p. 74.

10. Congressman John Cavanaugh; see note 6, above.

11. See Joseph Califano, "Playing the Draft Card," *The Washington Post*, 27 January
1980, B7; and the remarks by Roger Landrum and Harris Wofford, in National Youth
Service, *What's at Stake. Report of a Conference Sponsored by the Committee for the
Study of National Service* (Washington, D.C.: Potomac Institute, 1980), pp. 4, 14.

12. Aristotle, *The Nichomachean Ethics*, Book III, 1110^{a}10–^{b}2.

13. But this "seeming" may be in error. See the discussion by Adrian Piper in Chapter 8,
this volume, of rationality and the circumstances for rational choice of service.

14. We may regret I have a potentially fatal malady, but don't we rejoice that curative
surgery is available?

15. For negative views of military service, see Adrian Piper, Chapter 8, this volume; and Sara Ruddick, "Drafting Women: Pieces of a Puzzle," Chapter 14, this volume.

16. For a discussion of "taking advantage of," see Jules Coleman, Chapter 7, this volume.

17. The idea of *paying* for the rigors and risks of military service is what offends some. The all-volunteer policy, in their view, "makes military service seem like just another job" by emphasizing monetary incentives for enlistment. This corrupts the view of the military as a calling or vocation, to the detriment of the military itself (Fallows, *National Defense*, p. 126). An especially vigorous critic of the AVF along these lines is Charles Moskos. See, e.g., his "Making the All-Volunteer Force Work: A National Service Approach," *Foreign Affairs* 60 (Fall 1981): 17-34.

18. See the emphasis on this aspect of military life by Piper, Chapter 8.

19. But they will likely not die out of proportion to their numbers in the Army. Blacks make up 31.5 percent of combat occupational specialties in the Army and 33.6 percent of divisional strength. Blacks are not distributed evenly throughout divisions, however, and the number of black casualties in battle will depend upon the theater of conflict, the order in which divisions are deployed, and the duration of fighting. If, for example, fighting took place in the Middle East, then principal exposure would be to the 82nd Airborne Division, which is 26 percent black, and the 101st Airborne Division, which is 33.8 percent black. If fighting broke out in Korea, the initial exposure would be to the 2nd Division, which is 41.1 percent black. The divisions deployed in Europe are, in total, a little over 32 percent black. Heaviest black casualties would come from deployment of the stateside 197th Infantry Brigade, which is 51.8 percent black. In the event of a protracted war, black casualties in the Army would tend toward the average, and as reserve units and draftees were deployed, black casualties might well drop below 30 percent. See Martin Binkin and Mark J. Eitelberg with Alvin J. Schexnider and Marvin Smith, *Blacks and the Military* (Washington, D.C.: The Brookings Institution, 1982), pp. 56, 78-80.

20. During peacetime, how should a recruit estimate his chances of dying? Assuming he enlists in the combat arms, he must weigh the odds against the nation going to war during his term and, if it does, the chance he will die in combat. This last chance will vary according to the nature of the conflict: a full-scale war against the Warsaw Pact forces in Europe will be intensely lethal, a Vietnam-type conflict somewhere in the Third World very much less so. During the Vietnam War only about 6 percent of active-duty troops were committed to combat. "Overall, the risk of combat service was so low for Vietnam-era servicemen that life insurance companies did not charge extra premiums for military personnel, except for pilots and others on unusually hazardous missions" (Baskir and Strauss, *Chance and Circumstance*, p. 52).

21. Richard V. L. Cooper, *Military Manpower and the All-Volunteer Force* (Santa Monica, Calif.: The Rand Corporation, 1977), pp. 218-19.

22. For an explanation of mental categories employed to sort prospective enlistees, see Chapters 1 and 2, this volume.

23. The Veterans Educational Assistance Program provides contributory and noncontributory schemes for amassing a college fund.

24. See Jerald G. Bachman, John D. Blair, and David R. Segal, *The All-Volunteer Force: A Study in Ideology in the Military* (Ann Arbor: University of Michigan Press, 1977), pp. 33, 36-37, 38 (Table 2).

25. See John Sibley Butler and Malcolm Holmes, Chapter 10, this volume; and Butler, "Symposium: Race and the United States Military," *Armed Forces and Society* 6 (Summer 1980): 598-99.

26. Gates Commission, p. 145.

27. Ibid.; Cooper, *Military Manpower*, pp. 213 (Table 10-6), 214 (Table 10-7).

28. News Release No. 528-81 (Office of the Assistant Secretary of Defense for Public Affairs), 17 November 1981, p. 4.

29. One may believe that military service is such an objective bad that young blacks are not made worse off by being kept out even where they have no other economic opportunities. See Sara Ruddick, Chapter 14, this volume. On the alternative of improving the conditions of service, see Jules Coleman, Chapter 7, this volume.

30. Fallows, "The Draft," p. 79.

31. See David Segal, Chapter 1, this volume; and Bachman, Blair, and Segal, *The All-Volunteer Force:* "our own view is that the paramount issue in American civil-military relations in the all-volunteer era is the ideological rather than the demographic representativeness of the armed forces" (p. 17).

32. Under a *compulsory selection* system, of course, we will want to be concerned about demographic representativeness, because it will generally be a sign of fairness in the selection procedure. At least this is so if we think that among the eligibles, selection should be more or less random. Random selections recommend themselves as fair when we must distribute to some an unwanted burden, and when no one especially deserves the burden or has a special claim to be free from it. Under a system of *self-selection,* however, where outcomes will reflect the distribution of desire, there is no a priori reason to expect the outcomes to match what would have been achieved in a random selection.

33. See Adrian Piper, Chapter 8, this volume.

34. See Ronald Dellums, "Don't Slam Door to Military," *Focus,* 1975, p. 6.

12

The Manning of the Force and the Structure of Battle: Part 2—Men and Women

DAVID H. MARLOWE

In this chapter I consider the questions of the employment of female troops by the military and the conscription of women. I argue that women should be excluded from offensive ground combat roles, but not from combat roles in the air or at sea, and not from ground combat support and service support roles that may require possible defensive combat operations.

War and Biology

Throughout all of recorded history, war has been a male occupation, a fact that seems to be firmly rooted in the biology of our species. Human beings, like the other primates, are products of an evolutionary process that has taken place within the context of biological and social systems that define divisions of labor and function. Until the Neolithic period and the rise of specialized division of function within communities, male evolution was controlled to a great degree by fighting ability. Women, as bearers and rearers of young and as gatherers of foodstuffs, evolved within what some have called a more domestic and less agonistic framework. Different, rather than identical, selective pressures have operated upon men and women. In response to these pressures, the evolutionary process has defined biologically ordered gender differences that extend beyond those of simple primary and secondary sexual characteristics. Such differences do indeed interact with culture to produce a wide range of behavioral possibilities, competences, and repertoires. The range of possibilities remains constrained, however, by the biological substrate that characterizes each gender. Behavioral possibilities for humans, as for all animals, are an end product of the interaction of organism and environment. No organism is infinitely plastic, and the biological substrate of each defines the limits to which the environment may alter it.

Sexual dimorphism characterizes our species. Women average 86–89 percent of the bulk and volume of males; however, the differences are not those of scale alone, but involve body architecture as well. Muscle mass, upper-shoulder girdle structure, capacity for burst energy output, and a host of other factors all exemplify those differences imposed by the male hunter-fighter template, as opposed to the female nurturer-gatherer one.

Testosterone, the male hormone, is responsible not only for differences in brain structure between male and female mammals, but also has, in most primates, significant relationships to aggressive behavior.[1] While human studies are not conclusive, one recent Swedish study demonstrated a significant relationship between plasma testosterone levels and self-reports of physical and verbal aggression, the changes in testosterone level mainly reflecting responsiveness to provocation and threat.[2] Males also apparently differ from females in their response to external stress or threat, since male adrenaline levels are more readily raised than those of females, a probable advantage in the response to assault and attack.[3] Corinne Hutt has outlined the basic differences between human males and females:

> From infancy to senescence males have a consistently higher basal metabo-
> lism and greater vital capacity, they develop proportionately larger hearts
> and lungs, have a higher concentration of hemoglobin, notably after puberty,
> and have a greater capacity for neutralizing metabolites. . . . Since the male
> body has less fat and more muscle per unit volume, its inertia will be less and
> hence speed of movement greater. Muscular development and efficiency too
> are far superior in boys. Moreover, the greater length and smaller "carrying
> angle" of the male's arm ensures greater velocity and precision in aiming and
> throwing skills. Such differences in physical and physiological features equip
> the male for a more active and strenuous life, the evolutionary advantage of
> which is self-evident.[4]

It is unfortunately necessary to point out that these differences are not differences in the political, social, moral, or human worth of men and women, as is at times mistakenly inferred when such differences are noted. They are differences in capacity, biological design, and ability to perform certain kinds of actions between males and females as populations. While the populations evidence some overlap, the means remain widely divergent. Cultural changes that lead to higher female physical capacities tend to take place among a small group that overlaps the lower levels of normative male ability, while increased physical training of males tends to maintain the same relationships between group means. It is unfortunate that both an androcentric culture and its feminist critics treat such abilities as expressions of inherent value rather than of exoteric biological difference. To say that men and women are biologically different and have differing capacities to perform certain kinds of actions and master certain skills should in no way imply that either men or women are better or worse than each other; only that as populations they are indeed better or worse at doing certain kinds of things. One of these things is fighting, certainly in the forms required in land combat. The male's greater vital capacity, speed, muscle mass, aiming and throwing skills, his greater propensity for aggression, and his more rapid rises in adrenaline make him more fitted for physically intense combat. The issue is neither an ideological nor a political one, although both ideologists and politicians have seized positions in respect to it. The adult human being is the result of a sequence of interactions between fundamental phyletic biology and culture and the social system; each poses limits and introduces possibilities for change, but the fundamental parameters remain the same transculturally, no matter how different cultural conceptions of maleness or femaleness may be.[5]

Combat and Masculinity

The question of women in the services is further complicated by the powerful relationship between "maleness" and the self-percept of the combat group among American soldiers. While undoubtedly a number of women possess physical skills and abilities that do overlap into the normal male distribution, physical competence alone does not demarcate the successful combat soldier or combat group. The combat soldier has historically defined himself in terms of his masculinity.

> It is probable . . . that the young male has a biologically given need to prove himself as a physical individual, and that in the past the hunt and warfare have provided the most common means of such validation.[6]

A widespread relationship links male sexual validation and validation in war, combat, and aggression. Until recent times, many human groups' definition of the male as sexually mature and eligible for marriage and intercourse was contingent upon his having proven himself as a warrior in battle. For example, the Afar and Issa peoples of the Horn of Africa required the slaying of an enemy in combat before a male was eligible for marriage.[7] Among the Somali the demand for blood vengeance following assault is underlined by threats to withdraw sexual access and taunts about sexual unworthiness made by the women of the group to goad the men into combat.[8] The examples can be multiplied for human groups on every continent and at almost every level of societal complexity. Combat in all human groups is and has been an almost exclusively male preserve, and organized warfare has been, in a sense, the expression of the male-bonded groups that constitute armies and their analogues. As Lionel Tiger put it, "Males are prone to bond, male bonds are prone to aggress, and therefore aggression is a predictable feature of human groups of males."[9] The military group is, in this sense, a reflection of the myriad other adolescent and youthful male groups that in most cultures traditionally play either a formal or informal role in the process of maturation and the acquisition of full male sexual and social identity. These institutions range from the *poro* and other age-graded groups in African societies, including circumcision and warrior-age class groups, to the men's societies and men's houses of the Circum-Pacific and other specialized groups. Horizontally bonded, exclusive groups of young males have also characterized the social developmental process in Western Europe. These range from groupings of apprentices and students to those of young professionals, all based upon highly elaborated and complex percepts and images of male brotherhood.[10] The United States has since its founding been marked by many like groups in the form of gangs, militias, volunteer fire companies, and other organizations that partake of elaborate sets of constructs of masculinity and male behavior. Most have included agonistic behavior as an aspect of their raison d'être.[11] These male-bonding and agonistic behaviors are remarkably close to many of those exhibited by the infra-human primates, as is the predilection for more highly aggressive play on the part of the human male as compared to the female. To carry the illustration further, not only is the capacity to carry out aggression—i.e., to fight—related to the nature of the male bond, but a great part of the bond's sustaining power lies in the language of male sexual identity. As one sociologist stated, just after World War II:

> In the purely masculine surroundings of the Army, the values associated with the ideal of virility play a determining role in molding the soldier's image of himself and in creating his inner tensions and the channels for their release.[12]

The soldier's world is characterized by a stereotypical masculinity. His language is profane, his professed sexuality crude and direct; his maleness is his armor, the measure of his competence, capability, and confidence in himself.

The self-image of strength is evidenced in both the manner of expression and the expressions used. That the expressions may be more clever, more picturesque, or more obscene than the civilian equivalents is not relevant here; it is only relevant that to the soldier they are stronger ways of saying things and so manifest the image of a stronger self.[13]

Hamburg and Washburne put forward the interesting hypothesis that language plays the same role for the human male, in respect to aggression and agonistic behavior, that display plays for the primate (e.g., baring of the canines, chest thumping, display of the ruff, and so forth).[14] Such a homologue would provide another biologically based explanation for the compelling and aggressive use by males of obscenities in military groups.

This stronger self is built through the metaphor of the soldier's masculinity. He is "big balled"; his image of toughness, endurance, aggressiveness, and fighting skills is structured in good part upon his maleness and his being a "man among men." Tests of his maleness are symbolic tests of his combat potential, and the belief in his masculinity and toughness provide mechanisms that enable him to prepare for and accept the terrors of combat. These tests lie at the heart of incorporation of new members into the combat group, as Bey described it, in Vietnam:

The combat unit is an intensely close knit group. Initially, the "f.n.g's" [fucking new guy] anxiety is likely to be increased by the group's asking him extremely personal questions and telling him "war stories." One unit, for example, held "court" and sat around the new man while one of the old timers asked him whether or not he performed and enjoyed cunnilingus.

In another unit the members of the company sang the following song to the newcomer:

> You're going home in a body bag, doo da, do da
> You're going home in a body bag, oh, doo da day.
> Shot between the eyes, shot between the legs,
> You're going home in a body bag, oh, doo da day.

Bey then goes on to point out that, "Surprising as it may seem to the reader, in most instances these group confrontations tend to quickly establish closeness and a counterphobic stance towards the combat situation in the new arrival."[15]

Male sexual metaphor comes to symbolize aspects of the self and of the group and its power and consequently becomes an aspect of maintaining the group in combat. It divides the soldier from the civilian and defines the combat group both to itself and to others. An example of this use of sexual symbolism was related to the author in Vietnam in 1964, where certain special forces units quasi-publically defined themselves through their sexual behavior. Several massage parlors in South Vietnam were considered their regular territory; they never engaged in vaginal intercourse; the women in the massage parlors were engaged exclusively to perform fellatio upon them. This was the diacritical that contrasted them with other American groups in Vietnam, as it was widely believed that Vietnamese prostitutes had an abhorrence of oral sex and normally refused to perform it.

The Brotherhood of Soldiers

Some, of course, consider that the masculine ethos of the combat group has been markedly attenuated in recent times. This view seems to be based upon what I would consider to be a misreading of Moskos's observations in *The American Enlisted Man*.[16] Binkin and Bach assert that Moskos's data indicate a shift from a "primary group" modality to an individually centered one within the combat unit. They then infer that male bonding has been vitiated as an active principle of primary group structure. Several points are appropriate here. The shift that Moskos described as characterizing relationships between enlisted men in combat groups in Vietnam represented not an end to the primacy of primary group male bonding in maintaining the combat group, but more probably a shift in the language, i.e., the justificatory metaphor used to describe the bonding of combat groups by their members. What Moskos observed can be described as an *instrumentally* based bonding between individuals in the combat group, that is, a set of relationships described in essentially economic terms by many of the participants when characterizing the basis of the ties that hold the group together (e.g., "I will look out for and fight for the other guy because he will look out for and fight for me"). This description differs from descriptions of primary group bonding in World War II and Korea, which most commentators portrayed in terms of close affective and cathectic bonds between given individuals. In point of fact, this in no way vitiates a male-bonding basis for the combat group. Relationships in previous wars were as much relationships between roles as between real people, and most descriptions from World War II and Korea, as well as from World War I and preceding wars, can be recast in the same instrumental mold. Essential aspects of the bond between soldiers are intensity and transience, reflecting a context defined by constant loss and personnel turnover. The military unit consists of dyads and triads that constantly change and reform because of personnel turbulence created by personnel policies, such as rotation, and the exigencies of combat. What apparently has changed, when one compares the combat groups of previous wars with those in Vietnam, is the descriptive language used to classify relationships and the willingness to speak somewhat less "self-lessly" for public consumption than did soldiers in previous wars. One of the characteristics of the late sixties and early seventies was, I believe, an accelerated movement away from a descriptive language of "sentimentality" and "affect," such as that which characterized descriptions of relationships in the first half of the century, to a cooler, hipper language of cynicism. A World War I song such as "My Buddy" or the German *"Ich hatt eine Kamerad"* would have been cause for acute embarrassment and hoots of derision. While, in the cool culture of the sixties, as Moskos quite correctly points out, the exaggerated masculinity of the combat unit attenuates after it has been bloodied and ground down by fire, this does not shift the group's perceptions of combat from the masculine to the genderless.[17] Bravado is tempered, but as Mauldin's *Stars and Stripes* cartoons of dogfaces Willy and Joe attested, combat remains quietly and bitterly a man's world.[18]

The underlying profundity of the relations among combat soldiers was well put by Philip Caputo in his introduction to *A Rumor of War:*

> I have also attempted to describe the intimacy of life in Infantry battalions, where the communion between men is as profound as any between lovers. Actually, it is more so. It does not demand for its sustenance the reciprocity,

the pledges of affection, the endless reassurances required by the love of men and women. It is, unlike marriage, a bond that cannot be broken by a word, by boredom or divorce, or by anything other than death. Sometimes even that is not strong enough. Two friends of mine died trying to save the corpses of their men from the battlefield. Such devotion, simple and selfless, the sentiment of belonging to each other, was the one decent thing we found in a conflict otherwise notable for its monstrosities.[19]

In the world of the combat soldier, then, masculinity is an essential measure of capability. In an interaction between male bonding and widespread cultural norms, the maleness of an act is the measure of its worth and thus a measure of one's ability. While many may disapprove of these norms, they have been and are, as a matter of ethnographic fact, the operative ones in much of military society and particularly in the combat group. In observations made at a basic-training center during the period in which it was being gender-integrated, the importance for the male of definition by maleness and therefore toughness became clear. Almost universally the males felt that they had been subjected to less intense physical training and less challenging soldierly training than they would have been in an all-male environment. Men in units with women in them contrasted their training unfavorably with that of exclusively male neighboring units. The neighboring units were seen as producing tougher, more competent, militarily better trained, and "harder" soldiers. Long discussions were carried on about the challenge of bayonet training, for example, which was debarred to the integrated units but still carried out in the units not yet integrated. Many young men voiced the feeling that they had somehow been cheated. They had neither been stretched to their limits nor challenged in their masculinity, and conse- quently were poorer soldiers than they might otherwise have been. In reality, the training programs in all the companies were essentially identical, operating to the same physical training standards and exercise requirements. No basic-training unit at the post in question had received bayonet training for almost ten years. The issue involved was one of self-image and self-esteem. The presence of women lowered the perceived value of the training to many of the men, who asked themselves, "If women can do it, how much of a challenge can it be?" It is interesting that most of the young men felt that the women were good soldiers as well as friends and there was a fair amount of cross-gender cooperative behavior. Almost all agreed that women should be in the Army and almost all, of both sexes, agreed that women should not be "combat soldiers." At the same time, the males had judged *themselves* wanting. If women could do all of the things they could do, how good could they be? The answer of most was, "Not very good."

While we may characterize such attitudes as sexist, disapproval does not change the fact that they are a significant part of our common culture, nor does it speak to the high probability, given our present state of knowledge, that such attitudes and behaviors might well be grounded in those fundamental biological structures that underlie gender difference. One need not go to the extreme view that "biology is destiny" to recognize that biology shapes and may control certain aspects of destiny. It is fair to say that interactions of biological and sociocultural evolution have combined to make men more competent fighters to begin with. The absence of any reliable historical data indicating that women have ever served as part of the regular forces of organized combat in any human society does not preclude the possibility that women might so serve effectively. But it does present a powerful inductive and probabilistic argument that the lack of such participation reflects a deep-seated set of sociocultural and biological differences between the genders. The charge often made that such "sexism" simply reflects culturally based attitudes is, I believe, scientifically ill-grounded. Fighting groups, armies, and warriors have always been male. While women have participated in irregular warfare, in the defense of invaded homelands or as symbolic leaders, they have never been part of the actual land fighting forces of group, clan, tribe, or state. The image of the woman warrior has, in fact, been more an image of the alien, as in the Amazons of Greek mythology and Herodotus, or of a horrific reversal of the natural order, a world turned upside down and made preternaturally threatening, as in Chinese legend. As Walter Burkert puts it: "A combat of men with women is a startling inversion, the Amazon myth, or wife killing her husband."[20] Perhaps for this reason the most terrifying aggression in the myths of the West is embodied in female forms, the Erinnyes, the Maeneads, the Gorgons. But we must remember that the warriors serving even the most blood-thirsty of mythic creatures were almost invariably males.

It is sometimes averred that these biologically based arguments against the use of women in combat are analogous to the racist arguments that were invoked against the employment of black troops and the integration of blacks in the U.S. Army in the past. Prejudice against blacks in the armed forces, however, was the creation of a social system and culture during a single temporal period. The issue of the competency of blacks to fight was almost a distinctly American problem as, to a lesser degree, was that of integration. It involved biological assertions of inferiority and incapacity made in the face of thousands of years of black success as warriors and in the face of a history of combat success on the part of integrated fighting units in the classical world in the armies of Islam or even in *Othello*.[21] No such evidence exists for either the combat competency of women or the successful integration of women into fighting armies.

Many who advocate posting women to combat units seem to have little conception of the physical, as well as psychological and emotional, demands of ground combat. Women can indeed fire most weapons as well as men can; however, firing weapons is only a small part of ground combat. The larger part consists in getting the weapon, ammunition, and other equipment to those places from which the weapon can be used most effectively. The combat infantryman moves with combat pack, weapons, ammunition, grenades, and other equipment. At times he moves steadily; at times he must make short rushes over broken terrain, doubled over to minimize his size and bearing between 60 and 120 pounds of gear.[22] The combat arms soldier must, at the same time, be capable of killing with his clubbed weapon, with a knife, and with his hands and feet. As an old Army saying goes, "The object in war is not to die for your country, but to make the other fellow die for his." If we are serious about the missions that are mandated for the combat arms, we cannot afford to make them a locus of social experimentation. The reason is simple: we can afford to do nothing that would lessen their combat potential and power, else we run the risk of losing the war and sacrificing a force that was not the best structured to perform its job.

A Place for Women?

If those physiological traits conducive to success on the battlefield and those sociocultural aspects of the combat group critical to cohesion and endurance in battle seemingly preclude women from the combat *arms,* two questions still remain. Should women be drafted, and should women serve in combat (if not in the combat arms)? The latter question is, in effect, moot. In the worst-case war defined by Soviet tactical thought all forces in the theater are combatants.

Arguments about women in combat that hinge on images of "dead daughters at the front" are built out of the metaphors of past wars, not future wars. Long-range rocketry, long-range artillery, fighter-bombers and gunships, tactical missiles, and theater tactical nuclear weapons make the potential front as deep and as wide as Europe. Women in combat support and combat service forces will be under regular enemy fire and attack. Since Soviet doctrine calls for massive deployment of airborne forces, its enemies' depots, maintenance areas, communications and intelligence units, airfields, and ports may also come under direct as well as indirect attack. To debate whether women should be in combat is really to debate whether women should be in the armed forces at all, and that debate is, I think we would all agree, closed. Those who engage in the debate seem to forget that women served overseas in support functions during World War II and that they suffered casualties at the same rate as noncombatant men (0.5 percent).[23] Female casualties would, of course, be extremely high in the course of any ground conflict with the Soviet Union, but this would be equally so for all noncombatant support personnel. Possible "smaller" wars may well involve equally widespread combat, if the enemy forces are armed by and follow Soviet doctrine. Guerilla and terrorist wars place all at risk, regardless of job in the armed forces, since the entire nation is the battleground. Indeed, it may even strike some as strange that those who oppose the deployment of women overseas by invoking the image of daughters dead in battle do not usually use the same sentimental language to describe the dead dependents of our male personnel and the dead female citizens and children of our allies. If women are not, for many of the reasons adduced above, to be posted to combat arms or certain combat support units (infantry, armor, artillery, combat engineers, combat military police), what should the roles for women be?

Here I must say that I believe that women should be drafted in any new Selective Service System. The argument is the same one I offered in Chapter 3 for drafting men. An army capable of winning and, perhaps more important, of deterring the kind of warfare set forth in the Soviet scenario must have the most competent and highly skilled personnel available manning its force, its weapons, and its support systems. Because the demands of war are inequitable, demands for personnel will be inequitable. Equity in war cannot imply equal opportunity for all regardless of capabilities. One would, to put it simply, not put a 98-pound weakling in the ring with Mohammed Ali unless one began with the premise that we should all have equal access to defeat. If we are to staff our military force in a way that will ensure optimal competence, skill, and ability, women will have to provide a significant part of that force, particularly if that force is ever expanded significantly. The declining size of the male youth population will require in future years at least one out of every three eligible males of nineteen just to maintain present force levels. In the past two years the Army seems to have reached a limit in tapping the number of women available for service as voluntary enlistees, despite the recent lowering of standards. In point of fact, if the Israeli experience is any guide, the available pool of women for conscription will be markedly lower than for men. Women will be ineligible for service not only on the same physical and mental grounds for which vast numbers of men have been and will be excluded, but also on grounds of pregnancy and, particularly, religious commitments. In Israel 18 to 20 percent of women are excused from the draft because of declarations of fundamentalist orthodoxy.[24] It should be anticipated that an almost equivalent percentage may request deferment in the United States based upon fundamentalist religious objections to such "violations" of traditional female roles.

Many social and psychological barriers to the wider employment of women in the Army have already been broken down both in terms of traditional jobs (hospital and clinic-based medical, clerical, secretarial) and many nontraditional ones (diesel mechanics, telephone wiremen, military police, etc). The critical question is, in what array of jobs within the force will women not only perform well but enhance the overall combat power of the organization? We must not forget that the majority of women in the United States and the overwhelming majority of women in the services desire more "traditional" (female) jobs and actively indicate a preference for such jobs. Military occupational specialty (MOS) analysis should be cognizant of the special skills, competencies, and strengths that women bring to the armed forces and the workplace, as well as the values and sociocultural biases that they also bring. The basic barriers to assignment should then be rationally constructed in terms of effects on combat competence and power. It should be remembered that in the average run of noncombatant jobs there would be little to choose between the defensive skills and abilities of male and female personnel. Both would be partially trained and skilled at armed defense and at fairly equal risk if attacked by aggressive enemy combat troops.

Particular attention should be paid to women's skills that represent greater potential competency in critical areas. For example, women's finer-grained muscle movements and control would probably make them more effective repairers of complex electronic equipment. Girls have more sensitive touch thresholds and keener senses of smell, and are better at discriminating and localizing sounds than are boys. They are superior in recall and recognition memory and have better recall of auditory material. Women have better verbal skills and tend to process verbal data better than men do.[25] Many of these differences reflect differences in brain organization and left-right hemisphere dominance, presumably as differentially keyed between the two sexes by estrogen in females and testosterone in males. Again, our biological templates seem to provide for different and in some cases complementary innate capacities and potential skills. Women, then, should be drafted, trained for, and assigned to those MOSs that they are most able to fill. It is obvious that some jobs will be equally well performed by women and men; others, one would hypothesize, better by women; yet others, better by men. Jobs should be analyzed in terms of the primary and secondary abilities required to fill them, and of the other range of potential jobs which each individual might be asked or cross-trained to fill, and then opened to men or women on the basis of ability and potential. The better ability of women at processing verbal data and at verbal recall would, for example, probably make them more desirable as radio communicators in those ambients which control the battle—headquarters, command, control centers at levels of brigade, division, corps, etc. That those involved in communications at the company level must also function as combat infantry should, however, debar those jobs to women on the thesis that their lesser capacity as fighters and their intrusion as females into a male-based and -bonded combat group could threaten the competence and integrity of that group. Analyses of the entire repertoire of military roles and occupational specialties are required to determine those which women may effectively fill. Gender-free physical and mental criteria would then define the standards governing assignment. It is most probable that those criteria that would debar women from direct combat engagement roles in the land forces would not apply to direct engagement roles in the Navy and Air Force. Jobs with greater reliance upon technical skill than upon the physical, psychological, and social factors that ensure effectiveness in land warfare may well be efficiently staffed with female personnel. A broad spectrum of direct combat positions aboard combat naval vessels and combat aircraft could undoubtedly be performed equally well by women and men. Such restructuring would, of course, require revision of the Army's combat exclusion policy that bars women from all direct engagement roles, including the piloting of helicopters and light aircraft in the combat zone, and a change in the public law that bars women from direct combat service in the Navy and Air Force.

In summation: modern war involves no sharp discontinuities with modes of successful warfare in the past. The processes and capabilities that characterize the successful military group involved in direct engagement with the enemy will continue to make for combat success. A number of fundamental factors debar women from such groups, and their inclusion would threaten group efficiency and power. The consequences of such a threat could be costly. Technological change has vastly increased the complexity of modern war, however. In its myriad new functions, ranging from intelligence and electronic warfare to maintenance and repair of critical equipment, the skills, talents, and abilities of female personnel are vital.

Notes

1. See David A. Hamburg, "Developments in Research on the Psychobiology of Aggression," in *Developments in Psychiatric Research,* edited by James M. Tanner (London: Hodder & Stoughton, 1977), pp. 54-57; Robert M. Rose, "Testosterone Aggression and Homosexuality: A Review of the Literature and Implication for Future Research," in *Topics in Endocrinology,* edited by E. J. Sachar (New York: Grune & Stratton, 1975); Robert M. Rose, John W. Holiday, and Irwin S. Bernstein, "Plasma Testosterone, Dominance Rank and Aggressive Behavior in Male Rhesus Monkeys," *Nature* 231 (ll June 1971): 366; James A. Loyd, "Social Behavior and Hormones," and Arthur Kling, "Testosterone and Aggressive Behavior in Man and Non-Human Primates," in *Hormonal Correlates of Behavior,* edited by Basil E. Eleftheriout and Richard L. Sprott (New York: Plenum Press, 1975), pp. 185-204 and 305-24; and J. A. Gray, "Sex Differences in Emotional Behavior in Mammals Including Man: Endocrine Bases," *Acta Psychologica* 35 (1971): 29-46.

2. Dan Olewus, Åke Mattson, Daisy Schalling, and Hans Löw, "Testosterone, Aggression, Physical, and Personality Dimensions in Normal Adolescent Males," *Psychosomatic Medicine* 42, no. 2 (March 1980): 253-69.

3. John Z. Young, *Programs of the Brain* (Oxford: Oxford University Press, 1978), p. 161.

4. Corinne Hutt, "Biological Bases of Psychological Sex Differences," *American Journal of Diseases of Childhood* 132 (February 1978): 173.

5. Margaret Mead, *Sex and Temperament in Three Primitive Societies* (New York: William Morrow, 1963); *Male and Female* (New York: William Morrow, 1975).

6. Mead, *Male and Female,* p. xxvi.

7. Ian M. Lewis, *Peoples of the Horn of Africa* (London: International African Institute, 1955).

8. David H. Marlowe, "Commitment, Contract, Group Boundaries and Conflict," in *Science and Psychoanalysis,* edited by J. Masserman (New York: Grune & Stratton, 1963).

9. Lionel Tiger, *Men in Groups* (New York: Vintage Books, 1970), p. 241.

10. John R. Gillis, *Youth and History: Tradition and Change in European Age Relations, 1770–Present* (New York: Academic Press, 1974).

11. Frederick Thrasher, *The Gang,* 2nd ed. (Chicago: University of Chicago Press, 1927); J. F. Kett, *Rites of Passage: Adolescence in America 1790 to the Present* (New York: Basic Books, 1977).

12. Henry Elkin, "Aggressive and Erotic Tendencies in Army Life," *American Journal of Sociology* 51 (March 1946): 410.

13. Frederick Elkin, "The Soldier's Language," *American Journal of Sociology* 51 (March 1946): 418.

14. David A. Hamburg and S. Washburne, "Aggressive Behavior in Old World Monkeys and Apes," in *Primates: Studies in Adaptation and Variability,* edited by P. Jay (New York: Holt, Rinehart & Winston, 1968).

15. Douglas R. Bey, "Group Dynamics and the 'F.N.G.' in Vietnam—A Potential Focus of Stress," *International Journal of Group Psychotherapy* 22, no. 1 (1972): 211-26.

16. Martin Binkin and Shirley J. Bach, *Women and the Military* (Washington, D.C.: The Brookings Institution, 1977); Charles C. Moskos, Jr., *The American Enlisted Man* (New York: Russell Sage Foundation, 1970).

17. Moskos, *The American Enlisted Man*.

18. Bill Mauldin, *Up Front* (New York: Henry Holt, 1948).

19. Philip Caputo, *A Rumor of War* (New York: Holt, Rinehart & Winston, 1977), p. xv.

20. Walter Burkert, *Structure and History in Greek Mythology and Ritual* (Berkeley and Los Angeles: University of California Press, 1977), p. 19.

21. Frank Snowden, *Blacks in Antiquity* (Cambridge: Belknap/Harvard University Press, 1970); V. Lee, *The Employment of Negro Troops* (Washington, D.C.: Office of the Chief of Military History, U.S. Army, 1966).

22. See, for example, S. L. A. Marshall, *Battles in the Monsoon* (New York: William Morrow, 1967); S. L. A. Marshall, *Night Drop* (New York: Bantam Books, 1963); and M. Baker, *Nam* (New York: William Morrow, 1981).

23. Office of the Assistant Secretary of Defense, *Background Study: Use of Women in the Military* (Washington, D.C.: Department of Defense, 1977).

24. Lesley Hazleton, *Israeli Women* (New York: Touchstone/Simon & Schuster, 1977). See also Meville E. Spiro, *Gender and Culture: Kibbutz Women Revisited* (Durham, N.C.: Duke University Press, 1979); and Lionel Tiger and Joseph Shepher, *Women in the Kibbutz* (New York: Harcourt Brace Jovanovich, 1975) for a biologically oriented analysis of the changing work roles of Israeli women.

25. Hutt, "Biological Bases," pp. 173-74.

13

Women's Roles in the U.S. Armed Forces: An Evaluation of Evidence and Arguments for Policy Decisions

MADY WECHSLER SEGAL

The purpose of this essay is to discuss alternative policies with regard to the roles of women in the American armed forces and to evaluate the arguments and evidence bearing on such policy decisions and their potential consequences.* The basic question concerns the relative conditions of service for women and men. In theory, answers to this question range between two extremes, with the complete exclusion of women at one extreme and the irrelevance of gender at the other. In actuality, past and present debate has revolved around several specific interrelated policy issues. What proportion of military personnel should be female? What specific types of military roles should be open to women: "traditionally" female positions, traditionally male but "noncombat" positions, or combat positions? Should women be subject to a draft if men are?

The policy issues are interrelated because the decisions regarding each issue have consequences for the others. For example, if women are to serve only in traditionally female specialties (primarily clerical and medical), then the proportion of military jobs that can be filled by women would be quite low. If women are excluded from direct combat roles though permitted into other traditionally male jobs (such as equipment repair and military police), there would still be a ceiling on the proportion of female military personnel, but it would be higher than if women served only in traditionally female classifications. A decision to draft women would not obviate decisions about what jobs they would be required to take and what jobs would be open to them on a voluntary basis. If women were drafted in substantial numbers, however, this would necessarily increase their representation in traditionally male roles.

Past decisions about women's roles in the U.S. military have responded to

* The opinions or assertions contained herein are the private views of the author and are not to be construed as official or as reflecting the views of the Department of the Army or the Department of Defense.

perceived threats to national security, shortages of men to meet personnel requirements, and public opinion. A brief history of American women's participation in the military can illuminate the current discussion.

Women in the U.S. Military: 1940–1981

Before World War II, with some minor exceptions, women in the U.S. military served only as nurses and were under a separate command structure from regular military personnel. During World War II, each service established a women's unit, distinct from the nurse corps and also distinct from the rest of the force, with a separate command structure.[1] Only recently have the women's branches been integrated with the men's armed services: in 1978, Congress passed legislation abolishing the Women's Army Corps as a separate unit.

The number of women in the military has varied greatly, but the percentage has always been small. The largest number and concentration of women in the U.S. military, until recently, occurred in 1945, when approximately 265,000 women made up 2.2 percent of the force of over 12 million.[2] Legislation passed in 1947 and 1948 placed severe limitations on the numbers and functions of military women. A ceiling of 2 percent was placed on female enlisted personnel, and female officers (not counting nurses) could number at most 10 percent of enlisted women.[3] In the 1950s, the number of military women varied between approximately 22,000 in 1950 (1.5 percent) and approximately 35,000 in 1955 (1.3 percent). In 1967, the 2-percent limitation was removed, but by 1971 women still constituted less than 2 percent of the military.

From 1971 to 1980, the number and percentage of women in the U.S. military increased dramatically. At the end of fiscal year 1971, about 30,000 enlisted women and 13,000 female officers together constituted 1.6 percent of the total active-duty military personnel. By the end of 1980, about 151,000 enlisted women (8.6 percent of enlisted strength) and 22,000 female officers (7.9 percent of all active duty officers) made a total of 173,000 women in uniform (8.5 percent of the total active forces).

The variety of jobs performed by military women has paralleled the pattern of their numbers. That is, in the past during peacetime, women played only "traditionally" female roles in the military. During World War II, however, while "the vast majority were employed in health care, administration, and communications, women demonstrated their competences in virtually every occupation outside of direct combat—they were employed as airplane mechanics, parachute riggers, gunnery instructors, air traffic controllers, naval air navigators, and the like."[4] Thus, although women were still concentrated in a few job classifications, wartime necessity opened other jobs to them. The end of World War II saw a return to limitations on women's military jobs.

The past ten years have witnessed an increase in the number of job specialties open to women; currently, only the combat specialties are closed. In 1972, less than 10 percent of enlisted women held nontraditional jobs. By 1976, this figure had climbed to 40 percent; by 1979, it was 46 percent; by the end of 1980, it was 55 percent.

Current laws and policies regarding the positions that may be held by women vary among the different services. In all services, women are permitted to hold all jobs that do not involve direct combat. Women are permitted to and do serve in combat support and combat service support specialties which may involve service in a combat environment. The current prohibition against women in direct combat roles involves a combination of legal restrictions and military policies.

In the Navy and the Marines, until recently, women were restricted from serving aboard most ships by 10 U.S.C. 6015 (1976), which stated in part: "women may not be assigned to duty in aircraft that are engaged in combat missions nor may they be assigned to duty on vessels of the Navy other than hospital ships and transports." The effect of this statute was to bar women from service aboard ships (since the Navy currently has no hospital ships or transports). In *Owens* v. *Brown*, 455 F. Supp. 291 (1978), Judge John J. Sirica ruled that the Navy could not use this statute as the sole basis for excluding women from duty aboard ship. Congress modified the law to permit women to serve on hospital and transport ships and other such vessels not expected to be assigned combat missions, and to serve up to six months of temporary duty on other Navy vessels. The Navy is

> beginning to assign women to permanent duty on some ships. Women on temporary duty assigned to combat ships do not replace men. In case a vessel, with women on board, is assigned to a combat mission, every effort would be made to disembark the women but not in such a way as to interfere with the accomplishment of the mission. In the Navy, women still may not serve on vessels or aircraft engaged in combat missions.[6]

Women in the Air Force are similarly prohibited (by 10 U.S.C. 8459) from serving on aircraft engaged in a combat mission.

The Army has no statutory prohibition against women in combat. The current Army policy states:

> Women are authorized to serve in any officer or enlisted specialty, except some selected specialties, in any organizational level and in any unit of the Army except infantry, armor, cannon field artillery, combat engineer, and low altitude air defense artillery units of battalion/squadron or smaller size.[7]

In practice, this policy allows women to be assigned to a brigade headquarters or a brigade support unit of an infantry division. Women will serve in military police, mechanical repair, transportation, intelligence, signal, and other support specialties which bring them near the leading edge of a battlefield. A vehicle driver, for example, might be required to take a load forward into a battalion area one or two miles from the front, although typically the positions occupied by women keep them somewhat farther in the rear.[8] In case of war, such rear areas will themselves be lethal zones, and women soldiers will be exposed to death and injury and to the necessity, when rear areas are overrun or penetrated, of engaging in defensive fire. All women are trained in such defensive capability. Thus, the "combat exclusion" in the Army prevents women from entering units or jobs in which they would routinely be engaged in close combat, not from being in positions which subject them to occasional exposure to combat and risk. Similarly, the Air Force statutory restriction permits women to fly tankers (which would be targets of attack in war) but not fighter planes.

The Subcommittee on Military Personnel of the House Armed Services Committee held hearings in November 1979 on the utilization of women in the military. Included in their public hearings was consideration of the repeal of sections 6015 and 8549 of Title 10, which are the only laws prohibiting American women from serving in combat. While Congress did not act to change the laws, it is noteworthy that the Department of Defense favored such repeal at that time. Even if these legal restrictions were removed, it is still likely that Department of Defense policy would restrict the combat role of women, at least in the immediate future. The department's support of repeal reflected a desire to lodge at the level of the services the option of assigning women to combat roles. Some of the services might exercise the option on a very limited basis, with extensive study and evaluation of the performance of women in the combat roles. Some policymakers in the Army may also have been concerned that the current Army policy of assigning women to combat support and combat service support specialties, which would be likely to involve them in battle in the event of war, is a violation of congressional intent, given the statutory restrictions on the other services.

Through the end of 1980, the military planned to continue to increase the number of women to about 254,000 (223,700 enlisted and 30,600 officers) by 1985, with women constituting about 12 percent of active-duty personnel. At the beginning of 1981, the services (with the exception of the Navy) requested that the Reagan administration reexamine those goals and keep the number of women at the 1980 levels for the present time. The putative basis of this request is a concern about problems encountered with integrating women into the services and antici-pation that such problems would be exacerbated by increasing female representa-tion, especially in combat support units. Such concerns are at the core of the current policy debate and derive from the military's major goal of maintaining an effective and efficient fighting force. In discussing policy issues about women's military roles, this goal must be weighed along with the goal of equal citizenship. We turn now to a discussion of these goals.

Citizenship and Military Service

One of the basic principles publicly acknowledged in our country is the full participation of all citizens in the life of the nation. This entails both the rights of citizenship and civic responsibilities. Service in the military may be seen as both a right and a responsibility.

The view of military service as a right hinges primarily on its association with other rights and benefits. As noted by Janowitz, military service has been "seen as a device by which excluded segments of society could achieve political legitimacy and rights."[9] Their inclusion in military service establishes their social equality. Moreover, apart from group benefits, individuals who serve in the armed forces gain various benefits. Most obvious are training in job skills, veterans' preferences in civilian employment, and various veterans' benefits such as financial support for education under a G.I. Bill, insurance, health care, and home mortgages. Less tangible, but still important, is the socialization that takes place within the military, including learning to function in a large bureaucracy and developing feelings of self-esteem and personal accomplishment.

Two relatively recent examples demonstrate how groups can gain collective rights via the military service of individual members. The latest is the passage, in 1971, of the Twenty-Sixth Amendment to the U.S. Constitution, which lowered the age of political majority to eighteen. Some of the pressure for this move came from the argument that young men who were liable to military conscription should be eligible to vote.[10] The other example is the relationship between the racial integration of the armed forces and the subsequent civil rights movement. This latter example merits atention.

The effects of military service on women are likely to differ in some critical ways from the experiences of minority-race males. Nevertheless, the two cases have a number of striking similarities. The current stage of gender integration of the U.S. armed forces resembles, in several ways, an earlier stage of racial integration.

In the first half of this century, black men were underrepresented in the military and largely excluded from combat jobs. Moskos, in a summary of the history of the roles of black men in the U.S. military, observes that during World War II blacks served in segregated units and most were in combat support and combat service support jobs. Moreover, "even black combat units were frequently used for heavy-duty labor."[11]

The demand for recognition of their "right to fight" became a major slogan of black organizations that wanted to demonstrate the willingness of the black community to fulfill citizenship obligations. Yet as late as 1945 and 1950, reports by two Army boards "concluded that practical considerations required a mainte-nance of segregation and the quota system" and "recommended that black personnel be assigned exclusively to support units rather than combat units."[12] The end of racial segregation, the quota system, and the combat exclusion came as the result of President Truman's 1948 desegregation order and the combat manpower needs of the Korean War.

Many of the arguments now being advanced to justify limiting women's role in the military are reminiscent of those used in the past to limit the participation of black men. These arguments relate primarily to problems of interpersonal accept-ance and motivation to fight.

It might be argued, as David Marlowe does, that equality of citizenship rights among population subgroups, such as men and women, does not require that the subgroups perform identical functions. He cautions that sex differences in abili-ties should not be confused with "differences in the political, social, moral, or human worth of men and women."[13] While this may be true in theory, the problem in reality is that demonstrated, and even presumed, differences in abilities and functions do result in differing estimations of worth, at least in terms of rewards such as power, occupational status, and income. One may bemoan the cultural values that result in "women's jobs," however equal in importance for societal functioning, being compensated at substantially lower rates of pay than comparable men's jobs. If the goal is equality of citizenship benefits, "separate but equal" may be one avenue of social change. Integration of women into previously exclusive masculine domains such as the military is likely to accom-plish equality faster and more completely, since this involves access of previously excluded individuals into an existing social system, rather than core changes in the cultural value of differing social systems.

One benefit that men receive from military service is problematic for women. Military service, especially in combat roles, gives men the opportunity to develop and demonstrate masculine gender role identity. Throughout history and in almost all societies, the warrior role has been an avenue of proving one's manhood. Military service may be culturally transformed in the future into a mechanism for proving one's adulthood. Given current cultural values, however, military service (especially in traditionally male jobs, including combat) may serve to create ambivalence and psychological stress for women. The potential loss of feminine self-perception functions as a hazard for women.

On the other hand, the necessary redefinition of one's own femininity is present in most other roles previously defined as the province of men. This applies to an enormous array of social positions, including holding political office, financially supporting a family, or being in medicine, law, police work, mathematics, science, or sports. The potential hazard of redefining femininity should not deter policymakers from allowing women to choose to serve in the military in any capacity for which they can qualify. It does have implications for conscripting women, however, since women may thus be required to incur a loss which most men experience as a benefit.

This latter point involves the larger questions of whether men and women have equal obligations to serve in the military and whether equal service results in equal cost. The first question revolves around whether relatively disadvantaged groups have the same obligation to serve the state as those who enjoy greater benefits. Since this issue is discussed elsewhere in this volume, I will not deal with it here. The second question is whether equal conditions of military service for men and women would actually produce greater individual hardship for women, as well as risk losing a war. Marlowe argues that "equity in war cannot imply equal opportunity for all regardless of capabilities."[14] The less able soldier sent into combat incurs a greater risk. If one agrees with Marlowe that women, as a class, are less capable soldiers than men, then similar military service for men and women would exact greater cost from individual women. It would also risk greater societal cost. This brings us back to the major issue of the military effectiveness of alternative policies regarding military service for women.

Women and Military Effectiveness

The issue of the potential effects on military performance of the inclusion of women in nontraditional and even combat jobs is at least as critical as the issue of citizenship rights and responsibilities and to many observers and policymakers is of overriding importance. My goal here is to present some of the arguments about the potential military consequences of alternative women's roles and to survey some of the available evidence.

Most of the major arguments and issues can be classed into four categories. First are the arguments based on differences between men and women in certain individual characteristics related to the performance of many military jobs. Second, and related to the first, are concerns about the effect of personnel policies on efficiency and cost-effectiveness, including personnel selection costs and lost duty time. Third are arguments about the effect of the role of women on the perception of our military strength by our allies and potential adversaries. Fourth, and perhaps most problematic, are questions about the effect of women on interpersonal processes bearing on unit performance.

INDIVIDUAL CHARACTERISTICS

Some of the lingering concerns about women's capabilities in traditionally male jobs in the military, especially those in combat and combat support units, derive from observed differences between men and women in characteristics such as strength and endurance. Levels of physical strength, aerobic capacity, and adaptability to temperature extremes bear on the performance of many military jobs. We do not know precisely which jobs require particular levels of performance on these measures, but the services have begun research to establish such standards.

It is clear from research already done in the military and research by sports physiologists that the average young woman is inferior to the average young man on most measures of physical abilities, especially upper-body strength. It is also clear that performance is affected not only by innate capability, but also by life-long conditioning and physical fitness and can be substantially improved through training.[15] In many training programs, the women's percentage improvement is similar to men's and highly trained women outperform untrained men. Nonetheless, since average women begin training at significantly lower levels of physical performance than average men, the average performance of women after training remains lower than that of men.

Thus, we can conclude that in those military jobs requiring high levels of such abilities as physical strength and endurance, a smaller percentage of women than men will be capable of successful performance, even after training. Yet the potential physical performance of people entering the military is affected by prior athletic activity. If the current trend toward increased participation and success of girls and women in athletics continues,[16] we can expect some increases in the percentage of women capable of performing a variety of physically demanding jobs.

Most human cultures have so emphasized the differences between average males and average females that all members of each sex tend to be treated as if they represented the average for their sex. However, the general direction of social change in Western nations has been toward recognizing individual capabilities and differentiating the individual from the group. If the military's goal is to find the best fit between job requirements and individual abilities, individuals should be selected for jobs on the basis of measures of those abilities, not gender. If a certain level of physical strength is required for a particular job, then this should serve as one of the selection criteria for the job. We should not assume that all women are incapable of performance by virtue of the average woman's lesser capability, nor should we assume that all men are capable of performing jobs that require a high level of upper-body strength. Not all young men are strong enough to perform as combat infantrymen. We must be careful not to confuse a difference in average physical strength between men and women with a situation where all men are strong enough and no women are.

Jobs can also be redesigned and new technologies developed to allow for their performance by weaker people. This was commonly done for factory work during World War II, when women were performing jobs previously held only by men. The necessity of using women in jobs that men were not available to fill produced changes in the jobs, such as the substitution of lifting machinery for physical strength. While this type of redesign and technology development may not be possible for all types of military jobs currently requiring great upper-body strength, it is not inconceivable that some progress can be made.

Perhaps most important, not all military jobs now closed to women depend on their occupant's physical strength. Women are barred from service in any job aboard Navy ships with offensive combat missions and from flying combat planes in the Navy and Air Force. Such exclusions cannot be justified by citing differences in physical strength between men and women. Indeed, Navy women are permitted to perform some jobs in shore billets, but are excluded from the same jobs on ships. Such jobs require technical skills, not physical strength.

Another basis for excluding women from combat jobs has been the observed differences between the sexes in overt physical aggressiveness.[17] Much of the evidence used to demonstrate a biological basis for such sex differences comes from research on nonhuman primates and other mammals. Most research on humans, though still demonstrating that males are more aggressive than females, on the average finds greater differences within the sexes than between them.[18]

Another psychological trait related to successful performance in the military is the ability to perform under stress, an ability critical to survival in combat. It is sometimes assumed that women would be less capable of performing under the stress of combat than men,[19] yet no evidence currently substantiates such a claim. There is a great deal of evidence that military women have performed on a par with their male peers in difficult circumstances and in situations of severe psychological pressure. Instructive here are the well-known MAXWAC and REFWAC studies,[20] as well as documented descriptions of the reactions of women in World War II, including those who were prisoners of war.[21] Kalisch and

Scobey summarize the experiences of female American military nurses in war-time, including the "squalid and verminous living conditions" and having to "witness the pathetic results of the physical violence of modern warfare."[22] That "American nurses proved their physical and emotional stamina while performing their jobs under combat conditions"[23] is often forgotten in discussions of women's potential for withstanding the stress of combat.

In addition to such evidence on the ability of American military women to withstand psychological stress, there is some historical documentation that women in other countries have performed on a par with men in combat, albeit not in equal numbers.[24] Recent studies also document the ability of American policewomen to cope with situations of potential and actual physical violence.[25]

We have no direct evidence on how young American women today would behave in the extreme situation of infantry combat fighting side by side with young men. But if we have no evidence that women differ from men in their psychological stability to withstand the effects of combat, neither have we reason arbitrarily to assume that they are inferior. The conventional approach in research is to assume that no difference exists between groups until a difference is demonstrated.

Even if we find a difference between the *average* man and the *average* woman in ability to function under stress, we should use that ability and not the person's gender as the basis for selecting or rejecting the person for a job. Obviously, this requires us to develop a measure of this ability.

EFFICIENCY AND COST-EFFECTIVENESS

Two frequent arguments for restricting the use of women in the military appeal to efficiency and cost-effectiveness. The first argument is that it is more efficient to exclude all women from a specialty than to test each woman where the probabilities are low that many women will qualify. The second argument is that the average female recruit costs the military more than the average male recruit; so it is not cost-effective to increase the use of women.

For those military jobs that require high levels of traits on which the average young woman scores much lower than the average young man, such as physical strength and aggressiveness, certain situations might require the use of gender as a screening criterion. In the event of a rapid mass mobilization, where large numbers of potential recruits and/or conscripts have to be processed in a relatively short period of time, it might be inefficient to test large numbers of women for some jobs to identify the few who have the requisite capabilities; and it is legitimate under the circumstances to let efficiency override fairness to individuals. On the other hand, such a situation of mass mobilization does not currently prevail. Thus, this may be the optimum time to study ways to improve our selection, classification, and training systems to utilize most effectively the individual abilities of all personnel in the future, male and female. The military services are now conducting research to determine minimum levels and tests of strength and stamina to be used as gender-free standards.[26]

Measures of cost-effectiveness in the military include rates of attrition, job migration, and lost duty time. Attrition is defined for enlisted personnel as failure to complete an enlistment contract. Enlisted attrition rates have been higher for women than for men, partly because military policy, until 1975, required pregnant women to leave the services. Nevertheless, data on enlisted cohorts entering the services subsequent to the policy change still show higher attrition rates for women than for men, overall, with considerable variation among the services. For those enlisting in fiscal year 1977, the rate of attrition within three years was 30.8 percent for males and 37.4 percent for females, with most of the difference resulting from voluntary separation for pregnancy or parenthood.[27] Attrition rates for enlisted women in traditionally male military jobs (such as mechanical equipment repair) are higher than for women in more traditionally female jobs (such as medical and administrative.)[28]

Job migration is defined as "the movement of personnel out of the specific skill for which they were trained into another skill." Recent data show that "overall DOD migration rates are quite low on an annual basis, and slightly higher among men than women. However, important differences exist by Service and occupational area."[29] Like attrition, job migration is higher for women in the nontraditional than the traditional female skills.

Attrition and migration represent a cost to the military in money spent for training. Increases in the proportion of women in the military necessarily involve more women in the traditionally male jobs. In anticipating the effects of future policies, the services need to know the causes of attrition and migration. One factor likely to account for such losses is the women's lack of initial desire for the traditionally male jobs. Perhaps even more important are the problems that the women experience on the job.

Data on time lost from the job for enlisted personnel indicate that "while women lose more time due to pregnancy and medical care, males lose more time due to AWOL, desertion and other incidents of indiscipline."[30] Data on gender differences in total time lost have not been gathered by all the services. Studies on the Air Force show somewhat more lost time for women, while Navy studies show much more lost time for men.[31] Figures provided in a 1980 study show that for the Navy, at least, use of women is more cost-effective than use of men.[32]

PERCEPTION OF U.S. MILITARY STRENGTH

The degree of reliance on women in the U.S. military has potential effects on national security beyond the actual effects on military performance. The perception of our military effectiveness by our allies and potential adversaries is crucial to national security. The military is perceived in most national cultures as a masculine domain; women are seen as weaker than and in need of protection by men. Thus, the greater the proportion of women in our military services and the more traditionally male jobs they perform, the weaker and more ineffective our military may seem to other nations.

Little direct evidence is available to evaluate this argument. It is clear that the leaders of other nations have been closely observing U.S. policy on the role of military women. While some may regard their increasing role with disdain, other leaders are looking to the American experience in planning their own programs of increasing participation of women in the military. Many nations expect to experience social and demographic pressures similar to those that have led the United States to increased reliance on female personnel. This is most notably the case for the industrialized nations of the West.

INTERPERSONAL PROCESSES IN MILITARY UNITS

Interpersonal dynamics affect the degree to which a group functions effectively to achieve its goals. The performance of a group engaged in coordinated activities is more than the sum of the task performance of the individual members. The success of a military unit whose mission requires coordinated activity is affected by its cohesion and morale. In addition, individual performance is affected by interpersonal acceptance and integration into the group. The cohesion of a military unit affects the ability of the unit to function effectively in combat and the ability of its members to survive the psychological stress of combat.[33]

The critical question is how the presence of women in previously all-male military units affects unit performance. Empirical research completed to date shows basically no effect. The results of the MAXWAC and REFWAC studies showed that the proportion of women in combat support and combat service support units in the Army had no effect on measurable unit performance in field training exercises.[34] Preliminary reports on the Navy's Women-in-Ships program indicate a high level of performance by the women and acceptance by male crew members.[35]

These studies of gender-integrated military units do not involve performance in actual combat. Thus, they provide imperfect bases for inferences about the effects of integration on combat operations. The concern is often expressed that the battlefield is no place for social experimentation.[36] We need to consider if the evidence available is sufficient to encourage the integration of women into fighting units; that is, we need to understand how interpersonal relationships in actual combat might differ.

The willingness to engage in actual combat, to kill and to risk being killed, depends upon a very strong devotion to the group, which is seen by some as depending, among other motivations, on male bonding.[37] The presence of women would interfere with the devotion of the men to each other, as women are outsiders who are not privy to male subculture; competition might also arise among the men for the sexual favors of the women. No conclusive evidence supports or refutes these arguments. But one point *is* clear: if men believe that women are not part of their group and that they cannot function with women around, this belief will disrupt such functioning and may hinder actual ability to cope with the stress of combat, thereby serving as a self-fulfilling prophecy.

Let me offer an additional explanation for the resistance of men to allowing women in combat units. I conjecture that there is a psychological differentiation between the "real world" and combat that enables some men to survive the enormous psychological stress of combat. One survival mechanism is preserving a mental picture of the normal world back home to which one will return from the horror world of combat. After the elaborate game (albeit one with very high stakes) is over, one can go home to an intact world. One of the major components of the world back home is women, "our women," who are warm, nurturant, ultrafeminine, and objects of sexual fantasy. Women (at least "our women") are not part of war. Indeed, one of the reasons men have for fighting is to protect their women and the rest of their image of the world back home. If men allow their women into combat with them, this psychological differentiation cannot be maintained and this psychological defense is lost.

I would also conjecture that, in less extreme form, this differentiation exists for many men between work and family. It may be one of the reasons for resistance to women in various male-dominated civilian occupations. This would be especially true of blue-collar jobs where male subcultural norms govern interpersonal interaction (e.g., construction, fire fighting, auto mechanics). I also believe that this differentiation is one of the mechanisms used by male cadets/midshipmen at the military academies to survive the rigors of cadet training, especially during the first year.[38] This would account for some of the resistance to women cadets and for some of the reactions to them (especially negative stereotyping of them as too masculine).

The resistance of men to women has proven malleable in military units that used to be all male but now have women, including the academies. Various processes of social change resulting from gender integration have probably already begun and will continue to create new styles of interaction in face-to-face working units. DeFleur's study of the Air Force Academy shows that over the course of the first four years of gender integration, male acceptance of and interaction with the women has shown some increase. While women are far from being fully accepted and integrated, this is at least partially attributable to the lack of interdependence among cadets.[39] In units in combat, interpersonal interdependence is high and likely to foster cohesion, regardless of gender.

The concern that women in combat units will reduce unit cohesion is reminiscent of arguments used in the past to justify excluding women from other occupations. Not long ago women were excluded from law, medicine, police work, and firefighting (to name a few). This exclusion was based partly on women's supposed inability as individuals to perform the jobs adequately and partly on the potential disruption of men's interpersonal relations if women were included. While such arguments were accepted in the past, they have now been shown to be groundless. While women have certainly not been fully integrated into these occupations, and while some men are not happy with women's presence in these jobs, few would today be willing publicly to advocate their exclusion. This unwillingness is based on the normative changes in our society and on the evidence that women's performance in these occupations has been successful and not disruptive of interpersonal relations.

Outside of combat situations, certain interpersonal problems already existing in the military deserve attention. Their lack of acceptance by many military men creates problems for the women. As in other predominantly male settings, military women often face prejudice from male superiors, peers, and subordinates, as well as stress-creating male behavior. Such behavior includes differential treatment of women, which interferes with their job performance, and varying degrees of sexual harassment. These problems also exist in institutional settings other than the military, but they must be addressed in the military before we can expect women to function there most effectively. The potential effects of such problems on women must be considered in policy decisions about including women in a military draft.

During the racial integration of the armed forces, analogous interpersonal problems were addressed by service programs aimed at achieving racial equality and interracial harmony. Similar efforts directed at achieving gender integration could be expected to ameliorate the problems women encounter. For example, the services have initiated programs to combat sexual harassment, which should reduce a major obstacle to military women's effective functioning and psychological well-being.

Conclusion

With regard to military service, women are currently treated in many ways as a class of persons, rather than as individuals who differ from one another. All women are excluded, by law and/or by policy, from certain military positions, regardless of their individual motivations and capabilities. Women as a class are currently exempt from draft registration. Men, on the other hand, are treated as individuals: their acceptance or rejection by the military and for specific military jobs is based on their individual characteristics. With regard to draft registration and possible conscription, it is assumed that men, as a class, are eligible for assignment to any military role, subject only to limitations imposed by their individual characteristics (such as physical, mental, or cognitive disabilities or conscientious objection).

Given the ways in which military service is linked to citizenship rights and responsibilities, such unequal treatment of men and women can be justified only by very compelling reasons. The paramount question is whether this inequality is necessitated by some overriding value. An appeal to cost-effectiveness does not seem sufficient justification, because male-female differences are not consistent enough or great enough to warrant universal inclusion of men and universal exclusion of women.

The value of protecting women also fails as an adequate justification, on a number of counts. First, women are not currently excluded from the risk of warfare: they are already functioning in the military in positions that would involve them in combat. Second, the nature of modern warfare does not exempt civilian populations, male or female, from the hazards of war. Protection of women could have some credibility as a basis for certain policies, but only if the policies were applied equally to men with the same limiting individual characteristics. Both men and women who do not possess the requisite capabilities should not be allowed to fill military jobs that can be demonstrated to require high levels of physical strength and endurance.

In evaluating military personnel policies, we must consider the potential impact of the policies on the ability of the military to perform its mission. Indeed, the latest effort by the Department of Defense to review evidence and make policy recommendations on the participation of women states: "The main criterion by which any military personnel policy must be measured is its effect on the combat readiness and mission capability of the Armed Forces."[40] Much concern has been expressed by the services (but not the Navy) that increasing the representation of women, especially in traditionally all-male specialties and units, has already had detrimental effects on mission capability and that further increases should be delayed. Yet the evidence offered to substantiate these concerns is not convincing. Even the Department of Defense review states: "Except for the Navy, the services did not document for this review what effect military women have on mission accomplishment."[41]

The rapid expansion of women's roles in the U.S. military in the 1970s has not been without its problems. Many of the problems are logistical, such as shortages of uniforms and appropriate housing. Others are social and involve the kinds of adjustments to be expected in gender-integrating previously all-male environments. The services seem to be making serious attempts to solve these problems, as well as other personnel problems associated with an All-Volunteer Force.

The issue of drafting women raises other concerns. While equality of citizenship may demand that women not be exempt from draft registration and conscription, caution must be exercised in deciding what military roles women should be required to take. The reality is that the average young American woman is less prepared than the average young man, both physically and psychologically, for many of the traditionally male specialties and units. Thus, at least in the short run, we cannot expect women to be represented in the military in their proportion in the population, even under conscription. But all women should not be exempt solely because they are women, given the successful performance of most military women in a variety of capacities that include combat support and combat service support specialties.

Notes

1. For a thorough history of women's participation through World War II, see Mattie B. Treadwell, *United States Army in World War II; Special Studies; The Women's Army Corps* (Washington, D.C.: Office of the Chief of Military History, Department of the Army, 1954).

2. Nancy Goldman, "The Changing Role of Women in the Military," *American Journal of Sociology* 79 (1973): 895.

3. Martin Binkin and Shirley J. Bach, *Women and the Military* (Washington, D.C.: The Brookings Institution, 1977), pp. 10-12.

4. Ibid., p. 7.

5. Ibid., p. 17.

6. Department of Defense, *America's Volunteers* (Washington, D.C.: Office of the Assistant Secretary of Defense for Manpower, Reserve Affairs, and Logistics, 1978), p. 76. For the most recent description, see Department of Defense, *Background Review: Women in the Military* (Washington, D.C.: Office of the Assistant Secretary of Defense for Manpower, Reserve Affairs, and Logistics, October 1981).

7. Department of the Army, HQ DA Message, DAPE-MPE-C5, R082058Z (Washington, D.C., 8 September 1977).

8. See *Women in the Military,* Hearings Before the Military Personnel Subcommittee, Committee on Armed Services, House of Representatives, 96th Cong., 1st and 2nd Sess. November 1979 and February 1980, pp. 113, 127, 133.

9. Morris Janowitz, *Military Conflict* (Beverly Hills, Calif.: Sage Publications, 1975), pp. 77-78.

10. See Mady Wechsler Segal and David R. Segal, "Social Change and the Participation of Women in the American Military," in *Research in Social Movements, Conflicts, and Change,* Vol. 5, edited by Louis Kriesberg (Greenwich, Conn.: JAI Press, forthcoming).

11. Charles C. Moskos, Jr., "The American Dilemma in Uniform: Race in the Armed Forces," *The Annals of the American Academy of Political and Social Science* 406 (March 1973): 94-106.

12. Ibid., p. 96.

13. David H. Marlowe, "The Manning of the Force and the Structure of Battle," Chapter 12, this volume, p. 190.

14. Ibid., p. 196.

15. For extensive reviews of the literature, see H. Harrison Clarke, ed., "Physical and Motor Sex Differences," President's Council on Physical Fitness and Sports, *Physical Fitness Research Digest,* Ser. 9, no. 4 (October 1979); Barbara L. Drinkwater, "Physiological Responses of Women to Exercise," in *Exercise and Sports Sciences Reviews,* Vol. 1, edited by Jack H. Wilmore (New York: Academic Press, 1973), pp. 126 ff; Lloyd L. Laubach, "Comparative Muscular Strength of Men and Women: A Review of the Literature," *Aviation, Space, and Environmental Medicine* 47, no. 5 (May 1976):534 ff; Sarah A. Nunneley, "Physiological Responses of Women to Thermal Stress: A Review," *Medicine and Science in Sports* 10, no. 4 (Winter 1978):250 ff; Jack H. Willmore, "The Application of Science to Sport: Physiological Profiles of Male and Female Athletes," *Canadian Journal of Applied Sports Sciences* 4, no. 2 (1979):103-15.

16. Wilbert M. Leonard, II, *A Sociological Perspective of Sport* (Minneapolis: Burgess, 1980), p. 201; National Federation of State High School Associations, *High School Sports Survey* (30 December 1980); SPRINT, "Statistics from the SPRINT Files Showing Evidence of Growth in the Participation of Women in Sport" (Washington, D.C.: Women's Equity Action League Educational and Legal Defense Fund, January 1980).

17. See Marlowe, Chapter 12.

18. For reviews of the literature, see Irene H. Frieze et al., *Women and Sex Roles: A Social Psychological Perspective* (New York: W. W. Norton, 1978); Eleanor E. Maccoby and C. N. Jacklin, *The Psychology of Sex Differences* (Stanford, Calif.: Stanford University Press, 1974); John P. Seward and Georgene H. Seward, *Sex Differences: Mental and Temperamental* (Lexington, Mass.: D. C. Heath, 1980).

19. See "Women Don't Belong in Combat," *Conservative Digest,* April 1979, p. 9.

20. Cecil D. Johnson, Bertha H. Cory, Roberta W. Day, and Laurel W. Oliver, "Women Content in the Army—REFORGER 77 (REF WAC 77)" (Alexandria, Va.: U.S. Army

Research Institute for the Behavioral and Social Sciences, Special Report S-7, 1978); U.S. Army Research Institute, "Women Content in Units Force Development Test (MAXWAC)" (Alexandria, Va.: U.S. Army Research Institute, 1977).

21. Grace M. King, "Women in Combat: The New Reality," paper presented at the meetings of the Inter-University Seminar on Armed Forces and Society (Chicago, October 1980); Treadwell, *Women's Army Corps.*

22. Philip A. Kalisch and Margaret Scobey, "Female Nurses in American Wars: Help-lessness Suspended for the Duration," paper presented at the meetings of the Inter-University Seminar on Armed Forces and Society (Chicago, October 1980), p. 6.

23. Ibid., p. 15.

24. See, for example, Anne Eliot Griesse and Richard Stites, "Russian and Soviet Women in War and Peace," paper presented at the meetings of the Inter-University Seminar on Armed Forces and Society (Chicago, October 1980); and chapters in *Women in Combat,* edited by Nancy L. Goldman (Westport, Conn.: Greenwood Press, forthcoming).

25. Peter B. Bloch and Deborah Anderson, *Policewomen on Patrol: Final Report* (Washington, D.C.: Police Foundation, May 1974); Judith Greenwald, Harriet Connolly, and Peter Bloch, *New York City Policewomen on Patrol* (Washington, D.C.: Police Foundation, 1974).

26. Department of Defense, *Background Review,* p. 83.

27. Ibid., pp. 45-46.

28. Ibid., pp. 47-50.

29. Ibid., p. 50.

30. Ibid., p. 77.

31. Ibid., pp. 77-79, 134-40.

32. See Anne Hoiberg and Patricia Thomas, "The Economics of Sex Integration: An Update of Binkin and Bach," paper presented at the meetings of the Inter-University Seminar on Armed Forces and Society (Chicago, October 1980), Table 6.

33. For a review of the evidence, see David H. Marlowe, "Cohesion, Anticipated Breakdown, and Endurance in Battle: Considerations for Severe and High Intensity Combat" (Washington, D.C.: Walter Reed Army Institute of Research, 1980).

34. Johnson et al., "Women Content"; U.S. Army Research Institute, "Women Content."

35. Department of Defense, *Background Review,* pp. 74-75.

36. See, for example, Marlowe, Chapter 12, this volume p. 195.

37. Ibid., pp. 191-95; Seth Cropsey, "Women in Combat?" *The Public Interest* 61 (Fall 1980): 58-73; Richard A. Gabriel, "Women in Combat?" *Army* (March 1980): 45, 48-50, 52.

38. See, for example, Lucian K. Truscott IV, *Dress Gray* (New York: Fawcett Crest, 1978). The psychological survival mechanisms used by this novel's protagonist, a West Point cadet, illustrate how being with women (and thinking about women) functions as an escape from the world of the Academy.

39. Lois B. DeFleur, "Four Years of Sex-Integration: Changing Attitudes, Beliefs, and Interactions at the U.S. Air Force Academy," paper presented at the meetings of the Inter-University Seminar on Armed Forces and Society (Chicago, October 1980).

40. Department of Defense, *Background Review,* p. 96.

41. Ibid.

Drafting Women: Pieces of a Puzzle

SARA RUDDICK

Should women be recruited for military service and for combat?* Traditionally, in this country, women have relations to men, to their state, and to its wars that limit their participation in military service and exempt them from combat. Currently, we are questioning each of these relations. Our initial question raises at least five others: Do women have a right to fight, and if so, do they have a duty to serve that justifies recruiting them? Are women obligated to their state and its wars for the same reasons and to the same degree as men? Are women required to share the risks of battle out of fairness to men? Do women have a distinctive interest in peace and a distinctive capacity to bring it about? If so, should they be recruited for, or exempted from, the military in the interest of peace?

These are questions about the rights and obligations of women as citizens, warriors, and peacemakers. Each acquires new seriousness if we consider conscription—the forcing of women to act on their obligations to the state or to men by serving in the military.

Conscription for military service, and even more for combat, is prima facie an evil. All conscripted citizens suffer serious loss of liberty, while some may be forced into combat with its threat of injury or death. When it conscripts citizens either to support or to participate in battle, the state arrogates to itself central questions of moral life. When, if ever, am I permitted or obligated to kill another person in my own defense or for the common good? When, if ever, am I permitted or obligated to risk my life in self-defense? In defense of those close to me? For the common good? A state that denies its citizens the right to answer these questions for themselves infringes a liberty fundamental to their identity as moral persons. *Selective* service, no matter how fairly administered, requires a few to bear the burden of conscription while others, because of chance and circumstance, go free. To the burden of service is added the gall of inequity.

What, then, ever gives the state the right to conscript its citizens? Do the arguments that permit conscription in the first place apply to women? If no argument justifies conscripting any citizen, then, a fortiori, none justifies conscripting women. If, without justification, the state nonetheless imposes conscription on its citizens, who then should be conscripted? If the state violates the rights of some citizens, must it, paradoxically, out of *fairness,* violate the rights of as many citizens as possible?

* I am grateful to Carol Ascher, Peter G. Brown, William Ruddick, Marilyn Young, and especially Robert Fullinwider for careful reading and critical comments.

In this chapter, I examine women's relation to their state and its wars, and the implications of that relation for our military personnel policies. In the first section, I defend women's right to fight and argue that the right does not imply a duty to serve and consequently does not justify conscription. In the second section, I briefly sketch two accounts of women's obligation to their state, only one of which gives them equal responsibility with men for its wars. I argue, however, that this account of political obligation does not justify conscripting citizens and is incompatible with *selective* service.

In the third section, I consider issues of fairness. Many who believe that conscription cannot be justified in terms of the rights and duties of citizens nonetheless advocate it on the ground that a conscripted army is fairer than an All-Volunteer Force (AVF). In particular, the relatively poor male soldier fighting an unjust and unpopular war in a foreign land bears a heavy military burden that relatively affluent citizens do not. A draft, however, is an unreliable and morally costly instrument of fairness. I ask whether the benefit from conscription for the relatively poor male combat soldier is sufficiently weighty and predictable to justify a draft. I try to clarify the question but leave the question mark standing. Many who do not believe that conscription is justified argue that once a draft is implemented, women should be included out of fairness to men. I claim that women are required by fairness to share the burdens of battle with *conscripted* men. However, I am puzzled by the moral worth of fairly distributing burdens no one should bear.

In the last section I consider the implications of women's "peacefulness" for military personnel policies. I examine the claim that women have special interests in and capacities for resolving conflicts and resisting evil nonviolently, but I do not endorse drafting women in the interest of peace. I believe, however, that women's peacefulness might be effectively developed in pacifist movements. If so, there are grounds for excluding women from a draft in the interest of peace. On the other hand, if battles are left to men, it may be easier to let the fighting start.

I believe that the evil of violence outlasts the best intentions of the violent, that nuclear war is unconscionable, that conventional war is never wholly just and rarely justified, that it is imperative to develop effective nonviolent means of combating evil. I do not argue these points, though I do occasionally state or assume them. I have tried to consider the issue of women's relation to the military in such a way that those who anticipate fighting just wars are not excluded from the discussion. I do not consider the question of when or how to fight an easy one, nor believe that goodness lies only with those who answer it in a particular way. Nonetheless, my (near) pacifism inevitably shapes my discussion.

The Right to Fight

The "right to fight" is the right to train for and participate in combat.[1] It is a right conditional upon fulfilling qualifications established by military professionals. To fight and to command fighters, when qualified to do so, is a right conferred upon citizens and cannot be denied them because of their membership in a class or a group.

Women claiming the right to fight are claiming full citizenship. They argue that sex alone should not preclude them from any military tasks or ranks. Moreover, qualifications established by military professionals, almost all of whom are men, should be examined for sex bias unjustified by military needs.

The right to fight has a history and moral significance which I will not explore here. Suffice it to say that in our society assuming the burdens of combat has enabled previously despised groups to earn respect and some political-economic power. Correlatively, some groups have been denied the right to command and fight because they were considered socially powerless and stigmatized as inferior.

Many pacifists who are committed to resolving conflicts and resisting evil non-violently still recognize the importance of the right to engage in military combat. A *moral* decision to renounce weapons depends upon the ability and freedom to use them. The war-resister who breaks his gun must first have it in his hands. Moreover, people who are pacifists by default, as most women have been, may easily find themselves tempted by the apparent effectiveness and by the vicarious or direct pleasure of violent destruction.

The right to participate in any combat tasks for which they are qualified has special symbolic significance for women. A sense that we cannot protect ourselves or those we care for has undermined our independence. We need to be strong and to have our strength recognized. Moreover, the military institution, more than others, is a bastion and expression of masculinism. The grounds for excluding women from battle are familiar from other struggles: we are "too weak," "psychologically unreliable," "professionally incapable," and worst of all, "a trouble for men." But there is a special point in proving our ability to fight where stakes are high and where, hitherto, masculinity has prevailed. Military success would challenge the perception, common in civilian life, that women are weak, dependent, and powerless. Hence, for these and other reasons, it is not surprising to find women who worry about letting their sons play with water pistols nonetheless defending women's capacity to "carry the fight to the enemy" with our fiercest weapons.

Some have argued that if women claim the right to fight and command, they are morally required to assume the correlative duty to serve in the military and prepare for combat. But this seems wrong. Women who claim the right to fight are comparable to women who claim the right to have children. The latter argue that neither the needs of population control nor any other policy is sufficient to deny them the right to have children if they choose. Similarly, would-be fighters claim that discriminatory policies should not hinder them from participating in military activity for which they are qualified. But neither right entails that a woman in fact choose to participate in the activity to which she is entitled. Her correlative duty is to take upon herself whatever responsibilities follow from having acted on her rightful choice, from having joined the military or borne children. Indeed, it is often a virtue to refuse to act on legitimate rights. I can legitimately demand that the scholar on welfare who borrowed ten dollars from me last week should repay me, but it would be unseemly for me to do so. I might claim the right to choose to fight in front-line combat, but believe that it is almost always wrong for anyone to be fighting there.

If the right to fight does not imply the duty to do so, it does not, a fortiori, imply the state's right to enforce that duty. Yet proponents of equal rights make several plausible claims about the social connection of the right to fight and liability to conscription. If women were conscripted, women volunteers already enlisted in the services would be able to use the fact of conscription, as well as the greater female presence it would probably generate, as a rhetorical and practical aid in the struggles for equal treatment in the military. To suggest, as some have done, that women not be drafted because they cannot currently be fully utilized in combat positions puts the practical cart before the moral horse. If women have the right to participate in combat tasks for which they are qualified, that they are now illegitimately excluded from them provides occasion for military reform in which revised draft laws could play a role.

In civilian society, it is argued, conscription will aid women in achieving full citizenship, both because submission to conscription is thought to warrant full citizenship and because conscription, by increasing women's power and presence in the military, undermines our acceptance of gender division in the society at large. If, on the other hand, men are conscripted while women are not, women's power within the military will be weakened and their claims to full citizenship will suffer.

These are plausible hypotheses. I will express them, roughly, as the claim that conscription for women is an instrumental good because it tends to lead toward the realization of women's rights. If one believes on other grounds in the justifiability of conscription, then its benefit for women's citizenship rights gives an additional reason for its implementation. If, however, conscription is the evil it appears to be, then its likely benefit for women's rights will not outweigh the harm done to women or men. But if conscription is instituted despite its evil, then its benefit for women's rights, combined with consideration of fairness to the men affected, weighs heavily in favor of conscripting women. I will take up this question later when discussing issues of fairness.

Finally, the priority we should give to women's military or civil *rights* when addressing the issues of war and peace is problematic. Militarists might claim that, given the prejudices of men and women, even qualified women will, through no fault of their own, make less effective soldiers than men; they should not, therefore, take the time of Selective Service boards nor the place of male conscripts. In a similar way, pacifists might recognize the importance to women of the right to fight, but speak against their conscription. Forcing women into military training, they might argue, would change both them and the society they leave: women would no longer be, or be seen as, a distinct effective force for peace. I will take up this issue in the last section.

The Duty to Serve in the Military

If the right to fight does not imply the duty to serve, are there nonetheless other sources of obligation? If men are obligated to the state and its wars, are women obligated to the same degree and for the same reasons? People defending conscription usually argue that draft laws are merely the legal expression of a prior obligation. Hence, those favoring the conscription of women seek a gender-blind account of political obligation.

Women themselves have a far more ambivalent attitude toward citizenship than suggested by discussions of the right to fight. Many feminists self-consciously adopt the political identity of "outsider." While obeying criminal laws and paying their fair share of supportive social services, they want no part of nationalism. From their position as outsider, they criticize the very idea of "society" or "country" as it has developed:

> As a woman I have no country. As a woman I want no country. My country is the whole world.
>
> Inevitably, we look upon society, so kind to you, so harsh to us, as an ill-fitting form. . . . We look on societies as conspiracies that sink the private brother, whom many of us have reason to respect, and inflate in his stead a monstrous male, loud of voice, hard of fist.[2]

Many women who would never call themselves feminists believe that governments, and certainly their wars, are a male enterprise. Of men's making, they are terrible for everyone, but not women's responsibility. A woman's task in wartime is to maintain a "haven in a heartless world," preserving private decency and the lives of loved ones until the madness is past.

Political separatism is a force both within women's culture and in the smaller feminist community. Separatist attitudes affect discussions of conscription, although they may be voiced only in "women's space" behind the scenes of public debate. Those who would conscript women should look for an account of political obligation which the alienated woman and feminist outsider can take seriously as a requirement on themselves. I will consider two possible accounts of political obligation. The first bases obligation on the citizen-state relation; the second makes political obligation a consequence of general moral principles.[3]

According to the first account, citizens are obligated to their state because they stand in a special relation to it, that of participant-beneficiary.[4] Theories of democratic government and various forms of contractualism and consent theory describe a citizen's participation in ways that entail his obligation.[5] Briefly, the citizen is now obligated to serve the state because he has in the past consented to its system of legal and political obligations and, in a democracy, has participated in shaping their content. He is specifically liable to the drastic obligation of serving in the military because he has consented to or, more strongly, has participated in shaping the war policies of his government and the recruitment practices by which its wars are executed. As a beneficiary, the citizen receives two kinds of goods. The first is the minimal order and physical security necessary for any projects; the second, the supportive goods that enable his projects to succeed, which range from goods necessary for every project, such as adequate nutrition, health care, and basic education, to more optional enabling goods, such as graduate education and public television. Two criteria can evaluate the citizen as beneficiary. The first relates the degree of benefit to direct grants from the state, such as food stamps or income support. The more a citizen receives, the more obligated he is. The second criterion defines degree of benefit in terms of both direct grants and indirect benefits received from the state's political and economic organization. I will assume that the citizen most benefited is the one who directly or indirectly receives the greatest share of society's goods at the least personal cost.

A. John Simmons has joined others in arguing persuasively that the participant-beneficiary status of citizens cannot render them liable to conscription.[6] The participant-beneficiary status of citizens is probably inadequate to ground general political obligation and certainly does not yield the specific duty to serve in the military. Even if this theory did account for men's obligations, however, it would not obligate women to the same degree and for the same reasons. The point may seem obvious. Currently, women are not guaranteed equal legal rights with men nor equally represented in governing councils. As beneficiaries, women of every class are less protected and less supported in their independent projects than men of their class.

The attempt to account for women's obligations in terms of their participant-beneficiary status underlines a general weakness of the theory. Because there are many kinds and degrees of benefit and participation, the theory obligates citizens to different degrees. Only the most benefited and most fully participant citizens will be subject to a requirement as drastic as service in the military. If, on this theory, a state can legitimately force anyone into service, it will justifiably begin by drafting those men—and that class of men—who most directly control and

benefit from society's arrangements. Some may believe such differential obligation is just; others will find that it violates their moral intuitions about the
foundations of political life. But whatever one expects from accounts of political
obligation, this one will not obligate women.

The second account of political obligation directs our attention to the state of
which the citizen is a member.[7] The citizen owes service to a relatively just state
because such states are necessary instruments of moral good. A state's justice
turns upon the benefits citizens receive (both minimal and supportive) and upon
the degree to which the citizens participate in determining the content and manner
of distributing benefits and other state policies. We can say that the degree to
which its citizens are participant-beneficiaries largely determines the extent to
which a state is just. But despite the similarity of language, we should not
assimilate our two theories. On the second theory a citizen will be obligated to
fight (if he is) not because his state commands and he is beholden to it, but
because his state is just and he is moral. His obligation to a particular state is
twofold: to preserve it and to increase its justice. This obligation follows from a
natural duty to preserve states in their justice, because just states are necessary
for the implementation of moral principles and for the conduct of moral life.

In assessing a state's justice, we begin by looking at the participation and
benefits it offers its own members. Even this assessment is not merely an internal,
national matter. Citizens depend upon the security of an international order and
upon the benefits of reliable international economic exchange. But national and
international justice are not connected primarily through a state's self-interest. A
theory that bases political obligation on moral principle does not limit its scope to
the well-being of one national group. The moral subject is nationless, just as she
or he is classless and sexless. A state's justice is strongly determined by the
extent to which its policies abet or impede the security and benefits of the world's
citizens.[8]

On this second, moral account of political obligation, what are a citizen's
obligations in respect to the war policies of his state? If we focus on a just state
under attack, matters may seem simple. A citizen will usually be obligated to *his*
just state, because it is "efficient" to preserve justice where he lives and he is
obligated to the people he lives among to preserve the just institutions they share.
He can, however, with moral consistency escape the fight in order to devote his
energies (and life) to states whose justice is greater or at greater risk. Moreover,
not every attack threatens the survival or justice of a state. A citizen must
determine whether military defense is, for the state and for him personally, the
only or best way to fulfill his duty to preserve just states and their justice. His
evaluation will depend upon his interpretation of the circumstances of the attack
in the light of just-war doctrine and upon the ease with which he accepts or rejects
the use of organized violence.[9]

Most wars are not responses to direct attack. What can we say *in general* about
a citizen's relation to the wars of his state? I think he is obligated to assist in
prosecuting just wars so that they may achieve their aims as quickly and with as
little harm as possible. He is obligated to resist unjust wars, to bring them to a
close with as little harm as possible. He is obligated, as well, to assist and resist in
a way that maximizes the justice and security of the state. I will call this set of
obligations the *obligation to take responsibility for the violence of one's state.*

This obligation to take responsibility follows from the original obligation to
preserve just states. Just and unjust wars alike are a terrible curse which, among
other evils, decrease the participation of citizens in their government and lessen
their benefits. A citizen, even out of limited obligation to his own state, will try to

see that it wages war only as long as justice requires. Moreover, on the moral account of political obligation, a citizen's obligation to *his* state is a consequence of general moral principles and their requirement on him to preserve just states in general. A state that pursues unjust wars is undermining the moral well-being of citizens of the world. A citizen preserving the justice of the state is responsible for its uses of violence.

The obligation to take responsibility for the violence of one's state admits degrees. We have some discretion in construing our duty, depending upon the circumstances of our lives and upon our conflicting obligations, especially to children and other dependents. Moreover, in regard to such a serious duty we rightly allow degrees of virtue. We will admire the courage of both fighter and war resister, while being slow to condemn those who act in ways less costly to themselves.

But whatever the individual variation, it is wrong to expect a group to be less moral because it receives less than its fair share of benefits and has little power to shape the policies of its state. On the moral account of political obligation from which we derived the obligation to take responsibility, no basis exists *in theory* for distinguishing between the obligations of citizens on grounds of their status as participant-beneficiaries. More important, there is no basis in history for assuming that individuals have less courage, moral insight, or political perspicuity because they are women, poor, or members of oppressed groups. The responsibility for the violence of one's state derives from general moral principles binding on all moral subjects. On this theory, neither gentile nor Jew in Nazi Germany, neither black nor white in South Africa is required to preserve her/his state in its injustice. Similarly, if women are less participant in and benefited by the state than men, they are nevertheless still obligated to preserve their state and increase its justice. Indeed, working for social reform to increase the state's justice to women is one way for men and women to fulfill their general obligation to preserve their state and its justice.

If someone questioned whether women and men are equally obligated to take responsibility for the violence of the state, this would be tantamount to asking whether men and women are the same kind of moral being. Though the enterprise of morality is human, many believe that women have a distinctive moral voice.[10] Gender, they claim, is revealed in the most abstract principles, which display a male bias (when formulated publicly, by men) both in their content and in the manner in which they are articulated and justified. Gender differences may be even more evident in the application of moral principles. Women may, for example, have different concepts of the "justice" of a war, of the priority of "conscientiousness" over "objective" reason, of the conflict between duties to one's homeland and to the world's people.

Even if women speak in a different moral voice, the enterprise of morality may be universal. If moral thinking is common to both genders—and all races and classes—the concept of a moral person, whose characteristics are specified independent of gender, is central to it. Only separatists of the most radical sort, who believe and hope that women are essentially different moral creatures from men, will deplore the inclusion of women as full moral agents. Those who believe and hope, to the contrary, that there is a *human* moral enterprise, will include themselves in it and provide for gender differences by enunciating, refining, and applying moral principles in a style and with a content suitable to the culture from which they come and to which they are loyal.

There *are* separatists, and I have not argued against them nor even suggested the complexity of their position. I have only wanted to suggest that, on the moral account of political obligation, to say that women are different political creatures from men is to challenge the concept of moral personhood. I take it to be a virtue of this account that it pushes political separatism to its intellectual and moral limits.

What, then, does this moral account of political obligation have to do with conscription? If the obligation were to "repay" benefits to the state by complying with its demands, conscription laws might be the legal expression of one particular command, namely, to serve in the military when "called." However, no such direct relation exists between conscription and the obligation to take responsibility for the violence of one's state. When a state prosecuting a *just* war "calls" its citizens to fight, then responding to the call may be the best or only way to assist in the war effort. But it does not follow that a state has a right to force someone to answer the call, someone who may have conflicting obligations, great personal costs, or a different assessment of the cause or the uses of organized violence. Draft laws may, of course, be framed to accommodate just such objectors. If so, they will recognize that neither the military nor the peace movement has the right to force citizens to assist or resist wars against their judgment and will. Certainly, the state does not have the moral right to force citizens to assist in unjust wars, even though, under our Constitution, it has the legal power to do so.

Nonetheless, conscription might be seen as a means for inducing citizens to assume their obligation to take responsibility for the violence of their state. A conscription law could be framed to require all citizens to consider seriously the war policies of their state and to present their reflection before a duly appointed board. In peacetime, citizens would choose between military training or training in pacifist techniques of reconciliation and nonviolent resistance. Training could last a short time, but periodic refresher courses would be required. In the event of war, all citizens would be "mobilized." Those who believed the war was right and necessary would devote themselves to achieving its aims so that the fighting could cease. Those who believed that the violence was unjustified would either organize to achieve war aims nonviolently or, if the aims themselves were misguided, to put an end to battle. Some citizens would, however, be unclear about the justice of a war or the risk they felt it justified. They would be allowed to find "alternative" ways to preserve the state in its justice. Those few citizens who were prevented from any service because of severe handicaps or conflicting obligations could be exempted.

For a conscription law to encourage obligation, it would obviously have to be sex-blind. Indeed, if conscription reflects our obligation to take responsibility for the violence of our state, then all citizens must be subject to it. In the initial years of the law, efficiency would require selection as each citizen waited his or her turn for training. Such selection would have to cut fairly across race, class, sex, and age. In later years, it would be necessary to train only the young, all (or most) other citizens having already received their training. It would be important, however, to keep citizens of all ages in readiness for service. Some combat war tasks and some techniques of nonviolent resistance are appropriate only for the young and strong, but strength does not stop at 26, nor do all combat jobs require physical prowess. Any conscription law that places the greatest burdens of war and peace on our children who have the least responsibility for them is a perverse instrument of justice.[11] In war, efficiency would require both pacifists and militarists to be selected for some dangerous and unpleasant tasks, leaving other favored citizens to work for peace and/or victory in ways less personally disruptive. Such a selection may be made in many ways, taking into account abilities and professed willingness for dangerous service. The only requirement is that no group of citizens be exempted because of age, sex, race, or class, and that each individual citizen understand the reasons behind his or her particular service. The obligation to take responsibility for the violence of one's state cannot depend upon one's luck in a lottery, however fairly drawn.

It is obvious that no state will pass the kind of conscription law I have described. It is hard even to conceive of a state forcing citizens opposed to its policies to resist them actively. Conscription is used to get citizens to implement the war policies of a state, not to reflect upon them. Conscription has always worked to select some citizens, primarily males of a certain age, to do the fighting for the rest of us. It does not encourage the selected young men to question the violence they may perpetrate and suffer, but rather to engage in a battle others have initiated whose justice they may assume. The conscription law I have imagined is clearly a fantasy.

Even those drawn to the fantasy would find reasons to reject it. Libertarians would shudder at the state control such conscription would require. Many pacifists, although recognizing the need for training and discipline, would refuse to force anyone to participate even in nonviolent forces. Many militarists would oppose a citizen army, most of whose members would be of an age to think critically about the battles to which they were sent. And older citizens who can now cheerfully countenance training the young and requiring their service would find it quite "impractical" to have their own lives disrupted. Nonetheless, the fantasy is a useful one because it reveals what kind of conscription the moral account of political obligation would require. It shows that no conscription law we have had or are likely to have can be justified in terms of the obligations of citizens to take responsibility for the violence of their state.

Conscripting and Fairness

Even if conscription is not justified by political obligation, it may be introduced because, when all harms and benefits are taken into account, it is morally preferable to any other military personnel policy. The most commonly cited virtue of conscription is its fairness. Universal conscription, or conscription of all of a certain age group, is commonly thought to be the fairest policy. Many argue that even a selective draft would more fairly distribute military burdens than the AVF.

I am concerned primarily with issues of fairness that arise from the sex imbalance of the AVF. Without doubt, a sex-blind draft law would more fairly distribute military burdens now borne disproportionately by men. But most people who advocate conscription on grounds of fairness are not concerned with sex, but with the interconnected imbalances of class and race. Feminists sensitive to the unfairness visited upon women from gender discrimination are prepared, in intellectual and emotional consistency, to contest unfairness arising from class or race. Moreover, women as citizens are committed to military-staffing policies consonant with demands of justice.

In the following examination of fairness in relation to race and class, I will presume that AVF recruits see enlistment as in their own interest; and that the benefits offered by the AVF (economic gain, education, job training, patriotic service, a chance to fight, physical training) are deemed *by them* to be beneficial. If recruits are misled, misinformed, or ignorant about the character and burdens of military life, this is occasion for reform, not conscription.[12] The options of recruits may be severely limited by social-economic and personal conditions, over which they have no control. Some soldiers will hate the military life, which they undergo. Nonetheless, the AVF asks the recruit to match burden with promised benefit, and promises a measure of autonomy for those who enlist.

I will assume that there is now, and will continue to be, a disproportionate number of financially disadvantaged soldiers in the AVF and that a disproportionate number of these are members of racially or ethnically oppressed groups.[13] These soldiers are poor first because they have few options in civilian society; then because they have few options, they remain poor and oppressed. The class and race imbalance of the AVF reveals unpleasant truths both about the military and about the society from which it recruits. The composition of the AVF strongly suggests that the military offers unpleasant, unrewarding work which the affluent and ethnically privileged will avoid. Those who think of soldiers as "true volunteers" who like to fight and are moved by patriotic loyalties will not welcome this revelation. Even more serious, when the military is seen as an unpleasant job which those with other options avoid, the AVF clearly reveals the class divisions and racism which it embodies.

The AVF does not, of course, create the unpleasantness of military life nor the social injustices it reveals. Moreover, most of society's dirty, unpleasant, mind- and back-breaking jobs are done by poorer citizens, often of oppressed groups. Even those committed to redressing inequalities and fighting racism do not advocate conscripting for these jobs. Rather, they seek to improve the conditions of work and compensation for the worst jobs while striving for general social change. Similarly, we might improve the quality and rewards of volunteer military life at the same time as we redressed the inequities of civilian life embodied in, though not caused by, the AVF.

Why, then, do so many find the unfairness of the AVF intolerable? I cannot begin to answer this question here, but I will draw attention to two interconnected reasons for this intolerance. The first turns upon the relation of a state and its war policies to its citizens. Armies are meant to carry out the will of the state which, in a democratic society, is also said to be the will of a people. When soldiers fight for money and other advantages, armies seem external to the will of the state and unable to express the people's consent. Some would hold that the dominance of any group in the military—say, a group of technically trained, ethnically privileged men from families of the rich—would violate the ideal of a "citizen" army. Others would hold that conducting war policies with armies fighting for money rather than principle denies legitimacy to the policies and undermines the very idea of *patriotic* interest.

Unfortunately for advocates of conscription, an army of conscripts seems to many as illegitimate as an army of the poor. In their eyes, a state which forces its citizens to kill and risk injury or death has exceeded its authority. In any case, issues of legitimacy, consent, national will, and patriotic identity are not issues primarily of fairness—the equitable distribution of burdens and benefits. I bring up these concerns with legitimation here because they can be confused with issues of fairness and often underlie the refusal to tolerate the unfairness of the AVF.

The second reason given for refusing to tolerate the unfairness of the AVF is that the military burden is simply too great to be unfairly distributed. Three distinct ideals of fairness are invoked by proponents of this claim. The strictest insists that military burdens should be shared by everyone, with any minimal selection justified by clear military necessity; only universal military training and, in case of war, universal mobilization could fulfill this ideal. The second ideal does not require universality, but proportionality: admittedly unequal burdens should be distributed so that no identifiable group bears more than its proportionate share. A class-, race-, and sex-blind draft which cut across age wherever militarily feasible would satisfy this criterion. The third ideal allows, and sometimes requires, disproportionate representation, but insists that overrepresented groups be composed of the most powerful and advantaged members of society. A selective draft would have to exempt the poor to fulfill this ideal.

Clearly the AVF fails to meet each of these ideals of fairness. It selects, it selects disproportionately, and it selects citizens who bear a heavy share of society's burdens and have little power to shape its war policies. This is appalling. However, the unfairness of the AVF does not in itself justify conscription. Before we can take that step we must answer several questions, among them: How great is the burden of military service and who is to say? Who exactly will be relieved of military burdens by conscription, and how will they benefit from that relief? Will the draft prove a reliable instrument of fairness?

To start with the second question, how exactly will conscription benefit the victims of unfairness? Benefit from conscription will depend upon how the draft is used. One might draft relatively affluent citizens to supplement existing forces, still allowing relatively poor recruits to serve. Alternatively, one might use drafted soldiers to replace poor soldiers, thereby keeping the size of the forces fixed. Consider the case in which drafted soldiers are used to supplement existing forces. The same poor soldiers will serve, but they may benefit from the presence of affluent soldiers serving with them. In a society structured by race and class, all soldiers may be better treated when members of advantaged groups make up a large proportion of the ranks. Before resorting to a policy as serious as conscription in the interest of poor soldiers, however, we would have to determine the exact nature of their predictable benefit.

Poor soldiers will benefit from the presence of the affluent only if the draft is universal or designed to select the relatively affluent. Even its proponents now believe universal conscription is neither economically nor politically feasible. In the past, a selective draft allowed the affluent to avoid service. In fact, some arguments show that even a lottery will favor the affluent citizen.[14] Moreover, no one has yet endorsed the third ideal of fairness, which would exclude from conscription any poor or racially oppressed person who does not choose service. Therefore, in a conscript army some poor soldiers are likely to bear the double burden of military service and conscription, whereas in the AVF poor soldiers bear only the first.

Let us assume for the moment that we can and will enlarge our forces by means of a draft designed to select (only?) affluent citizens. To achieve the benefits envisioned for the poor soldier, force size would have to be *substantially* increased. The larger the force, the greater the chance to approximate the unrealizable ideal of universality and to realize the ideal of disproportionate burden-sharing by the affluent and powerful. But the larger the force, the greater the number subject to military training and indoctrination, and the larger the standing armies to which the nation would be committed. Someone who believes that compulsory military training and large standing armies are in the nation's interest might well enlarge the forces by conscription to provide potential benefits to the poor. Those, and I am one of them, who fear the consequences of greater militarization will ask: what moral price are we willing to pay for fairness?

Let me now turn to the replacement or poor volunteers with affluent conscripts. To do this we need only combine draft calls with recruitment policies that exclude the poor. This relieves some poor soldiers of a burden of military service, which is thought by some to be intolerably onerous. How great is the burden of service?

Are recruits well served when they are relieved of a burden that they themselves in some sense "chose"?

It is often assumed that poor recruits enter the military only because they have no tolerable, viable options in civilian life.[15] Rejection by the military does nothing, of course, to increase the poor citizen's civilian options. Some would argue that she or he is nonetheless better off in the worst civilian life than in the military. This assumes, but does not argue, that peacetime military service is indeed a dreadful burden, that its apparent advantages and pleasures are illusory. Moreover, the rhetoric suggests that only the worst-off civilians would ever choose the military, whereas in fact the "worst-off," most impoverished and demoralized "underclass" is usually rejected by the AVF.[16]

A comparison of the burdens of *peacetime* military life with impoverished civilian life, not easy in any case, is often skewed by an ignorant and intolerant antimilitarism. Moreover, it is misguided as well as arrogant for the affluent to do the comparing.[17] Those who wish to exclude poor soldiers from the military jobs they would choose must know them well enough and be sufficiently committed to their welfare to vouch for the benefit they will receive from the exclusion.

Those who find the unfairness of the AVF intolerable do not usually have *peacetime* military service in mind. The job of the military is to train for, and perhaps to engage in, battle. Peace cannot be sharply or reliably separated from war. Undeclared wars, gradual escalations, and sudden outbreaks give the peacetime soldier little time to reflect on or to escape battle. In war a soldier can be mortally endangered spiritually, physically, and psychologically. This is indeed a terrible burden.

The unfairness soldiers in wartime suffer in comparison to civilians is partly determined by the nature of war. In ground wars fought at home, or in air wars, civilians bear a large share of war's burden; however, we in America are used to fighting our wars in other people's lands. When we let our soldiers do our killing and suffering for us, their burden seems far larger than that of civilians. When a war is neither just nor popular (as seems to me likely for future American wars), then the soldier's burden becomes unconscionable. Quite aside from those who are killed or crippled, soldiers suffer longstanding damages from war experience. For a variety of reasons those damages are more extensive when their battle is, or is seen as, unjust.

If excluded from a battle for which he or she would volunteer, the poor soldier is indeed relieved of a terrible burden. Perhaps no group of citizens should be deliberately selected to bear that burden. But the ideal of universality is unrealizable. On both the second and third ideals of fairness, we are justified in relieving the poor soldier of a burden which the affluent replacement must bear instead. Nevertheless, we might still ask whether conscription is the only or the best way to redress the unfairness the poor soldier suffers. This question cannot be answered independently of at least two others.

First, what weight do we give to the burden of conscription itself and especially to the denial of freedom of conscience which conscription implies? I have said that a state which denies citizens the right to decide for themselves when to kill or risk their lives infringes a liberty fundamental to their identity as moral persons. Our draft laws allow some rights to conscience. But by refusing to allow conscientious objection to particular wars they encourage hypocrisy and prevent many young citizens from reflective, unfrightened deliberation about the most serious moral questions they are likely to confront. Moreover, the current law gives an advantage to better-off young people, who have the knowledge and support required to make good a claim of conscientious objection, or to make jail more survivable if the claim fails, or to make a good recovery after the jail term is over. I believe that conscription coerces the conscience of all classes and that such coercion is always wrong and can be tolerated only when it is necessary to redress a clear evil. The poor, however, have least defense against coercion.

Second, how does a draft affect a government's ability to prosecute and prolong a war? If a draft makes it more difficult to fight, then it relieves the burdens of all soldiers and many civilians as well as the poor soldier it may exclude. But if a draft makes it easier to prosecute or prolong a war, the benefit it provides for the excluded soldier may be outweighed by the burdens borne by all soldiers. In other words, the interests of fairness and of peace may conflict.

Fairness to Men

The AVF is now predominantly male and probably would continue to be so even in the absence of recruitment or other military policies that discriminate against women. Women are more likely to be poor than men, but they seem less likely to believe that the economic advantages of military service outweigh the concomitant burdens for them. Women seem less likely to want to fight or train to fight, and even when they are patriotic supporters of our government's war policies, they are less likely to find military service the best expression of their patriotism.

It is frequently argued that men are victims of a pervasive masculinist ideology which they neither understand nor control. Moreover, class and gender frequently combine to induce young men into especially dangerous forms of service. For example, one sociologist argues:

> The "manhood hustle" channels black males into the army because they have no viable options in civilian society. . . . Wanting to prove their manhood contributes toward [their] joining the more dangerous elite military units (such as the paratroopers and special forces) in far greater proportion than their numbers in the regular Army. In the Vietnam war, for instance, 26 percent of all casualties were black. The aftershocks of that war were even more devastating for the blacks who served in it. Even with the high rate of drug addiction, unemployment, crime and psychological problems of black male civilians, the Vietnam war veterans have an even higher rate. It is a terribly high price to pay for one's manhood.[18]

It seems to me likely that if women were drafted to supplement existing forces, the resulting degenderization would benefit all soldiers, including the women volunteers now in the service. Indeed, the benefits of degenderization seem somewhat easier to predict than those of gentrification through conscripting the affluent. The benefit of rejecting men who would otherwise volunteer depends again on whether we think primarily of peace or wartime service. The male soldier rejected for service is left to "prove his manhood" in ways that are presumably less effective in his eyes and, if he is a member of a poor or racially oppressed group, in fact may be more dangerous. But if women replaced male volunteers fighting foreign wars, some men would be relieved of an unconscionable burden, of which men as a group have always borne a disproportionate share.

The same questions about the relation of conscription to conscience and peace arise when speaking of sex imbalance. More important, despite the probable benefit to men of conscripting women, *fairness* seems not to be served if an unwilling female conscript were to replace a willing male volunteer. Many male volunteers may well be victims of a masculinist ideology dangerous to them; but whereas both men and women suffer from the effects of a masculinist ideology, men also benefit from them. The burden of military service chosen under the influence of masculinism is matched by the benefits maleness confers throughout civilian life. The conscripted woman would bear the double burden of military service and conscription, while being held responsible for saving her brother from a masculinism at least as much his doing as hers. Moreover, it is likely that once in the service, being female would bring the same kind of disadvantages with which women are familiar from civilian life, perhaps exaggerated by the masculinism that prevails in the military.

No one, as far as I know, has advocated conscripting women out of fairness to male volunteers. Some advocate conscripting affluent citizens of both sexes out of fairness to poor soldiers, who are in fact likely to be male. But these advocates seek to redress imbalances of race and class and are only coincidentally concerned with sex imbalance. Serious questions about sex imbalance arise only when a draft is presumed.

Some argue that greater liability to conscription is not unfair to men because men like battle and military life far more than women do. Conscripts, of course, do not want to join the military enough to enlist but, the argument runs, once resigned to the necessity of serving, men find military life far less burdensome than do women. Male traditions prepare them to fight, and a masculinist ideology that defines and elicits aggressive "maleness" makes it easier for them to do so. I find this unpersuasive. Men neither choose nor control male traditions and masculinist ideology. More important, a conscript has chosen *not* to fight, sometimes despite the pressures of masculinist ideology. And many young men find the thought of killing or dying in battle terrifying and appalling.

A greater predilection for fighting is only one of the "natural" differences that some think justify men's greater liability to conscription. It has often been argued that it is a fact of "nature" that burdens fall differently on men and women. Women suffer the pains and dangers of childbirth as well as its pleasures. Some people consider the burdens of warriorhood as "natural" for men as those of childbirth for women. But in our society the burden of forced warriorhood seems far greater than that of *chosen* childbirth. Nor does nature preclude women from sharing military service, including combat, as men are precluded from sharing childbirth. Women have, socially, borne an unfair proportion of the cost of raising children, and this burden is similar to the burden of warriorhood for men. It has been so long accepted that it seems natural, though its connection with nature is tenuous and malleable. Once we allow ourselves to question the natural femininity of childcare we will question the natural masculinity of battle. Moreover, even if there were a causal chain connecting male hormones with male aggression— with, say, the capacity to bomb cities—why should we respect rather than try to alter the connection? "Nature" gives us our cards but does not tell us how to shuffle or play them.

I am not denying that in our present culture men on the whole make more willing and able soldiers. (It is clear, however, that our belief in men's military capabilities and pleasures runs far ahead of the evidence.) I do not see that their ability and willingness allow us to *force* warriorhood on young men who do not want it. Moreover, many young men are looking for new ways to live "male" lives, ways in which self-respect and sexual identity do not depend upon one's ability to be warriorlike.

One peculiar argument has been advanced to support excusing women from combat and therefore from a draft intended to supply combat troops. We, the civilians, the argument runs, would find it intolerable to see young women wounded, mutilated, and killed; therefore, we will not support a battle in which they are at risk. I wish this were the case, although unfortunately we seem all too willing to bomb or shoot at young women, especially if they are at some distance from us. But in any event, our reluctance to endanger young women hardly justifies us in putting men at risk. The question we should be asking is not whether we would be able to sacrifice our daughters, but rather, why are we able to sacrifice our sons?

I believe that if only men are held accountable for war, and primarily young men are forced to fight it, we will continue to embody aggressive, "immoral" impulses in male bodies and punish them accordingly, thereby creating new motives for and consequences of unfairness. I do not know why we, as parents, allow men to do our fighting, nor why we pick on young, vulnerable men even for jobs where physical strength is not required. I suspect the sexual-psychological story behind our apparent acquiesence in the sacrifice of our sons is not a pretty one. But whatever the psychological explanation of our willingness to force men into battle, it cannot morally justify the burden we put upon them or the exemption we accord to women.

One argument does weaken the legitimacy of drafting women out of fairness to conscripted men; the same argument that, in another context, I believe justifies the preponderance of men in the AVF. In every class, the argument runs, men are more powerful economically and politically than women of that class. This inequity is neither natural nor inevitable, but as long as it exists, men deserve the greater burden of battle. Moreover, men have made societies, their armies, and their wars. Battle, as I myself will argue in the last section, has a decidedly masculine look. How can it be fair that women participate in activities they neither shape nor understand in defense of societies in which they are the victims of unfairness?

The quick objection to this argument is that not all men are powerful or advantaged—perhaps not even in relation to women of their class. Indeed, few men feel able to shape or control societies, their armies, and their wars. Those arguing for the exemption of women might extend their argument to include the exemption of relatively poor and powerless men. Or they might acknowledge some injustice to some men but insist that women, as a class, here and now, always and everywhere, have borne a disproportionate share of life's burdens while reaping a small share of its benefits and powers. To force them now to partake in an alien, "male," perhaps immoral activity is unfair. One might allow, perhaps even encourage, women to volunteer for the military, thereby perhaps making conscription of men unnecessary. But if there must be conscripts, then this heavy and unnatural burden is fairly borne by men who, as a group, are the privileged and powerful.

This argument persuades many women, who feel its force deeply. I, however, am not satisfied with it. To me, the burden of *forced* military service seems an extremely heavy one. If a man without other special privilege is forced into combat against his will and judgment, his masculine privilege does not seem to compensate for the burden. Nor can I see in the young men I know, even in the arrogant and affluent ones, sufficient power and privilege to justify such a special hardship. (Matters would be different if we drafted powerful men in their mid-thirties through fifties.) For the moment, however, I want only to acknowledge the seriousness and passion of the argument and let the reader decide its worth.

One final troubling question: should we distribute fairly burdens no one should bear? If conscription is bad for anyone, shouldn't we keep as many people free of the evil as possible? What of the burden of doing evil? Should we, for example, see that the order to kill in an unjust cause be fairly given to women and men of all classes? The question may seem to answer itself it we contemplate increasing the absolute number of people bearing a burden, for example, by adding conscripted women to the forces out of fairness to men already conscripted, or by increasing the number of immoral orders so that women too will be subject to them. The question remains puzzling if we consider restructuring the burdened group so that no class or kind of person is exempt. If women have been freed from participating in an admitted evil, should we out of fairness include them among its sufferers? Among its perpetrators?

Take the case of a combat soldier ordered to commit an immoral act, such as killing civilians.[19] This is a burden which, ex hypothesi, no one should bear. All of our efforts should go toward eliminating it altogether. But suppose we fail? When a burden is terrible and unjustified should we be all the more determined to distribute it fairly? Or should we insist that the burden is indefensible, mourn our failure, and let the people on whom it falls pay the heavy price of refusal or compliance? It will be their undeserved responsibility to disobey the immoral order, to refuse to fight the unjust battle. We must acknowledge, then, that at least in matters of war, the burden will probably continue to fall where it has always fallen—on a small group of men who are victims of chance, class, and gender. To this puzzle I have no solution.

Women and Peace

Militarists responsible for staffing policies often argue that moral issues should be subordinated to issues of effectiveness. Conscription may or may not distribute burdens fairly, infringe liberties, or compromise some citizens' right to fight. Its implementation or rejection should not depend upon these moral grounds, but upon its ability to produce an army better able to fight than an AVF. In producing such an army particular young men may be treated as means to achieve a general good. It is possible that their political obligations justify our use of these men. But if no obligation yields the right to conscript, we will conscript anyway, sacrificing individual lives and liberties to the war policies of the state.

Many people are now debating the implications of conscription for military strength. It is not clear that a conscripted army will fight more effectively than an AVF nor, even if it does, that its fighting ability will outbalance the social disruption of a draft that ultimately saps overall military effectiveness. I do not want to enter that discussion but to accept one of its premises, that the primary moral concern of military staffing policy is its effect on war and peace. Although fairness and liberty must never be ignored, some citizens may be treated unfairly, some liberties may be infringed, in the interest of the whole. Yet I would define the interest of the whole differently from many of those who raise armies. It is, as I see it, the primary interest of national and world citizens to render nuclear war impossible and to avoid conventional war. Consequently, if we decide to raise an army, the first task of our personnel policy is to raise an army that will refuse to fight an unjust war, that will fight a just war as humanely and briefly as possible, and that, in its fighting, will do nothing to increase the chances of nuclear war.

Many people who share this interest in peace argue in favor of conscription. Some "nuclear pacifists," for example, argue that a drafted army will be better able to fight conventional wars, thereby making nuclear war less likely. Some who reject both nuclear and conventional war argue that a draft provides a focus for resistance to any war; the wider the draft pool, the greater the base for resistance. Even if the number of soldiers remains fixed, it is important that no group of citizens be immune from the threat of conscription. Women and men of all classes and colors must realize they have to organize to end a war they don't want to fight. Moreover, proponents of conscription continue, drafted armies are less willing to go to battle and, once there, more eager to sue for peace. On this view, women make especially valuable conscripts just because they are less likely to want to be soldiers.

I myself am not convinced by arguments for conscription in the interest of peace. The "nuclear pacifist" argument depends upon an acceptance of conventional war and upon a faith in the separability of conventional and nuclear wars, neither of which I share. Because we are terrified of nuclear war we tend to underestimate the horror of conventional war and its weapons for our soldiers and the citizens in whose lands they fight. The more I understand of current battle plans, the more convinced I am of the danger that nuclear "exchanges" will grow out of conventional conflicts regardless of the presence of well-trained troops.

I believe that conscription makes it easier to fight wars, just as most of its proponents believe. Draft laws seem as likely to control effective protest as to arouse it. By misfocusing attention on a draft and its attendant conventional war, conscription makes it more difficult to organize for nuclear disarmament and to develop effective nonviolent ways of fighting evil which could replace conventional war. Moreover, conscription is a prima facie evil. Like the wars it services, it must be likely to achieve its just aims and it must be the "last resort" after other, less morally costly means of achieving them have failed. There seem to be ways of influencing military practices and government policy at least as likely to work in the interest of peace as conscription.

More could be said about the feasibility of conscripting for war in the interest of peace, but I want instead to focus on the particular issue of drafting women. It is widely believed that women have distinctive interests in and capacities for resolving conflicts nonviolently. Woman's "peacefulness," which militarists often deplore, might, from a peacemaker's point of view, make her an especially valuable conscripted soldier. Because women are, or are believed to be, especially peaceful, drafting them might "pacify" the military and its battlefields. "Peaceful" women would be slower than men to fight with weapons. When they did fight, they would do the least injury compatible with rendering their opponent harmless. They would always be on the look-out for ending the battle, thus saving soldiers on both sides from physical or psychic injury.

Drafted women are the most likely to be "peaceful." Unlike women in the AVF, they would not be self-selected and therefore would be less likely to be fighters or patriotic soldiers. They would be ordinary women, shaped by women's cultures and traditions out of which female peacefulness arises. Some argue that drafted women would be assigned service roles compatible with traditional female work. But women even now serve in support specialties which bring them into battle. If women were conscripted, pressures from volunteer women and male conscripts would bring women into various combat specialties. In any case, it is on the battlefield that peacemakers might want to see the "peaceful" female soldier.

Of course, few peacemakers actually argue for drafting women combatants just because they will fight less willingly and less fiercely than men. It is nonetheless useful to consider women's relation to the military from the perspective of those who believe women are radically different creatures from men. The popular belief that women are "peaceful" is sufficiently plausible to be taken seriously. If women are indeed more peaceful than men, or peaceful for different reasons and in different ways, both the militarist and peacemaker will want to take that peacefulness into account.

There is a widespread belief that women have distinctive interest in and capacity for peacemaking. Pacifists draw upon this belief to organize women against preparation for war.

> A woman's party for survival is being organized. . . . Women have tremendous power. As mothers we must make sure the world is safe for our babies. . . . Look at our growing children. Look at one child, one baby. I have three children. I am a doctor who treats children . . . I live with dying children. I live with grieving parents. I understand the value of every single human life. . . . I appeal especially to women to do this work [of peace] because we understand the genesis of life.[20]

On the other hand, feminists look at any alleged sex differences with a critical eye. No one denies that women and men now lead different social lives, nor that there is some biological basis for the difference. On the other hand, existing differences go well beyond those that biology can account for. They are largely the result of relegating childcare to women, educating children in sexist ways, training them for exclusive heterosexuality, and rewarding grown men and women for fulfilling expected sexual roles. They are also the result of economic inequities and the sheer force of men's institutionalized power. Moreover, whatever sex differences now exist are exaggerated and reified by those women and men who wish to maintain the gender division of power and work which sex differences seem to justify.

Nonetheless, since at least the suffrage movement, some feminists have insisted upon the distinctive character of women. Like other feminists, these "difference-feminists" (as I will call them) challenge sexual stereotypes and insist on women's citizenship rights. But they also believe that women, who now rightfully claim the instruments of public power, have cultures, traditions, values, and disciplines that we should bring to the public world. Women have, for example, learned to resolve conflicts nonviolently while at the same time resisting "evil" in their children and communities. They have acquired "disciplines" and "values" akin to those expected of pacifists.[21]

If women are believed to be peaceful, with equal certainty the military is believed to be male. That is, both the services and the wars they fight are male not just because fighters happen to be men, but because a masculinist ideology permits or coerces appropriately military attitudes and behavior. No one denies this. Indeed, it seems that soldiers are deliberately trained in maleness and misogyny: "Women are dinks. Women are villains. They are creatures akin to Communists and yellow skinned people and hippies.[22] Many marching chants include degrading references to women. Sexist terms for women and their bodies are commonplace in military discipline and play. Whatever the degree of explicit misogyny, it is agreed that

> The idea is manliness, crudely idealized. You liken dead friends to the pure vision of the eternal dead soldier. You liken living friends to the mass of dusty troops who have swarmed the world forever. And you try to find a hero.[23]

Just because the military is governed by a masculinist ideology, the mere presence of women who are believed to be peaceful could bring about changes. Commanders might be unable to encourage virtues allegedly "male," unable to coerce or permit actions on the grounds of gender identity. No one knows to what extent a change in ideology would change military practices. The change will be greater to the extent that women actually possess the characteristics they are believed to have. It is the combination of new ideology and actual femininity that is expected (hoped or feared) to be effective.

Many of the envisioned changes alter the style and method of military life, but not its values. Some of these changes may be quite trivial: tents are redesigned so that women as well as men can put them up. Others represent serious reforms. Once women are present in large numbers, military parents of both sexes may have their special needs recognized. Good day-care centers, health plans for parents and children, and flexible parental leaves could humanize the character of military life. Something like this seems to be happening in the AVF. But even serious reforms leave the ends and conduct of battle intact. The most promising (or worrying) claim is that when women are soldiers, values will change. Women might have a different conception of what it means to "win" a battle, what counts as an "acceptable" loss, or a "just" war. Or there might be a new priority between "winning" (newly defined) and the preservation of life and psychic health.

What can we make of the claim that women, just because they are more "peaceful" than men, will change the ends and conduct of battle? The argument for the greater pacifism of women has never claimed that women are born peaceful. Rather, women tend to become peaceful because many of us are, or expect to become, or identify with, mothers. Distinctive ways of conceptualizing, ordering, and valuing arise out of maternal practices. Some women, many of whom are not mothers, articulate and refine maternal thought, while actual mothers both develop and transmit it to their daughters. To describe the capacities, judgments, and values of maternal thought is not to presume maternal achievement. It is to describe a conception of achievement, the end to which maternal thinking is directed and the criteria by which success and failure are defined.

Although I will not attempt the task here, I believe that maternal thinking can be articulated with increasing precision and realism.[24] Moreover, and more important, the characteristics of maternal thinking can be accounted for by the theories that feminists are developing to explain sex differences.

If we assume that a distinctive kind of thinking has arisen out of maternal practices, can we connect that thinking to women's greater interest in and capacity for peacemaking? Though most people seem to make the connection, its legitimacy is not obvious. No one should claim that mothers don't get angry, though we do (I believe) manage, explain, and value anger differently from men. Mothers hate and they hit. They have also played their roles in the more organized violence of war. They have lent their blessings and sacrificed their sons to the most vile as well as to the most just of causes. When it has seemed appropriate for women to fight—to defend a besieged city or to take up arms when men have fallen—there is ample evidence that women fight no less fiercely than men. It has been argued that women fight only defensively in protection of their young and their home. But then, it is suggested, women fight "to the death," unrestrained by the rules of warfare that men, just because they are warlike, have had to develop.

Historically, women have played a dominant role in pacifist movements. Because of their courage and effectiveness as pacifists in a society where women had little voice and less power, these women publicized a pacifism which was womanly and, for them, self-consciously "maternal." But while women pacifists struggled against war and male dominance, countless other women prepared for war and countenanced the patriotic sacrifice of their sons. The militarist patriot, moved to protect her own children and homeland, or to rescue the victimized adults and children of other lands, is in no obvious way unmotherly. Both militarists and pacifists thought that their activism was justified by their responsibilities as nurturant mothers. Some wanted their sons forever freed from the threat of war; others wanted them to fight with the best guns and ships available. "Earlier I buttered bread for him, now I paint grenades and think, 'this is for him.' "[25] I will return later to the militarist mother. Let me now concentrate on the link between maternity and peacefulness which seems so obvious.

Can we identify features of maternal thinking that are contrary to behavior and attitudes we expect of men in battle? Let me take as an example women's "preservative love."[26] Maternal practice is governed by its primary demand that a child's life and psychic health be preserved. To a mother, committed to preserving a fragile being, life may seem "terrible, hostile, and quick to pounce on you if you give it a chance."[27] In response she develops an attitude toward human and nonhuman nature that I have called "holding." This attitude is characterized by the priority it gives to keeping over acquiring, to reconciling differences, to conserving the fragile, to maintaining the minimal peace and material conditions necessary to a child's life. Preservative love defines and rewards certain virtues, such as clear-sighted cheerfulness, because they enable a mother to "hold" and maintain the lives of others in an unpredictable world. A mother is faced with social and natural threats of psychic and physical damage and of death. Less dramatic, she deals daily with the independent and uncontrollable lives of the children whose growth she must foster. Typically, a mother develops a profound sense of the limits of action and of the unpredictability of her children and their world. She acquires the virtue Iris Murdoch calls "humility." "Humility is not a peculiar habit of self-effacement, rather like having an inaudible voice. It is selfless respect for reality. . . We cannot dominate the world."[28] As she engages in preservation, a mother is liable to the temptations of fearfulness and excessive control. Though necessarily controlling in their acts, reflective mothers themselves identify rigid or excessive control as the likely defects of the virtues they are required to practice.

We need no war memoirs to remind us that the humility of mothers is at odds with the self-righteous violence encouraged in soldiers. To recognize excessive control as a liability, and submissiveness of children as both an impossibility and a failure, distinguishes maternal from military practice. The "holding" of maternal practice seems directly opposed to the conquest of battlefields, the destruction of wills, bodies, landscapes, and artifacts routinely expected of soldiers. More than one writer has spoken of the typical warrior's "delight in destruction" and of animal aggression tamed in civilian life but encouraged in battle. Good generals are supposed to preserve the lives of their soldiers and are committed to preserving the lives of civilians, a commitment, however, that we no longer expect to be honored. I am (or, more accurately, would like to be) certain that many individual officers are humane, "maternal" men who achieve their aims with the least possible physical and psychological damage to their own soldiers or the enemy. And of course preservative policies necessary for victory are justified in military terms. But war memoirs from across the centuries as well as from recent decades make clear that people are "wasted" well beyond the requirements of victory. Moreover, victory itself is defined in such a way as to be compatible with immense psychological and physical damage to the victorious as well as the defeated.

In women's lives preservative love combines with a sexuality different from that of men in battle. It is widely believed that "sexual passion in isolation and the lust for battle are closely akin."[29] Nevertheless, the sexual love ascribed to soldiers seems distinctly male. The sexual love ascribed to females—or to be more exact, since it takes two to make the love, specifically feared and punished in the female—is sexual love between a woman and a soldier considered to be her "enemy." This love, like many female sexual fantasies and acts, seems to serve the cause of reconciliation. Other heterosexual passions of soldiers seem to various degrees narcissistic, assaultive (if not actually rapist), predatory, and demeaning to women. There is some reason to believe that women are less apt to eroticize combat than men, and more apt to eroticize union. Moreover, when women do eroticize combat they more often fantasize themselves in the role of submission than of conquest. If battle releases the conquistador in men who eroticize combat, the same stimulus might inhibit the combat fantasies of women. Whether they desexualize combat or sexualize submissiveness, typical female psychoerotic life seems at odds with the "lust for battle" encouraged in soldiers.

In a fuller treatment for sexuality in battle, we would have to consider the reported "ecstatic" bonding of men with each other that is held responsible for many of battle's appeals, triumphs, and cruelties.[30] The military seems to be frankly homophobic and homoerotic simultaneously. The combination of men's love for each other with their fear of that love is apt to be puzzling to civilians of both sexes. In any case, such bonding seems far less developed in women. Maternal love is individual. Sexual and nonsexual love between women seems more self-preservative and self-respecting than "ecstatic," more like the friendship between men that has been called the "true enemy of battle."[31]

The relation between homosexuality, heterosexuality, and battle is, however, obscure and in need of study. I believe the presumptive evidence that when women are soldiers in large numbers, combat will be both less eroticized and eroticized differently. Preservative love in combination with a different and lesser eroticism might lead soldiers to fight less often and less ruthlessly. These hypotheses depend, however, on a closer knowledge of men's battle fantasies, aggressive and sexual, than I possess. It is unclear to *me* that the typical soldier is excitedly battlelike. Often he seems (in memoirs) cold, dirty, numb, frightened, exhausted, and eager to get home. Conscripted, unwilling warriors of both sexes may have more in common with each other than either has with the voluntary soldier of legend who "lusts" for battle.[32]

Let me consider briefly a configuration of characteristics which *may* distinguish *homo furens* from the maternal woman. Abstraction, simplification, and separateness seem both male and warlike, whereas attention to the individual and respect for complexity and connectedness seem to arise from maternal practice.[33] Men are more likely, it is claimed, to be at home with sharply bonded abstract concepts. This capacity, which leads to male prominence in mathematics or science, may also have its place in war. Men may be more loyal to abstract causes and abstract states. They may be able to pray for a victory or to use a weapon that causes suffering they would not dare to imagine. Most important, they can develop an "abstract hatred for the enemy" that will allow them to kill.

Women, too, have their abstract hatreds and loyalties, but they are less direct. A woman acquires men's loyalties and hates with vehemence the enemies they fight. Often the loss of "her" men and boys is so painful that only the most inhuman brutal enemy, only the most just cause could legitimate it. Moreover, her very moralism and traditions of nonviolence require a greater evil to match the violence her men perpetrate. But freed from indirect participation with its attendant emotions and placed on a battlefield (or above the cities?) of those she would otherwise hate, she might develop a "concrete image" of the enemy as a soldier, like herself, with little control over his or her fate, an essentially decent person caught up in wars made by others. Women are said to eschew the clear-cut and unambiguous. Their thinking has been called "field-dependent," "holistic," "concrete"—different terms from different theories which seem to describe the same aspect of women's mental life. If these are indeed facets of the female mind, they may well be elicited by the demands of maternal practice. Mothers respond to a changeable, growing child, an "open structure" whose acts are irregular, unpredictable, often mysterious. They train themselves to look at and respond to complex individuals inseparable from the relations in which they grow. Such training *might* carry over to the battlefield, resulting in an imaginative grasp of the pain and hope of all combatants, which would make impersonal killing more difficult.

It may be that men's proclivities for abstraction affect both the content and style of their moral life. Lay observers, as well as psychologists, report that men are more able to dissociate themselves from the moral and human significance of their actions, more liable to compartmentalize various aspects of their morality and behavior. Women not only seem less able to bracket the moral implications of their actions; with the pervasiveness of morality goes a "different moral voice." Women are said, for example, to be less concerned with claiming rights, more with sharing responsibilities. They do not value independence and autonomy over connection and the restraints of caring, but rather assume that the conflict between rightful self-assertion and responsible interdependence is at the heart of moral life. Aware of the "danger of an ethics abstracted from life," the develop-ment of women's moral judgment "appears to proceed from an initial concern with survival (first of herself, then of her own) to a focus on goodness, and finally to a principled understanding of nonviolence as the most adequate guide to the just resolution of moral conflicts."[34]

It is frequently believed that rigid or compulsive concerns with autonomy, independence, and rightful ownership are warlike. At the very least these concerns, combined with abstract hatred and loyalty, give a peculiarly "male" cast to just-war theory. Women may well have developed a quite different theory of conflict, one suitable to maternal practices. Mothers, typically, are both socially and domestically powerless and, simultaneously, powerful keepers of unpredictable, often enraging beings. It is not surprising that physical and psychological violence is a temptation and frequent occurrence in maternal practice. It is also clear that violence is at odds with the interests a mother has in the preservation and growth of her child. Whatever their temptations and failures, mothers learn daily to make peace instead of fighting and then, when peace fails, to conduct necessary battles without resorting to violence. Their "theory of conflict" bears remarkable similarity to that of pacifists who refuse to separate means and ends, who treat enemies only as opponents with whom one struggles, who seek reconciliation rather than victory. Maternal thinkers, if forced to fight or even to look closely at and reflect upon battle, might well develop different conceptions of "victory" and its appropriate costs.

I have tried to specify a connection between women and "peacefulness" by identifying characteristics of women and mothers that are opposed to parallel characteristics encouraged in men at war. I am not saying that the military is in some simple sense bad, the maternal, good. Courage, risk-taking, and loyalties developed in military life are obvious examples of virtues quite different from, and sometimes at odds with, those called forth in maternal practices. The capacity for abstraction, which may be male and may play its role in war, is also a *human* capacity which, for women as for men, has its rightful place in moral as well as intellectual life. Nor am I claiming that all military men are male in the ways that I have specified. For example, something akin to preservative love is said to have its place on the battlefield. Soldiers are said to develop a kind of "maternal concern" for themselves, bits of nature, stray animals, fellow fighters, and the wounded enemy. Such concern may be the special province of the medic, but it is also necessary for the common soldier. "When soldiers lose this need to preserve and become impersonal killers, they are truly figures of terror."[35] Male soldiers, like the women fighters I am imagining, preserve their comrades, humanize their enemies, and resist excessive—and sometimes all—uses of destructive weapons. Anyone who doubts that maternal thinking can be expressed on the battlefield and preservative love flourish there should read the poetry of Wilfred Owen. For those interested in peace, the male peacefulness that survives the strain of battle and the masculinist ideology that prevails there is a source both of hope and profound admiration.

It is said that a male soldier who thinks maternally is "lonely and isolated on the battlefield." He grasps the impersonal cruelty of war but cannot be comforted by abstract hatred and fanaticism. The lonely soldier "longs for the end of war when reconciliation can begin and when he can help reconstruct what he has had a hand in destroying."[36] The difference-feminist hopes to make the lonely atypical soldier the ally of pacifists. Some hope that the conscription of women will bring about the abolition of increasingly cruel, impersonal, and wasteful battles.[37] Others hope that women, and the men who become their comrades, will fight as brave peacemakers, mournfully and humanely, doing the least harm to people or nature consistent with the requirements of justice. None of the differences I have suggested are sharp or extensive enough to justify the belief that women will not fight at all. Recent experience of women in battle shows that supposition to be clearly false. On the other hand, the most visible women warriors have been guerillas fighting for justice in their land and defenders of a besieged state (homeland) perceived to be under attack. I believe these types of battle are the most consonant with maternal thinking, although I won't make the case here.

We seem by now to have left the militarist mother far behind. Let me again recognize her existence. As I said at the outset, women, and especially mothers, have played their assigned parts in military scripts. On the sidelines of battle, women have been applauders and suppliers, plunder at the end of the day, "home" at the end of the war, mourners who let the fighting go on. The militancy of mothers has several sources which I can only touch upon here. Mothers' need for order, frustrated by the unpredictability of children and the messiness of their world, finds a relief in military discipline; disturbing eroticism is hidden or suppressed in war; unacknowledged violent impulses find a legitimate expression, vicariously safe. Nor should we forget that military leaders and ordinary soldiers, armed yet vulnerable, are quintessentially "male" and evoke in many women strong psychosexual desires to serve, sacrifice, and adore. Most important, for some women confined in domestic life, war offers real education, new training and job experience, economic power, travel, and a sense of shared communal life. It is no wonder then that they welcome its occurrence. "Consciously she desire(s) our splendid empire; unconsciously she desire(s) our splendid war."[38]

Even women who are true peacelovers, who dread war's horrors and value the texture of the lives it destroys, come to endorse the war policies of their government. Women, as a powerless group, may be especially fearful of alleged aggression. In the face of real or imagined threats, weapons can be wonderful, especially if carried by others, while to let one's "own men" remain unarmed can seem the epitome of vulnerability. And perhaps most important, even peaceloving women, especially if economically dependent, allow men, both the "leaders" and those at home, to judge for them the reality of a danger and the best method of meeting it. "The mother of her race, with all her fine emotions of sheltering care, comes through dependence to the opinions of the fighting male."[39]

Difference-feminists, unlike the antifeminists to whom they are ironically close, aim to increase women's independent economic and social strength. They believe that motherly militancy derives in large part from the confinements and power-lessness of maternal life. Consequently, womanly power, authentic female authority, and new possibilities in work and love will undermine the attraction and apparent necessity of war. In short, difference-feminists believe, paradoxically enough, that when women have the right and ability to fight on various battle-fields, the nonviolence now a part of maternal thought will truly prosper.

I have made the best case I can for the claim that women, being more peaceful than men, might pacify the military and change the nature of battle. The case would be more convincing in an extended treatment. But even at its most convincing, it would not justify the conscription of women.

Theories of gender are in an early stage of development. The sex differences they describe are changing as society changes. The research is far too tentative to justify a policy as serious as conscription. Moreover, except for distinctive female sexuality, the gender differences I have described are often elicited and strength-ened by actual care of small children or other "maternal" work. Conscripted women, unlikely to be mothers, are of an age when they are rightly concerned with developing the strength of self that will later counter the excesses of self-denial to which maternal life is liable. In the unpropitious circumstances of military life, these young conscripts will be unlikely to display the learning and thinking of maternal practice.

On the other hand, these young conscripts will as daughters be affected by maternal thinking. They may well exhibit a female cognitive style and morality. Still, they will have to reckon with the self-satisfaction of masculinist ideology. The pervasiveness of male values in the military makes it theoretically plausible but practically unlikely that the presence of women will bring about change. Moreover, the military is relatively powerless in respect to the civilian govern-ment. Unless women are as likely as men to be chiefs of staff, secretaries of state and defense, and corporation executives, it is unlikely that sex differences will affect overall war policies. Unlikely but not impossible. We occasionaly saw in Vietnam that, while you can force an army to battle, you cannot always make it fight. Such battlefield refusals affect the highest decisions back home, though not in predictable nor necessarily welcome ways.

If the likelihood of women pacifying the Army were even greater than it is, it would still not justify conscription in the interest of peace. Those committed to "peace"—that is, to resolving conflicts or resisting evil nonviolently—have their own "armies" to raise. It is more likely that distinctive interests in and capacities for peace will be developed in pacifist than in military organizations. Pacifists, more than militarists, acknowledge women's distinctive strengths and welcome women's power. And of course they are more apt to identify peacefulness with strength and power in both women and men.

Many pacifists cite women's special interests in and capacities for peace as reasons for excluding them from the military. They argue that within favorable institutions and social contexts, female peacefulness can be fortified and put to use. Belief in women's peacefulness, as well as the peacefulness itself, is fragile and likely to be destroyed by militarization. To force women into the military threatens a valuable resource of peace movements and peaceful states.

I myself believe that if peace were the primary issue, women should be excluded from conscription. But then I believe that no one should be conscripted for war in the interest of peace. The task for the peacemaker is to organize forces opposed to war, to train them to disarm the violent and to fight nonviolently. The task of feminists, from a pacifist point of view, is to make women independent, stronger instruments of peace. At best, a draft is a highly unreliable, risky means to that end.

Before excluding women from conscription, or for that matter from the military, we must reckon with one unwelcome consequence. If we insist that fighting is men's business, we will continue to embody immoral, warlike impulses in male bodies. Earlier I said that such a division of labor was unfair to men; now I would emphasize its danger to peace. When warriorhood is connected to masculinity, both men and women find it easier to accept the battles in which boys are sacrificed. Boys will go off to fight wars they barely understand and welcome special opportunities for macho aggression, because they fear feminization, or simply because fighting is and always has been their game. Men excluded from conscription by luck or age will find vicarious sexual confirmation in seeing their sons and brothers fight; most of them will find the battlefield a "normal," "natural" place even for boys they love. Women meanwhile can eschew responsibility for battles, refusing to acknowledge their many supportive roles. For us too, it may seem the "part of a man" to squander lives on battlefields from which we're safely distant. Only a feminist critique of gender stereotypes and of the sexual division of work and virtue can avert this danger.

Drafting Women

If we are deciding on moral grounds whether to draft women, what should our verdict be?

We should recognize the legitimacy of the "right to fight" and its historical significance for full citizenship. That right does not imply the duty to fight, however, nor, a fortiori, the government's right to enforce the duty. Nonetheless, the conscription of women would probably affect favorably women's economic and social power, whereas the exclusion of women would almost certainly have a deleterious effect. Commitment to women's rights, therefore, supports, though it does not require, their equal conscription. I believe, however, that in building an army concern with *rights*—of women or of citizens generally—has a lower priority than concerns for liberty, fairness, or peace.

In conscription, the state arrogates to itself central questions of moral life, thereby infringing liberties fundamental to the identity of moral persons. Typically, the state justifies this infringement in terms of citizens' obligations to serve in the military when called upon to do so. One theory derives political obligation from the participant-beneficiary relation of citizens to their state. If used to justify conscripting women, this theory is doubly deficient. It does not require any citizen to serve in the military, nor does it obligate women to the same degree and for the same reasons it obligates men. A second theory makes political obligation a species and consequence of moral obligation. On this theory women are justified to the same degree and for the same reasons as men because they are both moral persons. This theory yields the obligation of all citizens to take responsibility for the violence of their state but does not yield the narrower duty to serve in the military nor, a fortiori, the state's right to enforce that duty. Nonetheless, universal conscription which required *all* citizens to aid in just wars and resist unjust ones might be instrumental in inducing citizens to assume their rightful responsibility. Such a conscription law is clearly a fantasy, however, and perhaps a dangerous one. A *selective* service, especially one that discriminates by age or sex, works against the very obligation it seeks to promote.

If conscription cannot be justified from the obligation to serve, it will have to be defended from its consequences. Despite its infringement of liberties, a government may adopt conscription if, when all harms and benefits are considered, it is morally preferable to any other military staffing policy. There is a prima facie case for conscription if it distributes the burdens of military service more fairly. Although in the AVF military burdens are indeed unfairly shared, a draft is an unreliable and risky instrument of fairness. A draft could, however, relieve the poor soldier of the burden of combat and other dangerous wartime service by replacing him with an affluent conscript. For this reason, there is a prima facie case for a wartime draft of relatively affluent citizens in the interest of fairness. But if conscription violates conscience and makes it easier to fight or prolong unjust wars, a draft may not be worth the moral cost.

Fairness would not be served if male volunteers were replaced or supplemented by female conscripts. Yet if we are presented with conscription as a *fait accompli,* women seem required out of fairness to share the burden of compliance or resistance with conscripted men. Male privilege and power do not seem to justify the heavy burden of *forced* combat and other dangerous wartime work. In the event of unjustified conscription and conscription for unjust wars, we have to confront the paradox of requiring the fair distribution of burdens no one should bear.

For both militarists and pacifists, even issues of liberty and fairness are apt to be overshadowed by interests in wartime success or in peace. As a (near) pacifist, I myself would endorse conscription if I felt it would make war less likely or more humane. I do not believe, however, that conscription generally nor the conscription of women in particular is a wise strategy of resistance to war. Nor do women's special interests in and capacity for nonviolent resolution of conflict and resistance to evil justify conscripting them in the interest of peace. But a long tradition of preservative love and nonviolence does give women a basis and a hope for organizing ourselves outside the military in cooperation with the pacifist aims of men. Accordingly, a case can be made for excluding women from conscription in the interest of peace. On the other hand, the connection of battle with masculinity endangers us all. The recruitment of women for peace must go hand in hand with a feminist attack on conventional conceptions of gender.

The relation between alternative military staffing policies, peace, and fairness is obscure and controversial. I have tried to clarify arguments, to present pieces of a puzzle. Even so, my conclusions and the passions behind them often feel contradictory. An All-Volunteer Force that recruits both men and women seems less likely to lead to war than universal military conscription and is almost certainly less likely to do so than selective, age- and sex-biased conscription. The interests of peace are compatible with those of conscience. With an All-Volunteer Force, the state does not arrogate a central question of morality; each citizen decides for him or herself when it is permissible or obligatory to kill or to maim others, or to put one's own life and body at risk. But while respecting conscience and acting in the interest of peace, we run the risk of imposing on poor young men the unconscionable burden of fighting wars for which they have no responsibility and from which they will get no benefit. Even if we are successful in our peace efforts, relatively poor soldiers bear a disproportionate burden of peacetime service.

On balance, I oppose conscription of women and men. But opposition brings with it responsibilities to the volunteer soldier. As I see it, anyone opposing conscription is committed to redressing inequities that make society unfair, so that every citizen will have a viable civilian life. At the same time, so long as we maintain armies we are committed to making them more humane and personally rewarding to their members. Above all, while we work to make nuclear war impossible, we must not become callous to the possibility of conventional war, but try to ensure that no soldier bears the burden of combat. If, despite our efforts, the state does initiate a war, we must then, out of fairness to combatants and civilians, share the burden of ending the battles, some by fighting them, others of us by resisting in nonviolent ways the evils of our opponents or the war policies of our state.

Notes

1. In discussing the history and significance of women's struggle for the "right to fight" I have relied on the literature put out by the Women's Equity Action League. I have also used Martin Binkin and Shirley J. Bach, *Women and the Military* (Washington, D.C.: The Brookings Institution, 1977); and the following essays by Mady W. Segal: "Women in the Military: Research and Policy Issues," *Youth and Society,* vol. 10 (1978); and "Women's Roles in the U.S. Armed Forces: An Evaluation of Evidence and Arguments for Policy Decisions," Chapter 13, this volume.

2. Virginia Woolf, *Three Guineas* (London: Hogarth Press, 1938).

3. Both of the accounts I consider assume that nation-states exist and that their continued existence is morally justified. For a clear defense of this view and its importance for just-war theory, see Michael Walzer, *Just and Unjust Wars* (New York: Basic Books, 1977). Both accounts also assume that "individualism" is morally justified and that, therefore, the state's claims on its citizens require justification. I have not considered either the claims of anarchists, with which I have considerable sympathy, nor the claims of Hegelians whose political theory is less individualistic than the two I consider. The participant-beneficiary account of citizen obligation is discussed at length by A. John Simmons and briefly by Alan Gewirth, the moral account at length by Gewirth and briefly by Simmons. See Alan Gewirth, "Individual Rights and Political-Military Obligations," Chapter 6, this volume, and *Reason and Morality* (Chicago: University of Chicago Press, 1978); and A. John Simmons, "The Obligations of Citizens and the Justification of Conscription," Chapter 5, this volume, and *Moral Principles and Political Obligations* (Princeton, N.J.: Princeton University Press, 1979).

4. "Participation" is intended to cover both consent and contract and to underline the requirement of democratic participation that Gewirth emphasizes.

5. I use masculine pronouns, except to make a special point, in order to leave open the question whether these theories, developed with men in mind, also apply to women.

6. Simmons, "The Obligations of Citizens and the Justification of Conscription" and *Moral Principles and Political Obligations.*

7. I have derived the moral account of political obligation from the works of Alan Gewirth cited above (note 3). I do not consider, however, nor am I persuaded by the metaethical theory which, for him, underpins both moral and political theory.

8. See Charles R. Beitz, *Political Theory and International Relations* (Princeton, N.J.: Princeton University Press, 1979). Nationalism is as apt as not to lead to injustice for the world's citizens. On the other hand, if states are necessary to moral life, citizens should be slow to relinquish loyalties to their state, loyalties which have arisen out of shared history and responsibility. What is needed is a theory that locates the moral requirement for just states within a more general political theory articulating the requirements for international justice and freedom.

9. Throughout this paper I have relied on traditional and recent articulations of just-war theory. I myself believe that just-war theory serves warlike purposes. The theory makes it too easy, I think, to justify a particular war, too easy to underestimate or misdescribe the evils of the most just of wars. Moreover, the use of nuclear weapons, as well as some of the most destructive conventional weapons, would be outlawed by just-war theory, no matter how righteous the cause. I myself believe that pacifist theory has a firmer foundation than the denial that any war can now be a just one. To try to ground pacifism in just-war theories is like trying to build a ship with the tools and plans devised for buiding airplanes. Although some tools may be usable in both tasks, flyers and sailors may want to take different

journeys. Just-war theory provides the most useful framework for discussions between pacifists and militarists, however.

10. See especially Carol Gilligan, "In a Different Voice: Women's Conception of Self and Morality," *Harvard Educational Review* 47 (1977): 481-517.

11. Both draft and antidraft movements have developed lively discussions about the military and moral significance of sharing the burden of combat among citizens of every age. If the optimum military age lies somewhere between 19 and 30, as seems to be the case, then a majority of conscripts would have to be of that age. It would be all the more important to have older citizens predominate in jobs where youth was not so important. Disruption, economic sacrifice, and loss of freedoms can be borne by citizens of quite different physical constitution, strength, and age. For a discussion of the significance of age in a draft, see Sol Tax, ed., *The Draft: A Handbook of Facts and Alternatives* (Chicago: University of Chicago Press, 1967); and Martin Binkin and Irene Kyriakopolous, *Youth or Experience?: Manning the Modern Military* (Washington, D.C.: The Brookings Institution, 1979).

12. There is obviously room for reform in recruitment policies as well as for legal, economic, and social reforms within the military. See, for example, Binkin and Bach, *Women and the Military,* chap. 4; James Finn, ed., *Conscience and Command* (New York: Random House, 1971); Dina Portnay, *Women: The Recruiter's Last Resort* (RECON, 1974).

13. To be poor is at least to be in economic circumstances that make military offers advantageous. This makes poverty a relative matter, dependent upon current military offers. In discussions of fairness, however, to be "poor" means more—and worse—than this: to have no attractive options in civilian society, to be "forced" by poverty into the service. "Attractiveness" lies to some extent in the eye of the beholder, both the attractiveness of the civilian job and of the military job with which it is compared. We (I) need to know more about the actual choices volunteers make. How many of them are choosing between jail and service? Between supermarket checkout and service? Between assembly line and service? Between unemployment and service? How many are choosing between attractive offers for training and compensation offered by military and civilian work?

14. Richard V. L. Cooper presents evidence to this effect in his "Military Manpower Procurement: Equity, Efficiency, and National Security," presented at the Hoover-Rochester Conference on the All-Volunteer Force, Stanford University, 13-14 December 1979, pp. IV-14–16.

15. For a good discussion of this point, see Jules Coleman, "Liberalism, Unfair Advantage, and the Volunteer Armed Forces," Chapter 7, this volume.

16. See *Hearings on Military Posture and H.R. 2970,* Committee on Armed Services, House of Representatives, 97th Congress, 1st sess., Part 6, 26 February–1 April 1981, p. 22. United States military recruiting or drafting for the enlisted ranks has typically been skewed toward the lower middle-class youth. See Neil Fligstein, "Militarism, Not Service," *Society* 18 (March/April 1981), p. 43; and David Segal, "How Equal is 'Equity'?" ibid., p. 31.

17. What is dangerous and unpleasant for one class of citizens may be safer, healthier, and more rewarding than civilian life for another class of citizens. While we may deplore the class injustice such disparity reveals, a draft may increase misery while doing nothing to remedy the injustices. For a vivid expression of the different effects of military service on different classes, see Mary Lee Settle, *All the Brave Promises* (New York: Ballantine Books, 1966), especially p. 40.

18. Robert Staples, "Black Manhood in the 1970s: A Critical Look Back," *Black Scholar* 12 (May/June 1981): 5. See also Manning Marable, "The Military, Black People, and the Racist State: A History of Coercion," *Black Scholar* 12 (January/February 1981): 6-17; Representative Ronald V. Dellums, "Dellums Denounces Carter Proposals for the Resumption of the Draft," *Black Scholar* 11 (March/April 1980): 93, and various speeches available from Dellums's office. Although each of these writers recognizes the racial and economic imbalance of the AVF and deplores both military and civilian racism, none of them advocates a draft. It does not follow from the fact that the AVF exploits the poor and is shaped by racism that a drafted army will benefit the poor and provide some relief to the racially oppressed. The disease is clear; the remedy is not. See Jules Coleman, "Liberalism, Unfair Advantage, and the Volunteer Armed Forces," Chapter 7, this volume.

19. In the most just of wars, immoral orders will be given. Moreover, there seem to be

many burdens of combat that no one should bear because they are so costly physically, psychologically, and morally, and they occur in an unjust war or they occur in a just war but are not themselves justified militarily or morally.

20. Dr. Helen Caldicott, War Resisters League Calendar, 1981.

21. The literature of "difference-feminism" comes from many disciplines. I can only suggest its range here. Extensive work on a distinctive female morality has been done by Carol Gilligan. See especially "In a Different Voice: Women's Conception of Self and Morality," *Harvard Educational Review* 47 (1977): 481–517, and "Woman's Place in Man's Life Cycle," *Harvard Educational Review* 49 (1979): 431–46. Extensive work on the effect of masculinist ideology on the formation of scientific theory has been done by Evelyn Fox Keller. See especially "Gender and Science," *Psychoanalysis and Contemporary Thought* (1978); "Baconian Science: A Hermaphroditic Birth," *Philosophical Forum* II (Spring 1980): 299–308; and *Id in Scientific Discourse* (New York: Longman, forthcoming). Other writers include: Sandra Harding and Merrill Hintikka, *Discovering Reality: Feminist Perspectives on Epistemology, Metaphysics, Methodology and the Philosophy of Science* (Amsterdam: Dordrecht-Reidel, forthcoming; Nancy Chodorow, *The Reproduction of Mothering* (Berkeley: University of California Press, 1978): Dorothy Dinnerstein, *The Mermaid and the Minotaur* (New York: Harper & Row, 1976); Susan Griffin, *Woman and Nature* (New York: Harper & Row, 1978); Jean Baker Miller, *Toward a New Psychology of Women* (Boston: Beacon Press, 1976); Rayna R. Reiter, *Toward an Anthropology of Women* (New York: Monthly Review, 1975); Michelle Risaldo and Louise Lamphere, *Women, Culture, and Society* (Palo Alto, Calif.: Stanford University Press, 1974). Two of the many works in literary criticism influenced by and contributing to difference-feminism are Ellen Moeurs, *Literary Women* (New York: Doubleday, 1976); and Sandra M. Gilbert and Susan Gubar, *The Madwoman in the Attic* (New Haven: Yale University Press, 1979).

22. Tim O'Brien, *If I Die in a Combat Zone* (New York: Dell Publishing, Laurel Edition, 1979), p. 52.

23. Ibid., p. 146. See also David Marlowe, "The Manning of the Force and the Structure of Battle: Part II," Chapter 12, this volume. In trying to understand war and men in battle I have read several fictional and nonfictional accounts and memoirs of the Civil War, World War I, World War II, and Vietnam. I have found especially useful John Keegan, *The Face of Battle* (New York: Viking, 1976). I most often cite J. Glenn Gray, *The Warriors* (New York: Harper & Row, 1970). Nevertheless, I cite nothing from Gray that doesn't seem to be corroborated in at least two other accounts of battle.

24. I have made the case at some length in "Maternal Thinking," *Feminist Studies* (Summer 1980). I have dealt more extensively with these issues in "Preservative Love and Military Destruction: Reflections on Mothering and Peace," in *Mothering: Essays in Feminist Theory,* edited by Joyce Trebilcot (Totowa, N.J.: Rowman & Allanheld, forthcoming 1983).

25. The quotation is from a Nazi mother, cited in Leila J. Rupp, *Mobilizing Women for War* (Princeton, N.J.: Princeton University Press, 1978). See also Margaret Mead, "A National Service System as a Solution to a Variety of Problems," in Tax, ed., *The Draft*; Barbara J. Steinam, " 'The Mother Half of Humanity': American Women in the Peace and Preparedness Movements in World War I" in *Women, War & Revolution,* edited by Carol R. Berkin and Clara M. Lovett (New York: Holmes & Meier, 1980); and Jean Bethke Elshtain, "Women as Mirror and Other: Towards a Theory of Women, War, and Feminism" (unpublished manuscript, Institute for Advanced Studies, Princeton, N.J.).

26. I take the phrase from Harriot Stanton Blatch, *A Woman's Point of View: Some Roads to Peace* (New York: The Woman's Press, 1920).

27. The words are Mrs. Ramsay's in Virginia Woolf, *To the Lighthouse* (New York: Harcourt, Brace and World, 1927), p. 92.

28. Iris Murdoch, *The Sovereignty of Good* (New York: Schocken, 1971), pp. 95, 99.

29. Gray, *The Warriors,* chap. 3.

30. It may be that ecstatic comradery is less "ecstatic" since World War II (or, some would say, since World War I). See Paul Fussell, *The Great War and Modern Memory* (New York and London: Oxford University Press, 1975). Yet, recent memoirs from Vietnam continue to attribute both horrors and rewards of battle to men's love for each other.

31. Gray, *The Warriors,* chap. 3. Which is not to say that lesbian love is any less exciting or erotic than heterosexual or male homosexual peacetime love. The question is not what degree of excitement sexual love yields, but to what extent one loses self-consciousness and self-respect (both of one's own and the other's self).

32. I have treated the issue of maternal sexuality more extensively in "Preservative Love." I can just touch upon the complicated relation between sexuality and battle in these paragraphs.

33. I am relying especially on the work on Evelyn Fox Keller, Carol Gilligan, and Nancy Chodorow (see note 21). I have also dealt with this subject at greater length in "Preservative Love."

34. Gilligan, "In a Different Voice," p. 515.

35. Gray, *The Warriors,* p. 86 and chap. 3, passim.

36. Ibid., pp. 163, 164.

37. The "abolition of battle" is advocated by John Keegan, in *The Face of Battle.* I take both the phrase and the characterizations of battle from him.

38. Woolf, *Three Guineas,* p. 39.

39. Blatch, *A Woman's Point of View,* p. 169.

Index

Notes on Contributors

John Sibley Butler is Associate Professor of Sociology at the University of Texas. He has authored or coauthored several studies on race relations in the military, including *Inequality in the Military: The Black Experience* (Palo Alto, Calif.: R & E Research Associates, 1979).

James Childress is Professor of Religious Studies at the University of Virginia. Formerly Joseph P. Kennedy, Sr., Professor of Christian Ethics at the Kennedy Institute of Ethics, Georgetown University, he has published widely in medical ethics, including (with Tom Beauchamp) *Principles of Biomedical Ethics* (New York: Oxford University Press, 1979). He is also the author of *Civil Disobedience and Political Obligation: A Study in Christian Social Ethics* (New Haven, Conn.: Yale University Press, 1971), and "Francis Lieber's Interpretation of the Laws of War: General Orders No. 100 in the Context of this Life and Thought," *American Journal of Jurisprudence* 21 (1976): 34–70.

Kenneth J. Coffey is Associate Director, Federal Personnel and Compensation Division, General Accounting Office. Before joining GAO in 1979, he served as a consultant to the Office of the Secretary of Defense, to the Congressional Budget Office, and to the National Security Council, and directed recruitment studies for the Defense Manpower Commission, 1974–1975. He is the author of *Strategic Implications of the All-Volunteer Force: The Conventional Defense of Central Europe* (Chapel Hill, N.C.: University of North Carolina Press, 1979).

Jules L. Coleman is Professor of Philosophy at the University of Arizona. He was Visiting Professor of Jurisprudence and Social Policy at the Law School, University of California at Berkeley, in 1978. He is author of several influential essays in law and economics and of the forthcoming book *Justice and the Cost of Accidents: A Philosophical Analysis*.

Robert K. Fullinwider, Research Associate at the Center for Philosophy and Public Policy and director of the Center's Project on Voluntary versus Non-Voluntary Military Service, is the author of *The Reverse Discrimination Controversy: A Moral and Legal Analysis* (Totowa, N.J.: Rowman and Littlefield, 1980).

Alan Gewirth is Edward Carson Waller Distinguished Service Professor of Philosophy at the University of Chicago. A past president of the American Philosophical Association (Western Division), he has published extensively in ethics and political philosophy, including the widely discussed book *Reason and Morality* (Chicago: University of Chicago Press, 1978).

Richard W. Hunter is Senior Associate, Systems Research and Applications Corporation, Fairfax, Virginia. A graduate of the U.S. Naval Academy, he flew 175 missions in Vietnam as a Navy carrier pilot, earning a Purple Heart and a Legion of Merit award. From 1974–1980 he served in several positions in the Office of the Assistant Secretary of Defense for Manpower, Reserve Affairs, and Logistics, directing assessment of the All-Volunteer Force. As Director of Manpower Program Analysis, he was a principal author of *America's Volunteers: A*

Report on the All-Volunteer Armed Forces (Office of Assistant Secretary of Defense (MRAL), 1978).

David H. Marlowe is Chief, Department of Military Psychiatry, Walter Reed Army Research Institute, Washington, D.C. An anthropologist by training, he has more than twenty years' experience in observing the psychiatric effects of military training, drug use, and combat.

Adrian M. S. Piper is Assistant Professor of Philosophy at the University of Michigan. She has published "Utility, Publicity, and Manipulation," *Ethics* 88 (April 1978): 189–206, and "Property and the Limits of the Self," *Political Theory* 8 (February 1980): 39–64.

Sara Ruddick teaches in the Seminar College of the New School for Social Research, New York City. She has published essays in ethics, epistemology, and feminist thought, and is coeditor of *Working It Out: Twenty-three Women Writers, Artists, Scientists, and Scholars Talk About Their Life and Work* (New York: Pantheon, 1977).

David R. Segal is Professor of Sociology and Government and Politics at the University of Maryland. From 1973–1975, he was Chief, Social Processes Technical Area, U.S. Army Research Institute for the Behavioral and Social Sciences. He has published extensively on military manpower, including (with Jerald G. Bachman and John D. Blair) *The All-Volunteer Force: A Study of Ideology in the Military* (Ann Arbor: University of Michigan Press, 1977).

Mady Wechsler Segal is Associate Professor of Sociology at the University of Maryland, from which she was on leave in 1981 and 1982 doing research on military women and military families for Walter Reed Army Research Institute. She has published extensively on several topics in sociology, including military life, sports competition, and group effects.

A. John Simmons is Associate Professor of Philosophy at the University of Virginia. He is the author of several essays in political philosophy and ethics and of *Moral Principles and Political Obligations* (Princeton, N.J.: Princeton University Press, 1979), and is Associate Editor of *Philosophy & Public Affairs*.